LUTHER'S WORKS

American Edition

VOLUME 51

Published by Concordia Publishing House

and Fortress Press in 55 volumes.

General Editors are Jaroslav Pelikan (for vols. 1-30)

and Helmut T. Lehmann (for vols. 31-55).

LUTHER'S WORKS

VOLUME 51

Sermons

I

EDITED AND TRANSLATED BY
JOHN W. DOBERSTEIN

GENERAL EDITOR
HELMUT T. LEHMANN

FORTRESS PRESS / PHILADELPHIA

Library of Congress Catalog Card Number 55-9893

ISBN 0-8006-0351-6

Fourth printing 1980

8812K80   *Printed in the United States of America*   1-351

GENERAL EDITORS' PREFACE

The first editions of Luther's collected works appeared in the sixteenth century, and so did the first efforts to make him "speak English." In America serious attempts in these directions were made for the first time in the nineteenth century. The Saint Louis edition of Luther was the first endeavor on American soil to publish a collected edition of his works, and the Henkel Press in Newmarket, Virginia, was the first to publish some of Luther's writings in an English translation. During the first decade of the twentieth century, J. N. Lenker produced translations of Luther's sermons and commentaries in thirteen volumes. A few years later the first of the six volumes in the Philadelphia (or Holman) edition of the *Works of Martin Luther* appeared. But a growing recognition of the need for more of Luther's works in English has resulted in this American edition of Luther's works.

The edition is intended primarily for the reader whose knowledge of late medieval Latin and sixteenth-century German is too small to permit him to work with Luther in the original languages. Those who can will continue to read Luther in his original words as these have been assembled in the monumental Weimar edition (*D. Martin Luthers Werke*. Kritische Gesamtausgabe; Weimar, 1883-   ). Its texts and helps have formed a basis for this edition, though in certain places we have felt constrained to depart from its readings and findings. We have tried throughout to translate Luther as he thought translating should be done. That is, we have striven for faithfulness on the basis of the best lexicographical materials available. But where literal accuracy and clarity have conflicted, it is clarity that we have preferred, so that sometimes paraphrase seemed more faithful than literal fidelity. We have proceeded in a similar way in the matter of Bible versions, translating Luther's translations. Where this could be done by the use of an existing English version—King James, Douay, or Revised Standard—we have done so. Where it could not, we have supplied our own. To indicate this in each specific instance would have been pedantic; to adopt a uniform procedure would have been artificial—especially in view of Luther's own inconsistency in this regard. In each volume the translator will be responsible primarily for matters of text and language, while the responsibility of the editor will extend principally to the historical and theological matters reflected in the introductions and notes.

Although the edition as planned will include fifty-five volumes, Luther's writings are not being translated in their entirety. Nor should they be. As he was the first to insist, much of what he wrote and said was not that important. Thus the edition is a selection of works that have proved their importance for the faith, life, and history of the Christian church. The first thirty volumes contain Luther's expositions of various biblical books, while the remaining volumes include what are usually called his "Reformation writings" and other occasional pieces. The final volume of the set will be an index volume; in addition to an index of quotations, proper names, and topics, and a list of corrections and changes, it will contain a glossary of many of the technical terms that recur in Luther's works and that cannot be defined each time they appear. Obviously Luther cannot be forced into any neat set of rubrics. He can provide his reader with bits of autobiography or with political observations as he expounds a psalm, and he can speak tenderly about the meaning of the faith in the midst of polemics against his opponents. It is the hope of publishers, editors, and translators that through this edition the message of Luther's faith will speak more clearly to the modern church.

J. P.
H. T. L.

CONTENTS

C. R. — *Corpus Reformatorum*, edited by C. G. Bretschneider and H. E. Bindseil (Halle, 1834-1860).

CL — *Luthers Werke in Auswahl*, edited by Otto Clemen *et al.* (Bonn, 1912-1933; Berlin, 1955-1956).

EA — *D. Martin Luthers sämmtliche Werke* (Frankfurt and Erlangen, 1826-1857).

LW — American edition of *Luther's Works* (Philadelphia and St. Louis, 1955-   ).

MA³ — *Martin Luther*. Ausgewählte Werke (München, 1948-   ).

Migne — *Patrologiae, Series Latina*, 221 vols. in 222 (Paris, 1844-1904), J. P. Migne, editor.

PE — *Works of Martin Luther* (Philadelphia, 1915-1943).

St. L. — *D. Martin Luthers sämmtliche Schriften*, edited by Johann Georg Walch. Edited and published in modern German, 23 Vols. in 25 (St. Louis, 1880-1910).

WA — *D. Martin Luthers Werke.* Kritische Gesamtausgabe (Weimar, 1883-   ).

WA, Br — *D. Martin Luthers Werke.* Briefwechsel (Weimar, 1930-1948).

WA, TR — *D. Martin Luthers Werke.* Tischreden (Weimar, 1912-1921).

WA, DB — *D. Martin Luthers Werke.* Deutsche Bibel (Weimar, 1906-   ).

INTRODUCTION TO VOLUME 51

No full-scale monograph on Luther the preacher has yet been written in any language, though there are a number of important studies, both homiletical and hermeneutical, which have prepared the ground for such a monograph.[1] The reason for this lack seems to be the formidable task of studying and analyzing Luther's sermons of which more than two thousand are to be found in the Weimar edition (though it, too, does not contain all of the sermons of which transcripts are available). As Emanuel Hirsch has said, "Every Luther scholar knows that this requires years of labor." Luther's preaching activity was tremendous by any standards since it was carried out in addition to his proper vocation of lecturing to students and his astonishing literary output.

I

Luther's preaching ministry began officially in May, 1512, at a chapter meeting of the Augustinian order in Cologne when he was made sub-prior of the Wittenberg monastery. This entailed supervision of the monastery school, studies toward the degree of doctor of theology, and responsibility for the professorship hitherto held by Staupitz, who also committed to him the task of preaching in the monastery. However, he probably had already preached occasion-

---

[1] For example: Gerhard Ebeling, *Evangelische Evangelienauslegung. Eine Untersuchung zu Luthers Hermeneutik* (München, 1942); Heinrich Bornkamm, *Luther und das Alte Testament* (Tübingen, 1948); Walter von Loewenich, *Luther als Ausleger der Synoptiker* (München, 1954); Hermann Werdermann, *Luthers Wittenberger Gemeinde wiederhergestellt aus seinen Predigten* (Gütersloh, 1929); Georg Buchwald, *Predigten D. Martin Luthers auf Grund von Nachschriften Georg Rörers und Anton Lauterbachs* (2 vols.; Gütersloh, 1925-1926); Erwin Mühlhaupt, *D. Martin Luthers Evangelien-Auslegung* (5 vols.; Gütersloh, 1938-1954); Friedrich Gogarten, *Martin Luther, Predigten* (Jena, 1927); Emanuel Hirsch, *Predigten, CL 7* (Berlin, 1932); Emanuel Hirsch, "Luthers Predigtweise," *Luther, Mitteilungen der Luthergesellschaft,* Jg. 25 (1954), pp. 1-23; Paul Althaus, "Luther auf der Kanzel," *ibid.* (1921), pp. 17-34; Elmer Carl Kiessling, *The Early Sermons of Luther and Their Relation to the Pre-Reformation Sermon* (Grand Rapids, 1935).

ally even earlier than this, during his sojourns in Erfurt in 1510 and 1512. (On Luther's earliest sermons, see the introduction to Luther's First(?) Sermon, p. 5.) Having accepted the preaching office with great reluctance and even resistance, Luther began to preach regularly, first in the refectory and the old, dilapidated chapel in the monastery and then, at the request of the city council, in the parish church of Wittenberg, taking the place of the ailing pastor, Simon Heinz. About two hundred sermons of the period up to 1522 have been preserved. Though Bugenhagen became city pastor in 1522, he was sometimes absent for months and even years. During this time Luther took Bugenhagen's place in the pulpit. On special occasions he preached in the Castle Church, frequently in his own home, and also on his journeys in many other places. The frequency of his preaching is indicated by the fact that in the years from 1522 to his death in 1546 he preached an average of seventy sermons a year, though even this figure presents an inadequate picture, for, except when he was ill, he preached more often than this, and besides, for many periods we do not have transcripts of his sermons (e.g., Rörer's transcripts of the sermons of 1527 as well as the weekday sermons on Matthew 11-15 of 1528-29 are missing). The following samplings of the number of sermons preached in a year give a truer picture: 1522, 138; 1524, 100; 1528, 190; 1531, 180; 1534, 80; 1538, 100. After 1540 the number decreases but rises sharply again in 1544 and 1545. He preached on the average of two or three times, occasionally four times, a week. In his Table Talk on April 19, 1538, speaking of his preaching in the year 1517, Luther said, "Often I preached four sermons on one day. During a whole Lenten season I preached two sermons and lectured once each day in the early days when I was preaching on the Ten Commandments."[2] In 1529 he preached eighteen times in the eleven days from Palm Sunday to the Wednesday after Easter.

The Weimar edition contains more than two thousand sermons, transcripts of stenographic notes made by listeners, printings of individual sermons, various postils, and running expositions of books or parts of books of the Bible. This is estimated to be about two-thirds of the sermons actually preached between 1510 and 1546.

The sermons take up many volumes in the Weimar edition. The following sixteen volumes contain sermons exclusively: 10^{III}, 16, 24,

_____
[2] WA, TR 3, 3843.

27-29, 32-34, 36, 37, 41, 45-47, 49. Six volumes contain postils: $10^{I, 1}$, $10^{I, 2}$, 17^{II}, 21, 22, 52. Besides these there are numerous sermons in other volumes. Volume 22 contains a detailed index of the sermons.[3]

II

The preceding paragraph but one indicates how Luther's sermons were transmitted to us: through printed treatises, commentaries, and sermons published during his lifetime and after, the postils, and stenographic transcriptions made by various listeners.

In a very real sense, everything that Luther wrote could be called preaching, since his concept of preaching was a very broad one. Many of his treatises he called "sermons."[4] Thus his treatises on Trading and Usury, the Ban, the Estate of Marriage, and War Against the Turk are essentially sermons. The whole of the Large Catechism is sermonic, based on his actual preaching, and the Smalcald Articles, the great confession concerning the holy sacrament, and above all the treatise on Christian Liberty, are all powerful sermons. And in this sense all his commentaries and lectures are basically preaching.

Yet when all of Luther's sermons are taken into account, relatively few were published in his lifetime. The fact that a sermon was printed in his lifetime, however, is no guarantee that it represents what he actually said in the pulpit, even when it appears directly after it was preached. Very seldom do these printed versions stem from Luther himself. Indeed, whenever a first printing of a sermon appears outside of Wittenberg, in Augsburg, Nürnberg, or Erfurt, this may be accepted as clear proof that Luther had nothing to do with the form in which it appears. These contemporary prints are the product of notes and transcriptions by enthusiastic listeners and printers eager to profit by Luther's popularity. Luther was frequently obliged to protest that these printings misrepresented what he had said, and then proceeded to have them printed in an authorized form. But then he prepared a text from memory and often added much, so that the printed form still cannot

---

[3] Cf. also the survey in Ebeling, *op. cit.*, pp. 456-462.
[4] The Latin term, *sermo*, signifies more than a sermon in our sense, and yet its sermonic character is unmistakable. "Many people . . . say I write only little pamphlets and German sermons for the unlearned laity. . . . Would to God I had in all my life . . . helped one layman to be better." *PE* 1, 185.

be said to transmit what he actually uttered. Nevertheless, these printed versions are not altogether valueless, even though Hirsch makes the unqualified judgment that they give us a picture of Cruciger[5] and Veit Dietrich[6] but do not reflect Luther at all as far as form is concerned and only partially as far as content is concerned.[7] The printed versions, of course, contain language which is the transcriber's and not Luther's, and this often results, as one scholar has said, in a large admixture of water in Luther's wine. But if the sermon was elaborated from notes immediately after it was preached and the transcriber is a member of Luther's intimate circle, we may count upon a relatively high degree of dependability. Luther had good reasons for once admonishing the printers to print his sermons only "if they have been prepared by my hand or previously printed here in Wittenberg at my behest."[8] In the case of printed sermons, therefore, it is necessary first to discover how they were transmitted and then to compare the text with the manuscript transcription, if this is available, and arrive at a judgment as to how complete and accurate a reproduction it is. In any case, we can no longer judge Luther's preaching by the sermons printed in the Erlangen edition of his works.

The postils (*Kirchenpostille*) occupy a special position. Those published by Luther constitute the only "sermons" of his which we have in his own hand, but they are not strictly sermons at all. Rather they are expositions and sermon helps on the Gospels and Epistles of the church year intended to provide help for preachers with insufficient theological training, and for family reading. The so-called Wartburg postils, written by Luther himself, are "not model sermons but guides to the evangelical understanding of the Advent and Christmas Gospels and Epistles. Luther is concerned here that the preacher who has been won to the gospel should learn by means

---

[5] Like Dietrich and Poach, Kaspar Cruciger's (1504-1548) claim to fame rests chiefly on what he did to popularize Luther's ideas. A native of Leipzig, Cruciger was present, while a student, at the debate between Luther and Eck. After studying theology in Wittenberg he served as principal of a school in Magdeburg. Returning to Wittenberg in 1528, he became a professor in the theological faculty and pastor of the Castle Church.
[6] While studying theology in Wittenberg, Veit Dietrich (1506-1549) became Luther's amanuensis and one of his table companions. Even after he became pastor of the St. Sebaldus Church in his native Nürnberg his close association with Luther and Melanchthon continued.
[7] CL 7, vii.
[8] WA 10III, 176.

of these postils the right way to expound the Gospels and Epistles in preaching and to see very clearly the difference, even in details, between the traditional and the new piety and morality based upon the Bible. Thus the Wartburg postils are more applied homiletics than actual model sermons."[9] These postils extend from the First Sunday in Advent to the end of Holy Week. Luther wrote the Christmas and Advent postils (in that order) at the Wartburg in 1521 and these appeared in print in 1522. The so-called "winter portion" or Lenten postils, from Epiphany to Easter, appeared in 1525. This left a gap from Easter to the end of the church year which Stephan Roth[10] proceeded to fill with transcripts of Luther's sermons, publishing the "summer postils" in 1527, the "festival postils" for minor festivals in 1527, and in 1528 another series of "winter postils." Luther was put out over this last bit of presumption, since his own postils for this season were available, and only reluctantly was he persuaded to write a foreword to them. Roth's work is largely a hasty scrambling together of everything he could get hold of. He included previously printed sermons and occasionally, when Luther's sermons for particular Sundays were unavailable, even the sermons of others, such as Bugenhagen and Melanchthon. This has brought his collection into complete disrepute. In 1544 a new edition of the postils prepared by Kaspar Cruciger was published. The church postils are translated uncritically and inadequately in the J. N. Lenker edition of Luther's works. The so-called "house postils," church year sermons preached by Luther in his home from 1531 to 1535, when he was unable to preach in public because of his health, were published by Veit Dietrich in 1544, and also in a competitive edition by Andreas Poach,[11] based on stenographic notes of Georg Rörer, in 1559.

The third large group of sources for Luther's sermons is represented by the hundreds of stenographic reports by various listeners, including Veit Dietrich, Konrad Cordatus (1475 or 1476-1546),

---

[9] Hirsch, *Mitteilungen der Luthergesellschaft*, Jg. 25, *op. cit.*, p. 3 n.

[10] Like many of his contemporaries, Roth became an advocate and leader of "the new learning" in his native Zwickau and in Bohemia. A growing interest in the Reformation lead to his enrollment as a student in theology in Wittenberg in 1523. Returning to Zwickau in 1527, he became a recognized leader in civic, educational, and literary matters up to the year of his death in 1546.

[11] Though Poach (1516-1585) is known chiefly for his association with Luther, he became a protagonist of the Reformation in his own right as pastor in Halle, Jena, and Erfurt.

Anton Lauterbach (1502-1569), Johannes Schlaginhaufen (d. *ca.* 1560), Kaspar Cruciger, Andreas Poach, Johannes Stoltz, Johannes Aurifaber (1517-1568), Georg Rörer, and the work of two anonymous transcribers in a Nürnberg manuscript (Codex Solger) and a Copenhagen manuscript.

How Luther prepared his sermons we know from a few examples of his outlines in his own hand. They contain no elaboration of the text, only a brief outline with a few cues or catchwords. Frequently he had no time to jot down such notes, but even when he did, he often changed the prepared outline in the pulpit, adding new ideas, leaving out sections and transposing others. Consequently, we have his sermons in the form of stenographic notes and versions worked up from such outlines.

The most skilful of these note-takers was Georg Rörer (1492-1557), Luther's chief literary factotum and member and proofreader of the "Sanhedrim" which worked with Luther on the translation of the Bible. Rörer regularly recorded the sermons from 1522 on. The transcripts are not word-for-word records but full notes in a macaronic medley of Latin and German, employing a well-developed medieval system of shorthand, including such devices as omission and shortening of words and the use of signs for words and syllables.[12] Gaps occur and frequently transitions are lacking, and yet, since Luther was a deliberate preacher (*tardiloquus*), many of the transcriptions are so complete that it is not too difficult to reconstruct the sermon as it was spoken. It would seem beyond question that these texts bring us closest to the real preacher in the pulpit— far more direct, colorful, and concrete than the printed versions would indicate. Rörer's manuscripts were rediscovered in 1893 by Georg Buchwald, who edited them for the Weimar edition and published a large selection, carefully reproduced in German on the basis of the macaronic text.[13]

III

The year 1521 marks a change in Luther's preaching. Before this time he is still under the influence of his scholastic training and the homiletics of his time. The sermons of the first decade of his

---

[12] E.g., Luther's *der Glaub* (faith) and *die Sund* (sin) is rendered *der f[ides]* and *die p[eccatum]*. On Rörer's work, cf. WA 29, xvi-xxiv.
[13] See bibliography above, p. xi n. 1.

preaching indicate that he strove to give them the scholastic structure typical of the thematic sermon. This structure begins with the theme, a passage of Scripture or some other authority, which for Luther, who followed the strict rule, was usually the Gospel for the day. From this theme a clearly defined proposition (*suppositio*) is developed and then explained according to the rules of scholastic science with the aid of distinctions, bolstered at every point with authorities, and then applied, the whole being furnished with divisions, subdivisions, principal doctrines and subsidiary doctrines, and a long series of proof texts. Luther, however, never went to this extreme. A study of these early sermons shows that what distinguishes him from other scholastic preachers is that he (a) put more emphasis upon logic than learned prolixity, (b) preferred the Bible as his authority, adding at most a reference to one of the church fathers or a hymn, and (c) definitely tended toward more simplicity of form. The outline of these sermons is apparent; they do not require a chart to follow them, as is the case with many scholastic sermons. The introduction or *exordium* is omitted; he leaps directly into the subject and states the theme and the outline he proposes to follow. He kept the traditional form, but used it with freedom and a strong sense of what is essential. Allegorical interpretation in these sermons never exhibited the traditional, arbitrary whimsicalities of his own and earlier times; it is used with increasing moderation up to 1519, when he realized that there is "something altogether godless in so cutting up the Scriptures that the letter contains neither faith, moral, nor hope . . . as if Paul has not rightly said that 'all scripture is inspired by God and profitable for teaching, for reproof, for correction, and for training in righteousness.'"[14]

After 1521 Luther developed a completely new way of preaching. He begins at once with the main point and when his text or his time are used up he simply stops. His preaching is expository, not thematic or topical; instead of a theme the basis is a text of considerable length and the aim of the sermon is to help his hearers thoroughly to understand this text. The *suppositio* disappears and in its place Luther announces the text, makes a connection with the last sermon he has preached, points out that his listeners are familiar with the pericope, and comments on the theological importance of the lesson, or discusses its meaning in order to get it clear from the

---

[14] *WA* 5, 644, 39.

start. Sometimes he begins by pointing out the pastoral and practical implications of the pericope or by summarizing its content in a proposition; at other times he notes briefly the relation of the text to the church year or admonishes his hearers to give heed to its message. The goal is always that God may speak his Word to the congregation through the sermon. Then in practically all of his sermons the further development follows the text verse by verse or deals with its parts in a simple, direct flow of speech. The inner coherence that holds the sermon together is that everything he says serves to expound and proclaim the text, always keeping in mind the basic thought and thrust of the text. This type of sermon is usually called a homily (the nearest analogy to Luther's method is that employed in Augustine's homilies), but even this term is almost too precise, because he does not bind himself to treat the text exhaustively word by word, but moves freely, keeping to the important points, and also because his sermons have more unity than most homilies. In every sermon one is made aware of a definite point of view and, despite their seeming artlessness, they are unified in thought and mood.

As regards Luther's choice of texts, the great majority of the sermons are based on pericopes and especially the Gospel lessons. This is undoubtedly because he preached most frequently on Sunday mornings; when he preached in the afternoon the sermon would often be a continuation of the morning sermon or one based on the Epistle for the day. In spite of his sharply critical reservations with regard to the traditional lectionary, Luther preferred the Gospel pericopes. He maintained that the repetition of pericopes is profitable only for pedagogical reasons. Seldom does he choose free texts. Much of his preaching took the form of running sermonic commentaries; thus he preached series of sermons on Genesis, Exodus, Psalms, Matthew 5-7, 11-15, 18-24, 27-28, Luke 15-16, John 1-4, 6-8, 16-20. There is a large number of sermons without a text and these deal chiefly with parts of the Cathechism (mainly the Decalogue, Baptism, and the Lord's Supper) or with practical subjects like the problems of marriage, etc. These often became the basis of the published *sermones,* or treatises, mentioned above.

IV

A printed sermon is always a torso. It is only an objectivation of a part of an event committed to words. It is only the "offprint" of the event of worship, an interpersonal event in which the sermon is only one, though the most important, element. Many sermons which are printed lose the depth of the Word and the most vital thing in the sermon so easily vanishes the moment it is severed from its original situation: the listening congregation which gathered in a specific, unique place and time to hear it and respond to it. Words remain, but not always the Word. This is less true of Luther's sermons, for they breathe the atmosphere of the living congregation to which they were addressed and their one and only aim is to proclaim the text of Scripture as the living, present, effectual Word of God with all its demand and its promise. They can still "preach" to the reader today. Friedrich Gogarten comments on the "remarkable objectivity" of Luther's sermons, the fact that the biblical text becomes the living Word of God in the act of preaching (*viva vox Evangelii*), the voice of Christ himself addressing the hearer who cannot escape and must of necessity hear it and reject or accept it.

"Compared with what passes for preaching today, the peculiar characteristic of Luther's preaching is a remarkable objectivity, not only with respect to its object, the gospel, but also with respect to the hearers to whom it is addressed. But this objectivity does not mean the much-praised popular and illustrative quality of his speech and manner of expressing himself; for there is preaching like that today too. But we must not overlook the difference between this kind of popular and vivid preaching and that of Luther. That of Luther contains a measure of profound theology, or teaching, as he expressed it, such as present-day popular preachers apparently cannot produce even in the theological works they may write—if they ever even bother with what most of them would call 'theoretical' matters—to say nothing of their 'popular' sermons. Rather, what we mean by this objectivity that characterizes Luther's preaching is its completely contemporaneous concentration upon the gospel as well as the listeners. When Luther preaches the gospel the reference to the gospel which takes place in this preaching is *the* decisive and immediately operative event in one's whole life. And it is from this reference to the gospel that the reference to the listener derives its decisive meaning and its contemporaneity."[15]

Luther's sermons are therefore real battles in the eschatological struggle between Christ and the adversary; their aim is to make

---

[15] Gogarten, *op. cit.*, p. 523.

Christians of the hearers through the Word of God and thus hurl the power and victory of Christ against the power of evil.[16] "Nothing but Christ is to be preached," Luther says in his sermons on Exodus;[17] Christ himself is present and doing his work through preaching. For him, therefore, to preach Christ is not merely a hermeneutical principle or a homiletical method of stressing the kerygma, but an inner necessity of the message itself. Preaching continues the battle begun by the saving event and is itself the saving event. This is apparent in one of the most revealing of Luther's comments about his own method. In a sermon preached in his home on Whitmonday, 1532, he said, "When I preach a sermon I take an antithesis."[18] In other words, he never proclaims God's great Yes, God's acceptance of man in the gospel, without at the same time proclaiming his No, his rejection of all of man's presumption, work-righteousness, and the imaginations of his reason. This is apparent again in his characteristic use of direct address, dialogue, and the dramatic form. He has the persons of the text speaking to one another or goes into an imaginary dialogue between the preacher and his listeners or the preacher and his opponents. And every sermon is part and parcel of his own struggle, not only the dialogue he is carrying on with his opponents, the papists and the enthusiasts [Schwärmer], but also of that existential encounter which is constantly being enacted on the cosmic, eschatological level. One cannot read these sermons even today without realizing that they confront a man with ultimate decision.

Luther never wrote a systematic treatise on homiletics, though he once threatened to,[19] but there is a wealth of comment in the Table Talk and elsewhere.[20] What it all boils down to is a searching challenge to the preacher to believe that God speaks through preaching and preaching alone. For, as he says in the Advent postils, this is Christ's commission: "Go therefore, i.e., just go on preaching; don't worry about who will listen; let me worry about that. The world will be against you; don't let that trouble you. Nevertheless, there will be those who will listen to you and follow. You do not

---

[16] Cf. Ebeling, op. cit., p. 28.
[17] WA 16, 113, 7.
[18] Quando facio praedicationem, accipio Antithesin. WA 36, 181; CL 7, 18.
[19] "Some time I must write a book against the smart preachers." WA, TR 4, 4763.
[20] The best collection of Luther's homiletical wisdom is to be found in CL 7, 1-38.

know them now, but I know them already. You preach, and let me manage."[21]

V

This volume contains a selection of forty-three sermons arranged in chronological order, beginning with what is possibly Luther's earliest extant sermon and ending with the last he delivered before his death. It is obvious that, confronted by the enormous bulk of sources, an editor's most formidable task is that of selection. Almost anybody who is familiar with the sources might therefore quarrel with the selection; the editor can only say that he has endeavored to suppress his subjective propensities and make an objective choice within the limits imposed upon him. The selection covers the entire preaching ministry, from the "young Luther" to the "old Luther," including sermons on historic occasions, three sermons on the same text (Matt. 11:25-30) preached at widely different times, Christmas and Passion sermons, funeral, baptismal, marriage, and dedication sermons. Fortunately, the selection need not stand by itself, since other volumes in the whole edition contain many sermonic expositions and another volume or volumes will be devoted exclusively to sermons. The relevant facts concerning each sermon are given in brief introductions which locate time, place, text, source, transmission, etc. for each.

It remains only to express thanks to the librarians of the Lutheran Theological Seminary at Philadelphia, Union Theological Seminary in New York, and Wartburg Seminary in Dubuque for many courtesies, to Dr. Georg Merz, professor in the Augustana Hochschule, Neuendettelsau, and editor of the München edition of Luther's works (MA³), for counsel in the selection of these sermons, and to Miss Hope Treichler for many hours devoted to preparing the typescript.

J.W.D.

---

[21] WA I,² 51, 3.

LUTHER'S WORKS

VOLUME 51

EARLY SERMONS

1510(?)-1517

EARLY SERMONS, 1510(?)-1517

Luther's First (?) Sermon, Matt. 7:12,

1510(?) or 1512(?)

Luther's earliest sermons were probably given to friends, especially John Lang, and thus preserved. Two sermons, the one here chosen and another on John 3:16, discovered in Zwickau by Georg Buchwald, come from the remains of Andreas Poach, the Erfurt preacher, who prefaced his copy of them with the note: "From an autograph of Luther discovered in the monastery of the Augustinians, Erfurt." Buchwald leans toward the date 1512 (WA 22, xlvii), and Erich Vogelsang ("Zur Datierung der frühsten Lutherpredigten," ZKG, L, 3, Folge (1931), pp. 114-121, and CL 7, 19-20) suggests either 1510, during Luther's first sojourn in Erfurt, or 1512, during his second stay in Erfurt. Vogelsang says of this sermon: "It is the most penetrating sermon on Law and judgment which we have from the young Luther and is presumably the very earliest sermon of his we possess." There would seem to be no foundation for the remark in LW 22, ix that the sermon on John 1:1 (WA 1, 20) is the earliest sermon. The "first complete sermon of Luther's in his own hand" (Vogelsang) is probably the one embedded in the exposition of Psalm 60:8 (WA 3, 342-346). Cf. also Elmer Carl Kiessling, The Early Sermons of Luther, *pp. 68ff., and R. H. Fife,* The Revolt of Martin Luther *(New York, 1957), pp. 184ff.*

Text in Latin; WA 4, 590-595, compared with CL 5, 20-26 and German translation in Mühlhaupt, D. Martin Luthers Evangelienauslegung, *II, 213-19.*

"Whatever you wish that men would do to you, do so to them; for this is the law and the prophets" [Matt. 7:12].

This sermon will have three parts. First I shall say something which is noteworthy by way of introduction; secondly, I shall draw a useful conclusion for our own instruction; and thirdly, I shall answer some questions with regard to what has been said.

I

First, it should be noted that human goods are of three kinds.[1] The first are external, such as gold, silver, money, clothing, land, houses, servants, wives, children, family, sheep, oxen, horses, etc. These are called external goods because they lie outside of human nature. Secondly, there are the physical and personal goods, such as health, strength, beauty, the disposition of members, aptitude of the body and senses, and likewise, reputation and honor. These are also called intermediate goods, since they are not outside of the person like the first, but also are not internal goods, like those which will follow directly, but rather lie between these two. Thirdly, there are spiritual or internal goods, such as knowledge, virtue, love, faith. And these goods are called internal and spiritual because they lie solely in the mind and spirit. And the external and intermediate goods are symbols of these internal and spiritual goods, as gold signifies knowledge and wisdom, garments signify the virtues: love, chastity, patience, etc.;[2] if these virtues are in the soul, then one can say that the soul is adorned [with these], as the body is adorned with outward garments.

With these goods, then, each person can conduct himself toward his neighbor in two ways. First, with these goods he can do harm and evil to him, or, second, he can advance and benefit him. An example of the first is when one steals external goods or destroys the health of the body with blows and poison or takes from him his internal goods, such as knowledge, by seducing him into error; or virtue, by inciting him to evil, and so on. An example of the second way is when one gives him food and clothing, or heals his infirmities, or protects his body, or teaches him something better and incites

---

[1] The familiar classification of Aristotle's *Nichomachean Ethics*, I, 7 (Everyman's Library, p. 13).
[2] So in the *Glossa ordinaria* of Nicholas of Lyra (d. 1340), the commentary on the Bible used by Luther, e.g., glosses on Job 3:15 and Ps. 45:10.

him to do good, and so on. Therefore we have in the Scriptures two rules to guide us ·in the use of these goods: Psalm 33 [Ps. 37:27], "depart from evil," with respect to the first, and "do good," with respect to the second way.

II

As to the second part, this one doctrine is to be noted: It is not sufficient for salvation that a man merely refrain from doing harm and evil to his neighbor with these three goods. It is required rather that he be useful to him and benefit him with these three goods. This doctrine is proved by threefold authority: by reason, by authority, and analogy.

A

First, by *reason*:[3] If merely refraining from doing harm were sufficient for salvation, then much wood in the forest and many stones in the depths of the ocean would be saved, for they obviously do no harm or evil to anyone through these goods. But this is not true. Thus the one who merely does no harm would be like wood and stones, and this is not sufficient for salvation.

B

[Second,] by *authority*, in German, by passages of Scripture.

1

First is our text, which says, "Whatever you wish that men would do to you." It does not say: Whatever harm you wish that men should not do to you, do not this harm to them. This is true, of course, and it is necessary, but it is not sufficient; we must also do good to the other person. Now, let each one enter into his own heart and see whether he wishes that others would give him clothing, food, drink, shelter, and other external goods when he is in need; whether he wishes that others would defend his reputation and honor; whether he wishes that others would teach, comfort, and incite him to good, etc. And if he sees that this is the case and still does not do likewise to the other person, he sins and will never merit

---

[3] In the original the words, *teutonice aus der vernunft,* "in German, by reason," are added.

7

eternal life, for he does not wish to do to the other person in his need what he himself would wish for himself in his need. Therefore he acts contrary to the law and the prophets, which are all comprehended in this saying of the Lord.

2

Secondly, there is the parable of the rich reveller in Luke 16 [:19-31]. He was not damned because he robbed or did evil with respect to these goods, for he feasted and clothed himself sumptuously every day with his own goods. He was damned rather because he did not do good to his neighbor, namely, Lazarus. This parable adequately teaches us that it is not sufficient merely not to do evil and not to do harm, but rather that one must be helpful and do good. It is not enough to "depart from evil"; one must also "do good" [Ps. 37:27].

3

The third authority [i.e., passage of Scripture] is the parable of the slothful servant in Matt. 25 [:14-30], who received the one talent (in German, a pound) and hid it in the ground. He too was not damned because he took something away from others, but because he did not give to others. So it will be with us. To us has been given as a talent what we are able to do, our ability. For all that we are capable of in connection with external, internal, and intermediate goods we have, not of ourselves, but from God. And in all this we are required to do to our neighbor what we are able to do. If we do not do this, we hide the Lord's talent and are condemned along with that servant. Therefore the Apostle says, "Employ it for one another [I Pet. 4:10], that which the Lord has assigned to him [I Cor. 7:17]—in German, let each one be helpful to the other as God has given to him. This is love toward all and the true Christian life.

4

The fourth [word of Scripture] is that in the judgment the Lord will not speak of whether one has harmed or done evil to him with these goods, but rather that one has not done good. Therefore Matt. 25 [:42] says, "I was hungry and you gave me no food, I was thirsty

8

and you gave me no drink, etc." He does not say: I had food and you stole it from me, I had drink and you took it away from me, but rather, "You gave me no food, no drink." Therefore it is necessary to do good and not only refrain from doing evil. Similarly he says, "I was a stranger and you did not welcome me, naked and you did not clothe me, sick . . . and you did not visit me" [Matt. 25:43]. He does not say: I had a house and you expelled me. Granted, this too is condemnable; but it is not enough merely to refrain from this, as has been said. This must likewise be understood as applying also to the other goods. For example: I was defamed and you did not excuse me; I was in dishonor and you did not defend me. Likewise with regard to spiritual goods: I was sorrowful and you did not comfort me; I was in error and you did not instruct me, etc. We are bound to excuse, defend, console, and teach our neighbor, and what we do to him we do to Christ, as he says in the same passage: "As you did it to one of the least of these my brethren, you did it to me" [Matt. 25:40]. It is therefore not enough to be innocent of harming one's neighbor; we must also do good as far as we are able.

5

Fifthly, the blessed Augustine[4] says, "Feed the hungry; if you have not fed him, you have killed him." That is to say, if he dies of hunger, it is the same as if you had killed him; indeed, as far as you are concerned, you have killed him.[5] The same must be said concerning all other goods:

Clothe the naked		clothe him		robbed him
Welcome the stranger	if	take him in	it is	expelled him
Give the thirsty drink	you	give him drink	as if	made him thirsty
Console the sorrowful	were	console him	you	saddened him
Teach the erring	able and	teach him	yourself	led him astray
Reprove the sinner	did	reprove him	had	made him to sin
Excuse the defamed	not	excuse him		slandered him
Heal the sick		heal him		made him sick.

6

The reason for all this is that we would wish all this to be done to us by others if possible when we were in need. Therefore we are

---

[4] This saying is attributed by Gabriel Biel to Ambrose (d. 397), bishop of Milan and teacher of Augustine. Cf. CL 5, 22, note. Later Luther often quotes this saying, ascribing it to Ambrose; vid. Sermon July 20, 1533, WA 37, 113, 22
[5] The last part of this sentence in German.

held under God's command to do this as far as we are able to others also when they are in need. For this is the law and the prophets, as our text clearly says. Thus Ecclus. 17 [:14] also says, "He gave every man commandment concerning his neighbor." Likewise, there is that second commandment, which is like the first commandment because everything depends on it, namely, all the law and the prophets: "You shall love your neighbor as yourself" [Matt. 22:39]. This is the same as what is said here: "Whatsoever you wish that men would do to you, do so to them, etc."

C

Third, it is also to be proved by *analogy*. When a field is sown with good seed, it is not enough that it merely does not bear thistles, thorns, and weeds; it must rather bring fruit for its master and others from the seed which has been committed to it; otherwise it will be cursed. So it is with us, for we are God's field and the Father in heaven is the farmer [cf. John 15:1]. The Apostle also says that we are "God's field" [I Cor. 3:9]. He has given to us His seed, that is, the external, internal, and intermediate goods. It is not sufficient that we accept this and not produce thorns, offenses, and tribulations, not injuring our neighbor, but rather we must bring forth fruit by doing good to others. This is the way we become a good field.

A second analogy: Wild beasts and irrational animals keep this law. When a pig is slaughtered or captured and other pigs see this, we observe that the other pigs clamor and grunt as if in compassion. Chickens and geese and all wild animals do the same thing; when they see one of their own kind in trouble, they quite naturally grieve with it and are sad, and if they can, they help it. Only man, who after all is rational, does not spring to the aid of his suffering neighbor in time of need and has no pity on him. What a shame and scandal! Yea, more, they bring trouble upon one another rather than take it away. Therefore Seneca, when he was asked what is most harmful to man, quite rightly replied: Man, that is, one to another.[6] For one single man is able to injure another with respect to all three goods, and this is something which no element or physical creature

---

[6] Seneca, *Epistles*, 107, 7, *homo perniciosior feris omnibus*.

can do. For man kills, robs, wounds, defames, burns, seduces, and makes sad. Beyond this, he is also capable of cherishing hatred and jealousy. Fire and water, and the lion and the bear are not capable of all this at one time but only of one of them.

From this general lesson, it is possible to draw many special lessons and conclusions.

First, he who sees a naked man and does not clothe him, if he is able, will not be saved. This is proved by our text; for he does not do what he would have another do to him. For if he himself were thus naked, he would certainly wish to be clothed by one who was able to do so.

Second, he who sees a thirsty or hungry man and does not feed him, if he is able, will be damned. This too is clear, for this he too would wish to be done to him, but he does not do it to the other person. And thus he acts against the law and the prophets, for the law and the prophets consist in this, as the text says.

Third, he who hears one person slander another and remains silent and does not apologize for him, that person sins; for this is what he would wish to have others do to him. Therefore, if one does not resist the slander, this is to commit an "alien sin."[7]

Fourth, he who sees another person sinning or erring, morally[8] especially, and does not instruct and rebuke and admonish him, but rather laughs and applauds, that person sins the same sin. This too is clear, for he does not do in respect to spiritual goods what he would wish, or at least ought to wish, others to do to him.

Fifth, if those who merely do not do good to their neighbor, and do not further him in these goods, commit sin and are damned, where will they be who actually do evil and harm to others? Where will they be who deprive the other person of his external goods by robbery, usury, fraud, lies, force, and violence? Where will they be who mangle and tear down the good name of other persons, which now occurs so frequently that nobody pays any attention to it any more? Where will they be who draw others into sin, as often happens in drinking and gorging, when one makes another drunk and

---

[7] *Peccatum alienum.* The reference is to "presumptuous sins" (Ps. 19:13), the sin of associating oneself with the sin of presumptuous men.

[8] The original manuscript reads *mortaliter* (mortally), which may be the better reading, though it is crossed out and *moraliter* substituted.

thus injures his neighbor's spiritual and physical goods, for then the soul sins and the body is weakened by gluttony and excess? Where will they be, if even they sin who only look on and do nothing to stop it, and thus give their consent? From these our morals, one observes that nobody cares about the law and the prophets and there is almost no Christian life among us. Where will the flatterers and the sowers of discord among men be, if even they sin who fail to reconcile the discordant? Behold, we not only do not "do good," we have not yet "departed from evil" [Ps. 37:27], and thus keep neither of the two rules, but do everything that is contrary to them.

Therefore, sixth and last, let each one place this example of the Lord before his eyes like a mirror and note it well, for it is good and he would have it to be the whole law and the prophets. I am not saying this, but the Lord himself: "Whatever you wish that men would do to you, do so to them; for this is the law and the prophets." Look, here you have the whole of Scripture in one short saying! Hence this saying should be a mirror for every man and in it he should view all his works, whether he does to his neighbor as he would wish to have others do to him, and also whether for himself he would wish to have omitted what he omits to do to his neighbor. If he finds that this is so, he may hope that he will be saved. But if not, I beseech and admonish him to amend his ways that he may not perish. And he should pay no attention to the fact that there are many people, both secular and spiritual, who do not do this. They will have "their reward" [Matt. 6:5, 16]. The multitude of sinners will not be a patron or helper for any one on the day of judgment.

III

With regard to the third part there is a question. It is possible that one may think to himself: 1) Would it not be sufficient if I wish the other person well in my heart, especially if one is injured and offended by him? 2) Many say: I will let him go in peace, disengage myself from him, and do neither good nor evil to him. 3) Others say: Is not what I have my own? After all, I can do with it what I will.[9]

---

[9] It is apparent from Luther's letter to John Lang (WA, Br 1, 66) that he is here referring to the common scholastic tendency to qualify and weaken the commandment of love. Cf. CL 5, 318.

The answer to the first question is this: Just see whether what you wish is that the other person be favorable toward you in his heart and is content to leave it at that, without doing anything for you in deed. If not, then it is not sufficient for you either. For the Lord did not say: Whatever you wish that men would do to you, grant it to them in your heart; but rather "*do* so to them." But who is content with good will if something can be done? Therefore it is not enough. Rather look into the mirror of this saying, namely, whether you wish that this be done to you.

The answer to the second question is this: One cannot always know the reason why the offended one does not do good to the offender, whether the motive is love of revenge, or love of justice, or fear of danger or some other evil, such as fear that this may only strengthen and give comfort to the offender in his wickedness and impudence, as is the case with drunkards, mockers, and brawlers. Therefore one can say nothing better than this: Hold up the mirror of these words to your conscience and see whether any such motive would prompt you not to wish any good to be done to you by others if they cherished any such motive toward you. Then you are saved. Otherwise I advise you to beware. For the Lord will keep this rule: "The measure you give will be the measure you get" [Matt. 7:2]. For he well perceives the heart and the motives we cherish. Therefore, if we wish to be requited by God as we do to our neighbor, then it is well with us. But if in our ill will we say: I will let him go, disengage myself from him, then I ask whether you also wish that God should say to you: I will let you go, I will disengage myself from you and neither give nor take anything from you? Who would wish that? But this is precisely what he will do to us, if this is what we do to our neighbor without sufficient cause.

To the third question I reply that all the goods we have are from God and they are not given to us to retain and abuse, but rather to dispense. Therefore when a person retains, when he should not retain, or abuses them, then by this act itself they are no longer his, even if he has them in his power, but rather belong to the Lord, who is God. We, however, are all his servants, etc.

Sermon on the Tenth Sunday after Trinity,

Luke 18:9-14, July 27, 1516

This is one of the introductory sermons to a series of sermons on the Ten Commandments which Luther preached from June, 1516 to February 24, 1517 in the parish church in Wittenberg. (Cf. Fife, op. cit., pp. 232-235). Along with the three following pre-Reformation sermons it breathes the spirit of Luther's "theology of the cross," which he summed up in a statement occurring in a fragment of a sermon on St. Martin's Day, Nov. 11, 1515: Unum praedica: sapientiam crucis!—"Preach one thing: the wisdom of the cross!" (WA 1, 52).

Text in Latin; WA 1, 63-65.

[The Psalter says], "who is like unto the Lord our God, who dwelleth on high, who humbleth himself to behold the things that are in heaven and in the earth" [Ps. 113:5-6]. And again: "Though the Lord is high, he regards the lowly; but the haughty he knows from afar" [Ps. 138:6].

How wonderful is this God above all other gods! He sees what is remote and far off; the others, however, see only what is right next to them. He does not recognize what is close to him; they do not recognize what is remote from them, just like the rulers of this world. Therefore it is the true nature of humility to retire far off from God and from all that is God's. On the other hand, it is the true nature of pride to approach as close as possible to God and all that is God's, as Isa. 58 [:2] says of the proud Jews: "They delight to draw near to God." And both of these things are clearly disclosed in those two men in the Gospel, the Pharisee and the publican. But whatever is to be like God and the being of God, which is life, wisdom, power, righteousness, riches, beauty, and all good, must conform with the rule of the Apostle in Rom. 12 [:16]: "Associate with the lowly"; no matter how humiliating and difficult it may be for the rich man to put himself on the same level with any beggar who comes along, for the virgin to identify herself with a harlot, the chaste woman with an adulteress, the wise man with a fool, the strong man with a weakling, the living person with a dead one, the beautiful with an ugly one, the superior with an inferior one. If you say, I can not do it; very well, then erase this statement: "Who is like unto the Lord our God . . . who humbleth himself to behold the things that are in heaven and in the earth!" [Ps. 113:5-6]. How will it ever happen that the proud will do this? My answer is that they will do this only through this one word: "Take what belongs to you and go" [Matt. 20:14], or through this other saying: "What have you that you did not receive? If then you received it, why do you boast as if it were not a gift?" [I Cor. 4:7].

This drawing away from God and drawing near to God occurs in two ways, that is, inwardly and outwardly, or through acknowledging God and not acknowledging God. Acknowledging God results in drawing away in fear and reverence, and this is humility, in which a man recognizes his own nothingness and leaves all good to God, not daring to claim anything for himself. Not acknowledging God results in drawing away from God in contempt and security, and this is pride. Thus, for example, an utter pauper in the presence of a prince flees into a corner. The one who flees recognizes and reverences the majesty of the prince; but another turns his back and draws far away because he despises the prince.

So, learn here the characteristics of a proud man.

In the first place, he asks nothing of God. He imagines that he has no need of anybody and so he thinks that he does not even need God. He is rather sufficient to himself; for if he felt any lack in himself, he would plead with God and have need of him. If he removes the necessity for God and attributes to him only contingency, he is laying aside his own deficiency and ascribing sufficiency to himself. The truly humble person is the opposite. He despairs of being sufficient of himself. He fervently longs that there be a God and prays for what he lacks; indeed, he gives the glory to God, and so he is justified. But it is a very good thing that the Lord did not pass over in silence the hypocritical words of the proud. For they too return thanks to God, they too say that everything they have comes from God, that of themselves they are nothing and lacking in every respect. On the whole, they imitate as closely as possible the truly humble, even down to their gestures; that is, they have

15

the form of humility but deny its power [cf. II Tim. 3:5], which is proven when they compare themselves with others.

Secondly, this blindness and ignorance of oneself goes even further, as St. Augustine says: It is not enough for them not to petition God; they must praise themselves. Even though they may quite wonderfully blame themselves in words, they are nevertheless pleased with themselves in their hearts. They do not groan over themselves, they do not accuse themselves, but always keep on saying: I was not conscious of doing anything wrong. Have I not done well, even better than this person and that person? The humble man, on the contrary, when he had prayed to God to be merciful to him, went on and accused himself, saying, "to me a sinner." Behold, he calls himself, confesses himself a sinner. He draws away from the righteousness and holiness in which the proud man wraps himself.

Thirdly, he completes his wickedness, not only by praising himself, but also by deriding and accusing the one who is praying and accusing himself. This is a horrible monstrosity, which alone ought to humble all who are proud, for, of course, every proud person tears down and accuses his neighbor when he sits in judgment. Then just look at the evil he involves himself in. First, he fails to perform a work of mercy, for he ought to have compassion on his neighbor, pray for him, and help him in every way possible. Therefore he is worthy of eternal death (Matt. 25 [:41]). Then, mind you, he goes after him with his tongue, which is a sword worse than one of iron [cf. Ps. 57:4], and this he does before God and men and himself. And finally, he commits a lie and an injustice by doing this to one who is praying and confessing and thus is already justified. And he would be committing a lie and an injustice against his neighbor, even if he actually were what he accuses him of being. Then he even attacks Christ, who received all sinners, for thus Christ is judged, accused, and pilloried as a sinner, since every one whom one accuses is a sinner. But he who judges Christ, judges his own judge, and he who judges his own judge is violently denying God. You see where this furious and foolish pride comes out! On the other hand, the humble man declares his neighbor just; he really accuses only himself, for he says, "to me a sinner," not "to us sinners." Do you think he was so jealous that he did not want God to be merciful to the other sinners also? Then he certainly would not have been justified, but rather damned. But he sees none who is a sinner except himself alone. Everybody with whom he compares himself is just. So "to the pure all things are pure," but to the impure nothing is pure [Titus 1:15].

It is clear, then, that this Pharisee did not keep the first commandment. On the contrary, he had another God—if he had not had another God, he would certainly have been justified—I mean the idol of his own righteousness erected in his heart. But now let each one who hates and despises this Pharisee take heed lest he put himself above the Pharisee, just as the latter put himself above the publican. I believe that few are afraid of being like the Pharisee, whom they hate, but I know that the majority are like him; for who is so proud that he can boast of being free of all pride and can claim for himself this utter humility of the publican? Therefore we shall rather acknowledge that we are like the Pharisee and shall groan over ourselves and hate ourselves more than he did, and not presume so confidently that we are like the publican; for he was blessed beyond measure and was a child of grace. We, however, are children of nature and, therefore, children of wrath.

Sermon on St. Thomas' Day, Ps. 19:1,

December 21, 1516

This sermon contains one of the first detailed expositions of what Luther later called the "theology of the cross" and further developed in the Lectures on Hebrews *(1518) and the* Heidelberg Disputation *(1518). For a discussion of Luther's theologia crucis, see Philip S. Watson, Let God be God (Philadelphia, 1949), pp. 156-160 and for an analysis of this sermon, see Kiessling, op. cit., pp. 96-97.*

Text in Latin; WA 1, 111-115, compared with CL 5, 419-424.

"The heavens are telling the glory of God; and the firmament proclaims his handiwork" [Ps. 19:1].

The gospel is nothing else but the proclamation of the works of God, for it preaches what God does, and this in itself preaches his glory, since God is glorified through the very telling of the works of God. Glory and praise is nothing else but a proclamation of his power and a telling of his works. It follows that the heavens reprove and censure human glory and put to silence the works of men's hands, as Ps. 17 [:3-4] says, "My mouth does not speak of the works of men." For the glory of God makes us to understand that human glory is vanity, nay, shame; and the works of God declare and show that the works of men, which they glory in, as if they were good, right, wise, and useful, are nothing, or better, actually sins. For it is the works which are the substance and foundation of praise and glory. Therefore, where the substance is destroyed, the house which stands upon it is also destroyed. Therefore, the gospel, since it proclaims the glory of God, reveals human shame, and, since it manifests the works of God, discloses the idleness and sin of men. But proud man can bear neither of these indignities; for here his works, in which he was so pleased with himself and which he gloried in, because he felt that they were just and faultless, are shown to be polluted, even shameful. As Wisd. of Sol. 2 [:16] says, "He abstains from our ways as from filthiness." The wicked man hears it "and is angry; he gnashes his teeth and melts away" [Ps. 112:10]. Thus glory arouses anger and envy in men, and grace provokes indignation, mercy provokes cruelty, pity provokes tyranny, and salvation provokes perdition; in short, good becomes the cause of evil. Who would not wonder at this? The sun, when it rises, offends the eyes of the owl, and wine kills those who are fevered.

In order that this may be more clearly understood, we must know what is meant by the work of God. It is nothing else but to create righteousness, peace, mercy, truth, patience, kindness, joy, and health, inasmuch as the righteous, truthful, peaceful, kind, joyful, healthy, patient, merciful cannot do otherwise than act according to His nature. Therefore God creates righteous, peaceful, patient, merciful, truthful, kind, joyful, wise, healthy men. These are his handiwork, or his creations, as Ps. 111 [:3] says, "Full of honor and majesty is his work." That is to say, praise and comeliness, or glory and brightness is the work of God. It is praiseworthy and very beautiful, without any blemish whatsoever, as Ps. 96 [:6]

says, "Honor and beauty are before him; strength and majesty are in
his sanctuary," that is, in his church. The acts of God are therefore
the righteous and the Christians; they are his new creation. The
new works, however, are the righteousness, truths, etc., which he
performs in his acts, as the psalm says: They have proclaimed the
works of God and understood his acts,[1] that is, they caused them to
be understood. And again: "They have not understood the works
of the Lord, or the work of his hands" [Ps. 28:5].

But He cannot come to this his proper work unless he under-
takes a work that is alien and contrary to himself, as Isa. 28 [:21]
says: An alien work is his that he may work his own work. His alien
work, however, is to make men sinners, unrighteous, liars, miserable,
foolish, lost. Not that he actually makes them such himself, but that
the pride of men, although they are such, will not let them become
or be such, so much so that God makes use of a greater disturbance,
indeed, he uses this work solely to show them that they are such, in
order that they may become in their own eyes, what they are in
God's eyes. Therefore, since he can make just only those who are
not just, he is compelled to perform an alien work in order to make
them sinners, before he performs his proper work of justification.
Thus he says, "I kill and I make alive; I wound and I heal" [Deut.
32:39]. But they who deem themselves just and wise and think they
are somebody are most violently hostile to this alien work, which is
the cross of Christ and our Adam. For they do not want what is
theirs to be despised and regarded as foolish and evil, that is, they
do not want their Adam to be killed. So they do not come to God's
proper work, which is justification or the resurrection of Christ.

God's alien work, therefore, is the suffering of Christ and sufferings in Christ, the crucifixion of the old man and the mortification
of Adam. God's proper work, however, is the resurrection of Christ,
justification in the Spirit, and the vivification of the new man, as
Rom. 4 [:25] says: Christ died for our sins and was raised for our
justification. Thus, conformity with the image of the Son of God
[cf. Rom. 8:29] includes both of these works. This is what I said
not long ago[2] concerning John [the Baptist] and the gospel of which

---

[1] It is not clear what psalm is referred to here. The Weimar editor suggests
Ps. 97:6 and the reference in CL 5, 420, is quite irrelevant.
[2] Cf. end of Luther's sermon on the Gospel for the Second Sunday in Advent,
Dec. 7, 1516. WA 1, 104-106.

he is a figure. For just as the work of God is twofold, namely, proper and alien, so also the office of the gospel is twofold. The proper office of the gospel is to proclaim the proper work of God, i.e. grace, through which the Father of mercies freely gives to all men peace, righteousness and truth, mitigating all his wrath. Therefore it is called a good, delightful, sweet, friendly gospel, and he who hears it finds it impossible not to rejoice. But this happens whenever the forgiveness of sins is proclaimed to grieving consciences, as Rom. 10 [:15] says: "How beautiful," that is, how amiable, delightful, and, as the Hebrew reads, desirable [cf. Isa. 52:7], "are the feet of those who preach the gospel," that is, those who bring the good and pleasant news, who proclaim peace, and therefore, not the law and the threats of the law, not something which must still be fulfilled and performed, but rather the forgiveness of sins, peace of conscience, the message that the law has been fulfilled, etc. "Who preach good news," that is, the altogether sweet and delightful mercy of God the Father, the Christ who is given to us.

But the strange work of the gospel is to prepare a people [cf. Luke 1:17] perfect for the Lord, that is, to make manifest sins and pronounce guilty those who were righteous in their own eyes by declaring that all men are sinners and devoid of the grace by God [cf. Rom. 3:23]. But such a message may appear to be the worst kind of a message, and therefore one might much rather call it a *Cacangelium,* i.e. bad news, sad news. Just as one who awaits death in sadness and desperation hears nothing more sweet than to be told: Look, you shall be free, now live! so they who live securely hear nothing sadder than to be told: Look, you shall die!

So the gospel sounds exceedingly harsh in its alien tones, and yet this must be done, in order that it may be able to sound with its own proper tones. This must be made manifest through examples, as I have done previously.[3] Behold, the law says: "You shall not kill, you shall not steal, you shall not commit adultery" [Exod. 20:13-15]. Here the proud, who are righteous with the righteousness of works, and have not done these works,[4] already live in security, as though they had fulfilled the law, nor are they conscious of any sin in themselves, but of much righteousness. To those who

---

[3] I.e., in the sermon of the previous Sunday, WA 1, 106, 15; see note 2 above.
[4] I.e., have not transgressed these commandments.

are so presumptuous, the interpreter of the law, namely, the gospel, comes and says: "Repent, for the kingdom of heaven is at hand" [Matt. 4:17]. In saying to all men, "repent!" it undoubtedly declares all to be sinners, and so its brings sad and unwelcome tidings, which is *Cacangelium*, i.e. bad news and an alien office. When, however, it says: "The kingdom of heaven is at hand," this is good news, and a pleasant and joyous preaching; it is the proper office, namely, of the gospel. So John comes as "the voice of one crying" [Matt. 3:3], i.e., the gospel, and preaches to all men a baptism of repentance, and by this preaching he claims unceasingly that all men are sinful.

But here the Lord rises up "as on the mount of division,"[5] as Isa. 28 [:21] says. For some believe John as the voice of the gospel. They hold this mournful message to be true and thus are humbly and tremblingly obedient, recognizing that they are sinners. Whether they are conscious of it themselves or not, they nevertheless believe John more than themselves. And here already they are prepared by John to be a perfect people [cf. Luke 1:17], elect of the Lord, for they are capable of receiving grace; they hunger for righteousness; they mourn for consolation; they are poor in spirit [Matt. 5]; they are mild and biddable. Therefore, Christ, the kingdom of heaven, he who comes to save sinners, comes into them.

Others, however, who consider themselves just, do not believe that John's message is true, nor that those words, "repent ye," apply to them. On the contrary, they say: We are just; we are not aware of any sin; we are already reigning, since the kingdom of heaven is at hand, indeed, it came a long time ago. So when John proceeds to demonstrate their hard-heartedness and says: "You brood of vipers! Who warned you to flee from the wrath to come? Bear fruit that befits repentance" [Matt. 3:7-8], they immediately say, "He has a demon" [Matt. 11:18]. They say this, not only because he contends that these altogether just and worthy people have sins, but also because he calls them a brood of vipers in the presence of others and thus arouses anger.

Such are, now and always, all who put their trust in their own righteousness, who are bent solely on hearing—from themselves, not from Christ—the gospel, that is, the good news that they are just and

---

[5] The Vulgate translation of Mount Perazim, where by God's intervention David won a victory over the Philistines.

that they are doing what is right. Again, they do not want to hear the alien tone of the gospel, which declares that they sin and are fools. On the contrary, they believe that the gospel is false, that it is a lie. That is why they are the most irritated of all men, prompt to defend themselves and to be vindictive against others, to justify themselves and judge and condemn others, complaining and charging that they are being done an injustice when they are actually doing what is right.

But it was Christ and Paul who taught us how to show that these too are sinners, namely, by showing that they do not fulfil the law in spirit, that at all events they sin and have evil desires in their hearts. And even though they do not kill anybody, they are nevertheless angry. They may not steal, but they are avaricious. They may not commit adultery, but they have evil desires. This is so, because without grace concupiscence does not disappear, as Rom. 7 [:24] says, "Wretched man that I am! Who will deliver me from this body of death?" He does not say "disposition,"[6] or "constantly repeated acts," but rather, "Thanks be to God through Jesus Christ!" [Rom. 7:25]. Therefore the gospel magnifies sin in that it so broadens the law that no man can be found just, that there is none who does not transgress the law. And as all sin and have sinned, so it is obvious that all must receive the baptism of repentance before the baptism of remission of sins. Accordingly, it is not only written concerning John that he preached a baptism of repentance, but "into" or "for the forgiveness of sins" is added. That is to say that through it men are prepared for grace, which effects the remission of sins. Sins are remitted only to those who are dissatisfied with themselves, and this is what it means to repent. But only those are dissatisfied with themselves who know this. But only those know it who understand the law. But no one understands the law unless it be explained to him. This, however, the gospel does. Thus, "through the law comes knowledge of sin [Rom. 3:20]; apart from the law sin lies dead [Rom. 7:8]; but when the commandment came, sin revived [Rom. 7:9]; for I should not have known what it is to covet if the law had not said, 'You shall not covet'" [Rom. 7:7]. Therefore

---

[6] Derived from Aristotle, the term, disposition (*habitus*), is a concept basic to ethics in Roman Catholic theology. Cf. Anton Pegis, *Basic Writings of Saint Thomas Aquinas* (2 vols; New York, 1945), II, 366-411.

the law is an excellent thing, in so far as it points out sins and makes us realize our own misfortune, and thus moves us to seek the good. For the first step to health is to admit that one is sick, and the beginning of wisdom is the fear of the Lord [Prov. 9:10]. But the law excites fear, so that a man is humbled when he sees that he does not keep the commandments and thus is incurring the judgment of God. But grace infuses love, by which he is made more confident, because, while he sees that he wants to keep the commandments and yet is not able to keep them at all, the fulness of Christ is accepted instead, until he too is finally made perfect. Therefore, "thanks be to God who gives us the victory through Jesus Christ" [I Cor. 15:57].

Sermon on the Fourth Sunday after the Epiphany,

Matt. 8:23-27, February 1, 1517

The original text of this sermon on the stilling of the tempest begins with the tag of the pericope, "even winds and sea obey him." In accord with the plan adopted for this volume of not printing out the Scripture texts except when they are a part of the original text, the sermon text is omitted.

Text in Latin; WA 1, 128-130.

There can be no doubt that in this Gospel the sea is a symbol of this world, that is, this troubled, unstable, and transitory life. The storm and the winds are the "rulers of this present darkness, . . . the spiritual hosts of wickedness in the heavenly places" [Eph. 6:12]. The ship is the church and as many of us as are in the true faith; indeed, faith itself is the ship in which Christ is seated, which is constantly being tossed about by perils. Because we must necessarily be constantly tossed about in peril, blessed is he who perceives his perils and unhappy he who sees no dangers. Not as if he had no perils—there is no man without many and exceedingly great perils—but rather because he does not see that he is in the midst of perils, indeed, that he is dead and drowned in perils. For just as every temptation is not merely a double temptation but is rather all one temptation, so no peril is the greatest peril of all. The greatest security is the greatest temptation, the greatest wealth is the greatest poverty, the greatest justice is the greatest injustice, the greatest wisdom is the greatest stupidity, and every excess drives one to excess in everything, and this becomes the greatest peril. To have many temptations is no temptation,[1] the greatest disturbance is the greatest peace; the greatest sin is the greatest righteousness;[2] the greatest foolishness is the greatest wisdom. For in the former [i.e., in righteousness, wisdom, etc.] the fool reposes in himself and has forgotten God, whereas in the latter [i.e., in disturbance, sin, foolishness, etc.] the wise one forsakes himself and takes refuge in God. But to repose in oneself and forget God is the very cesspool of all evil; on the other hand, to seek after God is the sum of all good. As St. James says in the first chapter, "Count it all joy, my brethren, when you meet various trials" [Jas. 1:2]; and yet, on the other hand, he says, "Come now, you rich, weep and howl for the miseries that are coming upon you" [Jas. 5:1]. And Isa. 47 [:8-9] says, "Now therefore hear this, you lover of pleasures, who sit securely, who say in your heart, 'I am, and there is no one besides me; I shall not sit as a widow or know the loss of children': these two things shall come to you in a moment, in one day; the loss of children and widowhood, etc." And again he says, "Ruin shall come on you suddenly, of which you know nothing" [Isa. 47:11].

Therefore it is well with those who find water breaking into their ship, for this moves them to seek help from God. Wherefore, observe how Christ in all things is seeking our profit and is serving us even while he sleeps. The while he abandons us he is upholding us and while he is allowing us to go through storms in terror he is bringing us forward. Thus he brings it about that we do not perish but rather turn back to him, so that more and more we are constantly being saved. Indeed, he wants to arouse in us a desire for him, so that we may continue to cry out to him; he wants us to cry out to him in order that he may hear and answer us. He wants to

---

[1] Luther often expressed this in a different way: "No temptation is the worst temptation." Cf. WA 6, 223, 33.

[2] Compare this paradox with Luther's paradoxical, often misunderstood *pecca fortiter* and Augustine's *O felix culpa*.

hear us in order that he may save us, and thus he teaches us to distrust ourselves and put our confidence in him. And what he says is really true: "I kill and I make alive" [Deut. 32:39], which means that here the words, "woke him," mean our deliverance. Thus we are taught that we perish when he sleeps. For he for whom Christ is not sleeping will not perish. He who does not perish does not cry out. He who does not cry out will not be heard. He who is not heard receives nothing. He who receives nothing has nothing. And he who has nothing will perish. So it happens that he who does not perish really perishes;[3] and he for whom the Lord does not sleep never rightly wakes him. Therefore, sleep on, Lord Jesus, that thou mayest awake, and let us perish, that thou mayest save us.

Accordingly, even if the whole world outside leaves us in peace, behold, each one of us is himself a very great and spacious sea, full of reptiles and animals, large and small. Indeed, even the great dragon is in us. Just consider how many storms the eye alone stirs up, how many the ear, and the tongue! And besides, our slippery soul—how many deadly and reptilian thoughts it cherishes! How many beasts, large and small, are there—the various and constantly changing desires, cares and hatreds, fears, hopes, pains, and vain delights! Here is where the dragon comes in, that is, the tyranny of the flesh, the tinder of concupiscence, the law in our members [cf. Rom. 7:23]. When this beast rages and storms, who is safe, who is quiet? Behold, then, what great miseries we are filled with! Truly, such a person cries out, "My eyes cause me grief" [Lam. 3:51], and again, "Death has come up into our windows" [Jer. 9:21]. He who does not feel this, is dead, and as I have said, he who really feels it is certainly the one of the disciples who wakens Jesus and says, "Save, Lord; we are perishing." But oh, sorrow! how many people, even almost all Christians, do we see sinking, and how few crying out for help! Yea rather, we too are the same and we too act according to our own righteousness, so we are saved not by calling upon Christ but by the power of our works. We make ourselves secure in order to escape trials. We do not want perils which will drive us to

---

[3] Cf. Kierkegaard's motto, taken from the German philosophical writer, Johann George Hamann (1730-1788): *periissem nisi periisem* (I should have perished, if I had not perished). *The Journals of Søren Kierkegaard*, ed. and trans. Alexander Dru (New York: Oxford University Press, 1938), no. 767, p. 245.

cry out. We would rather perform good works in order to have peace. But this is to perish a thousand thousand times. Woe to those who do this!

Sermon on St. Matthew's Day, Matt. 11:25-30,

February 24, 1517

Luther's concern over the sale of indulgences finds passionate expression in this sermon. (Cf. Kiessling, op. cit., p. 100 and H. Boehmer, Road to Reformation, *trans. by John W. Doberstein and Theodore G. Tappert (Philadelphia, 1946), p. 177.*

Text in Latin; WA 1, 138-142, compared with CL 5, 424-428.

Man hides what is his own in order to conceal it, but God conceals what is his in order to reveal it. That is to say, he hides it from the wise and the great in order that they may be humbled and become fools and thus reveal it to babes; for such was his gracious will, and his will is the best, just, righteous, and holy. And where is there any better will than that which, because it hides itself, removes what impedes the gospel, namely, pride? Two questions should be asked here. Who are the ones who are wise and understanding, from whom it is hidden? And what is it that is hidden?

The usual answer to the first question is that the wise and understanding are those who think they are wise but actually are not. Many declare that this explanation is true enough, but that it is more obscure than the text itself. Those who say this are the ones who are themselves of this stripe but will not admit it and yet want to deprecate such people. For this explanation sounds as if some were actually wise, whereas others only think themselves wise. Such an explanation is dangerous; it comes very close to pride and is characteristic of those who imagine themselves wise. Therefore a Christian should say: Wise are those who, in so far as they are wise at all, are especially wise in the wisdom of God and in the holy Scriptures. All such are wise and appear to be wise only in their own eyes. On the other side are those whom the Christian calls truly wise, those who do not consider themselves wise, who have no wisdom of their own but rather are fools, lacking wisdom and understanding, because without any self-deception whatsoever they see that they are empty and know absolutely nothing. These, I say, the ones who are really foolish but thirst for wisdom, these are truly wise. All others, whether they be those who only think they are wise, like dolts and complete ignoramuses, or whether they possess wisdom, like subtle hypocrites, are wise only because they are not fools, not empty, not hungry for wisdom, and not babes [before God]. Therefore the Apostle, that excellent doctor, does not say: If any one among you thinks he is wise, let him consider himself a fool; he says rather, "let him become a fool that he may become wise" [I Cor. 3:18]. For this is a true statement: The fool is the wise man and the wise man a fool, a fool, of course, in his own wisdom and a fool in another's wisdom, namely, the wisdom of God who adjudges and imputes it to him. For he who acknowledges himself to be a fool in the sight of God to him this humility will be accounted as the highest wisdom.

Therefore the truly wise—I mean the fools—are always saying, "Make thy way straight before me" [Ps. 5:8] and "keep steady my steps" [Ps. 119:133]. But one who prays in this way is acknowledging himself to be blind and a fool, and yet he does not think of himself as being foolish but as if he were really wise after all. The wise, on the contrary, that is, the fools, say: "Who shall show us any good?" [Ps. 4:6]. We are what we are; we follow the dictates of our pious intentions and right reason—as Cicero in his work, "On Old Age,"[1] boasts that the wise are wise because they follow reason as their best guide. This right reason, this dictate, this wisdom of nature, which now resounds and is being vaunted from every pulpit, this is the wisdom and prudence which the Father has hidden from those who are his, in order to make them fools and defendants and thus compel them to seek for grace to guide them. And again one can distinguish the wise and intelligent by the fact that the wise are masters of youth and others, able to teach others, and the intelligent are capable of grasping what is being taught them. But both are fools in the sight of God.

---

[1] *Cato maior de senectute.*

To the second question the answer that is given is that what is hidden is Christ himself and God the Father. But Christ himself immediately resolved the question when he said, "All things have been delivered to me by my Father; and no one knows the Son except the Father, and no one knows the Father except the Son and any one to whom the Son chooses to reveal him" [Matt. 11:27]. Therefore the knowledge of God and Christ, the Father and the Son, is that which is hidden, against which the wise and holy make their greatest assaults, as John says, "And they will do this (that is, they will kill you and think they are offering service to God) because they have not known the Father, nor me" [John 16:3]. They think they are offering service to God by being wise and understanding, not babes. It follows, however, that the wise, because this is hidden, know neither the Father nor the Son. What, then, is the knowledge of God which is taught by Christ? Is everything taken away from us and nothing left to us? Where, then, is wisdom? Where is righteousness? Where is virtue? Not in us, but in Christ. It is outside of us, in God. Thus we have been made babes, fools, sinners, liars, weaklings, and nothing, since everything was given over to Christ. No one knows the Father except the Son and no one knows the Son except the Father because everything belongs to the Father alone and has been given only to the Son. Thus we have been utterly emptied of all knowledge and thus made so altogether childlike and fit that the Father reveals to us what is his own and likewise the Son reveals to us what is his own. This means, however, that both reveal the same thing and there is only one revelation and only one revealer. The Father glorifies the Son and the Son the Father, as is said in John [17:1]. Therefore, learn where wisdom, virtue, and understanding is to be found. Baruch says in chapter three: "This is our God . . . he found out the whole way to knowledge." It is therefore neither of us nor in us, but is to be sought in God. "He has given it to Jacob his servant and to Israel his elect" [Bar. 3:35, 36]. And John 12 [:32] says, "I, when I am lifted up from the earth, will draw all men to myself." Thus he leaves nothing to us. Really nothing! Where then does this leave the wise?

Therefore, know that Christ himself was made our righteousness, virtue, and wisdom by God [cf. I Cor. 1:30]. In him God the Father reposed all his wisdom, virtues, and righteousness in ordei

28

that they might become ours. This is what it means to know the Son. Moreover, you should know that the Father in his mercy reckons to us his Son's righteousness, which is his own righteousness; for the righteousness of the Father and the Son are one; it is one life and one virtue which is given to us. This is what it means to know the Father of Christ. But this is so hidden from the wise that, immediately they hear it, they begin to babble: "We shall not do good. 'Why not do evil that good may come?' [Rom. 3:8]. If we are justified through a righteousness outside of us and solely through God's mercy, then let us take our ease, since our work is all in vain and our wisdom is nothing." So say those who are all too wise and righteous. If only they would first become babes, in order to be able to accept the Father and the Son, who reveals himself, they would easily solve the question as to why it is not the do-nothings to whom wisdom, that is, Christ, is revealed, and that he who no longer lives to himself but Christ in him [cf. Gal. 2:20] need not fear that Christ is doing nothing. No, on the contrary, he is supremely active and present with all sweetness and ease, whereas these others drudge and sweat in their own wisdom and righteousness and burden themselves in vain with tremendous misery. For they want to attain peace of conscience through their own counsels and accomplishments and their own self-chosen ways, and they will not cease doing so until they see that their sins have been purged through satisfaction and their self-will has been satisfied, which is impossible and is only to build on sand [cf. Matt. 7:26].

Therefore, no matter how much they work, labor, and speculate, they accomplish nothing else except to increase the restlessness of their souls, which is just what they are seeking to escape through all their efforts. But one cannot escape it except through knowing the Father and the Son, that is, through knowing the grace and mercy of God which is freely given to us in Christ and the merits of Christ which are imputed to us. To these Christ now says, "Come to me, all who labor and are heavy-laden, and I will give you rest" [Matt. 11:28]; for you cannot refresh yourselves, you cannot give yourselves rest, but I can. What is there left in you? Get out of yourselves and come to me. Despair of yourselves and hope in me, just as Abraham went out from his country, his kindred, from his and his father's house [Gen. 12:1]. For we ourselves are a father's house, we ourselves are the world. Therefore we must go out of ourselves, for we labor and are heavy-laden. More fittingly the Greek text says: Come to me, all who are fatigued and heavy-laden. That is, it would be less hard if we labored as burden bearers, so that the burden would be the labor. But here the labor too is the burden, that is, we labor to find rest and this very labor only burdens us more, since the sin is only increased through our righteousness and works. The conscience is neither relieved nor freed from fear thereby, but only more greatly wearied, as the Preacher says, "The toil of a fool wearies him, so that he does not know the way to the city" [Eccles. 10:15]. And immediately preceding, "He who quarries stones is hurt by them; and he who splits logs is endangered by them" [Eccles. 10:9]. This is the business and labor of work righteousness. In ordinary speech we also say of difficult labor: I'd rather lug stones and chop wood.[2] And yet, what do both of these labors accomplish except that they serve others and not oneself?

Therefore, let us hear something about the rest of souls: "Take my yoke upon you" [Matt. 11:29]. He does not say: Do this or that; but rather, come to me, get away from yourselves, and carry your cross after me. "He who does not take his cross and follow me is not worthy of me" [Matt. 10:38]. For to come to Christ and go out from oneself is the great cross, which no one dreads more than he who is seeking to wash away his sins through his own works. Because all these desire to escape, not their sins, but the punishment of their sins—for they are slaves, they hate, not the sin, but the penalty of sin—therefore they seek to extinguish the fire of hell and escape the judgment by all kinds of sanctifications.[3] But because the sin always remains, the punishment of conscience does not pass over.[4] In other words, they are looking after their own interests [Phil. 2:21]. Therefore the wicked have no peace [Isa. 48:22; 57:21]. If they would give up themselves and hate their sins, they would have no punishment and would not need to fear it; for when the sin is taken away the punishment ceases of itself. But they do not want to give up themselves and are afraid of Christ's easy yoke. So they go on labor-

---

[2] This sentence in German.

[3] Löscher suggests that this should be *satisfactionibus*, satisfactions, instead of *sanctificationibus*, sanctifications. WA 1, 141.

[4] *Non transit;* Luther is alluding, as he often does, to the Passover (Exod. 12); Hebrew, *pesah,* Latin, *transitus.*

ing under their burden, being afraid where there is nothing to be afraid of, and dragging their sin like a heavily laden wagon.

Then in addition, the very profusion of indulgences astonishingly fills up the measure of servile righteousness. Through these nothing is accomplished except that the people learn to fear and flee and dread the penalty of sins, but not the sins themselves.[5] Therefore, the results of indulgences are too little seen but we do see a great sense of self-security and licentious sinning; so much so that, if it were not for the fear of the punishment of sins, nobody would want these indulgences, even if they were free; whereas the people ought rather to be exhorted to love the punishment and embrace the cross.[6] Would that I were a liar when I say that indulgences are rightly so called, for to indulge means to permit, and indulgence is equivalent to impunity, permission to sin, and license to nullify the cross of Christ. Or, if indulgences are to be permitted, they should be given only to those who are weak in faith, that those who seek to attain gentleness and lowliness through suffering, as the Lord here says, may not be offended. For, not through indulgences, but through gentleness and lowliness, so says he, is rest for your souls found. But gentleness is present only in punishment and suffering, from which these indulgences absolve us. They teach us to dread the cross and suffering and the result is that we never become gentle and lowly, and that means that we never receive indulgence nor come to Christ. Oh, the dangers of our time! Oh, you snoring priests! Oh, darkness deeper than Egyptian! How secure we are in the midst of the worst of all our evils!

---

[5] Cf. Thesis 40, *Ninety-five Theses*, LW 31, 29.
[6] Cf. Theses 94 and 95, *Ninety-five Theses*, LW 31, 33.

TWO LENTEN SERMONS

1518

TWO LENTEN SERMONS, 1518

Sermon on the Man Born Blind, John 9:1-38,

Preached on the Wednesday after Laetare,

March 17, 1518

This and the following sermon, preached in the midst of the uproar of the indulgence controversy, are warm, simple, practical, positive expositions of the central content of faith, with no reference, except an announcement appended to the second, to the controversy or Luther's part in it. The first was preached on the day the Witten-berg students publicly burned some eight hundred copies of Tetzel's Frankfurt theses which had been prepared by Wimpina (cf. Boeh-mer, op. cit., p. 204). These are also the days when Luther was completing his lectures on Hebrews. Neither of these sermons is a direct transcript. They were translated into Latin by his students and were not published until 1702, when they appeared, translated into German, in the Halle edition of the collected works.

German text; WA 1, 267-273, compared with MA[3] 1, 113-124.

You well know, dear friends of Christ, that I do not understand much about preaching and therefore I shall preach a foolish sermon; for I am a fool and I thank God for it.[1] Therefore I must also have foolish pupils; anybody who doesn't want to be a fool can close his ears. This Gospel compels me to take this attitude; for you have heard in this Gospel that Christ is dealing only with the blind. And Christ also concludes that all who see are blind and all the wise and prudent are fools. These are his words. If I were to say it, I

---

[1] Luther is referring to the paradoxical character of the Christian faith, expressed in such passages as I Cor. 3:18; 4:10 and Rom. 1:22. Cf. the paradoxes in the *Heidelberg Disputation*, 1518, WA 1, 353-365; LW 31, 39-70.

would be reviled as a new prophet. But Christ will not lie. Now listen to what St. Augustine says in his exposition of this Gospel: All that Christ did is both works and words; works, because they happened and were done by him; words, because they signify and teach something.[2] Now this is an event, because the blind man received his sight. But it is also a word, for it signifies every man born of Adam. For we are all blind and our light and our illumination comes solely from Christ, our good and faithful God.

To distinguish these from one another, works and words, requires an enlightened mind; for how many there were who saw this work and yet did not see its significance. They looked upon it as a work, but the word, the significance, remained hidden from them. But if they had recognized it, they undoubtedly would have said, "Oh, I am far more blind than he is." And that's the right understanding of it; and so it is to this day, that the number of them is great even among those who shine before the world in their great power, culture, wisdom, piety, holiness, chastity, purity, and so on. But it is certain that always it has been so ordained that with a powerful man there is found an outcast, with the wise a fool, with the pious an impious, with the holy an unholy, with the healthy a sick man, with the handsome an ugly man, and so on. Just look at the human race and you will find rich and poor, beauty and ugliness, gaiety and dreariness, joy and sorrow, culture and stupidity, wisdom and foolishness, piety and wickedness, and whatever else you may name, crooked and straight, high and low, and so on.

And it is not without cause that God in his unspeakable wisdom should so desire to cast down the rule of the proud and the wise. Therefore let each one take heed, whether he be blessed with many or few of these gifts, that he by no means regard himself, but rather his neighbor, who does not possess the gift. Then he will say, "Ah, dear God, I am learned, or devout, and so on; but in the sight of

---

[2] *Lectures or Tractates on the Gospel According to St. John* in *A Select Library of Nicene and Post-Nicene Fathers of the Christian Church,* ed. Philip Schaff, First Series (New York, 1888) VII, Tractate 44, 1, p. 245. Migne 35, 1713. The passage reads as follows: "All, certainly, that was done by our Lord Jesus Christ, both words and works, are worthy of our astonishment and admiration: his works, because they are facts; his words, because they are signs. If we reflect, then, on what is signified by the deed here done, that blind man is the human race."

God I am ignorant and full of sin, like this my brother"; then that person will find out what is his real condition. For God has established a fixed rule: everything that is high and praised of men is disregarded and abominable in the sight of God. Isaiah writes: God does not judge by the sight of his eyes or the hearing of his ears, but rather he will judge righteously [cf. Isa. 11:3-4]. It is as if he wanted to say: A man, because he is a man, judges no further than he sees or hears. So if he sees a rich man, a powerful man, a handsome man, a devout man, etc., that's what he calls him, just as he sees him. If he hears something amusing, sweet, lovely, that's what he calls it. But God turns all this upside down. Everything we call beautiful, jolly, rich, etc., he calls poor, sick, weak, impotent.

So let every man, if he has received a blessing or gift from God, learn to divest himself of it, shun it, give it up, in order that he may not look to himself, but rather note how his neighbor looks and how his neighbor is reflected in himself. Then he will surely say, "Ah, there God has hung a mirror before my eyes, and a book in which I am to learn to know myself. Ah, God, now I see clearly that what my brother is outwardly, I am inwardly." Thus he learns to know himself and not to exalt himself. So it is ordained and nobody can evade it. For we see in all the words and works of Christ nothing but pure humility.

That's what happened also in this Gospel. The blind man was a sign of the blindness that lay hidden in our hearts. And it follows from this that what Augustine said is true, that the works of Christ are words and the words are works. Therefore at the end of this Gospel, when the aloof and spiritual Jews said, "Are we also blind?" our Lord concludes, "If you were blind, you would have no guilt; but now that you say, 'We see,' your guilt remains" [John 9:40-41]. Look, what an upside-down judgment that is for Christ to make! Therefore one must try to understand all the gifts that a man can have. Those whom we think are learned are ignorant in the sight of God. And anybody who does not know this will have a bad time of it in the judgment of God.

This is what Paul says to the Ephesians [Phil. 2:5-8]: Oh, dear brethren, your attitude should be like that of Christ, who did not exalt himself in the form of God, even though he could be equal with the Father, but emptied himself and utterly lowered himself, and took on the form of a servant, and was found in every degree and way a man and like a man, like him even in that he died for the sake of obedience to his Father.[3] Note, dear friends of Christ, what a choice, profound saying that is. We should all be equal. For he speaks, not as a mere man, but as one in whom is the form of God, the very presence of power, honor, righteousness, wisdom, piety, and purity, who never did evil, who is full of every virtue even in his humanity, who desired to be equal with us, not with God, not like Lucifer who desired to snatch the image of God, nor like the proud, who so look down on their neighbors that they can scarcely recognize them as grasshoppers. This Christ did not do: he put off the form of God and was found in the form of man, in sinful flesh, though he never sinned; nor could he ever sin. So he became a fool, the object of mockery, reproach, and derision by all the people; he bore our misfortune, and in him were found all the titles of our poverty. And this he did in order that we might freely follow him.

This, then, is the meaning: He who finds in himself the form of God, that is, has title to the gifts we spoke of above, let him not exalt himself but rather abase himself and sincerely believe that he is the lowest in all the world. And this must happen, if he is ever to get to heaven, whether it happen voluntarily or against his will. Thus his works are words. And therefore he [i.e., Augustine] is right when he says, "He who does not see the mystery of God is blind. Therefore this man is not merely blind, but is rather a figure of the blindness which is within the soul." This means that he who does not see and know God's hidden holiness is blind. And therefore this man in the Gospel is only a figure of that other blindness which is in the soul.

But then, the reason why all this is said and what causes it, says Augustine, is the transgression of Adam, to whom the devil said, "Your eyes will be opened, and you will be like God, knowing good and evil" [Gen. 3:5]. Oh, you villain, scoundrel, and betrayer! You see what he is doing; he is trying to lead them to the form of God, so he says, "Your eyes will be opened," that is, they will become blind. Before their eyes were closed, but after the Fall they were opened.

---

[3] Cf. Luther's letter to George Spenlein, April 8, 1516, in Theodore G. Tappert, *Luther: Letters of Spiritual Counsel* (Philadelphia, 1955), pp. 109-111.

The consequence of this, as Origen, the wise and acute school-master teaches,[4] is that man has two kinds of eyes, his own eyes and God's eyes. But the fact is that both kinds of eyes, our inward eyes and outward eyes, are God's. Indeed, all our members and every-thing that is in us are instruments of God and nothing is ours if they are ruled by God. But they are ours when God forsakes us. This means that, as Christ says, we must pluck out the eye that scandal-izes and offends us and throw it away [Matt. 5:29]. That's why it is that we would rather see what is fine and pretty and well formed rather than what is gold or silver, rather a young Jill or a young Jack than an old woman or an old Jack. And this is the mousetrap that dupes our minds, as is written of Adam in the book of Genesis. So our eyes have been opened, which really means that we have become totally blind, so that, as was said a moment ago, we consider the sham to be good and what is poor and misshapen to be evil. This the devil taught us, and it is his eyes that do it. But Christ came to teach these eyes to see and to take away the blindness, in order that we should not make this distinction between young and old, beauti-ful and ugly, and so on. Rather all are equal, wise man or simpleton, sage or fool, man or woman; it is enough that he is a man with our flesh and blood, a body common to all. For such perception one must have a fine, acute, and well-trained mind.

Christ pays no attention to distinctions we make, for he bestows children and honor upon an old unattractive woman just as readily as upon a beautiful woman, which is clearly illustrated in Rachel and Leah [Gen. 29:21–30:24]. It makes no difference to him wherein he allows his work to appear. Therefore God says, "I will destroy the wisdom of the wise, and the cleverness of the clever I will thwart" [I Cor. 1:19; Isa. 29:14]. Isaiah says, "I will choose what they mock at and despise."[5] Also Paul says, "Thus is the call of God, that it receives the sick and the fools, in order that he may confound and shame the wise" [I Cor. 1:27].

So because Christ does this and considers that evil which we consider good and vice versa, he takes away that which we delight

---

[4] Luther was especially conversant with Origen's commentaries. He early rejected him and later condemned him because of his lack of a Christ-centered exegesis.

[5] Cf. Isa. 66:4. Luther's mistranslation.

in and gives everything that vexes us. This Christ practiced and proved; for God became man, as was said above. And in his last days we find what we consider the worst of all evils: we find him dying a shameful death. And when we view his whole life, we do not find that he undertook anything that the world considered good. Once he rode into Jerusalem with great honor, but his joy was embittered with sorrow. Now the most precious thing God has is death and dying; and Christ accepted it in love, joyfully and voluntarily, out of obedience to his Father. We flee it and consider life more precious than death. He embraced it as a thing of sweetness and gave his life unto death, and just because he is to ascend to the throne of glory and reign eternally with the Father, he must (and he does it willingly) die on the cross; he lets go of life and accepts death.

Now, if Christ did this, then fie on everyone who would try to get to heaven without following his example. And this is the true holy relic,[6] of which the prophet says, *"In reliquiis tuis praeparabis vultum eorum."*[7] "In thy relic," or in thy testament, which consists

---

[6] For this and the argument following compare Luther's letter to Georg Leiffer, April 15, 1516, WA, Br 1, 37 (Preserved Smith and Charles M. Jacobs, *Luther's Correspondence and Other Contemporary Letters* (Philadelphia, 1913-1918), I, 35-36) and "The Fourteen of Consolation," 1520, *Works of Martin Luther*, PE 1, 139. Luther is accepting the fact of the cult of relics as a starting point, but transcends its external form. We come into fellowship with Christ, not by putting a sliver of his cross in a golden monstrance, but by sharing in his suffering. As he entered into glory by choosing the cross, so we too can have fellowship with God by accepting cross and suffering. Thus Luther at this time is not rejecting the veneration of relics and images, but would permit them for the sake of the "sucklings," who require milk (I Cor. 3:2, Heb. 5:12). Cf. also Watson, *Let God Be God, op. cit.*, pp. 170, 187 n. 174.

[7] Ps. 21:12, cited from the Vulgate (Ps. 20:13). An example of medieval exegesis, whose influence Luther had not yet thrown off. The whole verse, which is obscure in the Latin of the Vulgate, based on the Greek Septuagint, reads: *"Quoniam pones eos dorsum, in reliquiis tuis praeparabis vultum eorum,"* literally, "Thou wilt make them turn their back; in those whom thou dost leave over, wilt thou prepare their face." In his later translation of the Bible from the Hebrew text, Luther's rendering is essentially the same as the RSV: "For you will put them to flight; you will aim at their faces with your bows." Luther's christological interpretation of this passage is made clearer in the "Lectures on the Psalms" (1513-1516), WA 3, 134, where his comment on this verse reads: "You will inflict punishment upon your enemies and subject them to evils, make them asses and martyrs. 'With your residuum,' that is, with the sufferings and evils which were left behind after the ascension, which he did not take with him, 'You will prepare their face,' in order that they may ever contemplate and feel them." In this sermon Luther is still interpreting the passage in this way.

in cross and suffering, "wilt thou prepare their face." This is so holy and so sublime that it cannot be put into any monstrance, in any silver or gold. It is not the wood, stone, or vesture which he touched, but rather the suffering, the cross, which he sends to his devout children. All the goldsmiths together cannot make a vessel to enclose this relic. It requires a spiritual, living, eternal monstrance. For this sacred relic is a living thing like the soul of man. Therefore, it is the inward relic we must seek, not the outward. Nevertheless, we ought to encase the bones of saints in silver; this is good and proper. Many things, like images and the like, may be permitted for the sake of the sucklings which must be forbidden to others.[8] Therefore those who are farther along should pay little regard to these things and lift their eyes higher; for Christ will bring to their very door something better than they can find anywhere in the world. For he will send them reverses, tribulation, anxiety, care, grief, poverty, ill will, and so on. He will send you sickness, and at the end of your life, in the throes of death, the devil will assault you unceasingly and terrify you so cruelly that you will well nigh despair. Indeed, he will press you to the point where he will snap his fingers at you and jeer: Yes, good pal, do what you will, you are mine anyhow. You have to listen with Christ to this mockery: "If he is the son of God, let him come down from the cross" [Matt. 27:40]. He will read you a lecture all right, and with spite too! Then let each one of us pay heed to what is pleasing to God in order that we may joyfully say: Oh, my dear God, I firmly believe that thou art sending this to me. Welcome, beloved relic. I give thanks to thee, my faithful God, that thou dost consider me worthy of what was most precious in thy life. Ah, my beloved, faithful Christ, help me and I bravely accept it, and freely imitate thee in the surrender of my will. Then all the power of the devil will forthwith fall to the ground.

This is the most precious relic of all, *quod obviis ulnis et osculis debemus accipere,*[9] which we ought to accept lovingly and gratefully. For this relic God himself hallowed and blessed with his most precious will, and with the approval of his Father. But now—God save the mark!—we see our bishops and leaders fleeing from this

---

[8] Cf. p. 40 n. 6.
[9] Literally, "which we ought to accept with open arms and kisses."

relic. If you take something away from them or speak too plainly to them, they would rather tear the whole place down than give in. So far has this childish veneration and holiness gone that they have started this game of excommunication, and the letters are flying about like bats, all because of a trifling thing. Their defense of this is: It is proper that we should guard and preserve the patrimony and legacy of Christ and St. Peter; we are doing it because it is right. O you poor Christ, O you wretched Peter! If you have no inheritance but wood and stone and silver and gold, you are of all the most needy.

Ah, but the good God wants what Isaiah speaks of in the last and also the first chapter [Isa. 66:1-2 and 1:10-17]. These things are all the works of his hands, which he has made. Therefore he does not need our goods, say David and Job [Ps. 34:16-21; 40:8-11; 50:8-15; 51:18-19; Job 22:23-27; 5:17-19; II Sam. 7:6-11; 18-29]. But when God sends it to us, we run away and flee from it. He wants to give it to us, but we don't want it. Nor are all of us worthy of it. In fact, it is the peculiar mark of faithful children of God. He bestows it often, but we do not know what to do with it. And so it comes about that we think we see clearly and yet are totally blind, so that we call evil what Christ calls good.

Therefore God the Father adorned his Son, as the bride in the Song of Solomon says, "Go forth O daughters of Zion, and behold your King, Christ, with the crown and the ornament with which his mother adorned and crowned him on the day of his espousal and wedding and on the day of the gladness of his heart" [cf. Song of Sol. 3:11]. That is, because Christ was about to receive the kingdom and the power to reign, and be a king above all kings, he had the greatest honor and glory and joy in his heart when he died on the cross. This we do not see and therefore we are rightly called blind and foolish by Christ.

But we persist in our evil way of seeing things and see no difference whatsoever. Augustine says, "Christ speaks of the blind man and of birth, whereby he clearly indicates that this is what we are from Adam's birth and that blindness adheres to us by nature,"[10] and this blindness can be taken away by none but Christ. Here is where all who undertake to do something of themselves are com-

---

[10] Cf. p. 36 n. 2.

pelled to submit and be conquered. For the blind man did not imagine that he would be made whole, as the text says, "Never has it been heard that a blind man should receive his sight" [John 9:32]. We must despair of everything that we can do. But those who say: Ah, but I have done as much as I possibly can; I have done enough, and I hope that God will give me grace—they set up an iron wall between themselves and the grace of God. But if you feel within yourself the urge to call upon God and pray and plead and knock, then grace is already there; then call upon it and thank God. Grace can never forsake him who despairs of himself. For many passages declare: To the humble He gives grace, but He denies it to the proud [Prov. 3:34; Jas. 4:6; I Pet. 5:5]. The fact is that nobody can do anything except freely surrender himself to God no matter what happens, and despair of himself. But those who say: All right, then I'll wait until grace comes, are turning it around. Ah, you fool, when you feel what has been effected within you, then grace is already there; just go on and follow. Thus you retire and you no longer stand and walk by yourself. God cannot endure our wanting to see; we needs must be blind. For God is wholly present in all creation, in every corner, he is behind you and before you. Do you think he is sleeping on a pillow in heaven? He is watching over you and protecting you. But as soon as Christ anointed the eyes of the blind man with spittle his will concurred and desired what he had never dreamed of before, as the Evangelist shows. What the spittle is and the meaning of the washing in the pool of Siloam we shall save for another time.

Sermon on The Raising of Lazarus, John 11:1-45,

Preached on the Friday after Laetare,

March 19, 1518

This sermon on the redeeming love of Christ, preached two days
after the preceding sermon, contains a miniature soteriology. God
comes to us only in Christ, who alone is the Father's "epistle, book,
and image," the "door, anchor, and path" to him; therefore works
which we think we can perform and thus find the way to God are
rejected. (Cf. Thesis 19 in the Heidelberg *Disputation, which*
Luther debated in the following month, April 26, 1518, LW 31, 52.)

Text in German; WA 1, 273-277, compared with MA³ 1, 113-124.

Dear Friends of Christ. I have told[1] you the story of this Gospel
in order that you may picture in your hearts and remember well that
Christ our God, in all the Gospels, from beginning to end, and also
all writings of the prophets and apostles, desires of us nothing else
but that we should have a sure and confident heart and trust in him.

Augustine[2] writes that we find in the Scriptures three dead
persons whom Christ restored to life. First, a twelve-year-old girl,
when he was alone in a house, behind closed doors, and in the presence only of the parents of the deceased girl and his intimate disciples [Matt. 9:18-26]. Second, the only son of a widow, who was
being carried out through the gate in the presence of all the people
[Luke 7:11-17]. Third, Lazarus, of whom this Gospel tells us, is
not raised by Christ privately in a house or at the gate, but one who
had been in the grave for four days and is raised in the presence of
many Jews and near Jerusalem.

According to Augustine's teaching, these three dead persons are
to be understood as three kinds of sinners. The first are those whose

---

[1] *erzelet.* Whether this means that Luther began this sermon with a paraphrase
of the text or whether the word should be rendered "read" cannot be determined; the latter is most probable. Cf. Hermann Werdermann, *Luther's*
Wittenberger Gemeinde (Gütersloh, 1929), pp. 177-181.
[2] *Lectures or Tractates on the Gospel According to St. John, op. cit.,* Tractate
49, 1-3, pp. 270-271. Migne 35, 1746.

44

souls[3] have died. This is when temptation comes and conquers and captures the heart, so that one consents to sin. Then follows a sense of pleasure and the evil poison begins to work its way in, kills the soul, and subjects it to the devil. This is represented by the twelve-year-old girl. This kind rises up without too much difficulty after a fall. With persons of this kind God deals in a very tender way. He speaks to them secretly, sends inward instruction to their hearts, which they alone hear and cannot evade, and prepares for them a rod of chastisement, which they must suffer to their grief.

The second dead person signifies those who have fallen into works, so that they have to be carried, since they cannot walk by themselves.[4] These must take heed; otherwise, since one thing leads to another, they may, as St. Gregory says,[5] be completely overborne by the weight of sins. It is the bier in which the dead person is carried.

Lazarus, finally, signifies those who are so entangled in sin that they go beyond all bounds; they drift into a habit [of sinning] which then becomes their very nature. They know nothing but sin; they stink and are buried in sin. It takes a lot of work [to save them]. This is shown by the fact that in the case of the maiden Christ had only to take her by the hand and she immediately became alive [Matt. 9:25]. The young man, however, sat upright, but not so easily as in the case of the maiden, for Luke writes that Christ first touched the bier and afterwards said, "Young man, I say to you, arise" [Luke 7:14]. This had to be accomplished through a command. But in this story, Christ looked up to heaven and said, "Father, I thank thee that thou hast heard me," and then cried with a loud voice, "Lazarus, Lazarus, come out" [John 11:41, 43]. And he came out, bound hand and foot, and his face also, and the apostles had to unbind him. This is the grave, the tomb: habituation in sin.

A question. If it is true that Lazarus and the other dead persons

---

[3] The soul as mind and heart which assents to sin before the act is committed.
[4] Augustine, *op. cit.*, p. 271; "If thou hast not only harbored a feeling of delight in evil, but hast also done the evil thing, thou hast, so to speak, carried the dead outside the gate: thou art already without, and being carried to the tomb." Migne 35, 1746.
[5] Pope Gregory I (590-604), whose letters and dialogues Luther was familiar with and often cited. The precise passage here referred to cannot be traced.

must be understood as signifying sin, how does this accord with the Gospel when the evangelist says in the speech of Martha, "Lord, he whom you love is ill" and "See how he loved him"? [John 11:3, 36]. Is it not true that Christ does not love the sinner but rather the truth, as the Scriptures says, "You love righteousness and hate wickedness" [Ps. 45:7] and "In my sight the sinner is scorned"? [cf. Ps. 5:5]. The answer is this: My dear man, [comfort yourself with this saying,] "I came not for the sake of the righteous, but to make righteous what is unrighteous and sinful and to lead the sinners to repentance" [cf. Matt. 9:13].

The whole human race was worthy of hatred, and yet Christ loved us. For if he had not loved us, he would not have descended from heaven. For the prophet says in the psalm: "There is none that does good," except one; "they have all become corrupt and sinners" [cf. Ps. 14:3] except Christ alone. So Christ loves the sinner at the command of the Father, who sent Him for our comfort. So the Father wills that we should look to Christ's humanity and love him in return, but yet in such a way as to remember that he did all this at the bidding of Father's supreme good pleasure. Otherwise it is terrifying to think of Christ. For to the Father is ascribed power, to the Son, wisdom, and to the Holy Spirit goodness, which we can never attain and of which we must despair.

But when we know and consider that Christ came down from heaven and loved sinners in obedience to the Father, then there springs up in us a bold approach to and firm hope in Christ. We learn that Christ is the real epistle, the golden book, in which we read and learn how he always kept before him the will of the Father. So Christ is the "access to the Father" [Eph. 2:18] as St. Paul says. And John too bears witness that Christ said, "I am the way, and the truth, and the life" [John 14:6]. "I am also the door" [John 10:7] and "no one comes to the Father, but by me" [John 14:6]. Now we see that there is no shorter way to the Father except that we love Christ, hope and trust in him, boldly look to him for everything good, learn to know and praise him. For then it will be impossible that we should have a miserable, frightened, dejected conscience; in Christ it will be heartened and refreshed. But the Scriptures say concerning the sinners: "The wicked shall perish and be driven away like dust" [cf. Ps. 1:4, 6]. Therefore the sinners flee and know not where to go; for when the conscience does not hope and trust in God it cowers and trembles before the purity and righteousness of God. It can have no sweet assurance; it flees and still has nowhere to go unless it finds and catches hold of Christ, the true door and anchor. Yes, this is the way that all Christians should learn. But we go plunging on, taking hold in our own name, with our understanding and reason, and do not see or ever take to heart how kindly, sweetly, and lovingly Christ has dealt with people. For the Father commanded him to do so. This tastes sweet to the faithful soul and it gives all the glory, praise, and honor to the Father through the Son, Christ Jesus. So God has nothing but the best and he offers it to us, weeds us, sustains us, and cares for us through his Son. That's the way our hearts are changed to follow Christ.

This is the way that Peter and Paul, the two leaders of the church, and all the other apostles taught with great diligence. Above all, they love the Father, as they declare in many passages: "Blessed be the Father, who has blessed us with every heavenly blessing through Jesus Christ" [Eph. 1:3]. Therefore, let no one undertake to come to God except over this bridge. This is the path that does not lead astray. Christ says, "Everything that my Father commands me I do" [John 14:31], and "I thank thee, dear Father, that thou hearest me always; but not for my sake, but for the sake of those who are standing down here, that they may believe that thou didst send me" [John 11:41-42]. What he is saying is: If they see my love and my works, and that thou are effecting them, and that thou hast commanded me to do them, then they will be at one with thee and will know thee through me and my works; out of which then will grow thy love toward them, O Father. The reason why Christ loves sinners is that his Father commanded him to do so. For in Christ the Father pours himself out in his grace. And all this serves to the end that we freely hope in Christ and trust him unafraid.

Therefore, let the works go, no matter how great they may be, prayers, chants, yammering, and yapping; for it is certain that nobody will ever get to God through all these things. Besides, it is impossible. Rather the heart must have love for Christ, and through him, for the Father. It's all lost if the heart is not cleansed. It must all be left behind, and we must freely, boldly, and with sure confidence take the leap into God. That's what he wants of us.

But when we put forward our works, the devil will use them for his own end,[6] and that's just what he does do with them. Let us therefore learn to know from the Gospel how kindly Christ deals with us; then we shall without a doubt love him and avoid sinning, and so see everything in a different light. See how kindly he draws our hearts to himself, this faithful God. He loves Lazarus, who was a sinner. He tolerates the timid faith of his disciples when they say, "Oh, Lord, don't go to Jerusalem, they will kill you" [John 11:8]. All this he would have condemned, if he had wanted to deal harshly. "Ah," said his disciples further, "if Lazarus is sleeping, as you say, then it isn't necessary for you to go there" [John 11:12]. And what about Mary and Martha? "Oh, Lord," they said, "if you had been here, our brother would not have died" [John 11:21]. And also they were earthly, so that they were unable to refrain from weeping and the people had come to them to console them because of the death of their brother, as the evangelist describes so skilfully. From this we learn that they were all in unbelief and sin. And then we see how kindly the Lord deals with them, praying and weeping with them, and all this at the behest of his Father. This is the true guidebook, from which we learn the will of the eternal Father.

Take note, then, all you who have a timid conscience, that you will not be saved by this or that work. For it will fare with you as with one who works in a sandpit: the more sand he shovels out the more falls upon him. That's why many have gone mad, as John Gerson[7] says, so that they began to imagine things, one that he was a worm, another that he was a mouse, and so on. Just commit it to God and say: "Oh, my dear God, I have sinned, but I confess it to thee, I pour it out to thee and pray thee for help; do thou help me!" This is what God wants of us.

That's why I should like sermons about the saints to be more moderate in the sense that we would also tell how *they* fell, in accord with the gospel, not the books of rhetoric. For there can be no doubt that they too tripped and stumbled over great humps. They

---

[6] *so sol der Teufel den Ars dran wischen.*
[7] John Gerson (1363-1429). Probably in his *De cogitationibus blasphemiae;* cf. *WA,* TR 2, 1349.

were of one flesh with us, one faith, one baptism, one blood. But we
have now set them so high above us that we must despair of imitat-
ing them. Thus, for example, the gospel speaks of Peter after his
confession concerning Christ, when he said to him, "You are the
Christ, the Son of the living God" [Matt. 16:16]. But soon afterwards he had to take these words: "Get behind me, Satan, you
devil!" [Matt. 16:23] whereas just a while before he had been told,
"Blessed are you, Simon Bar-Jona!" [Matt. 16:17]. Just look; first
he is blessed and holy, and afterwards he topples into hell and is
called a devil.

So it is: every one of us by himself is a devil, but in Christ we
are holy. So when we thus connect the saints with Christ, they are
Christ's true saints; but if we are not to despair, we must follow him.

This Gospel therefore expresses nothing but the sweetness of
Christ in his obedience to the Father and that he bestows nothing
because of merit. Therefore, when the devil assaults us with temptation, you say this: "Ah, even though I have done nothing that is
good, nevertheless I will not despair, for He always dealt with men
sweetly," and that is true. Only the damned must remain until they
have paid the last penny [Matt. 5:26]. This the Scriptures show
again and again. In Ecclesiasticus [2:10] it is written, "Who was
ever forsaken by God?" Jerome says, "Cursed be he who holds that
Christ's power is flesh," and again, "Blessed be he who hopes in
God."[8] And to Jeremiah[9] God says, "Hear me, because you have
hoped in me, I will deliver you with power, and even though the
city go down, I will preserve you" [Jer. 39:16-18]. From this we
should learn how Christ loves us, even though he might justly be
angry, in order that we should also love our brethren. Look, this is
the way God treats you! What are you going to do? You too must
have a heart that is sweet toward him. Do this, then, forthwith!
This I say in order that . . .[10]

---

[8] These quotations cannot be traced to Jerome's writings.

[9] The text here reads "*Anania.*"

[10] The text breaks off here and adds the following in Latin: "He was annoyed
because the students burned Tetzel's theses in the market place, etc." Cf.
Luther's letter to John Lang, March 21, 1518, Smith and Jacobs, *Luther's
Correspondence*, I, 75-76.

SERMONS AT LEIPZIG AND ERFURT

1519; 1521

SERMONS AT LEIPZIG AND
ERFURT, 1519; 1521

Sermon Preached in the Castle at Leipzig
on the Day of St. Peter and St. Paul,
Matt. 16:13-19, June 29, 1519

Luther arrived in Leipzig for the disputation with Dr. Johann Eck on June 24, 1519. Karlstadt began the disputation with Eck on June 27, but the debate was adjourned to allow for the observance of the festival of St. Peter and St. Paul on Wednesday, June 29. Duke Barnim of Pomerania had arranged for Luther to preach in the castle chapel but because of the crowd the service had to be transferred to the disputation hall. The text Luther chose is the Gospel for the day and, as he said, "contains all the materials of the disputation." The sermon treats first the grace of God and free will and second, the power of Peter. The text and the sermon are therefore closely related to the main point of controversy in the disputation, Luther's proposition concerning the power of the pope, Thesis 13. On the Leipzig Debate and this sermon, see LW 31, 309-325; Fife, op. cit., pp. 327-394; Letter of Luther to Spalatin, July 20, 1519 is preserved in Preserved Smith, The Life and Letters of Martin Luther *(Boston and New York, Houghton Mifflin, 1911), p. 67.*

The sermon with its preface was given to the printer in Leipzig by Luther himself after the disputation. It was toned down for publication and "in published form gives no adequate idea of the power with which the ardent monk must have set forth his position" (Fife, op. cit., p. 359).

Text in German; WA 2, 244-249, compared with CL 7, 356-362.

[Luther's Preface to the Sermon]

JESUS[1]

It is doubtless known to almost every one that I, Dr. Martin Luther, have been attacking the abuse of the Roman indulgence, having been moved to do this by Christian faithfulness and good intentions; since I have seen how the poor common people were being misled by the excessive enterprise of some preachers, and in their simplicity were not only slipping into dangerous error under the cloak of the indulgence but also being derprived of their scanty livelihood. From this my good intention and public service I have incurred much discomfort and danger and been put to trouble and expense, and besides, I have had to suffer grievous insult and defamation of my Christian honor by some sages and saints in the pulpit, on street corners, alleys, and everywhere else; and this has been going on now for almost two years without ceasing.

And yet, in all this what has grieved me most is that such preaching and slanders have moved and prompted so many Christian people to hatred, jealousy, backbiting, frivolous judgment, and similar grievous sins, when, if it were not for this damnable greed, indulgences in themselves are not and cannot ever become worth the price of having one heart poisoned or a commandment of God broken on their account, especially since neither God nor man has commanded indulgences and salvation gets along very well without indulgences. But now, through God's grace and help, the truth and reason for indulgences has become apparent, so that it is no longer necessary to defend my opposition. For the light itself reproves their dark work, so that one can see and understand why they have made such a hullabaloo and uproar against me, to the detriment of the truth and my condemnation. And though I might justly attack this past master [i.e., Dr. Johann Eck] of their vice, I have refrained from doing so, seeing that God, who has forgiven me many thousands of times more and, as I hope and believe, will continue to do, and from whom the real indulgence comes, has commanded us so to do [cf. Matt. 18:32-35]. I have also been content that I have experienced the fact that the envier may assail the truth, but he will never gain the upper hand.

---

[1] Common medieval salutation and invocation; cf. Col. 3:17.

So now that the storm is almost over, a new game is being started,[2] and since the recent disputation held at Leipzig they have undertaken to cover up and palliate all their previous wickedness and faults, introducing new tricks and accusing me of wanting to champion the Bohemian heresy.[3] And in order to put the seal on this properly, as such lies should be sealed, they add many other wanton, childish points: this one says that I do not accept any pope; another says that I tore up a rosary; one says that I wore a golden ring, another that I carried a garland; and like things, which are not worth telling before honest people. Therefore, the miserable, paltry envier, because he has no argument on his side, will find it far harder to invent lies than to insult me, as has happened before in this indulgence business.

Any honorable man can easily understand that it is to be expected that as they have unjustly told lies about me before so they will not tell the truth now; especially since they betray by such childish fables how eagerly they would do so if they could. And if in the past I have acted Christianly and been found innocent, contrary to all their slanders, it is to be hoped that I shall not act otherwise than as a Christian now, even though I must yield for a time to the malice of the envier and cheerfully resign myself to bear the defamation of my Christian name.

It seems fitting, however, that I should do what I can to warn and admonish every devout Christian person to guard his soul against these slanderous tongues and not to sin against God by indulging in wicked judgment or backbiting. Therefore I hope that I have demonstrated my innocence to everyone in this writing; for, upon my conscience, I know that everything which I have maintained at Leipzig is Christian and therefore I trust that I am willing, with God's help and grace, to die for it. And in due time I shall also demonstrate it and maintain it well, indeed, far better than I can maintain the traffic in indulgences.

Nor is there any good man who can say to me that I have been convicted of a single heretical point, whether it be Bohemian or

---

[2] Cf. letter of Johann Eck to Elector Frederick of Saxony, July 22, 1519, Smith and Jacobs, *Luther's Correspondence, op. cit.*, I, 202-205, and Eck's *Excusatio*, July 25, 1519, *C. R.* 1, 97-103.

[3] The heresy of John Huss.

Italian [*Welsch*], and will gladly see or hear the person, be he learned or unlearned, who would venture to bring it out into the open. Therefore I have defended myself; if anybody wants to say otherwise concerning me, he will do me no harm, but he will surely find his judge.

In order that I may not serve myself alone, but also be of some profit to him who reads this, I am presenting the sermon, delivered at the castle in Leipzig, which almost blew up a conflagration, and yet in such a way that I may moderate what I think may be too close to ill temper, and appeal more to basic understanding.

A Sermon on the Festival of St. Peter and St. Paul by Doctor Martin Luther

The Gospel, Matthew 16 [:13-19],[4] reads as follows:

"Jesus came into the region of the city of Caesarea, which Philip had built, and there he asked his disciples, 'What are the people saying about the Son of man?' And they said, 'Some say you are John the Baptist, some say you are Elijah, others Jeremiah or one of the other prophets.' Then Jesus said to them, 'What then do you say of me?' And Simon Peter answered and said, 'You are Christ, the Son of the living God.' And Jesus answered him and said, 'Blessed are you, O Simon Bar-Jona! For flesh and blood has not revealed this to you, but my father who is in heaven. And I tell you also: You are Peter (that is, a rock), and on this rock I will build my church, and the powers of hell shall not prevail against it. And I will give you the keys of the kingdom of heaven: whatever you bind on earth shall be bound in heaven; whatever you shall loose on earth shall be loosed in heaven.'"

[The First Part: The Grace of God and Our Free Will]

The Gospel includes all the materials of the whole disputation, for it speaks primarily of two matters: First, the grace of God and our free will; second, the power of St. Peter and the keys. The first part strikes at the great, the wise, and the holy, and would destroy them altogether, because they think they can accomplish everything through their own skill and works. But here the Lord teaches that everything that flesh and blood is or is capable of doing is futile.

[4] Luther's own translation from the Greek.

For no one can know, much less follow, Christ by flesh and blood; the Father in heaven must rather reveal him, as happened here to St. Peter. This is also indicated when he asks what the people are saying about him and no sure and settled answer was given, but only various unsettled opinions and fancies of the people were recounted. This shows that without the grace of God one wavers to and fro and has only an inconstant notion of God, until the Father reveals it; then a person knows what Christ is.

It follows from this that the free will of man, praise and extol it as you will, can do absolutely nothing of itself and is not free in its own volition to know or to do good, but only in the grace of God, which makes it free and without which it lies bound in sin and error and cannot get loose by itself. As Christ also says in John 8 [:32, 36, 34]: If the truth makes you free, you will be free indeed; but he who commits sin is a slave to sin. And Paul too says the same thing in Rom. 3 [:10, 11, 12, 23]: There is no man on earth who is good and who understands God and does good; rather they all need God's grace. Even though we of ourselves may want to begin something that is good, why then does Christ bid us to pray for grace and in the Lord's Prayer teach us to say: "Thy will be done, on earth as it is in heaven"? In order that it may be proved that we are not capable of doing God's will by our free will.

It follows, further, that one never speaks of the free will or understands it aright unless it be adorned with God's grace, without which it should rather be called one's own will than free will; for without grace it does not do God's will, but its own will, which is never good. It is true that it was free in Adam, but now through his fall it is corrupted and bound in sin. However, it has retained the name of free will because it was once free and, through grace, is to become free again.

If, then, you want to know how one becomes good and how one does good, which is the universal question, I have said that the first and foremost thing is for a man to know that of himself he cannot become or do good, and therefore he must despair of himself, let hands and feet go, declare himself an unprofitable man in the sight of God, and then call upon his divine grace, in which he should steadfastly trust. And anybody who teaches or seeks any way to begin other than this way errs and deceives himself and others [cf.

Gal. 1:8]. As they do who say: Why sure, you have a free will; do as much as in you lies, God will do his part. They say one should not bid the people to despair. Yes, of course, one should not bid them to despair; but the despair must really be pictured in its fulness. Nobody should despair of God's grace, but rather steadfastly rely upon God's help despite all the world and all sin. But one should despair completely of oneself and by no means rely upon one's free will, even to perform the smallest of works.

Therefore St. Jerome well says concerning this Gospel that it should be noted how Christ asks his disciples what men are saying of him and then afterwards asks them what they say of him, just as if they were not men. For it is true that man helped by grace is more than a man; indeed, the grace of God gives him the form of God and deifies him, so that even the Scriptures call him "God" and God's son. Thus a man must be extended beyond flesh and blood and become more than man, if he is to become good. And this begins when a man acknowledges that of himself this is impossible, humbly seeks the grace of God, and utterly despairs of himself; only then do good works follow. Thus, when grace has been obtained, then you have a free will; then do what in you lies.

It is not possible that God will deny his grace to a man who thus sincerely acknowledges his inability and utterly despairs of himself. This is the best and nearest preparation for grace, as the mother of God teaches and says in her Magnificat: "He has filled the hungry with good things" [Luke 1:53]. This is what should be preached; first rid the people of their own false trust and then fill them with good works. But the way it is, they[5] teach us to do many good works and very little about the beginning of doing good works, which is more important than good works. For when the beginning is not good the end will seldom be good; but when the grace of God is obtained, works will follow almost of themselves.

This despair and search for grace should not last only for an hour or a period of time and then cease. Rather, all our work and words and thoughts as long as we live should be directed solely toward despairing of oneself at all times and abiding in God's grace, longing and yearning for it, as the prophet says in Ps. 42 [:1-2], "As

---

[5] The text reads "do not teach us"; correction to restore the sense supplied from variant text. WA 1, 248 n. to line 15.

a hart longs for flowing streams, so longs my soul for thee, O God. My soul thirsts for God, for the living, strong God. When shall I come and behold the face of God?" This yearning for God and yearning to be good is initiated by grace and it continues until death. Therefore, despair of oneself must also continue along with it and false trust in oneself must be left behind.

[The Second Part: On the Power of St. Peter]

It is not necessary for the ordinary man to dispute much about the power of St. Peter or the pope. What is more important is to know how one should use it for salvation. It is true that the keys were given to St. Peter; but not to him personally, but rather to the person of the Christian church. They were actually given to me and to you for the comfort of our consciences. St. Peter, or a priest, is a servant of the keys. The church is the woman and bride, whom he should serve with the power of the keys; just as we see in daily use that the sacrament is administered to all who desire it of the priests.

Now, in order that we may understand how to use the key savingly, I have said above that if one desires to be good and is made receptive to grace through the forgiveness of what we can do by our own ability, then it is important to know whether one has received God's grace or not. For one must know how one stands with God, if the conscience is to be joyful and be able to stand. For when a person doubts this and does not steadfastly believe that he has a gracious God, then he actually does not have a gracious God. As he believes, so he has. Therefore no one can know that he is in grace and that God is gracious toward him except through faith. If he believes it, he is saved; if he does not believe it, he is damned. For this confidence and good conscience is the real, basically good faith, which the grace of God works in us.

This, you see, is what the keys do for you; this is what the priests were ordained for. When you feel your heart wavering or doubting whether you are in grace in God's eyes, then it is high time that you go to the priest and ask for the absolution of your sin, and thus seek the power and the comfort of the keys. So when the priest makes a judgment and absolves you, that is as much as to say: Your sins have been forgiven; you have a gracious God. This is a comforting statement and it is the Word of God, who has bound himself to loose in heaven the one whom the priest looses [Matt. 16:19].

See to it then, that you never doubt that this is so, and you should rather die many times than doubt the priest's judgment, for it is Christ's and God's judgment.

If you can believe this, then your heart must laugh for joy and it must cherish the power of the priest and praise and thank God for so comforting your conscience through the medium of men. But if you cannot believe and you think that you are not worthy of such forgiveness, you have not done enough. Then you must ask God to give you this faith; for you must have it or you will perish everlastingly; otherwise it is a good sign that you have been too little instructed in faith and too much instructed in works. A thousandfold more depends on your firmly believing the judgment of the priest than your being worthy and doing sufficient works. Indeed, this selfsame faith makes you worthy and helps you to make a proper satisfaction. Thus the power of the keys helps, not the priest as a priest, but only the sinful and abashed consciences, which receive grace through faith, and their hearts are set at peace and good confidence toward God. The result then is that all life and suffering is light, and a man, who otherwise never does any good because of the unrest of his heart, can serve his gracious God with joy. This means then the sweet burden of our Lord Jesus Christ [Matt. 11:30]. Amen. Praise and glory to God.

Sermon Preached at Erfurt on the Journey to Worms, John 20:19-20, April 7, 1521

The title of this sermon in its original printed form reads: "A Sermon by Dr. Martin Luther on his way to His Imperial Majesty at Worms, preached at Erfurt at the request of eminent and very learned men without previous preparation or special study, owing to the shortness of time. . . ." The Gospel for the day, Quasimodo Geniti, was John 20:19-31, but Luther limited his sermon to the first two verses.

On his way to Worms Luther was received with great enthusiasm in Erfurt; the church of the Augustinians where he preached could not contain the tremendous crowd that gathered to hear him. The sermon emphasizes the core of Christianity: faith in Christ on the foundation of the Word of God, and contains sharp strictures upon Rome, philosophy, and pulpit "fables." Eoban Hess, professor at the university, declared that, "by the power of his mouth hearts were melted like snow by the breath of spring as he showed the way to heaven's goods which had been closed for centuries." (Cf. Fife, op. cit., pp. 651-652; Boehmer, op. cit., pp. 401-402.) A recent translation of this sermon, undependable and riddled with errors, appeared in Bertram Lee Woolf (ed.), Reformation Writings of Martin Luther *(New York, 1953), II, 110-116. The transcriber of the sermon is unknown and the printed version indicates that it was "published by a layman" and printed by Matthes Maler in Erfurt. Seven prints appeared in the year 1521.*

Text in German; WA 7, 808-813.

Dear friends, I shall pass over the story of St. Thomas this time and leave it for another occasion, and instead consider the brief words uttered by Christ: "Peace be with you" [John 20:19] and "Behold my hands and my side" [John 20:27], and "as the Father has sent me, even so I send you" [John 20:21]. Now, it is clear and manifest that every person likes to think that he will be saved and attain to eternal salvation. This is what I propose to discuss now.

You also know that all philosophers, doctors and writers have studiously endeavored to teach and write what attitude man should take to piety. They have gone to great trouble, but, as is evident, to little avail. Now genuine and true piety consists of two kinds of works: those done for others, which are the right kind, and those done for ourselves, which are unimportant. In order to find a foundation, one man builds churches; another goes on a pilgrimage to St. James'[1] or St. Peter's[2]; a third fasts or prays, wears a cowl, goes barefoot, or does something else of the kind. Such works are nothing whatever and must be completely destroyed. Mark these words:

---

[1] St. James of Compostella.
[2] Rome.

none of our works have any power whatsoever. For God has chosen a man, the Lord Christ Jesus, to crush death, destroy sin, and shatter hell, since there was no one before he came who did not inevitably belong to the devil. The devil therefore thought he would get a hold upon the Lord when he hung between two thieves and was suffering the most contemptible and disgraceful of deaths, which was cursed both by God and by men [cf. Deut. 21:23; Gal. 3:13]. But the Godhead was so strong that death, sin, and even hell were destroyed.

Therefore you should note well the words which Paul writes to the Romans [Rom. 5:12-21]. Our sins have their source in Adam, and because Adam ate the apple, we have inherited sin from him. But Christ has shattered death for our sake, in order that we might be saved by his works, which are alien to us, and not by our works.

But the papal dominion treats us altogether differently. It makes rules about fasting, praying, and butter-eating, so that whoever keeps the commandments of the pope will be saved and whoever does not keep them belongs to the devil. It thus seduces the people with the delusion that goodness and salvation lies in their own works. But I say that none of the saints, no matter how holy they were, attained salvation by their works. Even the holy mother of God did not become good, was not saved, by her virginity or her motherhood, but rather by the will of faith and the works of God, and not by her purity, or her own works. Therefore, mark me well: this is the reason why salvation does not lie in our own works, no matter what they are; it cannot and will not be effected without faith.

Now, someone may say: Look, my friend, you are saying a lot about faith, and claiming that our salvation depends solely upon it; now, I ask you, how does one come to faith? I will tell you. Our Lord Christ said, "Peace be with you. Behold my hands, etc."[3] [John 20:26-27]. [In other words, he is saying:] Look, man, I am the only one who has taken away your sins and redeemed you, etc.; now be at peace. Just as you inherited sin from Adam—not that you committed it, for I did not eat the apple, any more than you did, and yet this is how we came to be in sin—so we have not suffered [as Christ did], and therefore we were made free from death and sin

---

[3] In the original these words are in Latin.

by God's work, not by our works. Therefore God says: Behold, man, I am your redemption [cf. Isa. 43:3]; just as Paul said to the Corinthians: Christ is our justification, redemption, etc.[4] [I Cor. 1:30]. Christ is our justification and redemption, as Paul says in this passage. And here our [Roman] masters say: Yes, *Redemptor*, Redeemer; this is true, but it is not enough.

Therefore, I say again: Alien works, these make us good! Our Lord Christ says: I am your justification. I have destroyed the sins you have upon you. Therefore only believe in me; believe that I am he who has done this; then you will be justified. For it is written, *Justicia est fides*,[5] righteousness is identical with faith and comes through faith. Therefore, if we want to have faith, we should believe the gospel, Paul, etc., and not the papal breves, or the decretals, but rather guard ourselves against them as against fire. For everything that comes from the pope cries out: Give, give; and if you refuse, you are of the devil. It would be a small matter if they were only exploiting the people. But, unfortunately, it is the greatest evil in the world to lead the people to believe that outward works can save or make a man good.

At this time the world is so full of wickedness that it is overflowing, and is therefore now under a terrible judgment and punishment, which God has inflicted, so that the people are perverting and deceiving themselves in their own minds. For to build churches, and to fast and pray and so on has the appearance of good works, but in our heads we are deluding ourselves. We should not give way to greed, desire for temporal honor, and other vices and rather be helpful to our poor neighbor. Then God will arise in us and we in him, and this means a new birth. What does it matter if we commit a fresh sin? If we do not immediately despair, but rather say within ourselves, "O God, thou livest still! Christ my Lord is the destroyer of sin," then at once the sin is gone. And also the wise man says: "*Septies in die cadit iustus et resurgit*." "A righteous man falls seven times, and rises again" [Prov. 24:16].

The reason why the world is so utterly perverted and in error is that for a long time there have been no genuine preachers. There are perhaps three thousand priests, among whom one cannot find

---

[4] In the original these words are in Latin.
[5] Righteousness is faith. Cf. Rom. 4:5.

four good ones—God have mercy on us in this crying shame! And when you do get a good preacher, he runs through the gospel superficially and then follows it up with a fable about the old ass[6] or a story about Dietrich of Berne,[7] or he mixes in something of the pagan teachers, Aristotle, Plato, Socrates, and others, who are all quite contrary to the gospel, and also contrary to God, for they did not have the knowledge of the light which we possess. Aye, if you come to me and say: The Philosopher says: Do many good works, then you will acquire the habit, and finally you will become godly;[8] then I say to you: Do not perform good works in order to become godly; but if you are already godly, then do good works, though without affectation and with faith. There you see how contrary these two points of view are.

In former times the devil made great attacks upon the people and from these attacks they took refuge in faith and clung to the Head, which is Christ; and so he was unable to accomplish anything. So now he has invented another device; he whispers into the ears of our Junkers that they should make exactions from people and give them laws. This way it looks well on the outside; but inside it is full of poison. So the young children grow up in a delusion; they go to church thinking that salvation consists in praying, fasting, and attending mass. Thus it is the preacher's fault. But still there would be no need, if only we had right preachers.

The Lord said three times to St. Peter: *"Petre, amas me? etc.; pasce oves meas"* [John 21:15-17]. "Peter, feed, feed, feed my sheep." What is the meaning of *pascere?* It means to feed. How should one feed the sheep? Only by preaching the Word of God, only by preaching faith. Then our Junkers come along and say: *Pascere* means *leges dare,* to enact laws, but with deception. Yes, they are well fed! They feed the sheep as the butchers do on Easter eve. Whereas one should speak the Word of God plainly to guide the

---

[6] *Von dem alten Esel.* A variant text reads, *von dem alten Ezel (Etzel),* "about the ancient Attila," which was probably what Luther originally said. Cf. WA 7, 810 n. 1.
[7] The cognomen of Theodoric I (493-526), king of the Ostrogoths, whose capital was in Verona-Berne; he appears in the Nibelungenlied associated with Attila. Cf. C. M. Gayley (ed.) *The Classic Myths in English Literature and in Art* (Boston, 1911), pp. 409, 537. Cf. WA 9, 620.
[8] Cf. Aristotle, *Nichomachean Ethics,* Book II, chap. I (Everyman's Library, pp. 26-27).

poor and weak in faith, they mix in their beloved Aristotle, who is contrary to God, despite the fact that Paul says in Col. [2:8]: Beware of laws and philosophy. What does "philosophy" mean? If we knew Greek, Latin, and German, we would see clearly what the Apostle is saying.

Is not this the truth? I know very well that you don't like to hear this and that I am annoying many of you; nevertheless, I shall say it. I will also advise you, no matter who you are: If you have preaching in mind or are able to help it along, then do not become a priest or a monk, for there is a passage in the thirty-third and thirty-fourth chapters of the prophet Ezekiel, unfortunately a terrifying passage, which reads: If you forsake your neighbor, see him going astray, and do not help him, do not preach to him, I will call you to account for his soul [Ezek. 33:8; 34:10]. This is a passage which is not often read. But I say, you become a priest or a monk in order to pray your seven canonical hours and say mass, and you think you want to be godly. Alas, you're a fine fellow! It [i.e., being a priest or monk] will fail you. You say the Psalter, you pray the rosary, you pray all kinds of other prayers, and say a lot of words; you say mass, you kneel before the altar, you read confession, you go on mumbling and maundering; and all the while you think you are free from sin. And yet in your heart you have such great envy that, if you could choke your neighbor and get away with it creditably, you would do it; and that's the way you say mass. It would be no wonder if a thunderbolt struck you to the ground. But if you have eaten three grains of sugar or some other seasoning, no one could drag you to the altar with red-hot tongs.[9] You have scruples! And that means to go to heaven with the devil. I know very well that you don't like to hear this. Nevertheless, I will tell the truth, I must tell the truth, even though it cost me my neck twenty times over, that the verdict may not be pronounced against me [i.e., at the last judgment].

Yes, you say, there were learned people a hundred or fifty years ago too. That is true; but I am not concerned with the length of time or the number of persons. For even though they knew something of it then, the devil has always been a mixer, who preferred the pagan writers to the holy gospel. I will tell the truth and must

---

[9] Because of the rule that the priest must say mass fasting.

tell the truth; that's why I'm standing here,[10] and not taking any money for it either. Therefore, we should not build upon human law or works, but rather have true faith in the One who is the destroyer of sin; then we shall find ourselves growing in Him. Then everything that was bitter before is sweet. Then our hearts will recognize God. And when that happens we shall be despised, and we shall pay no regard to human law, and then the pope will come and excommunicate us. But then we shall be so united with God that we shall pay no heed whatsoever to any hardship, ban, or law.

Then someone may go on and ask: Should we not keep the man-made laws at all? Or, can we not continue to pray, fast, and so on, as long as the right way is present? My answer is that if there is present a right Christian love and faith, then everything a man does is meritorious; and each may do what he wills [cf. Rom. 14:22], so long as he has no regard for works, since they cannot save him.

In conclusion, then, every single person should reflect and remember that we cannot help ourselves, but only God, and also that our works are utterly worthless. So shall we have the peace of God. And every person should so perform his work that it benefits not only himself alone, but also another, his neighbor. If he is rich, his wealth should benefit the poor. If he is poor, his service should benefit the rich. When persons are servants or maidservants, their work should benefit their master. Thus no one's work should benefit him alone; for when you note that you are serving only your own advantage, then your service is false. I am not troubled; I know very well what man-made laws are. Let the pope issue as many laws as he likes, I will keep them all so far as I please.

Therefore, dear friends, remember that God has risen up[11] for our sakes. Therefore let us also arise to be helpful to the weak in faith, and so direct our work that God may be pleased with it. So shall we receive the peace he has given to us today. May God grant us this every day. Amen.

---

[10] Cf. Luther's words before the Diet eleven days later, "Here I stand." *LW* 32, p. 113.

[11] Is there an allusion here to the bull, *Exsurge Domine* (Arise, Lord), which threatened Luther's excommunication?

EIGHT SERMONS AT WITTENBERG

1522

EIGHT SERMONS AT WITTENBERG
1522

*The title of the earliest printed version of these sermons reads:
"Eight Sermons by Dr. M. Luther, preached by him at Wittenberg
in Lent, dealing briefly with the masses, images, both kinds in the
sacrament, eating [of meats], and private confession, etc."*

*In December, 1521, Luther returned secretly to Wittenberg
from the Wartburg for a three-day conference on how to meet the
turbulence and confusion caused by the radical reformers. Soon
after his return to the Wartburg, Karlstadt put himself at the head
of those who favored immediate abolition of Roman practices. At
Christmas Karlstadt administered communion in two kinds for the
first time in the parish church. (This had been done as early as
September in the Augustinian monastery where Gabriel Zwilling
conducted mass in the vernacular and abolished private masses.)
Karlstadt also declared that confession before communion was unnecessary, that images were not allowable in the church, and that
rules of fasting were not binding, and this led to outbreaks of actual
destruction of images and altars. He also taught the doctrine of
direct illumination by the Spirit, which made scholarship and learning unnecessary for the understanding of the Scriptures. The consequence was that the city schools were closed and the university
threatened with collapse. Allied with Karlstadt's followers were the
Zwickau prophets, Storch, Drechsel, and Stübner, adherents of
Thomas Münzer.*

*Luther, who hitherto had relied upon Melanchthon's leadership
to keep order, returned to Wittenberg on March 6. On March 8 he
conferred with Melanchthon, Justus Jonas, Nicholas Amsdorf, and
Hieronymus Schurf. On March 9, Invocavit Sunday, he mounted
the pulpit in the parish church and preached each day from the
ninth to the sixteenth. This remarkable series of sermons, which are
powerful, inspired preaching of the gospel, had the effect of re-*

storing tranquility and order almost at once. His task was to lead his congregation away from fanatical enthusiasm back to the spirit of the gospel and to answer the questions that were agitating his people in the light of the gospel. (Further details may be found in an excellent introduction to the sermons in PE 2, 387-390 and in the biographies of Luther and the church histories.)

The sermons were transcribed by an unknown amanuensis and printed in many editions. Later versions by Stephan Roth, in the church postils, and Aurifaber, in the Eisleben edition, are simply free expansions of this oldest transcript. The present translation is a revision of that by A. Steimle in PE 2, 390-425. The minor differences, apart from style, are due largely to the fact that Steimle more frequently resorted to the undependable Aurifaber text.

Text in German; CL 7, 363-387, compared with WA 10^{III}, 1-64 and MA^3, 4, 33-58, 332-337.

The First Sermon, March 9, 1522, Invocavit Sunday[1]

The summons of death comes to us all, and no one can die for another. Every one must fight his own battle with death by himself, alone. We can shout into another's ears, but every one must himself be prepared for the time of death, for I will not be with you then, nor you with me. Therefore every one must himself know and be armed with the chief things which concern a Christian. And these are what you, my beloved, have heard from me many days ago.

In the first place, we must know that we are the children of wrath, and all our works, intentions, and thoughts are nothing at all. Here we need a clear, strong text to bear out this point. Such is the saying of St. Paul in Eph. 2 [:3]. Note this well; and though there are many such in the Bible, I do not wish to overwhelm you with many texts. "We are all the children of wrath." And please do not undertake to say: I have built an altar, given a foundation for masses, etc.

---

[1] In the original there follow the words "Sermon, "D.M.L."

Secondly, that God has sent us his only-begotten Son that we may believe in him and that whoever trusts in him shall be free from sin and a child of God, as John declares in his first chapter, "To all who believed in his name, he gave power to become children of God" [John 1:12]. Here we should all be well versed in the Bible and ready to confront the devil with many passages. With respect to these two points I do not feel that there has been anything wrong or lacking. They have been rightly preached to you, and I should be sorry if it were otherwise. Indeed, I am well aware and I dare say that you are more learned than I, and that there are not only one, two, three, or four, but perhaps ten or more, who have this knowledge and enlightenment.

Thirdly, we must also have love and through love we must do to one another as God has done to us through faith. For without love faith is nothing, as St. Paul says (I Cor. 2 [13:1]): If I had the tongues of angels and could speak of the highest things in faith, and have not love, I am nothing. And here, dear friends, have you not grievously failed? I see no signs of love among you, and I observe very well that you have not been grateful to God for his rich gifts and treasures.

Here let us beware lest Wittenberg become Capernaum [cf. Matt. 11:23]. I notice that you have a great deal to say of the doctrine of faith and love which is preached to you, and this is no wonder; an ass can almost intone the lessons, and why should you not be able to repeat the doctrines and formulas? Dear friends, the kingdom of God,—and we are that kingdom—does not consist in talk or words [I Cor. 4:20], but in activity, in deeds, in works and exercises. God does not want hearers and repeaters of words [Jas. 1:22], but followers and doers, and this occurs in faith through love. For a faith without love is not enough—rather it is not faith at all, but a counterfeit of faith, just as a face seen in a mirror is not a real face, but merely the reflection of a face [I Cor. 13:12].

Fourthly, we also need patience. For whoever has faith, trusts in God, and shows love to his neighbor, practicing it day by day, must needs suffer persecution. For the devil never sleeps, but constantly gives him plenty of trouble. But patience works and produces hope [Rom. 5:4], which freely yields itself to God and vanishes away in him. Thus faith, by much affliction and persecution, ever increases, and is strengthened day by day. A heart thus blessed with virtues can never rest or restrain itself, but rather pours itself out again for the benefit and service of the brethren, just as God has done to it.

And here, dear friends, one must not insist upon his rights, but must see what may be useful and helpful to his brother, as Paul says, *Omnia mihi licent, sed non omnia expediunt*, " 'All things are lawful for me,' but not all things are helpful" [I Cor. 6:12]. For we are not all equally strong in faith, some of you have a stronger faith than I. Therefore we must not look upon ourselves, or our strength, or our prestige, but upon our neighbor, for God has said through Moses: I have borne and reared you, as a mother does her child [Deut. 1:31]. What does a mother do to her child? First she gives it milk, then gruel, then eggs and soft food, whereas if she turned about and gave it solid food, the child would never thrive [cf. I Cor. 3:2; Heb. 5:12-13]. So we should also deal with our brother, have patience with him for a time, have patience with his weakness and help him bear it; we should also give him milk-food, too [I Pet. 2:2; cf. Rom. 14:1-3], as was done with us, until he, too, grows strong, and thus we do not travel heavenward alone, but bring our brethren, who are not now our friends, with us. If all mothers were to abandon their children, where would we have been? Dear brother, if you have suckled long enough, do not at once cut off the breast, but let your brother be suckled as you were suckled. I would not have gone so far as you have done, if I had been here. The cause is good, but there has been too much haste. For there are still brothers and sisters on the other side who belong to us and must still be won.

Let me illustrate. The sun has two properties, light and heat. No king has power enough to bend or guide the light of the sun; it remains fixed in its place. But the heat may be turned and guided, and yet is ever about the sun. Thus faith must always remain pure and immovable in our hearts, never wavering; but love bends and turns so that our neighbor may grasp and follow it. There are some who can run, others must walk, still others can hardly creep [cf. I Cor. 8:7-13]. Therefore we must not look upon our own, but upon our brother's powers, so that he who is weak in faith, and attempts to follow the strong, may not be destroyed of the devil. Therefore, dear brethren, follow me; I have never been a destroyer. And I was also the very first whom God called to this work. I cannot run away, but will remain as long as God allows. I was also the one to whom God first revealed that his Word should be preached to you. I am also sure that you have the pure Word of God.

Let us, therefore, let us act with fear and humility, cast ourselves at one another's feet, join hands with each other, and help one another. I will do my part, which is no more than my duty, for I love you even as I love my own soul. For here we battle not against pope or bishop, but against the devil [cf. Eph. 6:12], and do you imagine he is asleep? He sleeps not, but sees the true light rising, and to keep it from shining into his eyes he would like to make a flank attack—and he will succeed, if we are not on our guard. I know him well, and I hope, too, that with the help of God, I am his master. But if we yield him but an inch, we must soon look to it how we may be rid of him. Therefore all those have erred who have helped and consented to abolish the mass; not that it was not a good thing, but that it was not done in an orderly way. You say it was right according to the Scriptures. I agree, but what becomes of order? For it was done in wantonness, with no regard for proper order and with offense to your neighbor. If, beforehand, you had called upon God in earnest prayer, and had obtained the aid of the authorities, one could be certain that it had come from God. I, too, would have taken steps toward the same end if it had been a good thing to do; and if the mass were not so evil a thing, I would introduce it again. For I cannot defend your action, as I have just said. To the papists and blockheads I could defend it, for I could say: How do you know whether it was done with good or bad intention, since the work in itself was really a good work? But I would not know what to assert before the devil. For if on their deathbeds the devil reminds those who began this affair of texts like these, "Every plant which my Father has not planted will be rooted up" [Matt. 15:13], or "I have not sent them, yet they ran" [Jer. 23:21],[2] how will they be able to withstand? He will cast them into hell. But I shall poke the one spear into his face, so that even the world will become too small for him, for I know that in spite of my reluctance I was called by the council to preach. Therefore I was willing to

---

[2] Scripture passages in Latin, though Luther undoubtedly spoke them in German.

accept you as you were willing to accept me, and, besides, you could have consulted me about the matter.

I was not so far away that you could not reach me with a letter, whereas not the slightest communication was sent to me. If you were going to begin something and make me responsible for it, that would have been too hard. I will not do it [i.e., assume the responsibility]. Here one can see that you do not have the Spirit, even though you do have a deep knowledge of the Scriptures. Take note of these two things, "must" and "free." The "must" is that which necessity requires, and which must ever be unyielding; as, for instance, the faith, which I shall never permit any one to take away from me, but must always keep in my heart and freely confess before every one. But "free" is that in which I have choice, and may use or not, yet in such a way that it profit my brother and not me. Now do not make a "must" out of what is "free," as you have done, so that you may not be called to account for those who were led astray by your loveless exercise of liberty. For if you entice any one to eat meat on Friday, and he is troubled about it on his deathbed, and thinks, Woe is me, for I have eaten meat and I am lost! God will call you to account for that soul. I, too, would like to begin many things, in which but few would follow me, but what is the use? For I know that, when it comes to the showdown, those who have begun this thing cannot maintain themselves, and will be the first to retreat. How would it be, if I brought the people to the point of attack, and though I had been the first to exhort others, I would then flee, and not face death with courage? How the poor people would be deceived!

Let us, therefore, feed others also with the milk which we received, until they, too, become strong in faith. For there are many who are otherwise in accord with us and who would also gladly accept this thing, but they do not yet fully understand it—these we drive away. Therefore, let us show love to our neighbors; if we do not do this, our work will not endure. We must have patience with them for a time, and not cast out him who is weak in faith; and do and omit to do many other things, so long as love requires it and it does no harm to our faith. If we do not earnestly pray to God and act rightly in this matter, it looks to me as if all the misery which we have begun to heap upon the papists will fall upon us. Therefore I could no longer remain away, but was compelled to come and say these things to you.

This is enough about the mass; tomorrow we shall speak about images.

The Second Sermon, March 10, 1522, Monday

after Invocavit[3]

Dear friends, you heard yesterday the chief characteristics of a Christian man, that his whole life and being is faith and love. Faith is directed toward God, love toward man and one's neighbor, and consists in such love and service for him as we have received from God without our work and merit. Thus, there are two things: the one, which is the most needful, and which must be done in one way and no other; the other, which is a matter of choice and not of necessity, which may be kept or not, without endangering faith or incurring hell. In both, love must deal with our neighbor in the same manner as God has dealt with us; it must walk the straight road, straying neither to the left nor to the right. In the things which are "musts" and are matters of necessity, such as believing in Christ, love nevertheless never uses force or undue constraint. Thus the mass is an evil thing, and God is displeased with it, because it is performed as if it were a sacrifice and work of merit. Therefore it must be abolished. Here there can be no question or doubt, any more than you should ask whether you should worship God. Here we are entirely agreed: the private masses must be abolished. As I have said in my writings,[4] I wish they would be abolished everywhere and only the ordinary evangelical mass be retained. Yet Christian love should not employ harshness here nor force the matter. However, it should be preached and taught with tongue and pen that

---

[3] The title reads: "Another sermon of D. M. Luther's on Monday after Invocavit."

[4] In the *Open Letter to the Christian Nobility* (1520), *PE* 2, 61-164, and *The Babylonian Captivity of the Church* (1520), *PE* 2, 170-293.

to hold mass in such a manner is sinful, and yet no one should be dragged away from it by the hair; for it should be left to God, and his Word should be allowed to work alone, without our work or interference. Why? Because it is not in my power or hand to fashion the hearts of men as the potter molds the clay and fashion them at my pleasure [Ecclus. 33:13]. I can get no farther than their ears; their hearts I cannot reach. And since I cannot pour faith into their hearts, I cannot, nor should I, force any one to have faith. That is God's work alone, who causes faith to live in the heart. Therefore we should give free course to the Word and not add our works to it. We have the *jus verbi* [right to speak] but not the *executio* [power to accomplish]. We should preach the Word, but the results must be left solely to God's good pleasure.

Now if I should rush in and abolish it by force, there are many who would be compelled to consent to it and yet not know where they stand, whether it is right or wrong, and they would say: I do not know if it is right or wrong, I do not know where I stand, I was compelled by force to submit to the majority. And this forcing and commanding results in a mere mockery, an external show, a fool's play, man-made ordinances, sham-saints, and hypocrites. For where the heart is not good, I care nothing at all for the work. We must first win the hearts of the people. But that is done when I teach only the Word of God, preach the gospel, and say: Dear lords or pastors, abandon the mass, it is not right, you are sinning when you do it; I cannot refrain from telling you this. But I would not make it an ordinance for them, nor urge a general law. He who would follow me could do so, and he who refused would remain outside. In the latter case the Word would sink into the heart and do its work. Thus he would become convinced and acknowledge his error, and fall away from the mass; tomorrow another would do the same, and thus God would accomplish more with his Word than if you and I were to merge all our power into one heap. So when you have won the heart, you have won the man—and thus the thing must finally fall of its own weight and come to an end. And if the hearts and minds of all are agreed and united, abolish it. But if all are not heart and soul for its abolishment—leave it in God's hands, I beseech you, otherwise the result will not be good. Not that I would again set up the mass; I let it lie in God's name. Faith must not be chained and imprisoned, nor bound by an ordinance to any work. This is the principle by which you must be governed. For I am sure you will not be able to carry out your plans. And if you should carry them out with such general laws, then I will recant everything that I have written and preached and I will not support you. This I am telling you now. What harm can it do you? You still have your faith in God, pure and strong so that this thing cannot hurt you.

Love, therefore, demands that you have compassion on the weak, as all the apostles had. Once, when Paul came to Athens (Acts 17 [:16-32]), a mighty city, he found in the temple many ancient altars, and he went from one to the other and looked at them all, but he did not kick down a single one of them with his foot. Rather he stood up in the middle of the market place and said they were nothing but idolatrous things and begged the people to forsake them; yet he did not destroy one of them by force. When the Word took hold of their hearts, they forsook them of their own accord, and in consequence the thing fell of itself. Likewise, if I had seen them holding mass, I would have preached to them and admonished them. Had they heeded my admonition, I would have won them; if not, I would nevertheless not have torn them from it by the hair or employed any force, but simply allowed the Word to act and prayed for them. For the Word created heaven and earth and all things [Ps. 33:6]; the Word must do this thing, and not we poor sinners.

In short, I will preach it, teach it, write it, but I will constrain no man by force, for faith must come freely without compulsion. Take myself as an example. I opposed indulgences and all the papists, but never with force. I simply taught, preached, and wrote God's Word; otherwise I did nothing. And while I slept [cf. Mark 4:26-29], or drank Wittenberg beer with my friends Philip[5] and Amsdorf,[6] the Word so greatly weakened the papacy that no prince or emperor ever inflicted such losses upon it. I did nothing; the Word did everything. Had I desired to foment trouble, I could have brought great bloodshed upon Germany; indeed, I could have started such a game that even the emperor would not have been safe. But what would it have been? Mere fool's play. I did

---

[5] Melanchthon.
[6] Nicholas von Amsdorf (1483-1565).

nothing; I let the Word do its work. What do you suppose is Satan's thought when one tries to do the thing by kicking up a row? He sits back in hell and thinks: Oh, what a fine game the poor fools are up to now! But when we spread the Word alone and let it alone do the work, that distresses him. For it is almighty and takes captive the hearts, and when the hearts are captured the work will fall of itself. Let me cite a simple instance. In former times there were sects, too, Jewish and Gentile Christians, differing on the law of Moses with respect to circumcision. The former wanted to keep it, the latter not. Then came Paul and preached that it might be kept or not, for it was of no consequence, and also that they should not make a "must" of it, but leave it to the choice of the individual; to keep it or not was immaterial [I Cor. 7:18-24; Gal. 5:1]. So it was up to the time of Jerome, who came and wanted to make a "must" out of it, desiring to make it an ordinance and a law that it be prohibited.[7] Then came St. Augustine and he was of the same opinion as St. Paul: it might be kept or not, as one wished. St. Jerome was a hundred miles away from St. Paul's opinion. The two doctors bumped heads rather hard, but when St. Augustine died, St. Jerome was successful in having it prohibited. After that came the popes, who also wanted to add something and they, too, made laws. Thus out of the making of one law grew a thousand laws, until they have completely buried us under laws. And this is what will happen here, too; one law will soon make two, two will increase to three, and so forth.

Let this be enough at this time concerning the things that are necessary, and let us beware lest we lead astray those of weak conscience [I Cor. 8:12].

---

[7] A note in *MA*[3], 4, 334 reads: "Luther correctly discerns that about the time of Jerome (*ca.* 345-420), the creator of the Latin translation of the Bible (the Vulgate), the peculiarly Roman character of the Christian church began to develop."

The Third Sermon, March 11, 1522, Tuesday

after Invocavit[8]

We have heard the things which are "musts," which are necessary and must be done, things which must be so and not otherwise:
the private masses[9] must be abolished. For all works and things,
which are either commanded or forbidden by God and thus have
been instituted by the supreme Majesty, are "musts." Nevertheless,
no one should be dragged to them or away from them by the hair,
for I can drive no man to heaven or beat him into it with a club. I
said this plainly enough; I believe you have understood what I said.

Now follow the things which are not necessary, but are left to
our free choice by God and which we may keep or not, such as
whether a person should marry or not, or whether monks and nuns
should leave the cloisters. These things are matters of choice and
must not be forbidden by any one, and if they are forbidden, the
forbidding is wrong, since it is contrary to God's ordinance. In the
things that are free, such as being married or remaining single, you
should take this attitude: if you can keep to it without burdensome-
ness, then keep it; but it must not be made a general law; everyone
must rather be free. So if there is a priest, monk, or nun, who cannot
abstain, let him take a wife and be a husband, in order that your
conscience may be relieved;[10] and see to it that you can stand before
God and the world when you are assailed, especially when the devil
attacks you in the hour of death. It is not enough to say: this man
or that man did it, I followed the crowd, according to the preaching

---

[8] The title reads: "Another sermon of D. M. Luther's on Tuesday after Invocavit."
[9] *Winkelmessen oder sonderlichen Messen.*
[10] The contradiction of genders and the switch from impersonal to personal
address reflects Luther's spoken style and is here retained.

of the dean,[11] Dr. Karlstadt,[12] or Gabriel,[13] or Michael.[14] Not so; every one must stand on his own feet and be prepared to give battle to the devil. You must rest upon a strong and clear text of Scripture if you would stand the test. If you cannot do that, you will never withstand—the devil will pluck you like a parched leaf. Therefore the priests who have taken wives and the nuns who have taken husbands in order to save their consciences must stand squarely upon a clear text of Scripture, such as this one by St. Paul, although there are many more: "In later times some will depart from the faith by giving heed to deceitful spirits and doctrines of the devil (I think St. Paul is outspoken enough here!) and will forbid marriage and the foods which God created" [I Tim. 4:1-3]. This text the devil will not overthrow nor devour, it will rather overthrow and devour him. Therefore any monk or nun who finds that he is too weak to maintain chastity should conscientiously examine himself; if his heart and conscience are thus strengthened, let him take a wife and be a husband. Would to God all monks and nuns could hear this sermon and properly understand this matter and would all forsake the cloisters, and thus all the cloisters in the world would cease to exist; this is what I would wish. But now they have no understanding of the matter (for no one preaches it to them); they hear about others who are leaving the cloisters in other places, who, however, are well prepared for such a step, and then they want to follow their example, but have not yet fortified their consciences and do not know that it is a matter of liberty. This is bad, and yet it is better that the evil should be outside than inside.[15] Therefore I say, what God has made free shall remain free. If anybody forbids it, as the pope, the Antichrist, has done, you should not obey. He who can do so without harm and for love of his neighbor may wear a cowl

---

[11] Justus Jonas (1493-1555), dean (*Probst*) of the Castle Church and professor in the Wittenberg faculty, at this time a radical advocate of liturgical reform. However, the omission of the comma in the original text may indicate that Luther did not refer to Jonas at all, since Karlstadt was dean of the faculty. Cf. *WA* 10III, 438.

[12] Andreas Bodenstein Karlstadt (1480-1541).

[13] Gabriel Zwilling (Didymus) (*ca.* 1487-1558), Augustinian monk and champion of immediate reform of the mass.

[14] Zwilling's first name, Gabriel, probably suggested to Luther the addition of the name of the archangel Michael. Cf. Gal. 1:8.

[15] Namely, of the monasteries.

or a tonsure, since it will not injure your faith. The cowl will not strangle you, if you are already wearing one.

Thus, dear friends, I have said it clearly enough, and I believe you ought to understand it and not make liberty a law, saying: This priest has taken a wife, therefore all priests must take wives. Not at all. Or this monk or that nun has left the cloister, therefore they must all come out. Not at all. Or this man has broken the images and burnt them, therefore all images must be burned—not at all, dear brother! And again, this priest has no wife, therefore no priest dare marry. Not at all! For they who cannot retain their chastity should take wives, and for others who can be chaste, it is good that they restrain themselves, as those who live in the Spirit and not in the flesh [Rom. 8:4; I Cor. 7:40]. Neither should they be troubled about the vows they have made, such as the monks' vows of obedience, chastity, and poverty (though they are rich enough withal). For we cannot vow anything that is contrary to God's commands. God has made it a matter of liberty to marry or not to marry, and you, you fool, undertake to turn this liberty into a vow contrary to the ordinance of God! Therefore you must let it remain a liberty and not make a compulsion out of it; for your vow is contrary to God's liberty. For example, if I vowed to strike my father on the mouth, or to steal someone's property, do you believe God would be pleased with such a vow? Therefore, little as I ought to keep a vow to strike my father on the mouth, so little ought I to abstain from marriage because I am bound by a vow of chastity, for in both cases God has ordered it otherwise. God has ordained that I should be free to eat fish or flesh, and there should be no commandment concerning them. Therefore all the Carthusians[16] and all monks and nuns are departing from God's ordinance and liberty when they believe that if they eat meat they are defiled.

Concerning Images

But now we must come to the images, and concerning them also it is true that they are unnecessary, and we are free to have them or not, although it would be much better if we did not have them at all. I am not partial to them. A great controversy arose on the subject of images between the Roman emperor and the pope; the

---

[16] As he does frequently, Luther here names the strictest of the orders.

emperor held that he had the authority to banish the images, but the pope insisted that they should remain, and both were wrong. Much blood was shed, but the pope emerged as victor and the emperor lost.[17] What was it all about? They wished to make a "must" out of that which is free. This God cannot tolerate. Do you presume to do things differently from the way the supreme Majesty has decreed? Surely not; let it alone. You read in the Law (Exod. 20 [:4]), "You shall not make yourself a graven image, or any likeness of anything that is in heaven above, or that is in the earth beneath, or that is in the water under the earth." There you take your stand; that is your ground. Now let us see! When our adversaries say: The meaning of the first commandment is that we should worship only one God and not any image, even as it is said immediately following, "You shall not bow down to them or serve them" [Exod. 20:5], and when they say that it is the worship of images which is forbidden and not the making of them, they are shaking our foundation and making it uncertain. And if you reply: The text says, "You shall not make any images," then they say: It also says, "You shall not worship them." In the face of such uncertainty who would be so bold as to destroy the images? Not I. But let us go further. They say: Did not Noah, Abraham, Jacob build altars? [Gen. 8:20; 12:7; 13:4; 13:18; 33:20]. And who will deny that? We must admit it. Again, did not Moses erect a bronze serpent, as we read in his fourth book (Num. 22 [21:9])? How then can you say that Moses forbade the making of images when he himself made one? It seems to me that such a serpent is an image, too. How shall we answer that? Again, do we not read also that two birds were erected on the mercy seat [Exod. 37:7], the very place where God willed that he should be worshipped? Here we must admit that we may have images and make images, but we must not worship them, and if they are worshipped, they should be put away and destroyed, just as King Hezekiah broke in pieces the bronze serpent erected by Moses [II Kings 18:4]. And who will be so bold as to say, when he is challenged to give an answer: They worship the images. They will say:

---

[17] Luther has reference to the Iconoclastic Controversy, initiated by Emperor Leo III, who prohibited the veneration of images in 718, contested by Pope Gregory II, and finally settled in 843. Invocavit Sunday is the "Feast of Orthodoxy" in commemoration of the Seventh Ecumenical Council of 783, which dealt with this question.

Are you the man who dares to accuse us of worshipping them? Do not believe that they will acknowledge it. To be sure, it is true, but we cannot make them admit it. Just look how they acted when I condemned works without faith. They said: Do you believe that we have no faith, or that our works are performed without faith? Then I cannot press them any further, but must put my flute back in my pocket; for if they gain a hair's breadth, they make a hundred miles out of it.

Therefore it should have been preached that images were nothing and that no service is done to God by erecting them; then they would have fallen of themselves. That is what I did; that is what Paul did in Athens, when he went into their churches and saw all their idols. He did not strike at any of them, but stood in the market place and said, "You men of Athens, you are all idolatrous" [Acts 17:16, 22]. He preached against their idols, but he overthrew none by force. And you rush, create an uproar, break down altars, and overthrow images! Do you really believe you can abolish the altars in this way? No, you will only set them up more firmly. Even if you overthrew the images in this place, do you think you have overthrown those in Nürnberg and the rest of the world? Not at all. St. Paul, as we read in the Book of Acts [28:11], sat in a ship on whose prow were painted or carved the Twin Brothers [i.e., Castor and Pollux]. He went on board and did not bother about them at all, neither did he break them off. Why must Luke describe the Twins at this point? Without doubt he wanted to show that outward things could do no harm to faith, if only the heart does not cleave to them or put its trust in them. This is what we must preach and teach, and let the Word alone do the work, as I said before. The Word must first capture the hearts of men and enlighten them; we will not be the ones who will do it. Therefore the apostles magnified their ministry, *ministerium* [Rom. 11:13], and not its effect, *executio*.

Let this be enough for today.

The Fourth Sermon, March 12, 1522, Wednesday
after Invocavit[18]

Dear friends, we have now heard about the things which are "musts," such as that the mass is not to be observed as a sacrifice. Then we considered the things which are not necessary but free, such as marriage, the monastic life, and the abolishing of images. We have treated these four subjects, and have said that in all these matters love is the captain. On the subject of images, in particular, we saw that they ought to be abolished when they are worshipped; otherwise not,—although because of the abuses they give rise to, I wish they were everywhere abolished. This cannot be denied. For whoever places an image in a church imagines he has performed a service to God and done a good work, which is downright idolatry. But this, the greatest, foremost, and highest reason for abolishing images, you have passed by, and fastened on the least important reason of all. For I suppose there is nobody, or certainly very few, who do not understand that yonder crucifix is not my God, for my God is in heaven, but that this is simply a sign. But the world is full of that other abuse; for who would place a silver or wooden image in a church unless he thought that by so doing he was rendering God a service? Do you think that Duke Frederick, the bishop of Halle,[19] and the others would have dragged so many silver images into the churches, if they thought it counted for nothing before God? No, they would not bother to do it. But this is not sufficient reason to abolish, destroy, and burn all images. Why? Because we must admit that there are still some people who hold no such wrong opinion of them, but to whom they may well be useful, although they are few. Nevertheless, we cannot and ought not to condemn a thing which may be any way useful to a person. You should rather have taught that images are nothing, that God cares nothing for

---

[18] The title reads: "A Sermon preached by M. L. on Wednesday after Invocavit."
[19] Duke Frederick is Elector Frederick the Wise of Ernestine Saxony (1463-1525). The "bishop of Halle" is probably Albrecht of Hohenzollern, archbishop of Mainz and of Magdeburg; the cathedral was located in Halle.

them, and that he is not served nor pleased when we make an image for him, but that we would do better to give a poor man a gold-piece than God a golden image; for God has forbidden the latter, but not the former. If they had heard this teaching that images count for nothing, they would have ceased of their own accord, and the images would have fallen without any uproar or tumult, as they are already beginning to do.

We must, therefore, be on our guard, for the devil, through his apostles, is after us with all his craft and cunning. Now, although it is true and no one can deny that the images are evil because they are abused, nevertheless we must not on that account reject them, nor condemn anything because it is abused. This would result in utter confusion. God has commanded us in Deut. 4 [:19] not to lift up our eyes to the sun [and the moon and the stars], etc., that we may not worship them, for they are created to serve all nations. But there are many people who worship the sun and the stars. Therefore we propose to rush in and pull the sun and stars from the skies. No, we had better let it be. Again, wine and women bring many a man to misery and make a fool of him [Ecclus. 19:2; 31:30]; so we kill all the women and pour out all the wine. Again, gold and silver cause much evil, so we condemn them. Indeed, if we want to drive away our worst enemy, the one who does us the most harm, we shall have to kill ourselves, for we have no greater enemy than our own heart, as the prophet, Jer. 17 [:9], says, "The heart of man is crooked," or, as I take the meaning, "always twisting to one side." And so on—what would we not do?

He who would blacken the devil must have good charcoal, for he, too, wears fine clothes and is invited to the kermis.[20] But I can catch him by asking him: Do you not place the images in the churches because you think it a special service to God? And when he says Yes, as he must, you may conclude that what was meant as a service of God he has turned into idolatry by abusing the images and practicing what God has not commanded. But he has neglected God's command, which is that he should be helpful to his neighbor. But I have not yet caught him, though actually he is caught and will not admit it; he escapes me by saying: Yes, I help the poor,

---

[20] *Kirchmess:* service for the consecration or commemoration of the consecration of a church, an occasion for placing images or embellishments in the church.

too; cannot I give to my neighbor and at the same time donate images? This is not so, however, for who would not rather give his neighbor a gold-piece than God a golden image? No, he would not trouble himself about placing images in churches if he did not believe, as he actually does, that he was doing God a service. Therefore I must admit that images are neither here nor there, neither evil nor good, we may have them or not, as we please. This trouble has been caused by you; the devil would not have accomplished it with me, for I cannot deny that it is possible to find someone to whom images are useful. And if I were asked about it, I would confess that none of these things give offense to one, and if just one man were found on earth who used the images aright, the devil would soon draw the conclusion against me: Why, then, do you condemn what may be used properly? Then he has gained the offensive and I would have to admit it. He would not have got nearly so far if I had been here. Proudly he scattered us, though it has done no harm to the Word of God. You wanted to blacken the devil, but you forgot the charcoal and used chalk. If you want to fight the devil you must know the Scriptures well and, besides, use them at the right time.

Concerning Meats

Let us proceed and speak of the eating of meats and what our attitude should be in this matter. It is true that we are free to eat any kind of food, meats, fish, eggs, or butter. This no one can deny. God has given us this liberty; this is true. Nevertheless, we must know how to use our liberty, and in this matter treat the weak brother quite differently from the stubborn. Observe, then, how you ought to use this liberty.

First, if you cannot abstain from meat without harm to yourself, or if you are sick, you may eat whatever you like,[21] and if anyone takes offense, let him be offended. Even if the whole world took offense, you are not committing a sin, for God can approve it in view of the liberty he has so graciously bestowed upon you and of the necessities of your health, which would be endangered by your abstinence.

---

[21] For a discussion of this and related questions cf. also Luther's *Explanations of the Ninety-five Theses* (1518), LW 31, 86-87; 109-110.

Secondly, if you should be pressed to eat fish instead of meat on Friday, and to eat fish and abstain from eggs and butter during Lent, etc., as the pope has done with his fool's laws, then you must in no wise allow yourself to be drawn away from the liberty in which God has placed you, but do just the contrary to spite him, and say: Because you forbid me to eat meat and presume to turn my liberty into law, I will eat meat in spite of you. And thus you must do in all other things which are matters of liberty. To give you an example: if the pope, or anyone else were to force me to wear a cowl, just as he prescribes it, I would take off the cowl just to spite him. But since it is left to my own free choice, I wear it or take it off, according to my pleasure.

Thirdly, there are some who are still weak in faith, who ought to be instructed, and who would gladly believe as we do. But their ignorance prevents them, and if this were preached to them, as it was to us, they would be one with us. Toward such well-meaning people we must assume an entirely different attitude from that which we assume toward the stubborn. We must bear patiently with these people and not use our liberty; since it brings no peril or harm to body or soul; in fact, it is rather salutary, and we are doing our brothers and sisters a great service besides. But if we use our liberty unnecessarily, and deliberately cause offense to our neighbor, we drive away the very one who in time would come to our faith. Thus St. Paul circumcised Timothy [Acts 16:3] because simple-minded Jews had taken offense; he thought: What harm can it do, since they are offended because of their ignorance? But when, in Antioch, they insisted that he ought and must circumcise Titus [Gal. 2:3], Paul withstood them all and to spite them refused to have Titus circumcised [Gal. 2:11]. And he stood his ground. He did the same when St. Peter by the exercise of his liberty caused a wrong conception in the minds of the unlearned. It happened in this way: when Peter was with the Gentiles, he ate pork and sausages with them, but when the Jews came in, he abstained from this food and did not eat as he did before. Then the Gentiles who had become Christians thought: Alas! we, too, must be like the Jews, eat no pork, and live according to the law of Moses. But when Paul learned that they were acting to the injury of evangelical freedom, he reproved Peter publicly and read him an apostolic lecture, saying: "If you, though a Jew, live like a Gentile, how can you compel the Gentiles to live like Jews?" [Gal. 2:14]. Thus we, too, should order our lives and use our liberty at the proper time, so that Christian liberty may suffer no injury, and no offense be given to our weak brothers and sisters who are still without the knowledge of this liberty.

The Fifth Sermon, March 13, 1522, Thursday

after Invocavit

We have heard of the things that are necessary, such as that the mass is not to be performed as a sacrifice, and of the unnecessary things, such as monks' leaving the monasteries, the marriage of priests, and images. We have seen how we must treat these matters, that no compulsion or ordinance must be made of them, and that no one shall be dragged from them or to them by the hair, but that we must let the Word of God alone do the work. Let us now consider how we must observe the blessed sacrament.

You have heard how I preached against the foolish law of the pope and opposed his precept,[22] that no woman shall wash the altar linen on which the body of Christ has lain, even if it be a pure nun, except it first be washed by a pure priest.[23] Likewise, when any one has touched the body of Christ, the priests come running and scrape his fingers, and much more of the same sort. But when a maid has slept with a naked priest, the pope winks at it and lets it go. If she becomes pregnant and bears a child, he lets that pass, too. But to touch the altar linen and the sacrament [i.e., the host], this he will not allow. But when a priest grabs it, both top and bottom, this is all right.

Against such fool laws we have preached and exposed them, in order that it might be made known that no sin is involved in these

---

[22] Reference to *On the Abuse of the Mass* (1521). WA 8, 477-563, especially pp. 508, 540.
[23] *Decretum Gratiani*, dist. 23, cap. 25.

foolish laws and commandments of the pope, and that a layman does not commit sin if he touches the cup or the body of Christ with his hands. You should give thanks to God that you have come to such clear knowledge, which many great men have lacked. But now you go ahead and become as foolish as the pope, in that you think that a person must touch the sacrament with his hands. You want to prove that you are good Christians by touching the sacrament with your hands, and thus you have dealt with the sacrament, which is our highest treasure, in such a way that it is a wonder you were not struck to the ground by thunder and lightning. All the other things God might have suffered, but this he cannot allow, because you have made a compulsion of it. And if you do not stop this, neither the emperor nor anyone else need drive me from you, I will go without urging; and I dare say that none of my enemies, though they have caused me much sorrow, have wounded me as you have.

If you want to show that you are good Christians by handling the sacrament and boast of it before the world, then Herod and Pilate are the chief and best Christians, since it seems to me that they really handled the body of Christ when they had him nailed to the cross and put to death. No, my dear friends, the kingdom of God does not consist in outward things, which can be touched or perceived, but in faith [Luke 17:20; Rom. 14:17; I Cor. 4:20].

But you may say: We live and we ought to live according to the Scriptures, and God has so instituted the sacrament that we must take it with our hands, for he said, "Take, eat, this is my body" [Matt. 26:26]. The answer is this: though I am convinced beyond a doubt that the disciples of the Lord took it with their hands, and though I admit that you may do the same without committing sin, nevertheless I can neither make it compulsory nor defend it. And my reason is that the devil, when he really pushes us to the wall, will argue: Where have you read in the Scriptures that "take" means "grasping with the hands"? How, then, am I going to prove or defend it? Indeed, how will I answer him when he cites from the Scriptures the very opposite, and proves that "take" does not mean to receive with the hands only, but also to convey to ourselves in other ways? "Listen to this, my good fellow," he will say, "is not the word 'take' used by three evangelists when they described the Lord's taking of gall and vinegar? [Matt. 27:34; Mark 15:23; Luke 23:36].

You must admit that the Lord did not touch or handle it with his hands, for his hands were nailed to the cross." This verse is a strong argument against me. Again, he cites the passage: *Et accepit omnes timor,* "Fear seized them all" [Luke 7:16], where again we must admit that fear has no hands. Thus I am driven into a corner and must concede, even against my will, that "take" means not only to receive with the hands, but to convey to myself in any other way in which it can be done. Therefore, dear friends, we must be on firm ground, if we are to withstand the devil's attack [Eph. 6:11]. Although I must acknowledge that you committed no sin when you touched the sacrament with your hands, nevertheless I must tell you that it was not a good work, because it caused offense everywhere. For the universal custom is to receive the blessed sacrament from the hands of the priest. Why will you not in this respect also serve those who are weak in faith and abstain from your liberty, particularly since it does not help you if you do it, nor harm you if you do not do it.

Therefore no new practices should be introduced, unless the gospel has first been thoroughly preached and understood, as it has been among you. On this account, dear friends, let us deal soberly and wisely in the things that pertain to God, for God will not be mocked [Gal. 6:7]. The saints may endure mockery, but with God it is vastly different. Therefore, I beseech you, give up this practice.

Concerning Both Kinds in the Sacrament

Now let us speak of the two kinds. Although I hold that it is necessary that the sacrament should be received in both kinds, according to the institution of the Lord, nevertheless it must not be made compulsory nor a general law. We must rather promote and practice and preach the Word, and then afterwards leave the result and execution of it entirely to the Word, giving everyone his freedom in this matter. Where this is not done, the sacrament becomes for me an outward work and a hypocrisy, which is just what the devil wants. But when the Word is given free course and is not bound to any external observance, it takes hold of one today and sinks into his heart, tomorrow it touches another, and so on. Thus quietly and soberly it does its work, and no one will know how it all came about.

I was glad to know when some one wrote me, that some people here had begun to receive the sacrament in both kinds. You should have allowed it to remain thus and not forced it into a law. But now you go at it pell mell, and headlong force every one to it. Dear friends, you will not succeed in that way. For if you desire to be regarded as better Christians than others just because you take the sacrament into your hands and also receive it in both kinds, you are bad Christians as far as I am concerned. In this way even a sow could be a Christian, for she has a big enough snout to receive the sacrament outwardly. We must deal soberly with such high things. Dear friends, this dare be no mockery, and if you are going to follow me, stop it. If you are not going to follow me, however, then no one need drive me away from you—I will leave you unasked, and I shall regret that I ever preached so much as one sermon in this place. The other things could be passed by, but this cannot be overlooked; for you have gone so far that people are saying: At Wittenberg there are very good Christians, for they take the sacrament in their hands and grasp the cup, and then they go to their brandy and swill themselves full. So the weak and well-meaning people, who would come to us if they had received as much instruction as we have, are driven away.

But if there is any one who is so smart that he must touch the sacrament with his hands, let him have it brought home to his house and there let him handle it to his heart's content. But in public let him abstain, since that will bring him no harm and the offense will be avoided which is caused to our brothers, sisters, and neighbors, who are now so angry with us that they are ready to kill us. I may say that of all my enemies who have opposed me up to this time none have brought me so much grief as you.

This is enough for today; tomorrow we shall say more.

The Sixth Sermon, March 14, 1522, Friday

after Invocavit[24]

In our discussion of the chief thing we have come to the reception of the sacrament, which we have not yet finished. Today we shall see how me must conduct ourselves here, and also who is worthy to receive the sacrament and who belongs there.

It is very necessary here that your hearts and consciences be well instructed and that you make a big distinction between outward reception and inner and spiritual reception. Bodily and outward reception is that in which a man receives with his mouth the body of Christ and his blood, and doubtless any man can receive the sacrament in this way, without faith and love. But this does not make a man a Christian, for if it did, even a mouse would be a Christian, for it, too, can eat the bread and perchance even drink out of the cup. It is such a simple thing to do. But the true, inner, spiritual reception is a very different thing, for it consists in the right use of the sacrament and its fruits.

I would say in the first place that this reception occurs in faith and is inward and will have Christ. There is no external sign by which we Christians may be distinguished from others except this sacrament and baptism, but without faith outward reception is nothing. There must be faith to make the reception worthy and acceptable before God, otherwise it is nothing but sham and a mere external show, which is not Christianity at all. Christianity consists solely in faith, and no outward work must be attached to it.

But faith (which we all must have, if we wish to go to the sacrament worthily) is a firm trust that Christ, the Son of God, stands in our place and has taken all our sins upon his shoulders and that he is the eternal satisfaction for our sin and reconciles us with God the Father. He who has this faith is the very one who takes his rightful place at this sacrament, and neither devil nor hell nor sin can harm him. Why? Because God is his protector and

[24] The title reads: "Sermon of M. Luther preached on Friday after Invocavit."

defender. And when I have this faith, then I am certain God is fighting for me; I can defy the devil, death, hell, and sin, and all the harm with which they threaten me. This is the great, inestimable treasure given us in Christ, which no man can describe or grasp in words. Only faith can take hold of the heart, and not every one has such faith [II Thess. 3:2]. Therefore this sacrament must not be made a law, as the most holy father, the pope, has done with his fool's commandment: All Christians must go to the sacrament at the holy Eastertide, and he who does not go shall not be buried in consecrated ground.[25] Is not this a foolish law which the pope has set up? Why? Because we are not all alike; we do not all have equal faith; the faith of one is stronger than that of another. It is therefore impossible that the sacrament can be made a law, and the greatest sins are committed at Easter solely on account of this un-Christian command, whose purpose is to drive and force the people to the sacrament. And if robbery, usury, unchastity, and all sins were cast upon one big heap, this sin would overtop all others, at the very time when they [who come to the sacrament] want to be most holy. Why? Because the pope can look into no one's heart to see whether he has faith or not.

But if you believe that God steps in for you and stakes all he has and his blood for you, as if he were saying: Fall in behind me without fear or delay, and then let us see what can harm you; come devil, death, sin, and hell, and all creation, I shall go before you, for I will be your rear guard and your vanguard [Isa. 52:12]; trust me and boldly rely upon me. He who believes that can not be harmed by devil, hell, sin, or death; if God fights for him, what can you do to him?

He who has such faith has his rightful place here and receives the sacrament as an assurance, or seal, or sign to assure him of God's promise and grace. But, of course, we do not all have such faith; would God one-tenth of the Christians had it! See, such rich, immeasurable treasures [Eph. 2:7], which God in his grace showers upon us, cannot be the possession of everyone, but only of those who suffer tribulation, physical or spiritual, physically through the persecution of men, spiritually through despair of conscience, outwardly

---

[25] This law goes back to the Fourth Ecumenical Lateran Synod, 1215, under Innocent III. In the canon law: C. 12, X, de poenitentiis.

or inwardly, when the devil causes your heart to be weak, timid, and discouraged, so that you do not know how you stand with God, and when he casts your sins into your face. And in such terrified and trembling hearts alone God desires to dwell, as the prophet Isaiah says in the sixth chapter [Isa. 66:2]. For who desires a protector, defender, and shield to stand before him if he feels no conflict within himself, so that he is distressed because of his sins and daily tormented by them? That man is not yet ready for this food. This food demands a hungering and longing man,[26] for it delights to enter a hungry soul, which is constantly battling with its sins and eager to be rid of them.

He who is not thus prepared should abstain for a while from this sacrament, for this food will not enter a sated and full heart, and if it comes to such a heart, it is harmful.[27] Therefore, if we think upon and feel within us such distress of conscience and the fear of a timid heart, we shall come with all humbleness and reverence and not run to it brashly and hastily, without all fear and humility. So we do not always find that we are fit; today I have the grace and am fit for it, but not tomorrow. Indeed, it may be that for six months I may have no desire or fitness for it.

Therefore those who are most worthy, who are constantly being assailed by death and the devil, and they are the ones to whom it is most opportunely given, in order that they may remember and firmly believe that nothing can harm them, since they now have with them him from whom none can pluck them away; let come death, devil, or sin, they cannot harm them.

This is what Christ did when he was about to institute the blessed sacrament. First he terrified his disciples and shook their hearts by saying that he was going to leave them [Matt. 26:2], which was exceedingly painful to them; and then he went on to say, "One of you will betray me" [Matt. 26:21]. Do you think that that did not cut them to the heart? Of course they accepted that saying with all

---

[26] A quotation from Augustine, cf. *Enarratio in psalmos* XXI. Migne, 36, 178. Also quoted by Luther in *Treatise Concerning the Blessed Sacrament, etc.* WA 2, 746; PE 2, 15.

[27] This is a first indication of a doctrine which Luther later developed more emphatically, the doctrine of *manducatio impiorum*, i.e., to receive the sacrament unworthily, without faith, is to receive it to one's damnation. Cf. I Cor. 11:27-29.

fear and they sat there as though they had all been traitors to God. And after he had made them all tremble with fear and sorrow, only then did he institute the blessed sacrament as a comfort and consoled them again. For this bread is a comfort for the sorrowing, a healing for the sick, a life for the dying, a food for all the hungry, and a rich treasure for all the poor and needy.

Let this be enough for this time concerning the use of this sacrament. I commend you to God.

The Seventh Sermon, March 15, 1522, Saturday before Reminiscere[28]

Yesterday we heard about the use of this holy and blessed sacrament and saw who are worthy to receive it, namely, those in whom there is the fear of death, who have timid and despairing consciences and live in fear of hell. All such come prepared to partake of this food for the strengthening of their weak faith and the comforting of their conscience. This is the true use and practice of this sacrament, and whoever does not find himself in this state, let him refrain from coming until God also takes hold of him and draws him through his Word.

We shall now speak of the fruit of this sacrament, which is love; that is, that we should treat our neighbor as God has treated us. Now we have received from God nothing but love and favor, for Christ has pledged and given us his righteousness and everything he has; he has poured out upon us all his treasures, which no man can measure and no angel can understand or fathom, for God is a glowing furnace of love, reaching even from the earth to the heavens.

Love, I say, is a fruit of this sacrament. But this I do not yet

---

[28] The title reads: "A Sermon on the Eve of the Sunday or Saturday before Reminiscere. D. M. L."

perceive among you here in Wittenberg, even though you have had much preaching and, after all, you ought to have carried this out in practice. This is the chief thing, which is the only business of a Christian man. But nobody wants to be in this, though you want to practice all sorts of unnecessary things, which are of no account. If you do not want to show yourselves Christians by your love, then leave the other things undone, too, for St. Paul says in I Cor. 11 [I Cor. 13:1], "If I speak in the tongues of men and of angels, but have not love, I am a noisy gong or a clanging cymbal." This is a terrible saying of Paul. "And if I have prophetic powers, and understand all mysteries and all knowledge, and if I have all faith, so as to remove mountains, but have not love, I am nothing. If I give away all I have, and if I deliver my body to be burned, but have not love, I gain nothing" [I Cor. 13:2-3]. Not yet have you come so far as this, though you have received great and rich gifts from God, the highest of which is a knowledge of the Scriptures. It is true, you have the true gospel and the pure Word of God, but no one as yet has given his goods to the poor, no one has yet been burned, and even these things would be nothing without love. You are willing to take all of God's goods in the sacrament, but you are not willing to pour them out again in love. Nobody extends a helping hand to another, nobody seriously considers the other person, but everyone looks out for himself and his own gain, insists on his own way, and lets everything else go hang. If anybody is helped, well and good; but nobody looks after the poor to see how you might be able to help them. This is a pity. You have heard many sermons about it and all my books are full of it and have this one purpose, to urge you to faith and love.

And if you will not love one another, God will send a great plague upon you; let this be a warning to you, for God will not have his Word revealed and preached in vain. You are tempting God too far, my friends; for if in times past someone had preached the Word to our forefathers, they would perhaps have acted differently. Or if it were preached even now to many poor children in the cloisters, they would receive it more joyfully than you. You are not heeding it at all and you are playing around with all kinds of tomfoolery which does not amount to anything.

I commend you to God.

The Eighth Sermon, March 16, 1522,

Reminiscere Sunday

A Short Summary of the Sermon of D[r.] M[artin] L[uther]
Preached on Reminiscere Sunday on Private Confession

Now we have heard all the things which ought to be considered here, except confession. Of this we shall speak now.

In the first place, there is a confession which is founded on the Scriptures, and it is this: when anybody committed a sin publicly or with other men's knowledge, he was accused before the congregation. If he abandoned his sin, they interceded for him with God. But if he would not listen to the congregation [*häuffen*], he was cast out and excluded from the assembly, so that no one would have anything to do with him. And this confession is commanded by God in Matt. 18 [:15], "If your brother sins against you (so that you and others are offended), go and tell him his fault, between you and him alone." We no longer have any trace of this kind of confession any more; at this point the gospel is in abeyance. Anybody who was able to re-establish it would be doing a good work. Here is where you should have exerted yourselves and re-established this kind of confession, and let the other things go; for no one would have been offended by this and everything would have gone smoothly and quietly. It should be done in this way: When you see a usurer, adulterer, thief, or drunkard, you should go to him in secret, and admonish him to give up his sin. If he will not listen, you should take two others with you and admonish him once more, in a brotherly way, to give up his sin. But if he scorns that, you should tell the pastor before the whole congregation, have your witnesses with you, and accuse him before the pastor in the presence of the people, saying: Dear pastor, this man has done this and that and would not take our brotherly admonition to give up his sin. Therefore I accuse him, together with my witnesses, who have heard this. Then, if he will not give up and willingly acknowledge his guilt, the pastor should exclude him and put him under the ban before the whole assembly, for the sake of the congregation, until he comes to himself and is received back again. This would be Christian. But I cannot undertake to carry it out single-handed.

Secondly, we need a kind of confession when we go into a corner by ourselves and confess to God himself and pour out before him all our faults. This kind of confession is also commanded. From this comes the familiar word of Scripture: *Facite judicium et justitiam.*[29] *Judicium facere est nos ipsos accusare et damnare; justitiam autem facere est fidere misericordiae Dei.*[30] As it is written, "Blessed are they who observe justice, who do righteousness at all times" [Ps. 106:3]. Judgment is nothing else than a man's knowing and judging and condemning himself, and this is true humility and self-abasement. Righteousness is nothing else than a man's knowing himself and praying to God for the mercy and help through which God raises him up again. This is what David means when he says, "I have sinned; I will confess my transgressions to the Lord and thou didst forgive the guilt of my sin; for this all thy saints shall pray to thee" [Ps. 32:5-6].

Thirdly, there is also the kind of confession in which one takes another aside and tells him what troubles one, so that one may hear from him a word of comfort; and this confession is commanded by the pope. It is this urging and forcing which I condemned when I wrote concerning confession,[31] and I refuse to go to confession simply because the pope has commanded it and insists upon it. For I wish him to keep his hands off the confession and not make of it a compulsion or command, which he has not the power to do. Nevertheless I will allow no man to take private confession away from me, and I would not give it up for all the treasures in the world, since I know what comfort and strength it has given me. No one knows what it can do for him except one who has struggled often and long with the devil. Yea, the devil would have slain me long ago, if the confession had not sustained me. For there are many doubtful matters which a man cannot resolve or find the answer to by himself, and so he takes his brother aside and tells him his trouble.

---

[29] Do judgment and righteousness. Cf. Gen. 18:19.
[30] To do judgment is to accuse and condemn ourselves; but to do righteousness is to trust in the mercy of God.
[31] *Von der Beichte, ob die der Papst Macht habe zu gebieten* (1521). WA 8, 138-204.

What harm is there if he humbles himself a little before his neighbor, puts himself to shame, looks for a word of comfort from him, accepts it, and believes it, as if he were hearing it from God himself, as we read in Matt. 18 [:19], "If two of you agree about anything they ask, it will be done for them."

Moreover, we must have many absolutions, so that we may strengthen our timid consciences and despairing hearts against the devil and against God. Therefore, no man shall forbid the confession nor keep or draw any one away from it. And if any one is wrestling with his sins and wants to be rid of them and desires a sure word on the matter, let him go and confess to another in secret, and accept what he says to him as if God himself had spoken it through the mouth of this person. However, one who has a strong, firm faith that his sins are forgiven may let this confession go and confess to God alone. But how many have such a strong faith? Therefore, as I have said, I will not let this private confession be taken from me. But I will not have anybody forced to it, but left to each one's free will.

For our God, the God we have, is not so niggardly that he has left us with only one comfort or strengthening for our conscience, or only one absolution, but we have many absolutions in the gospel and we are richly showered with many absolutions. For instance, we have this in the gospel: "If you forgive men their trespasses, your heavenly Father will also forgive you" [Matt. 6:14]. Another comfort we have in the Lord's Prayer: "Forgive us our trespasses," etc. [Matt. 6:12]. A third is our baptism, when I reason thus: See, my Lord, I have been baptized in thy name so that I may be assured of thy grace and mercy. Then we have private confession, when I go and receive a sure absolution as if God himself spoke it, so that I may be assured that my sins are forgiven. Finally, I take to myself the blessed sacrament, when I eat his body and drink his blood as a sign that I am rid of my sins and God has freed me from all my frailties; and in order to make me sure of this, he gives me his body to eat and his blood to drink, so that I shall not and cannot doubt that I have a gracious God.

Thus you see that confession must not be despised, but that it is a comforting thing. And since we need many absolutions and assurances, because we must fight against the devil, death, hell, and sin, we must not allow any of our weapons to be taken away, but keep intact the whole armor and equipment which God has given us to use against our enemies. For you do not yet know what labor it costs to fight with the devil and overcome him. But I know it well, for I have eaten a bit of salt or two with him. I know him well, and he knows me well, too. If you had known him, you would not have rejected confession in this way.

I commend you to God. Amen.

TWO SERMONS PREACHED AT WEIMAR

1522

TWO SERMONS PREACHED AT WEIMAR, 1522

In October, 1522, Luther journeyed to Weimar and Erfurt, having been invited to preach in Weimar by Duke John of Saxony and his son John Frederick, through the court preacher, Wolfgang Stein. There he preached six sermons, two on October 19, one on the 24th, another on the 25th, and two on the 26th. (On October 21 and 22 he visited Erfurt, where he preached three times.) He was accompanied on the journey by Melanchthon, John Agricola, and Jacob Propst and the transcriber may have been one of these. The first two of these six sermons, published together in Weimar, are here translated. Julius Köstlin said of them: "These six sermons, which we possess in a careful transcript, provide one of the best examples of his ability to set forth in brief compass the sum of the Christian faith simply, clearly, vividly, and practically for those of both high and low estate" (Martin Luther, Sein Leben und seine Schriften *(1903), I, 521).*

Text in German; WA 10^III, 341-352.

The First Sermon, Matt. 22:37-39, the Morning
of October 19, 1522

The First Sermon Preached by Doctor Martin Luther at the Castle
in Weimar on the Nineteenth Sunday after Pentecost,[1]
October 19, 1522

The Gospel is written in Matthew 22 [:37-39],[2] "You shall love
. . . God with all your heart, and with all your soul, and with all
your mind . . . and your neighbor as yourself, etc."

And the Gospel consists in two questions. First, what is the
greatest commandment, by which one is saved, and second, what
the law requires; and these two must agree with each other. And
he who wants to be a Christian must know this, and this the unbeliever cannot understand and know, because he is blind and
hardened. This is also the reason, believe me and understand this,
why he is blind and has no understanding of the divine Word; and
these are the ones who want to be considered wise, and yet they are
obstinate fools.

Now we shall show what Christ here requires of us, and what
the commandment is, and which is the greatest.

It is the law and commandment of Christ that one must love
him with the whole soul, the whole mind, and all powers, and the
neighbor as one's self; and he who has this has everything and God
dwells in him; this is certain. But you may say: Oh, it is utterly
impossible for a person to keep these two commandments. Yes, it
is impossible for you to keep or perform them. You cannot do it;
God must do it in you, for him it is possible. Now we shall see what
the law requires.

The law requires that we love God with all our powers, etc..
and our neighbor as ourselves. Now, if it is true that the law requires that we love God and our neighbor with all our soul and all

---

[1] I.e., Eighteenth Sunday after Trinity, forenoon.
[2] The liturgical Gospel for this Sunday is Matt. 22:34-46.

our powers, then it is certainly true that a person is not rightly fasting, praying, crying to God, and doing other things, if he does not first love God and his neighbor. If the works are not done out of love, then they are absolutely nothing; then there is nothing good in this love, and the outward works are performed and put on in order that the person may prove that he loves God or his neighbor and that in all these things he is devoting himself to them.

Thus circumcision among the Jews was a commandment commanded by God. It was a foolish commandment and to Christ it was not at all an acceptable commandment and it was nothing in the sight of God; they were obliged to do it only in order to show that they loved God. But then it is a shameful, disgraceful, and ridiculous commandment in the sight of God and of men, and among us it would be a disgrace and a shame to keep it and especially here. Therefore all works must be performed out of love, and where there is a heart that loves God, there all works are good. What good would circumcision do me as far as salvation is concerned? But if God were to command it, even the most shameful thing, then I should do it gladly on account of love for him.

This we can see in the case of Abraham, who sacrificed his son because this is what God wanted [Gen. 22:1-19]. According to nature and also in other respects, it was a foolish, stupid command; but Abraham was willing to follow God, and because of the love he bore for God, it was pleasing to God. If he had been able to kill his son a hundred times for the love of God, he would have done it. But God does not care about his killing, about his wanting to sacrifice his only son to him; he was looking at his love and obedience. Thus, when the children of Israel came into the promised land, they gave praise to Abraham, and they too sacrificed their children in great heaps [Ps. 106:37-38]. If someone had said to them: God doesn't care about that, they would not have believed it. God had no use for it whatsoever because they did not do it out of love; and afterwards the prophets preached mightily against it, even giving up their lives over it, for God would not have it. No, he wanted the love which Abraham had, for Christ says: Your circumcising and killing is nothing to me; it is not pleasing to me, for you serve me by loving me and not otherwise. Therefore, for love of him, we should do even the most contemptible works commanded us by God, and on this law depend all the commandments. And those commandments which do not come through and out of love are to be broken and they should be left undone, for when God does not find love in a person, he has no desire for his works either.

Thus we find in the old law that when God led the children of Israel out of Egypt through Moses, he did not command circumcision at that time at all; nor had they had it before, and yet it was not displeasing to God, for he was indifferent to it. But when they came into the wilderness he did command them to do this [Gen. 17:10], for in the beginning they loved him exceedingly and therefore he gave them circumcision and other commandments in order that they might show that they loved him, and having love, all works were pleasing to him and in good use. Therefore, as we said before, all works must issue from love; otherwise they are nothing.

Thus we read that as the disciples of Christ were going through the grainfields they plucked ears of grain and ate them [Matt. 12: 1-8]. The Jews were angry over this, but Christ said: Your sabbath is no commandment to me; I don't care about that. The point is that his disciples were hungry and, having loved Christ and followed him, they preferred to break the sabbath rather than leave him. The Jews did not see the love. So one should break all the other commandments for the sake of love to God and one's neighbor. David also did this. When he came to the priest, being hungry, he demanded bread, and the priest said: We have only holy bread which the priests eat [I Sam. 21:1-6]; David took it and ate it and paid no regard to the commandment of the Jews. Therefore, in that same Gospel Christ says to the Pharisees: Have you not read what David did? The devout David was hungry, destitute, and poor [Matt. 12:3], and they had to give it to him and honor him.

Thus, all the commandments of the law depend on love [Matt. 22:40]. That is to say, if they are not done out of love, they are contrary to God and are nothing; that's what you should go by. It is not to be done for the sake of other works, for your eye should be kept only on the work of love, and you should break all the laws rather than see your brother suffer want or affliction. For Christ imputes everything to love and our whole life should consist in this. And if you could save a soul with a mass and you see your brother suffering want, you should help him and let the other go; there is no other way out.

But isn't it a pitiful thing? A priest has a commandment, not from God, but from the pope, such as praying the seven hours,[3] fasting the long fasts, doing this and doing that. He attaches more importance to fulfilling obedience to the pope than he does to doing this for the love of Christ; he would rather let his neighbor suffer hunger and want. Here is a lay person who is commanded as a penance to go to Rome, make a pilgrimage to this or that saint; he is to go barefoot and do a lot of other things. Now when he sees his neighbor suffering want, with wife and child, and the poor man asks him for help, he should look to the love of Christ, help him, and let the pilgrimage go. For love of one's neighbor is like the first commandment. Therefore a priest should let his "hours" go and help his neighbor; he should interrupt the outward work, which is of no consequence to God, and say quite freely: This I should let lie and help my neighbor; this is what God commanded me, the other is the pope's, and now I shall follow God's commandment and let the other go. This would be a real Christian and priest.

But nowadays when a pilgrimage is imposed upon a person and his brother and neighbor asks him to help him, he goes to confession and receives the penance that he should help his neighbor and that he is unable to perform the pope's commandment. Thus he has more regard for the pope's commandment than for Christ's.

This is what the preachers accomplish! Oh, we have had blind preachers for a long time; they have been totally blind themselves and leaders of the blind, as the gospel says; they have left the gospel and followed their own ideas and preferred the work of men to the work of God [cf. Mark 7:8-9]. Oh, how well we have done, how interested God is in this! So say the seducers and shameful scoundrels. Therefore we have left Christ and followed our own opinions. God has commanded us to love him and our neighbor, but we have esteemed outward work more than love. It is just as if a master said to his servant: Go and plow for me; and he went and washed the pails, and then sulks against his master as if he needed a box on the ears.

Thus all our works should be done in love. So, even if I am a Carthusian or a monk and find that I am not helping my neighbor

---

[3] Latin, *septem horas.*

therein, I should break free from the order and help my neighbor. God doesn't want any works without love. Let this be your guide. Therefore the monk's life is all wicked, for it does not help the neighbor and it is just because of this commandment of the pope that many of you know so little of what Christ and his Word is. And the same people know neither the smallest nor the greatest commandment of Christ. Therefore, the more spiritual and hypocritical, the more blind they are. And yet the spirituals boast that they are the most devout of all; there is no faith in them and they have no understanding of Scripture at all, and yet we must pay them great honor. They should remember, however, that what people do to them, they should do also to them. Thus they have been so led astray by human laws that not one of them patiently follows Christ. If one is struck by another, he will not forgive him. This is simply impossible. Christ teaches us to do things that are impossible, but God effects them in us. Therefore, let each one of us look into his heart and remember the love which is able to do this.

Now, what is meant by "with all your heart"? Nothing else but that I do willingly and gladly everything that my God commands me. This I do not accomplish, however long I pray the rosary and other prayers in a secret place. Now one who loves with his whole heart always says: O God, as thou wilt, so I will; should I die, live, be poor, should I be sick, saved, or condemned, I shall do so gladly with all my will; it is thy will; lead me, therefore, through all shame. That person loves with his whole heart.

Then, loving with one's "whole soul." This is to love with one's whole, inmost heart, spirit, and one's whole life. Where do you find that kind of a person? Man, whether he hears, sees, wakes, sleeps, walks, or stands still, wants always to live his life without being bothered at all. That person who loves best is the person who loves with his whole soul.

And then, to go on, loving "with all your mind." This is to surrender oneself to God with one's whole mind, so that even his commands become good and right. But in these days our minds have been utterly corrupted by man-made laws, for the evil spirit usually concentrates on seizing the human mind and spirit, and this is the blindness in which our spirituals are living and they have been leading us in it for a long time.

This, then, is the love which Christ would have. And here we find that we are all under condemnation; no one does or has this love. When this law is kept, one needs no other law. To the Jews a ridiculous, trifling commandment was given, that of wearing tassels and borders on their garments [Num. 15:38-39]. God cares nothing about this; for as we have said, unless one wears them for love of him, it does not help them at all. Hence, a person, confronted with this love, must feel his inability and powerlessness to perform the least letter of the law and know that he can do nothing good. Now this knowledge does not come through works; nor do these contribute to our salvation, as Paul shows that salvation does not come through works or issue from works [Rom. 3:20]. You cannot have this knowledge through your own nature, for your nature is so blind that it does not know what Christ and his law is, nor does it know how deeply it lies in sin. Therefore Luke, who also records this Gospel, says that the Jews said to Christ that the commandment of love was right [Luke 20:39; cf. Luke 10:28, Mark 12:32]. But they would not accept it; they were too blind.

Therefore we conclude, by the authority of this Gospel, that monks, nuns, and priests have all been led and turned to blind, outward works, and there they are stuck, though we can accomplish nothing through them. For anyone who does not do his work out of love is blind. So it was also with the Jews and the Pharisees; though they were fine persons and honest men, they nevertheless were blind. So we accomplish nothing whatsoever by outward works. To be a monk, nun, a Carthusian, to go to Rome or to St. James,[4] all this is nothing. He who does not acknowledge his sinfulness, like the Pharisees and Jews, is condemned. Christ came down from heaven to make himself known to us. He stepped down into our mire and became a man. But we do not know him, nor do we accept him, who came to help us out of every need and fear. But he who accepts Christ, acknowledges and loves him, he fulfils all things and all his works are good; he does good to his neighbor; he suffers all things for God's sake.

Therefore, this is what the law requires and says: You owe nothing except to love Christ and your neighbor; otherwise you are eternally condemned. But then afterwards Christ comes and says:

---

[4] St. James of Compostella, a place of pilgrimage in Spain.

I suffered, died, and rose again in order that I might fill you with the riches and grace of my Holy Spirit and thus strengthen you. So if you have the Spirit, then you are not an outward spirit; no, you have salvation. Then a person thinks this way: Now, Lord Jesus, I will serve you, die and live for you, and patiently suffer all that is disagreeable from you and from men; do with me as you will. That person will be washed of his sins by the blood of Christ.

Hence, if I have the Holy Spirit, I have faith, by which I cling to God. And if I believe in God, then I also have his love and I love God, foe, and friend. That is why Paul says: I can do all things through the Spirit of God [Phil. 4:13]. The Spirit does not come through fasting, praying, pilgrimages, running to and fro around the country; no, only through faith. So Christ bestows his gifts upon you without any merit whatsoever and what he did for him [i.e., Paul], he does for you also. Here, of course, you must guard against thinking that you are capable of faith; God must give it to you.

Therefore, this is what we say about the law; this is what it is and nothing else: The law kills; your God saves you. And he who does not believe is condemned. In short: Help us, O God, to this faith. Amen. Therefore, guard yourselves against the fool preachers who say: Yes, good works will do it. No, first faith must be present in a man. So he who does not follow Christ and also does not love him is condemned.

As for us, we shall call upon God. Amen.

The Second Sermon on the Same Text, the Afternoon

of October 19, 1522

The Second Sermon Preached by Martin [sic] at Weimar in the Parish [Church] on the Afternoon of the Above-named Sunday

This morning you heard the Gospel. Nevertheless we shall deal with its main point.

Now you know that we have all been baptized and are called Christians. Accordingly, we should endeavor to know what it means to be a Christian man and have the name of Christian, and also what one must do to be one. Similarly, when a shoemaker, a tailor, or some other craftsman wants to pursue his trade, he must know his trade, in order that he may fairly be called a tailor. If he could not establish his name it would be a disgrace. Likewise, if a person called himself a Carthusian, a Bernardine [i.e., a Cistercian], or a Benedictine and did not know the rule of the order, he would be a laughingstock. Accordingly, we, too, must establish our name and demonstrate that we are rightly called Christians.

Therefore a person must first guard against human teachings and human commandments, in order that they may not take root in him. He should first open his mouth wide [Ps. 81:10] to rejoice in the teaching of Christ and also cultivate it in his heart; which teaching is the Gospel, which Paul [Rom. 1:16], Peter [I Pet. 1:12], and especially Christ in all the Gospels call the Word of God, because God through Him gave it and sent it from heaven. Neither I nor anyone else can ever preach the Word adequately; the Holy Spirit alone must utter and preach it. It is not being preached these days, not by a long shot, God have mercy on us. And where it is not being preached, there you have tomfoolery, corruption, and the devil himself. Therefore, the first thing to learn is the teaching of Christ and not that of men. For these latter teachings should be thrown out, which is highly necessary at the present time, for through them

111

many a man is being led astray. Now we shall preach only the gospel, which came from God and was proclaimed and revealed from heaven.

Moreover, the gospel proclaims nothing else but salvation by grace, given to man without any works and merits whatsoever. Natural man cannot abide, hear, or see the gospel. Nor does it enter into the hypocrites, for it casts out their works, declaring that they are nothing and not pleasing to God. Therefore nature is constantly fighting against the gospel; it will not tolerate it. They keep saying: Ah, should we not do good works? After all, were there not devout people in former times who did good works? My father and mother believed this, and where they have gone I want to go too. These people preach against God and do wrong.

Saying such things, the teaching of Christ pleases them not at all, and finally it makes them furious. Now this is surely a sign that one is preaching the gospel and that it is beginning to be heard. Where the preaching or the preacher is not persecuted or spoken against it is not the gospel at all and the preacher is not preaching it. The gospel is always persecuted, and the hypocrites murmur against it, but their works are nothing. Direct yourself by that!

Thus you must prove your name as a Christian by faith and nothing else, that is, so as to believe that Christ's righteousness is yours, that his life, death, and everything that Christ is, is yours, given to you, as Paul says in Gal. 1 [2:20], "It is no longer I who live, but Christ who lives in me." It is as if Paul were saying: Christ gives me life, he lives in me; what I do I am not doing; what I say and preach is not my word; Christ is in me. Therefore, he who does not conduct and exercise himself in the Spirit and in the work of Christ is condemned. Thus Paul says in Rom. 8 [:9], "Any one who does not have the Spirit of Christ does not belong to him." Even though a person did everything, if the Spirit of God is not at work and in the person, it is all nothing. Therefore, let a man cast away all his works, for without faith they are all condemned.

This the world and human nature cannot tolerate, for they are constantly grumbling about our taking their good works away from them and saying: If our works are nothing, how can we get there? It is no good. In fact, you do not know what you are talking about. Do you think that you can perform the work? It is not your works.

If that were the case, you would have to despair of your works altogether; but it pains you. And yet we must not keep silent about the gospel on account of them. God will send a Spirit of truth (John 16 [:7-9]); he punishes us for our unbelief. Therefore we shall preach Christ and his faith even though it be a pain to everybody, as Paul says: We preach the crucified Christ, a stumbling block to the Jews, to the Gentiles folly or stupidity, and to believers salvation and consolation [I Cor. 1:23-24].

Therefore works are nothing. For our monks who think they will be saved by their works, Christ is foolishness. So it must needs be that in the world the gospel should be called folly. If we can so preach that the gospel is rejected, then things will be going as they should. So if you see that today some are saying that the gospel is right; others blaspheming and saying that it is wrong; some calling it a malediction, and so on, then you see that things are going well. So whomever the gospel hits, it hits, and whomever it saves, it saves; and we must act according to it and nothing else. It follows from this that a Christian name is an utterly unfathomable thing; and he is a Christian who believes in God and acknowledges and loves him above all things. The Christian knows all things, even what the devil has in mind.

So, does the Augustinian order make me a Christian, or is any other monk made a Christian by his order? No, we are all Christians through faith and baptism. Now Christ is called the Anointed, and through his name I, too, can be called an anointed one. It follows that that person is a Christian who has received Christ and believes in God with his whole heart. Take, for example, a faster, who fasts every day on water and bread. He should rather be called a faster than a Christian; his fasting does not make him a Christian, not at all. One who constantly prays much should rather be called a pray-er than a Christian. Likewise with a pilgrim, a flagellant,[5] a virgin, a founder of churches and altars—this does not make them Christians. What makes him a Christian is that he has God and everything that is God's, that is, that he has the unsurpassable

---

[5] *Trescher;* cf. Jacob and Wilhelm Grimm's *Deutsches Wörterbuch* (16 vols.; Leipzig, 1854-1954), II, 1403, where a derivative meaning of *dreschen* or *treschen* is that of inflicting pain.

treasure, Christ, who is called rich in grace. As we call a rich man rich because he has many guldens and goods, so Christ is called the richest of the rich.

How, then, do we have Christ? After all, he is sitting at the right hand of the Father; he will not come down to us in our house. No, this he will not do. But how do I gain and have him? Ah, you cannot have him except in the gospel in which he is promised to you, that gospel which is folly to the Pharisees and salvation and consolation to believers, as Paul declared [I Cor. 1:18]. And since Christ comes into our heart through the gospel, he must also be accepted by the heart. As I now believe that he is in the gospel, so I receive him and have him already. So Paul says: I carry Christ in my heart, for he is mine, etc. [cf. Eph. 3:17]. Thus Christ is given to us through the gospel in the same way as a person is given a letter in which he is promised a city or a kingdom, and now the letter is sealed as a sign that this promise should and will be kept. So we, too, become rich in all his goods and riches through faith in Christ.

There are some who say that faith is such a trifling thing always to be preaching about it. Yes, it is such a trifling thing that it can never be sufficiently spread abroad and understood! Would God that it had been well preached! But now we are going to make a beginning and preach it. Christ, too, must be abbot for once, and not man-made laws. Christ gives to a man a letter, which is the gospel, and this God seals with his baptism and faith. He says to this man: Look, I tell you and assure you that Christ Jesus, my Son, is yours, and I have given you baptism and the sacrament as a true sign and seal, in order that you may believe me when I say that Christ is yours. His grace and mercy is given to you without any merit of yours; only believe me, you will find eternal life in him. If you believe this, even though you have not seen the city which he has deeded to you, then you have in addition the letter and the seal as a true sign. Then you will say: If I have Christ, the great treasure and Lord over death, sin, devil, and hell, I shall not despair, and I know that I, too, shall be lord over these things, and I, too, have eternal life. Then blind nature opens up and recognizes Christ, and it is also glad that it is lord over death.

What could bring a person greater joy than to be told that he need not die? That's why this assurance of Christ is unfathomable.

Man, after all, is too fainthearted, our hearts are too small and we hear a lot of preaching, but still there is no faith there. This is the reason why we get other ideas and beliefs. When we hear the gospel we walk away and say: Yes, I believe in God and his gospel. No, that is no sufficient Christian faith. Listen to God; this is what he said through David, "O Israel, open your mouth wide, and I will fill it" with good [Ps. 81:8, 10]. It is as if Christ were saying: Oh yes, it is true that your heart is small and faint, but open it up and believe in me, I will give you all things. And Christ did say this: You faint-hearted, you little flock, you need not fear, for it has pleased God to give you the kingdom of heaven [Luke 12:32]. Therefore, for us men it is an altogether great thing for Christ to have given us a kingdom, but for him it is a small thing.

So you can see that human nature is always hostile to the gospel, for it is ambitious and wants to become good through good works. Wearing a black or a white or a blue cap, a long cloak, or a big tonsure doesn't make a Christian name. No, my monastic order is nothing; before Christ it must fall to the ground. But rejection of their works is something that will not go into the hearts of the Jews and monks. In short, through faith all things are subject to man, as Paul shows [Rom. 8:2].

Therefore, faith, eternal life, grace, mercy, and all good is to be sought in the everliving God. And this he wants to give to man. Man should freely count upon this and make bold to assume that all the things of Christ are his through pure grace without his works. For if we had to be saved through our works, then Christ would be nothing at all. So you see that works contribute nothing to salvation or to establishing the name of Christian. No Carthusian, no Franciscan, no preaching monk [Dominican] gives me salvation, as we have so long wanted it to be. No, they cannot do it; for they are subject to death, as Paul says: Death became my master [Rom. 7:10]. Therefore, I say very bluntly that all monks and nuns are the devil's (there is no other conclusion you can draw), because they all set their salvation on cowls, tonsures, or good works and expect to be saved through them, which is something that will never happen and will never save, for their works are nothing in the sight of God. Do you think the kingdom of heaven will be given to you because you sit home by the stove and say a couple of psalms? No;

nor will it be given to you if you go running around.[6]

Therefore, if we are going to have Christ, let us see to it that we receive him, that we may say: O thou heavenly Father, thou hast given thy Son to me in order that I might be saved and in him possess all good. Now I make bold to believe that he is mine and has been given to me. And for a seal upon it I also have thy true body, flesh and blood, thy sacrament and baptism; to this I firmly cling. Then all the desires of the flesh must be taken away in order that it may be kept under. That is why Christ bids men to take young women and the young women to take men. That is why the monks and nuns enter the monastery to preserve their chastity; they can hardly bear it there, however. They should take husbands.

When we have Christ by true faith, then he causes us to live in such a way that we are strengthened in faith, in such a way that I do these works which I do for the benefit and the good of my neighbor. For my Christian name would not be sufficient, despite my baptism and my faith, if I did not help my neighbor and draw him to faith through my works in order that he may follow me. Then a person, after he has given all glory to Christ, is always remembering to do to his neighbor as Christ has done to him, in order that he may help him and everyone else. Thus Christ lives in him and he lives for the betterment of his neighbor, giving to everyone a good example of doing all things in love. So princes and officials should also perform their office in love. If he rules well, he should not boast that he is gracious and good to his people. God will not forget to reward him. No, he should commit the matter of reward to God. So the monk should direct his whole life to his neighbor in love. He should not say: Oh, I have made the vow to my God in order to be saved. If he does this, he is denying Christ, for this is not helping his neighbor. And even if he brought with him to Christ a whole cloakful of rosaries, it would not save him. Even if he took with him all the fish he ate when he was fasting, and the bones too, they would not help him at all.

Without faith you will not be saved. That's why Peter says we should desire the gospel and faith as a child longs for milk [I Pet. 2:2]. The child drinks milk in order to become strong. It does not drink it in order to become a human being; it is a human being

---

[6] Luther has in mind the mendicant orders.

before it drinks. Thus, if I have faith, I am already saved, without any works or merit. It follows that it is faith alone that does it and not works. For God's work, the love which he teaches today in the gospel, goes on. And so, if somebody charges that we are forbidding good works, you say to them: We do not forbid them; we are only pointing out the abuse of them and showing that they should be done for the inspiration and good of our neighbor and that we should not put our trust in them.

So, when I help my neighbor, I prove my name as a Christian. God does not want our work. Guide yourself strictly by that. It follows from this that to us believers Christ is salvation and consolation, but to the monks he is foolishness, for the gospel does not bring anything into their kitchens, cellars, or closets, as their laws did before. That's why they are the ones who are persecuting us now. But patiently take the cross of Christ upon you in order to be able to suffer this patiently, if you want to be Christians. Take your faith and your Christian name to heart, for it is highly necessary for you and for me. In the whole gospel nothing is more clearly emphasized than faith and love, as I said this morning. This sinks very slowly into the heads of the lazy monks and sleepers; therefore you should pray to God for them constantly.

As for us, we shall call upon God. Amen.

SERMON ON ST. MATTHIAS' DAY

1525

SERMON ON ST. MATTHIAS' DAY
1525

Sermon on St. Matthias' Day, Matt. 11:25-30,[1]

February 5, 1525

This sermon, preached in the parish church in Wittenberg, is pre-
served in two texts, one by Georg Rörer, who dated it Dominica post
purificationis *and wrongly attributed it to Bugenhagen, and the*
other by Stephan Roth, who included it in his festival postils of
1528 as a sermon on St. Matthias' Day (Feb. 24). Both texts are
printed in the Weimar edition and Rörer's text is printed with excel-
lent critical apparatus in CL 7, 398-403. *The text chosen here is that*
of Roth, in this case more dependable than most of his postils since
it was worked up from his own notes. The sermon appears in a
sixteenth-century English translation as "A Sermon of D. Martin
Luther, upon the Gospell on Sainct Matthias Day" in Special and
Chosen Sermons of D. Martin Luther, Collected of his writings and
preachings for the necessary instruction and edification of such, as
hunger and seek after the perfect knowledge and inestimable glorie
which is in Christ Iesu, to the comfort and salvation of their soules.
Englished by W. Gace (London, 1578). On W. Gace, see H. E.
Jacobs, The Lutheran Movement in England *(Philadelphia, 1891),*
p. 356, and Gordon Rupp, The Righteousness of God: Luther Studies
(London, 1953), p. 42. Emanuel Hirsch says of this sermon that it
is "one of the richest and most thoughtful of all his sermons which
sum up his faith in Christ" (CL 7, 392).

---

[1] In Roth's text a brief summary of the Gospel, taken from John Bugenhagen's
summaries of the Gospels of the church year, follows; here omitted. The open-
ing sentence, obviously supplied for continuity by Roth, is also omitted.

Text in German; WA 17¹, 38-46, compared with Rörer's maca-
ronic text in CL 7, 398-403 and Roth's postil in WA 17¹¹, 388-397.

This Gospel[2] is one of the really genuine Gospels. Other
Gospels in which the miracles of Christ are described are not so
comforting as those which contain the sermons of Christ in which
he so lovingly teaches and entices us. I am not so certain of the
grace which I see in miracles shown to others as when I have before
me plain, clear words.

To me it is also more comforting to hear such loving admoni-
tions and allurements than to hear preaching on the miracles, although they too strengthen my faith and are examples of the fact
that as he helped these people so he will help me also. Now this
Gospel is nothing else but a knowledge of God the Father and Christ
his Son, and the power of this Gospel lies in these two words, "the
wise" and "babes."

But lest when we hear this we say that it has nothing to do with
us, that it is addressed to others, as the Jews did with the prophets,
interpreting everything they said as meaning the heathen, the preceding words make it clear to whom these words are addressed or
of whom they are spoken by Christ. For earlier he says of those who
despised the gospel and would not accept it—though they should
have been the first to accept it and were also the people who wanted
to be considered the only ones who were dealing with God's Word
and belonged to the people of God—of these people he says, "To
what shall I compare this generation? It is like children sitting in
the market places and calling to their playmates, 'We piped to you,
and you did not dance; we wailed, and you did not mourn'" [Matt.
11:16-17]; which the Lord then applied to himself and to John the
Baptist. It is as if he were saying: We have preached the gospel to
you, John with sternness and severity, but I with graciousness and
gentleness; but you despised it and would not accept it, and you
will come to no good end. It is also true that no matter how one
preaches to the people, sweetly or sourly, kindly or unkindly, they
are still not satisfied.

These the Lord here calls the wise and understanding, from
whom the gospel is hid. Here he does not call wise men those who

---

[2] The term is used here as the designation of a pericope of the so-called ancient
lectionary.

are really and truly wise in divine things. For it is a great favor to be called wise or understanding. True wisdom is nothing else than the knowledge of God, that is, when I know what I am to think of God and know his divine will. But understanding means that I am able to judge worldly things and what is right and wrong, as St. Paul frequently links these two words together, especially in Ephesians and Colossians [Eph. 1:18; Col. 1:9]. Christ is not speaking of this kind of wisdom here, but rather of worldly wisdom, which puffs people up and will not admit the true, divine wisdom. This kind of fellow we all are by nature; we rebel against God's wisdom.

By worldly wisdom you call good what brings pleasure, honor, and profit, but what is contrary to these, such as affliction, dishonor, and loss, you call bad; for human nature cannot do anything else but seek its own [cf. I Cor. 13:5]; what it likes and thinks is good, it considers the best. But what it does not like, it considers the worst, no matter how good it may be. So I say that the Lord is speaking here about the wise and understanding who set their wisdom against God's wisdom. For worldly wisdom is so constituted that it not only wants to rule temporal, worldly things, but also the things which are God's. It is always hatching out and devising something new, even in spiritual and divine things.

Thus, out of their own wisdom, they invented cowls and tonsures and almost everything that is practiced in the whole papacy: There each one chose his own work; one invented this and another that, and when one thing died down or failed to please they soon invented something else, as we, unfortunately, have seen and still see to this day. There is no end to it, and it all comes from the fact that we will not let God's Word and the truth have the right of way, but are always thinking up something new.

For it is certain that when we contrive a new service of God which is contrary to God's Word we become blinded and fall ever deeper from one error into another, which then turns out to be the worst of plagues and punishments. That is why Paul says to the Thessalonians, "Therefore God sends upon them a strong delusion, to make them believe what is false, so that all may be condemned who did not believe the truth but had pleasure in unrighteousness" [II Thess. 2:11-12]. Indeed, they finally come to the place where they know nothing about God, as the psalm says, "The fool says in his heart, 'There is no God'" [Ps. 14:1]. For it is impossible for the natural man, who is made of flesh and blood and has not been instructed by God's Spirit, to judge and understand the things that belong to God, as Paul says to the Corinthians, "The natural man does not receive the gifts of the Spirit of God, for they are folly to him, and he is not able to understand them because they are spiritually discerned" [I Cor. 2:14].

Anybody who wants to read more about this should look at the first chapter of Paul's letter to the Romans; there he will find what blindness does and what punishment ensues when we neglect the Word of God and follow our own inventions and ideas, all of which we see and, unfortunately, experience as true in our spirituals, monks, nuns, and priests. God grant that the day may come when they will repent and let God have his honor.

St. Paul says [Rom. 1:23] of the Gentiles that they have changed the glory of the immortal God into an image which is like that of mortal man and birds and fourfooted animals and creeping things.[3] This is what our papists do too, but even more foolishly and stupidly. They make of him a God who goes about with cowl, tonsure, and hempen rope, concerned with eating meat and eating fish. Therefore God has abandoned them also to the lusts and impurity of their hearts, like the heathen, so shameful that we can hardly speak of it. For if this kind of thing happened among the heathen, who, after all, possessed many wives and whores, why should it be lacking among the spirituals, to whom women were forbidden? In short, this is just what happens wherever the devil is and wherever God's Word does not hold sway. This any man can certainly see for himself. In fact, it is so obvious that the children in the streets sing and talk about it.

Now this is not to be understood as applying only to the spirituals; it also applies to the common man, when he does not accept the Word of God. We see citizens dealing in counterfeit wares and merchants who are swindlers, and there is so much trickery and deceit, so much usury and taking of advantage that it is hardly possible to enumerate it all. And yet they go on doing it while having masses said and providing candles, thinking that God will

---

[3] The Weimar text is defective at this point; sense supplied from EA (2d ed.) 15, 292.

allow himself to be propitiated in this way, concerned only that their reputation before the world remain untouched and unsullied, no matter what it is in the sight of God.

It is of these wise and understanding men that the Lord Christ is speaking here in the gospel, men who hear the gospel and see the miracles, but it does them no good for it does not enter their hearts. He says, therefore:

"I thank thee, Father, Lord of heaven and earth, that thou hast hidden these things from the wise and understanding and revealed them to babes; yea, Father, for such was thy gracious will" [Matt. 11:25-26].

Christ here calls foolish, simple people "babes"; he is not speaking of actual infant children, nor of people who are childish in the eyes of the world. It could be a great doctor whom he here calls a babe, and on the other hand it could be a peasant whom he here calls wise and understanding. In the Psalter, David also calls them babes and children when he says, "By the mouth of babes and infants, thou hast founded a bulwark because of thy foes" [Ps. 8:2]. These surely were not actually infant children by whom God established a power against his enemies and who were to praise and extol his glory in all the earth.

Here the Lord calls "babes" the people who count their own works as nothing, who attribute nothing to their own wisdom, and make nothing whatsoever of themselves, but consider only God to be wise and prudent. That is why they keep quiet and submit themselves completely to God and let themselves be taught by him alone. The others are too wise, they do not want to learn anything from God, indeed, they even presume to cavil at God's doctrine and works. You can read about this in the first and second chapter of St. Paul's first letter to the Corinthians [cf. I Cor. 1:19-31; 2:6-9].

Therefore Christ says in Luke [16:8], "The sons of this world are wiser in their own generation than the sons of light." But the foolish sons of light are more esteemed in the sight of God than the wise sons of the world. Concerning the babes the Lord says here in this Gospel: Now the wise must be foolish and the foolish wise. For this is just what was said: Father, thou hast hidden these things from the wise and understanding, but thou hast revealed them to babes, for the wise and understanding do not know them, but the babes and the fools do know them. Why is it that the wise do not know them? Thou hast hidden them from them. But why do the babes know? Thou hast revealed them to them.

But what he means by this saying must be understood in the light of what he has said previously, namely, that he had proclaimed the gospel of the kingdom of God in many places in Judea, such as Chorazin, Bethsaida, and in his own city Capernaum [Matt. 11:20-24], and they had not accepted it because of their great wisdom, which prevented them from accepting the foolish, silly message of the gospel.

The gospel is a good, joyful message which teaches me how to know God, through which knowledge I obtain the forgiveness of sins and eternal life. As Christ says to his Father in John [17:3], "This is eternal life, that they know thee the only true God and Jesus Christ whom thou hast sent." He says the same things here in this Gospel: "No one knows the Son except the Father, and no one knows the Father except the Son and any one to whom the Son chooses to reveal him" [Matt. 11:27]. He is speaking here of the knowledge of both the Father and of the Son. Now the one to whom this is revealed knows it, and he has eternal life. But this the Father has hidden from the wise and understanding, that they should know neither the Father nor the Son, and has revealed it to babes, that they might know the Father and the Son and thus have eternal life.

Now, if this is true, as it most certainly is true, then what becomes of free will? When you see that such shameful things are done in the body as are spoken of in the first chapter of Romans [1:24], well, go ahead and boast about your free will. I too would say: What a fine kind of a free will that is, to live in such a horrible, inhuman way, which is unheard of even among the animals which have no reason. It's all very well to boast about free will; we see very well what it accomplishes. But this is just what happens when we are forsaken by God. No sooner are we forsaken by God than immediately the devil is in us with his government. And such is life in that kingdom that nothing else can happen except vice and shame, and yet the devil is able to cover it up so masterfully with such fine shine and simulation that it is even looked upon as the holiest, indeed, an angelic, life. What can be accomplished here by human strength, by which some think they can do many things, even to gaining heaven, if they only put their minds to it.

But here you hear Christ saying that the Father "reveals" it, and again, that it is the Father's "gracious will"; and thus he actually nullifies all human merit. Here no satisfactions can help, here no works have any validity whatsoever. It is done only by the will and good pleasure of the Father. He does not look upon the person as it appears before the world; he neither disdains nor rejects the sinner, no matter how laden with sins he may be. So in Luke also Christ says to his disciples, "Fear not, little flock, for it is your Father's good pleasure to give you the kingdom" [Luke 12:32]. This the hypocrites and work-saints cannot stand; in fact it makes them furious, raving mad that the foolish and simple, the publicans and open sinners should go into the kingdom of God before them [cf. Matt. 21:31], and they, with all their holiness and beautiful, fine, glittering works, be excluded. After all, it is enough to make a person mad. But what can we do for him? This is God's good pleasure; the one to whom He reveals it, has it, and the one from whom He hides it, it is hidden from him. There is nothing to be done about it.

And note here especially that Christ says, "Yea, Father, for so it was well-pleasing before thee."[4] "Before thee," yes, before the world was created, as St. Paul says in Eph. [1:4-6], "Even as he chose us in him before the foundation of the world, that we should be holy and blameless before him. He destined us in love to be his sons through Jesus Christ, according to the purpose of his will, to the praise of his glorious grace which he freely bestowed on us in the Beloved." This excludes all merit; so don't let it enter your mind that you can earn anything here or brag about your works or your wisdom or your merits. Here all glorying is taken away, so that, as Paul says to the Corinthians, "Let him who boasts, boast of the Lord" [I Cor. 1:31]. Now let us go on in the Gospel:

"All things have been delivered to me by my Father; and no one knows the Son except the Father, and no one knows the Father except the Son and any one to whom the Son chooses to reveal him" [Matt. 11:27].

---

[4] Alternate RSV rendering of Matt. 11:26.

Here you see the security which is in the kingdom of Christ, through whom we have knowledge and light. Now, if Christ has all things in his hand [cf. John 3:35] and has power over all things just as the Father himself has, then no one can snatch anything from his hand, as he himself says in John [10:28-30], "I give them eternal life, and they shall never perish, and no one shall snatch them out of my hand. My Father, who has given them to me, is greater than all, and no one is able to snatch them out of the Father's hand. I and the Father are one." Therefore every Christian, if he has accepted the gospel, may well rejoice that he is in the hands of this Christ and need not be troubled by his sins, if he has accepted the gospel, for Christ, under whom he lives, will carry on from there. It is true, the devil will go on tempting him with this or that vice, with adultery, fornication, theft, slaughter, envy, hatred, anger, and whatever other sins there are, but there is no need to be troubled, for he has a strong, mighty King; he will defend him well. It will be hard for you, it will be bitter; therefore prayer will be needed and others too will have to pray for you, that you may have strong courage and a brave heart to withstand the devil. But one thing is certain; you will not be forsaken. Christ will surely save you. There is no need to worry, but only do not fall from his kingdom.

So now you see here in this Gospel that Christ is God and man; man in that he praises and thanks God, and God in that all things have been delivered to him by the Father.

But since he says, "No one knows the Son except the Father, and no one knows the Father except the Son and any one to whom the Son chooses to reveal him" [Matt. 11:27], this is all spoken against the free will, which wants to know God and Christ whenever and however it pleases. Here it is clear whence the knowledge of God and Christ comes. The Father, he says, knows the Son and the Son the Father. How then do we get to know it? Through this or some other preacher? No, they are only instruments; but "any one to whom the Son chooses to reveal him." Just before this he said that the Father reveals it; now he says here that the Son does it. Yes, both the Father and the Son reveal it. And as the Father reveals it, so the Son reveals it also, as Christ also says in John [14:26], "The Holy Spirit . . . will teach you all things." Therefore as the Father teaches, so the Son teaches, and so also the Holy

Spirit teaches. And where the Father and the Son and the Holy
Spirit do not teach, then doubtless there is no teaching or knowledge. Now proceed further in the Gospel:

"Come to me, all who labor and are heavy-laden, and I will
give you rest. Take my yoke upon you, and learn from me; for I
am gentle and lowly in heart, and you will find rest for your souls.
For my yoke is easy, and my burden is light" [Matt. 11:28-30].

Up to this point we have heard how God deals with the wise
and understanding, namely, that he blinds them and hides the
gospel from them, and likewise how he deals with the babes and
the simple, namely, that he gives them a real understanding and
reveals the gospel to them. Now somebody may say: "If that's
the way it is, then I must necessarily be in great peril of conscience
until I hear and know that the gospel applies to me also. I am a
sinner and maybe the gospel does not apply to me; I am unworthy
of it." That's why Christ goes on and says, in order to comfort such
timid, dismayed, troubled consciences, "Come to me, all who labor
and are heavy-laden, and I will give you rest." Here we are called
to come to this consolation, to the gospel. Here you must not
think about your worthiness; for this is just what he has been
saying, You "who labor and are heavy-laden," that is, with the
law, with sin, with anxiety and affliction, and with whatever else
may burden the conscience. That's why he does not give it any
special name. He does not say, with this or that difficulty, but
simply says, "all who labor and are heavy-laden." Nor will he have
any one excluded, for he says "all"; which is an excellent and mighty
comfort in temptation, no matter what temptation it may be. So
whoever feels his sinfulness and knows his inability to fulfil the
law of God, let him come confidently and boldly; he will surely
be helped. "I will give you rest," he says to those who are oppressed, as it were, with hard labor and toil. But see to it only
that you believe this friendly bidding and assurance.

So Christ cried out on another occasion in the temple at a
feast in Jerusalem: "If any one thirst, let him come to me and
drink. He who believes in me, as the Scripture has said, 'Out of
his heart shall flow rivers of living water.' Now this he said about
the Spirit, which those who believed in him were to receive" [John
7:37-39]. This is the way this happens: first he causes the gospel

to be preached to us, then I believe this preaching, and as soon as I believe and accept this preaching the Holy Spirit is present, and when the Holy Spirit is present my sins are forgiven. But you feel that the Holy Spirit is present when you believe and are certain that your sins are forgiven. Truly, this is really to give rest to those whose consciences are burdened, for them to feel that their sins are forgiven and that they have become heirs of the kingdom of heaven. Moreover, he not only refreshes us in the anxiety and assaults of sin, but he will be with us in all other troubles; in hunger, war, famine, and whatever other tribulations which may come, he will not leave us, as God never left the dear patriarch Joseph, even in a strange country, but was always with him in prosperity as well as adversity. It is a heavy burden when a man is weighed down by sins, and no one will be relieved of this except those whom the Son of God, Christ Jesus, delivers through the Holy Spirit, whom he secured for us from the Father. He then makes our hearts joyful, steady, and ready to do all that God requires of us.

But what does he mean by saying, "Take my yoke upon you"? Is it rest for me to take one burden from a man's neck and lay another upon him? This is what we have often said; at first the gospel terrifies and is contrary to the flesh, for it says that all our efforts are nil, our holiness and goodness count for nothing, everything that is in us is condemned, we are children of wrath and indignation. And this is hard on the flesh, an intolerable burden; this is why he calls it a burden or yoke.

But lest anyone should be terrified of this Man and think him so great, high, and mighty that he could not abide poor sinners and ordinary people or would deal unkindly with them, he goes on to say, "Learn from me, for I am gentle and lowly in heart." What St. Augustine says here, namely, that we should learn gentleness and humility from Christ,[5] is well spoken, but it does not fit in well at this point. Here Christ's intention is to lure us lovingly to his teaching concerning knowledge of the Father. It is as if he were saying: Flesh and timid natures look upon me as if I were cruel, stern, and severe, but I am not so; I am gentle and lowly in heart. I do not terrify people, as Moses did. I do not preach:

---

[5] Cf. Epistle 147. Migne 33, 597.

do this, do that; I preach the forgiveness of sins. I preach only that you should receive, not that you should give anything. I am not like the Pharisees, who wanted to be magnified; rather I am altogether kind and lowly in heart and ready to receive sinners. And even though they fall right back into sin, I still do not cast them away from me, if only they come to me and accept comfort and help from me. I do not put people under the ban, like the Pharisees, who put people under the ban even on account of their own ordinances and human inventions, and would sooner have all the commandments of God broken than see one of their statutes and ordinances go unobserved. Just as we have seen in the papacy, that it was a far greater sin to eat meat on Friday or for a priest to marry than to commit twenty adulteries or even ten murders. But here you hear that God even abrogates his own law in order to draw sinners to himself.

And Christ makes a special point of saying here that he is gentle. It is as though he were saying: I know how to deal with sinners. I myself have experienced what it is to have a timid, terrified conscience (as the letter to the Hebrews [4:15] says, he "in every respect has been tempted as we are, yet without sinning"). Therefore let no one be afraid of me; I will deal kindly and gently with him. I will not jump on him or frighten him. Let him come boldly to me, in me he will find rest for his soul. "His soul," he says, as if he were saying: It may well be that there will be outward tribulation and physical persecution and calamity may befall you, but all this you should bear easily and quietly (as he also says to his disciples in John [16:33]: In me you have peace, but in the world tribulation). Therefore, even though outwardly everything seems to be against us, as if it would crush and devour us, there is no need to be troubled; for inwardly, in our conscience, we have peace. And this peace of conscience is the first and most immediate fruit of faith, as Paul says in Rom. [5:1], "Therefore, since we are justified by faith, we have peace with God through our Lord Jesus Christ." And when our conscience is free and at peace with God, then nothing can move us nor hurt us, no matter how evil it may be.

But in order that no man may think and say: It doesn't solve the problem simply to take one burden from a man's neck and lay upon him another (as we said above), he goes on to say, "My yoke is easy, and my yoke is light." It is as if he were saying: Don't be afraid of my yoke. The yoke of the law, under which you have been living up to now, was heavy; but my yoke is not so heavy. It is a light and easy yoke, you can easily carry it. The wise fellows are still saying that Christ's yoke is heavier than the yoke of the law and they cite the fifth chapter of Matthew [cf. Matt. 5:22]. But there Christ is explaining how the law is to be understood, not making laws, but rather saying that murder comes from an evil heart and adultery issues from an impure heart [Matt. 15:19]. Therefore he is only interpreting the Law of Moses, not making laws.

But the yoke of Christ is easy and his burden light, not only because he takes away ceremonies and human ordinances, but also the whole law, the curse, the sin, the death, and everything that can happen to us on account of the law. All this Christ takes from me and gives me the Spirit, through whom I cheerfully, willingly, and gladly do everything I should do. And it is called gentle, sweet, and easy because he himself helps us carry it, and when it grows too heavy for us he shoulders the burden along with us. The world looks upon it as heavy and intolerable, but it is not, for then one has a good companion and, as the saying goes: With a good companion the singing is good. Two can carry a burden easily, though one alone may not carry it well.

TEN SERMONS ON THE CATECHISM

1528

TEN SERMONS ON THE CATECHISM
1528

The Last of Three Series of Sermons on the Catechism
Before the Publication of the Large and Small Catechisms,
November 30 to December 18, 1528

In 1528 Luther preached three series of sermons on the Catechism: the first series, consisting of eleven sermons, from May 18 to May 30, the second series of ten sermons from September 14 to September 25, and a third from November 30 to December 18. (The text of all three series may be found in WA 30¹, 1-122.) It is apparent that Luther is here forming the vocabulary into which he cast both his Large and Small Catechisms and that the Large Catechism particularly is a reworking of this catechetical preaching.

In his sermon on the Sunday preceding the first sermon of the series (First Sunday in Advent, Nov. 29), he made the following remarks, which are given here, not only to provide the setting of his catechetical instruction, but also as an example of the "announcements" which were a typical part of his congregational preaching.

"It has hitherto been our custom to teach the elements and fundamentals of Christian knowledge and life four times each year and we have therefore arranged to preach on these things for two weeks in each quarter, four days a week at two o'clock in the afternoon. Because these matters are highly necessary, I faithfully admonish you to assemble at the designated time with your families. Do not allow yourself to be kept away by your work or trade and do not complain that you will suffer loss if for once you interrupt your work for an hour. Remember how much freedom the gospel has given to you, so that now you are not obliged to observe innumerable holy days and can pursue your work. And besides, how much time do you spend drinking and swilling! You don't count that, but when you are asked to spend time on God's Word you are disgusted. Woe to you who scorn this treasure on account of your

135

greed and will not give your servants a free hour to hear God's Word. Give them an hour off that they may come to know themselves and Christ more fully.

"But you fathers who have given your children, servants, and maidservants time off and then found that they did not want to come to church, I give you the liberty to compel them to come. Don't think, you fathers, that you have fulfilled your responsibility for your households when you say, 'Oh, if they don't want to go, how can I compel them? I dare not do it.' Oh, no, this isn't so. You have been appointed their bishop and pastor; take heed that you do not neglect your office over them. If you neglect this office in your homes, we shall fall into public disgrace, as we have seen this happen already. For you will have to answer for your children and servants whom you have neglected. If you have neglected their education inwardly or outwardly, see to it that this is corrected! See to it, then, that they come to hear this preaching. I hold the office of pastor and I will preach these sermons; I will do my part and even more than we are obliged to do."

The text of the third series of sermons has been chosen here because the sermons bring us closer to Luther's final crystallization of his thought in the Large and Small Catechisms. Their relation to the findings of the visitation of the churches in Saxony in the summer of 1527 becomes apparent in Instructions to the Visitors of Parish Pastors in Electoral Saxony *(1528), LW 40, 263-320, and the revised "Church Ordinance" of 1528, for which see Emil Sehling,* Die evangelischen Kirchenordnungen des XVI Jahrhunderts *(1902-1957), pp. 142-174.*

Text in macaronic Latin and German; WA 30¹, 57-121, compared with Buchwald, Predigten D. Martin Luthers, op. cit., *I, 72-145. The translation, like Buchwald's German version, is a conflation of text "R" (Rörer) and text "N" (Cod. Solger 13).*

Introduction. The First Commandment

These portions, which you have heard me recite, were called by the ancient fathers the catechism, that is, an instruction for children, which the children and all who want to be Christians should know. And one who does not know them should not be counted among the number of Christians. For when a person does not know this, it is a sign that he has no regard for God and Christ. Therefore I have admonished you adults to hold your children and servants and yourselves to this; otherwise we shall not admit you to holy communion. For if you parents and masters do not help, we shall accomplish little with our preaching, and if I preach all year long and the crowd only comes in and looks at the walls and windows of the church, it is of no use. A person who wants to be a good citizen owes it to his family to urge them to learn these portions of the catechism, and if they will not, do not give them any bread to eat. If the servants grumble, then throw them out of the house. If you have children, train them to learn the Ten Commandments, the Creed, and the Lord's Prayer. If you urge them diligently to do this, they will learn much in a year's time. But when they have learned this, there are many excellent passages scattered throughout the Scriptures; these they should learn afterwards; if not all, at least some of them. God has appointed you a master and a wife in order that you should hold your family to this. And you can do this easily enough by praying in the morning when you rise, in the evening when you go to bed, and before and after meals. Thus they will be brought up in the fear of the Lord. I am not saying this for nothing; I am determined that you shall not cast it to the winds. I should never have believed that you were such ignorant people if I did not learn it every day. Every father of a family is a bishop in his house and the wife a bishopess. Therefore remember that you in your homes are to help us carry on the ministry as we do in the church. If we do this we shall have a gracious God, who will defend us from all evil and in all evil.

In the Ps. [78:5-8] it is written: "He appointed a law in Israel, which he commanded our fathers to teach their children, that the next generation might know them, the children yet unborn, and arise and tell them to their children, so that they should set their hope in God, and not forget the works of God, but keep his commandments; and that they should not be like their fathers." Note that well—that they learn to fear God and not become like their fathers!

In these sermons there will be five parts.[1] These we call the catechism, which must be taught for the sake of the simple, that they may first learn to recite it word for word but then afterwards learn to understand it. But one who does not know it should not call himself a Christian, but belongs body and soul to the devil, and it will never go well with him here and hereafter. First are the Ten Commandments, which forbid and teach what one must do and not do.

[The First Commandment]

"You shall have no other gods before me." This is a commandment which gives all the doctors trouble to understand. But it should be taught to the children just as it stands in the words, "I am your God," or, "You shall have no other gods before me." Anybody can learn this, no matter how ignorant he may be. But if you won't learn it, then you shall be of the devil. But what does this mean: not to have any other gods or "I am your God"? To have God is to fear God and trust him. I will say it as crudely as I can: He who fears God and trusts him is keeping this commandment, but he who fears something else and trusts it is transgressing. This is the way the prophets preached and explained the first commandment. And, taking it all in all, there is nothing to be found in it except that we must fear God and trust him. The Psalm [147:11] sums up the first commandment in one verse: "The Lord takes pleasure in those who fear him, in those who hope in his steadfast love." "Those who fear him" are those who keep the first commandment, which is to fear God and trust him. For he who fears God and trusts him has no other god.

From this there follows the greatest wisdom. One who fears something else and trusts it makes of it a god. That is why all

---

[1] The five parts of the catechism.

sorcerers transgress this first commandment; they neither trust God nor fear him. You see, then, what faith is and what idolatry is. If you fear the prince more than God, then the prince is your god. If you trust your wife or money more than God, then these are your god. But God is held not in the hand but in the heart. If you fear him and trust him then you need fear no one and trust no one except God. Therefore the first commandment claims the two parts of your heart: fear God and trust him. You learn from this that to fear God is not merely to fall upon your knees. Even a godless man and a robber can do that. Likewise, when a monk trusts in his cowl and rule, this is idolatry.

This you will learn when you have matured; you will be more learned than the whole world. You will know this: I should fear and trust none but God. If I do this I have the one God. My dear child, if you have learned only this first commandment, you have learned enough. Then in time you will also learn to put it into practice. But when you do not hear your God speaking you should not trust or fear him. But if you really hear him, then fear and trust him! When you hear a bishop preaching the Word of your God, then fear and trust! But if he is preaching not the Word of God but of the devil, let him pound, stamp, and curse and say: I do not fear you and I do not trust in you. So the princes these days are attempting to scare the devout away from the Word and faith. Then you must say: My God says that he wills to be gracious to me; him alone must I fear and trust. If they want to give you riches, you already have another treasure, which is trust in God alone. Fear is on the left side,[2] trust is on the right.[3]

Thus the first commandment requires that you fear no one and trust no one except God alone, who says: If you fear me and trust me, I will protect you and supply you with nourishment and all that you need and you shall have what is sufficient. Therefore fear nobody but me, for I can smite you, and put your trust in none but me, for I can help you. No prince will give you either good or evil, for both are in my hand. Therefore fear me and trust in me! This too is what Moses bade his Jews to do in Deut.

---

[2] Facing that which is evil.
[3] Facing the good which we hope for.

6 [:8-9], commanding them to write the commandments upon the walls and bind them upon their hands and keep them before their eyes. But we shall not do as the Jews did, who sewed the commandments on their hats and let it go at that; rather the Lord wills that we should practice them in all affairs of the household, so that when a servant does wrong the master may say: Don't fear me, fear God! You are not my servant but God's servant. You can very well do me an injury without my knowing it. If you will not obey me, then fear God and be obedient for his sake. It is of no account that you be obedient for my sake, but trust God and obey his commandment!

Thus there is always occasion for observing the commandment and practicing it daily in the home. If this is done, you will see the fruits which will come of it when the servants hear God's commandment set forth to them and learn that God has commanded that servants should be faithful to their master. It would be only a clod and a villain who would not be moved by this and worthy of being instructed by Jack Ketch.[4] We probably think that the Ten Commandments are there only to be preached from the pulpit, but they need rather to be applied to use. For God has commanded you to fear and trust him. So the young can be well brought up in the discipline of the Lord [Eph. 6:4]. For they must fear God if they are to cease from doing evil for his sake and [they must trust God if they are to do the good for his sake]. It is small wages when I give you three or four guldens, but God gives you a happy life here and, after that, eternal life. The fault lies with us householders. Necessity has forced us to engage teachers because the parents have not assumed this responsibility. But every master and mistress should remember that they are bishops and bishopesses for Gretel and Hans.[5]

All the wisdom which is in the Scriptures follows from the first commandment. David boasts in Ps. [119:100], "I understand more than the aged, for I keep thy precepts." Thus one becomes greatly learned through this [commandment]; for when the family fears and trusts God you will be able to deal well with every external situation. If my neighbor tries to alienate my servant or

---

[4] *Meister Hans,* the hangman.
[5] Boys and girls, sons and daughters.

maid from me, I immediately say, why do you trust this rascal more than God, who has given you to me to be my servant? In all of life such wisdom proceeds from a knowledge of the first commandment. No matter how many people teach you to go contrary to the first commandment, dismiss them and say, I must fear and trust God more than you. Then they will become fine people; otherwise they will grow up to be blockheads. The chief part of all wisdom and knowledge is the first commandment, namely, that you should fear and trust no one but God alone. He will richly reward you. In the course of time you will learn to apply it well in every situation and action.

The Second and Third Commandments

Yesterday, dear children, you heard that you should be able to recite these words [the first commandment] word for word. Any of you who cannot do this must learn them as you have heard me recite them; for this is the beginning. But when you are able to recite them then this must be followed by understanding. Yesterday we dealt with the first commandment. First you must know the words and then what the meaning of the words is, namely, that nobody should fear or put his trust in any other thing except God. I have stated this very clearly and not without purpose, for this commandment is the sum of all the commandments and the light that goes out into all the commandments and shines in all the others. Therefore learn that it means that you should neither fear nor trust anybody, neither man nor devil, except God.

[The Second Commandment]

The second commandment also requires, beyond its recitation, the understanding of it. And here you will find that the first commandment, fearing and trusting God, is mixed in with it. First, [this commandment teaches that you do not fear and trust God] if you swear and curse by his name or misuse it for wickedness, spite, and deception, as the pope did with his bulls, and those among the Brotherhood of St. Valentine who sold [indulgences], and the sectarians who say they teach God's Word, and the sorcerers who employ good words. But if you fear God, you do not misuse his name and you will not curse and practice sorcery, because you know the first commandment, which says you should fear and trust God.

Secondly, it is to be understood in this commandment that you should use the name of God well, to the honor and praise of God. This is done when you call upon his name in time of need, as he has commanded: "Call upon me in the day of trouble; I will deliver you, and you shall glorify me" [Ps. 50:15]. Likewise, the name of God is honored when an oath is required in court. There too the first commandment is intermixed. For he who does not trust God does not call upon God. Therefore the whole sum of this commandment is this: You should not curse, swear, or conjure by his name, but rather call upon him in trust in every need and praise and honor him.

The first point is that you should not swear, curse, conjure, lie, and deceive. To this the first commandment, which requires that you fear God, impels you. The second is that you should call upon God. And to this too the first commandment impels you, for it says that one should trust God, and he who trusts him calls upon him in every need and praises and thanks him. Therefore, if a person lives in God's fear and trust, he does not curse, but rather calls upon him. The true child of God is one who does not use God's name falsely but rightly. This commandment could be explained further as it is in the Scriptures, but I confine myself now to the short, compact form in order that you may grasp it. Otherwise I could also say that every head of a house should write this commandment on the walls, as is commanded in Deut. 6 [:9]. For when something evil happens, what do people say? Devil take it! [Then the head of the house should say,] why don't you say instead, may God forbid? So instead of cursing one should say, Come, help, O God! God forfend, God counsel me! Then the curses will disappear. The Lord's Prayer and the Creed will be easier when the Ten Commandments are understood. The first commandment says, Fear and trust God. The second says, You should not swear, curse, conjure, slander, lie, deceive, or teach falsely in my name, but on the contrary, you should fear and trust God, call upon him in every need, and praise and honor him.

This anybody can grasp. If you can learn a song of twenty stanzas, you can also learn this. God help me! God bless me! Aye, God save me! This means that a person is in need. But then we shall also call upon God when we are in the greatest of danger. I knew a fellow who whenever he struck against a stone would say, Yo-ho, in the name of a hundred thousand devils! When anybody warned him to stop it, lest he use the same words when he was in need or even dying, he would say, When I am in danger I will call upon the Lord. It so happened that one time he stumbled on a bridge, fell into the river, and was drowned. But as he was falling he cried out his customary invocation: Yo-ho, in the name of a hundred thousand devils. If he had been accustomed to call upon the Lord, however, he would have been helped. It is certain that this name does help as soon as it is uttered in time of need, for Satan is terrified of this name. Otherwise, if one has not called upon the name of God, the devil will have inflicted an even greater evil. It certainly does happen; anybody who immediately cries out, God help me! will not sustain such a dangerous injury as he would otherwise. These are things that happen suddenly to the children and things belonging to the household. For you have Satan in your houses, where he lies in wait for you with every kind of peril, he lurks upon stairs and stiles. Oppose him there with the name of God! I shall not at this time speak of the fact that we also misuse God's name in preaching.

[The Third Commandment]

God has appointed a day of rest and on that day our bodies are to rest from physical labor, likewise also the beasts of burden. It is not enough, however, that you only rest; you are also to keep this rest holy. The commandment does not say: You shall be idle or get into mischief on the day of rest; but rather, you shall keep it holy. What is the intent of this commandment? The answer is: I should live holily on this day; for this day is given to us in order that we may use it for the exercise of holiness. Exercise in the fields is not holy if the person himself is not holy beforehand. In the day of rest, however, you have an exercise through which you become holy. That is, you should concern yourself with the Word of God, devote yourself to it at home and especially in church, for the place, the person, and the time have been appointed for you.

Here again you have the first commandment in this third commandment. Fear God, in order that you may do no evil on the day of rest nor despise God's Word and say, What do I care about the sermon? The commandment therefore requires first that you fear God and second, that you trust God and hear his Word. If you do this, you perform for him a pleasing, precious work, nay, a godly, holy, Christian work, which God himself will deem holy. Therefore, earnestly and reverently hear God's Word! But if you do not do this, then you profane the place, the persons who teach there, and the time, for you are despising God's Word.

Therefore, the meaning of this third commandment is this: Take heed that you do not despise the preaching and neglect the Word of God! Secondly, see to it that you speak of it seriously, hear it, sing it, read it, use it, and learn it! Even though this is to be done every day, especially by me and those like me, since God has committed this work to us, God has nevertheless appointed this day especially in order that we may hear God's Word, his Commandments, the Lord's Prayer, and the Creed. Be sure, therefore, that you do not misuse the day! What you lose in work on this day you will recover in the other six. If masters and mistresses do not compel the servants to go during the week, they should compel them to go on Sunday, that they may hear, read, and sing God's Word for at least an hour. The preacher has his [work] in the church.

That is the sum of these first three commandments. The first requires a heart that fears and trusts God. This must run through all commandments because it is the sum and the light of all the others, for all of the commandments prohibit for the sake of the fear of God and command for the sake of trust in God. The third commandment says this: You shall not despise God's Word but rather go and learn it with all earnestness and humility.

There is one thing more, however. Formerly Sunday was observed in such a way that it was enough if one had heard mass. Now that the mass has been put away, we now put in its place the abuse of thinking that the ministry of the Word was instituted merely to permit people to go in and come out again. They come out no wiser than when they went in; they snore and sleep in church. This is not to keep the sabbath holy. But the ministry of the Word was instituted in order that people might learn the Word of God. For God will surely require that you give an account of what you have learned from the preaching. It is therefore necessary that you not only hear it but also receive it, for this commandment says, "Remember the sabbath day, to keep it holy"; do something holy on this day. But if you have learned nothing, then you have done nothing holy on the sabbath day. Secondly, hear the Word of God with humility and learn it! The fear [of God] constrains you not to despise it; trust [in God] constrains you to hear and learn it.

These first three commandments cover the works toward God; the first, that the heart should trust God; the second, that we should outwardly use his name well; the third, that we should not despise his Word, but on the contrary [hear it]. They are not mere idle talk, but commandments; therefore observe them! If we do this, we do enough so far as God is concerned.

The Fourth Commandment

We have now heard the first three commandments. Remember that you are to learn them and retain them in order that you may also live in accord with them. The first commandment was: "You shall have no other gods before me." That is, fear and trust God! That is saying it briefly and plainly enough. The second: "You shall not take the name of the Lord your God in vain." That is, you should call upon the name of God in every need and honor and praise it. The third: "Remember the sabbath day, to keep it holy." That is, you should so fear God as not to despise his Word, but rather hear and learn it; so you will have a gracious God. These are the first commandments of God, which refer to God himself. They are not mere talk but the commandments of God. Highly as you are commanded to fear God and not despise him, so highly you are also commanded to trust him. Therefore, you should not swear by the name of God; this is the fear of God; you must refrain for his sake. But likewise it is also commanded that you should call upon him in every need. This you do by reason of the first commandment that you should trust him. Likewise it is commanded that you should not remain idle at home and thus despise the Word, but go to church to hear it. If you do this, he will give you more than you have dared to ask him. So far we have preached on the first three commandments. Now comes the fourth.

[The Fourth Commandment]

Here he uses not the words "love," "obey," or "do good to," but rather the noble word "honor." He has put father and mother next to himself and uses the word with which one honors him. Therefore neither the pope nor the higher schools have understood this commandment, nor did I understand or was ever taught what you are being taught now. When you learn the Ten Commandments you are learning more than the pope and all the schools. But honor is paid not merely with the body, with bows and doffing the hat, but rather by respecting them, by honoring them [i.e., parents] with the heart. For God is well aware that the world does not respect parents, especially when they perform their office, that is, when they discipline their children and keep them from evil. Then the old Adam curses under his breath. God knows that there lurks in the children a poisonous resentment against the parents and therefore he commands not only that they should obey them but also honor them; that is, that the children think highly of them, not because they are strong or beautiful or well clothed, but because of the first commandment, which commands that we fear God and trust him. So when God speaks these words about your parents he knows what he is talking about. Therefore, for the sake of the Word of God, which he himself speaks, you should honor them. Even if your parents treat you unjustly, so long as it is not contrary to God, you should stop and consider: I must fear God and trust him who said, Honor your father and mother. The Jews and their Pharisees taught disobedience to parents as being in accord with the command of God, as in Matt. 15 [:5].[6] But when you hold your parents in honor, this honor will teach you not to let them suffer want, to lack food, and perish with hunger, but you will rather give them the best you have in the house, the most precious treasure, which God has given to you in order that you may honor them. Since the first commandment casts light upon the fourth commandment, it is for the sake of fearing him that God wills that you let your parents be your treasure.

The meaning of the commandment is this: Fear God and trust God in this commandment. This is done when, for the sake of the fear of God, you do not despise, defame, or contradict your parents, but rather when you show them honor, are helpful and obedient to them, and regard them so highly in your heart that there is nothing better in your heart than your parents. If you fear me, says God, you will honor your parents. Therefore God has also added the promise: "that your days may be long." If you honor them and serve them, then you have this promise that he will give you a long life. That is, I will give you a wife, a husband, I will supply you with food, house, and home; you will be a fine citizen; here in time you shall have sufficient and hereafter eternal life. Ah, should I not then be obedient? Especially since God promises eternal life and besides a long life here, which cannot endure if you do not have a wife, husband, house, and home; and he will take care of you. This the children especially should learn in order that they may honor their parents. Then they will be blessed children, saints; this is what he promises them.

This is why so few marriages turn out well, because they have not deserved to turn out well in the sight of God. They have not shown due honor to their parents, but rather have scorned their commandments and not feared them. This is not mere junk or talk, but a commandment of God, who demands it of you. Therefore, a mother should say to her daughter: My dear daughter, do not regard me, but take heed of him who commands you to honor your

---

[6] Text N (see WA 30[I], 68) reads: "Not as the Jews, who teach Corban with respect to deserting one's parents." Cf. Mark 7:9-13.

father and mother. If you despise me, you will come to no good end, but if not, you will have a gracious God who will give you long life.

Furthermore, everything which is called "father" belongs under this commandment, as the pope has quite rightly called bishops and preachers fathers. In the Scriptures the masters of the household are called *patres familias,* as the word indicates. The word is used of Naaman in II Kings 5 [:13]. In Greek and Latin they are also called *patres familias.* If you are a servant, then honor your master like a father; the commandment applies to you. If you are a maid, remember to let your mistress be your mother. It would not be a bad thing at all if servants called their masters and mistresses father and mother, especially the minors and orphans. This would please the father of a household.

The whole world these days is complaining about the wickedness of servants. The reason for it is that they consider the commandment a joke and think it does not apply to them. But if you are a servant or a maid, you owe to your master the honor which a son or a daughter owes to a father, which means that you will not only serve him but show him honor. God knows when a servant is unfaithful to his master. And the same goes for the maid; when she is given many things to do, she does nothing. Look out, you servants, and heed the first commandment: Fear God and trust in him! So a father of a household should speak to his servants: Don't look to me; I'll get along all right, but God has commanded you to fear him. If you show disrespect to God, it will not mean much to you if you despise me also. But if you are devout, you will have your consolation here. If you serve faithfully and pay honor to our Lord God, God will see to it that he will give you, servant, a fine maid for a wife and you, maid, a good husband. The terrible conditions in the world today are surely to be attributed to the disobedience of servants. They do not stay in one place; they are nothing but beggars, clods. Today husband and wife come together, after two months they separate. When a maid is careless, she thinks to herself: Oh, my master won't see it. The mistress is sick. If I don't milk the cow today, I'll do it tomorrow. And she thinks she is committing no sin. But there is one above who sees and says, Honor your master! I command this to you. If you do not, you shall die of pestilence, fever, or bloody flux, or remain a beggar all your life. But if you do, then you make of your master a father and of your mistress a mother, and besides you will have a gracious God. Note well that master and mistress are called fathers and mothers in the Scriptures!

This applies also to the government. The Romans called the princes *patres patriae*. We should be ashamed that we do not call our princes fathers or do not consider them as such. Our prince is our father. Likewise the burgomaster. For God gives us sustenance and guards our homes through the princes as through a father. Therefore one should so honor them, obey them, and love them that a subject should consider his prince his greatest treasure and guard against rebellion. The same applies to the citizen with respect to the burgomaster. This is the fourth commandment. But we say, What do I care about the prince and the burgomaster? But look who has commanded you to honor parents and what he says to you! It is easy to have contempt for persons, but look here: Fear and trust God! God has commanded that you should honor the government; even if you despise them for other reasons, you dare not do so any longer because of the Word of God. If you do not despise them, then you have the promise that he will be your God and will give you long life. Then we can have decent people on earth and we shall have peace. But if we do not do what God commands in the Ten Commandments, we shall see everything full of war.

Thus there are three kinds of fathers: [fathers by birth, in the household, and] fathers of the land. The fourth kind are the bishops, these one should dishonor.[7] But for those who are true Christians, it is right that they should honor their bishops, because they watch over their souls and administer the sacraments to them. I shall not preach much about this, for I too am one of these. In short, if you honor your parents, masters, princes, and bishops, [says God,] you must not worry about where you are going to get a wife, husband, house and home. Let Me take care of that. If you honor your prince, burgomaster, and preacher, let Me take care of how you will get enough to live on. The God who says, "that your days may be long

---

[7] That is, so the world believes. Cf. the corresponding section in the Large Catechism: WA 30¹, 155.

in the land which the Lord your God gives you" will not deceive you. He is not talking about five guldens; it includes everything: house and home, wife and children. This should make us melt with love and lift up our hands in gratitude that we have a master, a mistress, a prince, burgomaster, preacher in whom we honor only God. You see in the Ten Commandments the orders so gloriously established with such glorious benefits and promises. Nothing is more precious than long life. Emperor Charles and the Turks are not able to lengthen your life by even one hour or give you a good wife.

Anybody whom this does not move is not worthy to hear a single word [of God]. Therefore, honor all who can be called father —father and mother, master and mistress, prince, burgomaster, and preacher! If you honor them, God will richly reward you even here on earth. This is a bull which one could not write on twenty-four cowhides.[8] Therefore do it, in order that you may fear God. Always relate it to the first commandment!

The Fourth, Fifth, and Sixth Commandments

We have heard four commandments. The first three relate to God himself, the fourth to parents. The first is, "You shall have no other gods before me," which means: Fear and trust God and no one else. The second: Do not curse or swear, but rather call upon God, pray, praise, and give thanks. The third: Do not despise and neglect the Word, but rather go gladly to hear and learn it. The fourth is that you should not only obey your parents but also, because of the fear of God, think highly of them and share with them all that you have. Then you are promised a long life.

You parents, on the other hand, must remember to show yourselves to be parents toward your children! For the fourth command-

---

[8] I.e., a subject which cannot be dealt with briefly.

ment calls you fathers and mothers, not tyrants, rascals, and scoundrels. Therefore, if you are a father or a mother, this commandment
means you. If you are a burgomaster, or anyone who bears the
name of father, see to it that you carry out your paternal office.
You father, instruct your son, that he may fear God; you master,
your servants; you burgomaster, your townsmen; you prince, your
subjects. You too have been commanded. Your maids do not exist
merely to wash the pots for you. Listen! this commandment is for
you. If you are not diligently concerned that your children and
servants learn piety, then it serves you right if your children are disobedient and your servants unfaithful. For God does not give you
your children to play with, nor does he give you servants for you to
use them like asses for work. As you learn from me, so children and
servants should learn from you parents and masters. Remember and
help to raise up good people, that you, father, may raise up a devout
son, you, mother, a devout daughter, who in turn will raise up their
children in piety. Thus the servants will also be well trained. A
prince and the cities need good people. The prince needs coun-
cilors, the cities need pastors and learned men. Therefore, do not
say, as some people are saying these days: Priestcraft doesn't count
any more. If you note that your child can become an able boy, send
him to school.[9] If you do not do this, you will have to give an
account, and you are a rogue who is against the prince and the city
and disobedient to your God. Hitherto scholars have been educated
in order to become canons. Now we must devote far more care to
educating the children in order that we may find people who are
capable of serving a country in its secular government and the cities
in spiritual government as preachers and lectors. You see what mur-
derous harm you do to the sovereign prince and the fatherland when
you keep gifted boys away from study. The same applies to you,
the mother of a family, if you train your daughter or your maid
badly. It is a commandment which is laid upon you, not something
which is merely given to you. For if you are able to rear your
daughter well and do not do so, you are the one who has ruined her.
Conditions are such in Christendom that unfortunately no estate

---

[9] Cf. Luther's treatises, *To the Councilmen of All Cities in Germany That They
Establish and Maintain Christian Schools* (1524); and *A Sermon on Keeping
Children in School* (1530). *PE* 4, 103-178.

[*Stand*] knows what it is any more. It is no small thing when a young woman is well reared and becomes a good mother, who is then able to bring up her children in piety. Therefore you parents should learn that you are not excluded from this fourth commandment. There is no lack of learned men now, for at the present time you have learned men, such as the world has never seen before.

[The Fifth Commandment]

The following commandments refer to our neighbor, who is our equal. The first four refer to those who are over us. The first [of these] is: "You shall not kill." "Not to kill" means not to kill either with the tongue or the hand, or with a sign or in one's heart. This commandment is clearly explained by Christ himself, as you read in Matt. 5 [:21-26]. The greatest treasure your neighbor has on earth is his life and body. This God would have secured from all violence and assault and with this commandment he builds a wall around him and says, "You shall not kill." Thus the Lord cares for us by providing us with a protection. He says, Do him no harm, but rather show him all good; do not injure him physically, either with words or deeds or in your heart. For to have rancor in one's heart toward a neighbor, or to laugh in one's sleeve when he dies or has bad luck, is also to kill one's neighbor. If all the murderers were to be stoned, the streets would be flowing with blood. It means, therefore, that we must neither do him any evil or wish him any evil, but rather the contrary. If we do not do this, it is the same as if you had done harm to him. Therefore, in these commandments are contained the six works of mercy. If he is hungry, feed him, if he is naked, clothe him, if he is in prison, visit him, and so on [Matt. 25:35-36]; otherwise you are guilty of his death. If you can avert his danger, do so; if not, you become guilty. Therefore, mark these words well: You shall not do him any harm or injury, but rather do good to him and help him. The six commandments of mercy are quite plainly included here.

The fifth commandment therefore requires a heart that is gentle, friendly, and sweet toward everybody, ready to do good to everyone. Anger is forbidden to everybody; it is permitted only to those who stand in God's stead, such as parents, princes, and preachers. Those who are not acting in God's stead, must not be angry with their neighbor. If you want to be a knight, cutting and slashing, then attack yourself first, your own pride and all offenses against your neighbor's body and goods. But see to it that you are not found to be a murderer by neglecting your neighbor whom you are well able to help. How many there are, however, who laugh at their neighbor's misfortune! Here it stands: "You shall not kill." When evil thoughts come into your mind, remember this: God has commanded me to fear him and he bids me not to kill anyone, not to harm anyone. I must fear him who is above and not do this for his sake. You must look upon the fifth commandment as a wall which God has built against my anger. You see how hard this commandment is. Though many transgress it, they still go on wanting to be pious, though their hearts, mouths, and eyes are full of poison. Therefore, see to it that you fear God; and then afterwards, when you should give to the poor people and help them, see to it that you are not slothful. Feed the hungry; if you have not fed them, you have killed them.[10] So also in Matt. 25 [:42-45]. The tyrants who hound people and despoil them of their goods are well skilled in this. Help your neighbor with hand, mouth, and heart for the sake of God, who has commanded you to do this. Therefore, fear God and give to the needy in whatever he is lacking, as Moses says: "If there is among you a poor man, one of your brethren, in any of your towns within your land which the Lord your God gives you, you shall not harden your heart or shut your hand against your poor brother, but you shall open your hand to him, and lend him sufficient for his need, whatever it may be" (Deut. 15:7-8). Don't say, I don't have it. Here Moses himself is taking the fear of God from the first commandment and applying it in all ten of them. If we remembered God's Word in everything, we would often leave some things undone which we would otherwise do. Then you would again have a gracious God, as you have heard and will continue to hear.

[The Sixth Commandment]

Adultery includes all unchastity. Adultery is mentioned most frequently because it was the most common unchastity. The Jews were all married, for at that time there was no priesthood. God did not create man and woman in order that villainy should be per-

---

[10] A quotation of Ambrose, often cited by Luther. Cf. p. 9 n. 4.

petrated through celibacy, but rather gave to the body its nature of being able to be fruitful and multiply. It is a great and excellent blessing, which no human heart would ever have conceived. The Lord therefore wills that the body of the man and of the woman, which he has given, should be kept under discipline. He therefore also appointed that each should have his wife or her husband and remain faithful to each other.

Married life is not a subject for jest, but an excellent estate. God bestowed upon it all the goods of the earth, as is written in Gen. 1 [:28]. He honored it so highly that he reposed everything in it; for what he is concerned with here is that people should be raised up. Therefore, let each one see to it that he remains with his wife and vice versa, and that both keep their bodies pure, not only outwardly but also that you may not set your heart upon another. They shall "become one flesh," it is said [Gen. 2:24; Matt. 19:6], and this they do on account of the first commandment: Fear God! What you must say is: Even though I do have chances to kick over the traces, nevertheless, since God says, Fear me! I will not do it. Even though the emperor will not find it out, God who is above me will. Therefore say, O my God, grant me grace that I may not fall and that I may keep my marriage pure. This means that you are to live chastely in your marriage, in body, words, gestures, and heart. That's why God gave to each his wife.

The other filthy sins, such as the violation and defloration of virgins, I shall not mention, for by God's grace, I think that we have succeeded to the point where this estate, which is the best and highest estate, is again being held in honor. For if bishops and emperor desire to lead their lives in piety, they must become married, just as they also come but of this estate.

But let each one look to his own house and neither permit nor counsel fornication, but rather prevent it, because God's Word commands it: "Because of the temptation to immorality, each man should have his own wife and each woman her own husband" (I Cor. 7:2). Therefore, if you cannot be continent, take a wife. Then you will have the promise that God will not forsake you. Blessed be he who holds to this, that public prostitution may not take hold.

"You shall not kill." That is, you shall not do your neighbor any harm or wish him any evil, either in your heart or by signs, words, or deeds, but rather benefit and counsel him, no matter whether he is your friend or your enemy. At this point all the works of mercy flow together. The sixth commandment is this: You shall be chaste in words and deeds and keep to your wife and love her, and you shall honor your husband. If you avoid unchastity with another's wife and child and keep only to your own, you will have a gracious God; for he says, "I show steadfast love to thousands of those who love me and keep my commandments" [Exod. 20:6]. This applies to all the commandments.

The Seventh, Eighth, Ninth, and Tenth Commandments

You have recently heard the sixth commandment. In general, you should be admonished first to learn the words and then what they mean. The first commandment reads: "You shall have no other gods before me." That is, you should so fear God and trust in him that you neither despise him nor despair of him. The second is: You shall not curse, swear, or conjure, but call upon him in every need. The third: You shall not despise the Word of God on Sunday, or any other day for that matter, but rather willingly hear and learn it. The fourth is: Whoever bears the name of parent should not only not be dishonored, but served, honored, and highly esteemed. The fifth is: Do no harm to your neighbor, but rather help and advance him according to his need. The sixth is: Fear God and live chastely, and you shall not commit adultery but rather love your wife and honor your husband. Add to each and every one of the commandments: Fear and trust God!

[The Seventh Commandment]

The seventh commandment is one which was not given by a prince or burgomaster, but by your God, who holds your life and everything else in his hand, who can destroy you. The word "steal" includes every kind of advantage and this commandment applies in every trade and profession. One can commit a theft in these trades just as well as if you climbed in through a back window. It is as much as stealing for you to charge too much for the meat. It is stealing whenever I get my neighbor's goods into my possession by any means whatsoever. That's why there is no more common trade or larger craft on earth than thievery. And usually we hang the petty thieves; the big ones, however, go walking around in the highest esteem. But when you steal something from me or do me the slightest injury, you are not attacking me, but rather God. Therefore every artisan, butcher, and the like should write this commandment on his scales, the miller on his sacks, the baker on his bread, the shoemaker on his last. For He who will punish theft is great and is angry unto the third and fourth generation. On the other hand, if you carry on your trade fairly and do not steal, hear the God who says: You shall be rich and blessed. Otherwise he will scatter it all as dust.

There is a complaint that things are not just. I have warned you. To the rich you do no wrong; but here is the great mass of poor people; these are the ones you cheat and afflict. These are the ones who go out of the butcher's with weeping eyes and cry out to heaven. These are the ones to fear, the multitude of the poor does it, and God regards their tears. If you are successful, then may all the devils take me if you are not detestable. Beware of the neighbor who cannot endure your insolence, [when you say:] I won't give it to you cheaper; take it or leave it! If you despise God, he will despise you, so that neither you nor your descendants will be able to use your ill-gotten gains. You farmers and townsmen are, almost all of you, thieves and skinflints! Paul says in Eph. 4 [:28], "Let the thief no longer steal, but rather let him labor, doing honest work with his hands, so that he may be able to give to those in need." You should not skin him, but give to him. But you turn it around. When a poor woman comes to you with two pennies to buy a half a pound of meat, you dare not drive her away; you must give it to her or you will have an angry God. The same applies to tailors, brewers, and others. Don't think that God established the market to be a den of thieves. It is a market, not a skin-game. There are no more dangerous men in your market or butcher's stall than the wretched poor people. They will carry to heaven a complaint against you which will prove to be all too grievous for you, your house, and your children. Therefore, learn this commandment, that you may not commit any theft! If Jack Ketch[11] doesn't hang you, the devil will.

You servants and workers are also thieves. Your master gives you wages, food, bed, and protection, which means that here the master himself is the servant and the servant master. But you take the wages your master gives you in order to defend him from loss and do the opposite. Likewise, a maid should remember that she should preserve her mistress from harm. If she does not, she is a thief. It is just as much stealing if she lets a sow go to ruin as if she stole from the purse. But God says to her; Fear me! If you do not, then I am a jealous God. If one does not prevent the other from suffering damage, it is all as good as stolen.

Thievery, as I have said, is a great and powerful trade. This is what war and famine come from—to take away what has been ill-gained; for the Lord punishes the wicked. So the workers never bamboozle themselves more than when they sit around guzzling half the day and even brag about it. Such fellows are called thieves, and they are thieves, and they are worthy of being hanged. They lie when they say they work and get nothing for it. If you say a word to them, they let the work lie undone. Thieves, thieves, that's what you are! Just as if it were in your power whether you worked or not, as if there were no God who punishes! You must do it and not let it lie; for God says, "You shall not steal." That's why there is no prosperity, but rather war and pestilence. They think they have a right to work or not to work. Therefore, let every artisan, every carpenter write upon his adze: "You shall not steal." You must work as you have contracted to work. If you don't want to work, then don't hire yourself out to work, but stay home behind the stove and cook pears.[12] The Turk builds this way; he says, Come and get it done in three days! And see to it that the stable stands up, if not, off with your head! Their work is laid out for them, as much as a man can do. So the Romans did too. But we are nothing

---

[11] Cf. p. 140 n. 4.
[12] I.e., do some work that requires no effort.

but beer guzzlers. "You shall not steal," says God. Don't scorn it; if you work faithfully and sell your things [fairly], you will have a gracious God; he will reward you richly. Anyone may sell what he has for the highest price he can get, so long as he cheats no one. Solomon says, "A false balance is an abomination to the Lord, but a just weight is his delight" [Prov. 11:1]. That is, God cannot and will not abide it; but on the other hand he is heartily pleased when it is just. But if you do the opposite, you are not attacking a poor man or woman, but God himself. Just look at these words! But the other way pleases God and you will have a good trade. You should always be more pleased with a penny and God's approval than with a whole city full of guldens and his abomination. Then one drink of wine is as much as a whole big cellar full of Malvoisie. That is, you shall do no harm to his possessions, but rather promote them and help him to do so wherever and however you can. And you do this for the sake of God. Thus [a maid] will consider: I will do no harm to my mistress, not for her sake, but for the sake of him who said, "You shall not steal." So too the laborer and every man, let him apply the Ten Commandments in his life. Then he will have a gracious God, who gives him a hundred times more than he now has and, besides, a good conscience. For if you keep on scrimping and skinning for long, the time will come when you will lay your head [on the executioner's block] or the Junker's trooper will come and pay you a visit and take what you have unjustly amassed.

[The Eighth Commandment]

In the first place [we take the plain meaning of the commandment as pertaining to] when a person gives false testimony in court out of hatred and envy, accepts money and gives false witness, so that his neighbor is punished in body, property, or honor. And this happens often to the poor man. The fanatics [*Schwärmer*] also bear false witness; but this we will leave, since it pertains to the second commandment. The sum of this commandment is this: You shall bear true witness and speak the truth, and furthermore, you shall not judge your neighbor, not speak evil of him, as is the nature of women who cannot keep quiet about the weaknesses of a neighbor. Rather you shall speak the best about your neighbor, in the market, in conversation, and elsewhere, and likewise in court. If he is to be put to shame, cover up and bury his fault. Paul says in I Cor. 12 [:22-24], that we do not cover up noses and eyes, for they have their honor, but the dishonorable members we cover up and veil most carefully; for one attaches far more importance to eyes, hands, and all the honorable members than to the others. One who likes to hear about the shame and disgrace of others is a person who likes to look at others' backsides. In court speak the truth, outside of court speak the best, that is, do not speak evil of your neighbor, but the best! So you will guard your tongue in order not to sin against this commandment. But if you speak evil of him, God threatens not to forgive you. In the other case, however, he will be your gracious God and will reward you.

But in this matter the secular government, preachers, fathers, and mothers are excepted. For this commandment is meant to be kept in such a way that evil is not left unpunished; therefore, though it is commanded that you should do no physical harm to your neighbor, the government is nevertheless excepted. Thus parents likewise apply physical force to their children. The commandment is not laid upon them, because God bids them to correct their children; just as God also commands the government to wield the sword, since he does not wield it himself. God rejected Saul, because he spared the Amalekites.[13] You have not been commanded to take another man's wife. But if you were commanded from heaven to do so, you would have to do it, just as the government has the commandment, and therefore it proceeds to take a man's wife who has committed a crime and kills her. Thus nobody is permitted to speak evil of a neighbor except those to whom this has been committed, as a judge and his assessor are obliged to examine and call witnesses in order to correct faults. Therefore God has ordained the government to do this; it is its office to speak of the sins of others. So father and mother speak of their children; a sister may complain to the mother about a sister and a brother to the father about a brother. If one takes it to the ones who are authorized to punish, one does well. Therefore, if your neighbor does evil, tell it to the burgomaster or the judge. [Christ speaks of this in] Matt. 18 [:15-17]. Nobody should say: I will punish no one. But if you are not willing to

---

[13] Actually, God punished Saul for sparing Agag, the King of Amalek, and for keeping the booty won in the war with the Amalekites [I Sam. 15:1-35].

declare your neighbor's evil publicly to the government, then keep it to yourself, for if you carry it into all the houses with your scandalous, poisonous tongue, you do not improve it, but only make it worse. Therefore, declare it where you should declare it.

Besides [the government and parents], the preachers, who are to declare to the world its condemnation, are also excepted, save that they are not to expose anybody by name. It would not be proper for me to do this apart from my office. In summary: You shall declare the truth in court and speak no evil or falsehood concerning your neighbor, but the best. If you do this, you have a gracious God in heaven.

[The Ninth and Tenth Commandments]

These last two commandments were, strictly speaking, given especially to the Jews, although they also concern us. Above, in the seventh commandment, it is said, "You shall not steal" and not take anything from your neighbor by force. This has to do with a more subtle kind of fraud; therefore he says, "You shall not covet." When a person sees that his neighbor has a fine house, he does not steal it, of course; but he employs dodges and devices in order to get possession of it. For example, if a prince wanted to be the elector of Saxony, he might make a cunning deal with the emperor, procure letters from the emperor, and then pretend that he had not acted deceitfully. Cunning appears to have been very much the rule among the Jews. It is possible to deprive a man of his possessions with a fine title and a false law in such a way that the deceiver cannot be accused of fraud. So it was with wives also, for in the Old Testament a bill of divorce was given. So some rascal would begin to think: My neighbor has a beautiful wife, what can I do to get her? Therefore, it is here commanded that none shall thus shrewdly entice away another man's wife under the pretext of right. In the sixth commandment something else is said. Such a one was Herod, at first, when his brother Philip was living, and later, after his death. Among us this is not the way it is done; when a man wants to get another man's wife, he kills him. David likewise committed this sin. The same thing happens with servants. If a man has a good servant or maid, the neighbor's servants do not favor the master and they say, Why do you serve this master? He doesn't give you enough wages. But at that time the servants were bondsmen. With us, however, it often happens that a man will alienate another's servants or maid and think he is doing well! But this is contrary to the commandment. Always remember: You shall not covet another's servant and desire to have him as your servant. The same applies to his ass, his field, his garden, as in the case of Naboth's vineyard [I Kings 21:1-16]; that is, you shall not alienate his horse or his garden or anything else by guile or law, but rather assist him in order that he may keep them.

Now, tell me whether we do not have enough good works to perform! But contempt of the Ten Commandments has caused men to invent other orders.[14] Now let us weave all the commandments into a garland, the last into the first. In all of them you find these two things: you should fear God and trust God. If you fear God, you will not mistrust him, you will not blaspheme, you will not be disobedient to your parents, you will not kill anybody or do him physical harm, but rather help him; and so with all the rest of the commandments.

To the conclusion of the commandments add the threat and the promise of the first commandment. The reason why the generations and nations are going to ruin is because this word [i.e., God's threat] is not observed. On the other hand, however, it says: "showing steadfast love to thousands of those who love me and keep my commandments." There is set forth life and death, wrath and grace, blessing and curse, benefit and evil. These two, threat and promise, are the cord with which one binds the garland together.[15]

---

[14] Cf. Large Catechism, Conclusion of the Ten Commandments, Henry E. Jacobs (ed.), *The Book of Concord,* I, 435.

[15] Cf. *WA* 30[I], 180-181; Large Catechism, Conclusion of the Ten Commandments: "Thus the first commandment is to shine and impart its splendor to all the others. Therefore you must also allow this part [of the Decalogue] to run through all the commandments like the clasp or hoop in a garland, which joins the end and the beginning and holds them all together."

The Creed

You have heard the first part of Christian doctrine, namely, the Ten Commandments. And I have carefully admonished you to exhort your household to learn them word for word, that they should then obey God and you as their masters, and that you too should obey God. For if you teach and urge your families, things will go forward. There has never yet been a [perfect] learned man; the more he has studied the more learned he has become. (Here he recited the Ten Commandments in order.)[16]

Now we shall take up the second part. In former times you heard preaching on twelve articles of the Creed. If anybody wants to divide it up, he could find even more. You, however, should divide the Creed into the main parts indicated by the fact that there are three persons: God the Father, Son, and Holy Spirit; since I believe in God the Father, I believe in God the Son, and I believe in God the Holy Spirit, who are one God. Thus you can divide each separate article into its parts. The first article teaches creation, the second redemption, the third sanctification.' The first, how we are created together with all creatures; the second, how we are redeemed; the third, how we are to become holy and pure and live and continue to be pure. The children and uneducated people should learn this in the simplest fashion: the Creed has three articles, the first concerning the Father, the second concerning the Son, the third concerning the Holy Spirit. What do you believe about the Father? Answer: He is the creator. About the Son? He is the redeemer. About the Holy Spirit? He is the sanctifier. For educated people one could divide the articles into as many parts as there are words in it. But now I want to teach the uneducated and the children.

[The First Article]

The first article teaches that God is the Father, the creator of heaven and earth. What is this? What do these words mean? The

---

[16] A note of the transcriber.

meaning is that I should believe that I am God's creature, that he has given to me body, soul, good eyes, reason, a good wife, children, fields, meadows, pigs, and cows, and besides this, he has given to me the four elements, water, fire, air, and earth. Thus this article teaches that you do not have your life of yourself, not even a hair. I would not even have a pig's ear, if God had not created it for me. Everything that exists is comprehended in that little word "creator." Here we could go on preaching at length about how the world, which also says, I believe in God, believes this. Therefore, everything you have, however small it may be, remember this when you say "creator," even if you set great store by it. Do not let us think that we have created ourselves, as the proud princes do.

At this time I speak only of these things, for the creator, the Father almighty, has still more in store [than I enumerate here].[17] I believe that he has given to me my life, my five senses, reason, wife, and children. None of these do I have of myself. God is the "creator," that is, God has given everything, body and soul, including every member of the body. But if everything is the gift of God, then you owe it to him to serve him with all these things and praise and thank him, since he has given them and still preserves them. But, I ask you, how many are there in the world who understand this word "creator"? For nobody serves him. We sin against God with all our members, one after another, with wife, children, house, home.

Therefore, this first article might well humble and terrify us, since we do not believe it. Note that I am basing [everything] on the word "creator," that is, I believe that God has given to me body and soul, the five senses, clothing, food, shelter, wife, child, cattle, land. It follows from this that I should serve, obey, praise and thank him. A man who believes this article and looks at his cow says: This the Lord gave to me; and he says the same with regard to wife and children.

In short, the first article teaches creation, the second redemption, the third sanctification. The creation, it teaches, means that I believe that God has given to me body, life, reason, and all that I possess. These things I have not of myself, that I may not become proud. I cannot either give them to myself or keep them by myself. But why has he given them to you and what do you think he gave

---

[17] Cf. Large Catechism, Part II, par. 16-18; WA 30¹, 183-184.

them to you for? In order to found monasteries? No, in order that you should praise him and thank him. There are many who say these words, "I believe in God the Father," but do not understand what these words mean.

"And in Jesus Christ"

You have heard that for the simple and the children we divide the Creed into three articles. The first part deals with the Father, the second with the Son, the third with the Holy Spirit. The first teaches creation, the second redemption, the third sanctification, in order that each may know what he is saying when he says the Creed. I have emphasized the word "creator" in order that, when you are asked, you may answer: I believe that God is the creator, who has given to me my body and soul, all members, all physical goods, all possessions. Therefore I owe it to him to serve, thank, and praise him. This first article requires that you believe. This is most certainly true.

Now follows the second article. This too we want to treat for the children and I shall emphasize only the words "our Lord." If you are asked, What do you mean when you say, "I believe in Jesus Christ"? answer: I mean by this that I believe that Jesus Christ, the true Son of God, has become my Lord. How? By freeing me from death, sin, hell, and all evil. For before I had no king and lord; the devil was our lord and king; blindness, death, sin, the flesh, and the world were our lords whom we served. Now they have all been driven out and in their stead there has been given to us the Lord Christ, who is the Lord of righteousness, salvation, and all good. And this article you hear preached constantly, especially on Sundays, as for example, "Behold, your king is coming to you."[18] Therefore, you must believe in Jesus, that he has become your Lord, that is, that he has redeemed you from death and sin and received you into his bosom. Therefore I have rightly said that the first article teaches the creation and the second redemption. For after we had been created, the devil deceived us and became our Lord. But now Christ frees us from death, the devil, and sin and gives us righteousness, life, faith, power, salvation, and wisdom.

It is because of this article that we are called Christians, for

---

[18] Matt. 21:5, the Gospel for the First Sunday in Advent and Palm Sunday.

those who acknowledge and call upon Christ are called Christians. But the words which follow, "conceived by the Holy Ghost, born of the Virgin Mary," etc., are points which emphasize and show what Christ became, what he did as our Lord in order to redeem us, what it cost him, what he risked. This is what happened: He was conceived by the Holy Spirit without any sin whatsoever in order that he might become my Lord and redeem me. He did it all in order to become my Lord, for he must be so holy that the devil could have no claim upon him. These points show what kind of a God he is and what he paid in order that I might come under his lordship, namely, his own body, with which he established his kingdom. The whole gospel is contained in this article, for the gospel is nothing else but the preaching of Christ, who was conceived, born, [raised again, ascended, and so on].

Therefore learn to understand these words "our Lord." I should believe and I do believe that Christ is my Lord, that is, the one who has redeemed me, for the second article says that he has conquered death and sin and liberated me from them. At first, when I was created, I had all kinds of goods, body, [soul, etc.]; but I served sin, death, and the devil. Then came Christ, who suffered death in order that I might be free from death and become his child and be led to righteousness and to life. Thus the word "Lord" here is equivalent to the word "Redeemer."

The other points show what it was by which he accomplished this and what a price he paid for it, namely, not with gold, silver, or an army of knights, but with his own self, that is, with his own body. He was conceived by the Holy Spirit, born of the Virgin Mary, and so on. I shall not say any more about this article because I do not want to overwhelm you. It is true Christian article, which neither the Jews nor the papists nor the sectarians believe. For he who believes that he will be saved by his own works and not through Christ [does not believe that Christ is his Lord]. This belongs to the regular preaching.[19]

In these two parts we have heard what we have received from the Father and from the Son, namely, from the Father creation, from the Son redemption.

---

[19] Cf. Large Catechism, Part II, par. 32; WA 30^I, 187.

"I believe in the Holy Ghost"

The third article is about the Holy Spirit, who is one God with the Father and the Son. His office is to make holy or to vivify. Here again one must understand the words, "Holy Spirit," what "Holy Spirit" means, for there is the human spirit, evil spirits, and the Holy Spirit. Here he is called the "Holy Spirit." Why is he so called? Because he sanctifies. And therefore I believe in the Holy Spirit, because he has sanctified me and still sanctifies me. How does this happen? In this way; just as the Son accepts and receives his lordship through his death, so the Holy Spirit sanctifies through the following parts. In the first place he has led you into the holy, catholic church and placed you in the bosom of the church. But in that church he preserves [you] and through it he preaches and brings you [to Christ] through the Word. Christ gained his lordship through death; but how do I come to it? If [his] work remains hidden, then it is lost. So, in order that Christ's death and resurrection may not remain hidden, the Holy Spirit comes and preaches, that is, the Holy Spirit leads you to the Lord, who redeems you. So if I ask you: What does this article mean? answer: I believe that the Holy Spirit sanctifies me. So, as the Father is my creator and Christ is my Lord, so the Holy Spirit is my sanctifier. For he sanctifies me through the following works: through "the forgiveness of sins, the resurrection of the body, and the life everlasting."

The Christian church is your mother, who gives birth to you and bears you through the Word. And this is done by the Holy Spirit who bears witness concerning Christ. Under the papacy nobody preached that Christ is my Lord in the sense that I would be saved without my works. There it was an evil and human spirit that was preaching. That spirit preaches Christ, it is true, but along with it, preaches works, that through them a man is saved. The Holy Spirit, however, sanctifies by leading you into the holy church and proclaiming to you the Word which the Christian church proclaims.

"The communion of saints." This is of one piece with the preceding. Formerly it was not in the Creed.[20] When you hear the word "church" understand that it means group [Haufe], as we say

---

[20] Cf. Large Catechism, Part II, par. 47-49; WA 30I, 189.

in German, the Wittenberg group or congregation [*Gemeine*], that is, a holy, Christian group, assembly, or, in German, the holy, common church,[21] and it is a word which should not be called "communion" [*Gemeinschaft*], but rather "a congregation" [*eine Gemeine*]. Someone wanted to explain the first term, "catholic church" [and added the words] *communio sanctorum*, which in German means a congregation of saints, that is, a congregation made up only of saints. "Christian church" and "congregation of saints" are one and the same thing. In other words: I believe that there is a holy group and a congregation made up only of saints. And you too are in this church; the Holy Spirit leads you into it through the preaching of the gospel. Formerly you knew nothing of Christ, but the Christian church proclaimed Christ to you. That is, I believe that there is a holy church [*sanctam Christianitatem*], which is a congregation in which there are nothing but saints. Through the Christian church, that is, through its ministry [*officium*], you were sanctified; for the Holy Spirit uses its ministry in order to sanctify you. Otherwise you would never know and hear Christ.

Then, in this Christian church, you have "the forgiveness of sins." This term includes baptism, consolation upon a deathbed, the sacrament of the altar, absolution, and all the comforting passages [of the gospel]. In this term are included all the ministrations through which the church forgives sins, especially where the gospel, not laws or traditions, is preached. Outside of this church and these sacraments and [ministrations] there is no sanctification. The clerics[22] are outside the church, because they want to be saved through their works. Here we would need to preach about these individually.

The third point is that the Holy Spirit will sanctify you through "the resurrection of the flesh."[23] As long as we live here [on earth] we continue to pray, "Forgive us our trespasses, as we forgive those

---

[21] *Christenheit*. On the question of these terms, cf. notes in *The Papacy at Rome*, PE 1, 337-393; *On the Councils and the Churches*, PE 5, 264-265; and the Large Catechism, Part II, par. 47-52; WA 30^I, 189-190.

[22] *Clerici*, the spiritual estate, priests, monks, friars, etc. Cf. *The Papacy at Rome*, PE 1, 354.

[23] The German version of the Creed employs "flesh" insteady of "body."

who trespass against us"; but after death sin will have completely passed away and then the Holy Spirit will complete his work and then my sanctification will be complete. Therefore it will also be life and nothing but life.

This is a brief explanation of the third article, but for you it is obscure, because you do not listen to it. The third article, therefore, is that I believe in the Holy Spirit, that is, that the Holy Spirit will sanctify me and is sanctifying me. Therefore, from the Father I receive creation, from the Son redemption, from the Holy Spirit sanctification. How does he sanctify me? By causing me to believe that there is one, holy church through which he sanctifies me, through which the Holy Spirit speaks and causes the preachers to preach the gospel. The same he gives to you in your heart through the sacraments, that you may believe the Word and become a member of the church. He begins to sanctify now; when we have died, he will complete this sanctification through both "the resurrection of the body" and "the life everlasting." When we [Germans] hear the word "flesh," we immediately think that what is being spoken of is flesh in a meat market. What the Hebrews called "flesh," we call "body"; hence, I believe that our body will rise from death and thus live eternally. Then we will be interred and buried "in dishonor," as I Cor. 15 [:43] says, but will be raised "in glory."

These latter clauses show the ways in which he sanctifies me, for the Holy Spirit does not justify you outside of the church, as the fanatics, who creep into corners, think. Therefore immediately after the Holy Spirit is placed the Christian church, in which all his gifts are to be found. Through it he preaches, calls you and makes Christ known to you, and breathes into you the faith that, through the sacraments and God's Word, you will be made free from sin and thus be totally free on earth. When you die, remaining in the church, then he will raise you up and sanctify you wholly. The apostles called him the Holy Spirit because he makes everything holy and does everything in Christendom and through the church. On the other hand, an evil spirit does the opposite. The creation we have had long since and Christ has fulfilled his office; but the Holy Spirit is still at work, because the forgiveness of sins is still not fully accomplished. We are not yet freed from death, but will be after the resurrection of the flesh.

I believe in God, that he is my creator, in Jesus Christ, that he is my Lord, in the Holy Spirit, that he is my sanctifier. God has created me and given me life, soul, body, and all goods; Christ has brought me into his lordship through his body; and the Holy Spirit sanctifies me through his Word and the sacraments, which are in the church, and will sanctify us wholly on the last day. This teaching is different from that of the commandments. The commandments teach what we should do, but the Creed teaches what we have received from God. The Creed, therefore, gives that which you need. This is the Christian faith: to know what you must do and what has been given to you.

On Prayer and the First Three Petitions

of the Lord's Prayer

You have heard the Ten Commandments explained in the most simple way as what you must do and not do, and the Creed as what you should expect and receive from God. The Father gives his gifts by creation, the Son by redemption, the Holy Spirit by sanctification, as you have heard.

Now we must also take up the Lord's Prayer. In the first place necessity itself requires that we not only admonish you to pray but also teach you to pray. You should pray and you should know that you are bound to pray by divine command. For the second commandment teaches that you shall not swear, curse, or conjure, but call upon the name of God in every time of need, pray, praise, and exalt him; hence that it is commanded that we pray. Let no one think: If I do not pray, someone else will. You have been commanded to give honor to God's Name, to call upon him, and pray to him, and this is just as much a command as the other commandments, "You shall not kill," and so on. But you say: My prayer is nothing, and we get into such habits that it is thought that we do not teach that men should pray. But this is true: the prayers in the

Hortulus animae[24] and other prayer books were not prayers. This [i.e., the recitation of prayers] is suitable for young children, in order that they may learn and become accustomed to read and pray from a script. Therefore this is not praying, but droning and howling. But praying is rather what the second commandment says: Do not curse, swear, conjure, but call upon my name in every time of need. This is what God demands of you and it is not a matter of choice whether you do it or not; you must do it. Therefore, my beloved, I point it out to you, that you may know that prayer is required in the second commandment. And here you must repel such thoughts as: What does my prayer matter? This is just the same as if a son were to say to his father: What does it matter whether I am obedient or not? No, indeed, you must obey. That's why we are so barbarous; it is because we do not pray. We preach, however, that we should pray. By no means do I reject prayer, but only the abuse of prayer. It is true that Christ in Matt. 6 [:5] rejects useless and heathenish prayers, but elsewhere he commands that we should pray without ceasing. So you must not say that Christ has rejected prayer. He did reject prayers, but only those stupid prayers; on the contrary, he taught the true prayers.

Therefore, since it is commanded that we pray, do not despise prayer and take refuge behind your own unworthiness. Take an example from other commands. A work which I do is a work of obedience. Because my father, master, or prince has commanded it, I must do it, not because of my worthiness, but because it has been commanded. So it is also with prayer. So, when you pray for wife or children or parents or the magistrates, this is what you should think: This work I have been commanded to do and as an obedient person I must do it. On my account it would be nothing, but on account of the commandment it is a precious thing. So you should pray for the prince, the city, the burgomaster, and so on. Therefore I admonish you most faithfully, do not despise your prayers! But do not pray as the clerics do, who merely pray at a venture and think: I am not holy enough and fit enough to be heard. Or: If I were as holy as Peter and Paul I would pray too! You must rather say: The commandment which applied to St. Peter applies

---

[24] *Hortulus animae (Garden of the Soul)*, a widely used title of medieval prayer books. Cf. WA 30I, 47.

to me also, and Peter's prayer was no more holy than mine, for I have been given the same second commandment as he. Therefore my prayer is just as holy and precious as St. Peter's. Your prayer is not one cent less valuable than St. Peter's. And this is the reason: I will grant that he is holier as far as his person is concerned, but the commandment and obedience upon which St. Peter based his prayer I base my own also.

You have needs enough: You are lacking in faith, in love, in patience, in gentleness, in chastity; my wife, my children are sick. Then pray undauntedly and with sure confidence, because God has commanded you to pray. He did not command it in order to deceive you and make a fool, a monkey of you; he wants you to pray and to be confident that you will be heard; he wants you to open your bosom that he may give to you. So open up your coat and skirt wide and receive God's gifts for which you pray in your prayer. It would be a shame if he were to have to accept from you. The monks want to give something to God. Therefore, you should say: Lord, thou hast commanded that I should pray; if I do not pray and ask of thee what I need, I am damned. But do not pray the Lord's Prayer as the vulgar people do, as the vigils,[25] the seven canonical hours,[26] the *Deus in adjutorium*[27] are prayed. This is nothing, and if all the monasteries and foundations were put together in one heap, they still would not pray for so much as a drop of wine. But you must present your need to God, not the need of which you are not aware, but in order that you may learn to know yourself, where you are lacking, and to receive more and more the longer you hold open your sack.

Therefore, children right from the cradle on should begin to pray for the princes, for their brethren and companions. For here you hear the command and the promise: "Ask, and it will be given you; seek and you will find; knock, and it will be opened to you" [Matt. 7:7]. You have been commanded to pray and promised that what you pray for will be given, as in [Ps. 50:15], "Call upon me in the day of trouble; I will deliver you, and you shall glorify me";

---

[25] Wakes for the dead.
[26] The daily prayers of the clergy, fixed by canon.
[27] Ps. 70:1, "O Lord, make haste to help me"; which occurs repeatedly in the breviary.

and [Ps. 91:15], "When he calls to me, I will answer him." So, go on that and say: Now I know that my prayer is not to be despised; for if I despise it, I despise the command and the promise of God. But God does not despise prayer, but rather has commanded it and promised that he will hear it. Why then should I despise it? But we live like the wild beasts who do not pray.

Let this be said as an introduction and admonition to prayer, for all our protection lies in prayer. We are too weak to withstand the princes, the kings, the world, and the devil; they are much greater and more powerful than we. Therefore we must resort to Christian weapons and say: "Hallowed be thy name." Then Christ says: So shall it be! If the prayer of devout people had not accomplished it, Münzer[28] would probably not have been put down and the princes would now be raging in a different way. It was two or three Christians who prayed in earnestness and faith: "Thy will be done!" And Christ said: So shall it be. But if you do not know and you ask what or how you should pray, then listen to Christ, who enumerates seven successive petitions. Therefore, you must not plead that you feel no need. Look behind yourself for what makes you angry and remiss. Here he has combined all the needs which cause us to cry out to him. Therefore it is not only commanded that we pray, but promised that we shall be heard. And then also what and how we are to pray is prescribed as in a table. Therefore there is no doubt that our prayer will please God. The first need which ought to impel us to pray and call upon the name of God is [expressed in the words]:

"Hallowed be thy name"

This manner of speaking is unfamiliar to us [i.e., not in good German idiom], and it is the equivalent of: O dear Father, may thy name be holy! But what does this mean? Is it not already holy? It is holy in its nature, but not in our use. God's name has been given to us. By what means? We have been baptized in his name, we have the Word which makes us God's children, we have his sacraments, which unite us with him. He has implanted his name, Word,

---

[28] Thomas Münzer, a religious radical who was beheaded in 1525 for his leading role in the Peasants' War.

and sacrament among us. Therefore it is of the highest necessity that we pray to our Father. I will gladly endure poverty and sickness if only the heavenly Father has his glory, and I will gladly suffer want if this were to be the result, namely, that the name of God, which is altogether holy in heaven, would also be precious and holy among us.

What, then, does it mean to hallow the name of God? This: when our teaching and life are Christian and godly. The purpose of the second commandment is to cause us not to curse, swear, and lead people astray, as the sectarians do, but rather to praise and call upon this name. Those who misuse the name of God for deceiving and lying profane and desecrate the name of God, just as it used to be said that churches were desecrated when a fight had taken place in them. God's name is hallowed, therefore, when one calls upon him, prays, praises, and magnifies him, preaches about the Lord, that he is merciful and helps us in peril and otherwise. Therefore the first petition in the Lord's Prayer is explained by the second commandment. In short, when one teaches and lives Christianly, that is, when one does not curse, swear, and so on.

This is the first need which ought to move us to prayer. For in the world there are so many sectarians, all of whom impose upon and deceive the people by using this name, preach the Word of God falsely and say that what they preach is the name and the Word of God. Therefore, in this petition you pray against all who preach, teach, and believe falsely, against the pope and all sectarians, against the tyrants who persecute the Word of God by violence, and against those who lie, deceive, revile, and curse against us, who so coolly listen [to the Word of God]. God's name is never sufficiently praised and preached. Therefore, [we pray]: Let thy name become holy, that is, that the whole world may not curse and swear by thy name, but rather pray and call upon thee according to the second commandment. In short, grant that we may teach and live Christianly.

This is purely Hebrew speech; we are not accustomed to the language; but we must preach about it in order that you may learn it and become accustomed to it. The first petition is that God's name be honored, that his name never be put to shame by us either in teaching or in life.

"Thy kingdom come"

The second need which drives us to prayer is that we pray that God's kingdom may come. This, too, is somewhat Hebraically expressed, but it is not so obscure as the first petition which means: Grant that the world may not lie and deceive by thy name, nor curse and conjure, which is shame and dishonor to thy name, but rather that we may proclaim and praise [thy name]. The second petition is: "thy kingdom come." You must learn to understand the word "kingdom," what is the Father's kingdom, God's kingdom, the kingdom of heaven. Just as the name of God is holy in itself and we still must pray that it may be holy among us, so the kingdom of God comes, whether we pray or not. But we should pray, in order that I too may be a part of those in whom the name of God is hallowed, that God's kingdom may come also to me and his will be done in me. Christ is the king of righteousness and life against the devil, sin, death, and all evil conscience. He has given us his holy Word, that it may be preached, in order that we might believe in him and live holy lives. Therefore we must pray that this may become effective and powerful, that the Word may go out into the world with power, that many may come into this kingdom and learn to believe and thus become partakers of redemption from death, sin, and hell. The first petition is that God's name be not blasphemed, but rather [honored]. The second is that this may also bear fruit, that his name be so hallowed that his kingdom will come in us and we become members of his kingdom. But God's kingdom comes to us in two ways: first, here, through the Word, and secondly, in that the future, eternal life is given to us. This is a strong petition when it is expressed in German: Dear Father, grant thy pure Word, that it may be purely preached throughout the world, and then grant grace and power that it may also be accepted and the people believe. The first concerns the Word and the second the fruit of the Word. For, if the Word is preached but not accepted, the kingdom of God does not come. It is an obscure prayer because it is so Hebraically expressed. These are the two greatest needs. Here on [earth] God's kingdom comes through the beginning of faith and there [in eternity] through the revelation of eternal life. These are the two greatest petitions of this prayer, both of which are comprehended [in Christ's saying:] "Seek first his kingdom" (Matt. 6:33). Here we pray that his name and kingdom may remain with us.

"Thy will be done"

When you pray this petition you must look askance at a gang, which is called the devil and his mates, who would hinder the kingdom of God. For the father of a household should not only support his own but also defend them. And so it is here; even if we already prayed the first two greatest petitions, the devil nevertheless cannot endure that the Word should be preached and people accept it. Here he has his poisoned arrows: he has the opposing world and our flesh, which is lazy. The will of the pope, the emperor, the princes, the devil, and our flesh prevents the will of God from being done. What we pray is: Dear Father, defend us from the devil and his cohorts and from our lazy flesh which would hinder thy will, and grant grace that thy gospel may go forth unhindered. Thus we are shown in these three petitions our need with regard to God, but in such a way that it redounds to our benefit. God's name is not only hallowed in itself, but in me. Likewise, God's kingdom not only comes of itself and his will is done not only of itself, but rather in order that God's kingdom may come in me, that God's will may be done in me, and his name be hallowed in me. In German, the first [petitions would be:] O Lord, grant grace that the gospel may be purely preached; let thy name be hallowed in us through thy Word; let thy Word be proclaimed to us. The second [petition:] Grant grace that we may diligently accept it, that it bring power to us, and that the people may sincerely adhere to it. The third: Restrain, O Father, all tyrants, devils, all those who would hinder and oppose it and let only thy will be done. In this petition the Christians are our wall and destroy all the counsels of the adversaries. This prayer demolishes the devices of all the tyrants who say, This is the way we will do it: our will must be done! We will shoot down Wittenberg, we will destroy the heretics! But we say one little petition: Dear Father, thy will be done! That is, Say to them, that not their, but thy will be done! Then whatever our enemies counsel will not prevail. But our will too must be broken;

otherwise God's name will not be hallowed in us and his kingdom will not come to us.

Today we see the whole world raging against the gospel, and even many among us do not have the gospel. Therefore the name of the Father is constantly being profaned. This should move us Christians. When you feel that your own flesh, your slothfulness, avarice, fornication, and passion is hindering you, then say: "Thy will be done!"

Let this be sufficient for this time on these first three petitions.

The Fourth, Fifth, Sixth and Seventh Petitions

Thus far you have heard the first three petitions.[29] This is Hebrew speech, to which we are not accustomed. The matters of which the petitions speak are hidden from reason. Christ therefore commanded that they be preached, because he knows that we do not know them. The first [petition is:] God's name is holy in itself, but we pray that it may be hallowed in us and in the whole world and that the Word and the honor of God may be kept holy against all fanatics and blasphemers of his name. This is done when his name and his honor is in our teaching and life. The second: His kingdom comes when his Word increases and is powerful among us. In short, when we have God's power, which begins here through the Word and then becomes an actuality when we are buried. The third: That all those be restrained who oppose the name and kingdom of God, for Satan assails all its members. Will of God, John 6 [:38-40].

The fourth: "Give us this day our daily bread." This is beginning to be understood, though there are few who do understand it. When you pray this petition turn your eyes to everything that can prevent our bread from coming and the crops from prospering. Therefore extend your thoughts to all the fields and do not see only

---

[29] The text reads *praecepta*, commandments.

the baker's oven. You pray, therefore, against the devil and the world, who can hinder the grain by tempest and war. We pray also for temporal peace against war, because in times of war we cannot have bread. Likewise, you pray for government, for sustenance and peace, without which you cannot eat: Grant, Lord, that the grain may prosper, that the princes may keep the peace, that war may not break out, that we may give thanks to thee in peace. Therefore it would be proper to stamp the emperor's or the princes' coat-of-arms upon bread as well as upon money or coins.[30] Few know that this is included in the Lord's Prayer. Though the Lord gives bread in sufficient abundance even to the wicked and godless, it is nevertheless fitting that we Christians should know and acknowledge that it comes from God, that we realize that bread, hunger, and war are in God's hands. If he opens his hand, we have bread and all things in abundance; if he closes it, then it is the opposite. Therefore, do not think that peace is an accidental thing; it is the gift of God.

This petition, therefore, is directed against everything that hinders bread, including also base coinage. It is not well with the man who has lost the common prayers.[31] Beware of this, but even more if it[32] is against you. It is the greatest of losses if you are cut off from the church and no longer a member, of it and besides, have the prayers of the church against you. Therefore, he who hinders bread and injures the people, let him be afraid of this petition. Thus it is a petition against tempest, war, false buyers and sellers; against all of these this prayer cries out. Do not be afraid of the rich people; Duke Hans gets enough to eat from them;[33] but fear the groans and tears of those who pray: "Give us this day our daily bread," i.e., defend us from famine and evil men, that they may not deprive us of bread.

Bread cannot come to me if there is no peace, so that there are just prices in the market, so that there is no bloodshed. Defend us from skinners and usurers! [The explanation of] "daily" and "this

---

[30] The opposite is suggested in the Large Catechism: "Therefore it would be very proper to place in the coat-of-arms of every pious prince the figure of a loaf of bread, etc. Cf. WA 30I, 204.

[31] One who is not included in the intercessions of the church.

[32] The prayer of the church.

[33] Elector John of Saxony, in consequence of the usurious practices of the rich, suffers no want.

day" belongs in the sharp sermons.[34] The Lord does indeed give bread, but he also wants us to pray, in order that we acknowledge it as his gift. This again is a great need, which pertains to the body.

"Forgive us our debts, as we also have forgiven our debtors"

In the fourth petition you pray against that need which the poor body has for bread, which it cannot get along without. It includes every peril which may hinder bread from coming to us. Now comes our life, which we cannot lead without sinning. Here is the greatest need of all, and we pray: "Forgive us our debts." Not that he does not give it without our prayer, for he has given us baptism, and in his kingdom there is nothing but forgiveness of sins. But it is to be done in order that we may acknowledge it. For the flesh is anxious for the belly and has evil lusts and loves, hatred, anger, envy, and wicked whims, so that we sin daily in words, deeds, and thoughts, in what we do and fail to do. No one does what he should do. So we get stuck in the mire of being proud and thinking that we are thoroughly holy people. Therefore he says here: None of you is good. All of you, no matter how holy and great you are, must say: "Forgive us our debts." Therefore one must pray God to give us a conscience unafraid, which is assured that its sins are forgiven.

Anyone, therefore, who has a burdened and sorrowful conscience prays here for grace and forgiveness of sins, that is, for the strength of the name, the kingdom, and the will of God. This petition therefore serves those who are conscious of their sins. May everyone acknowledge the need which he feels! I do not do enough in my office of preaching. You, burgomaster, captain, prince, husband, wife, you do not do enough in your office either. I do not do enough for my neighbor. Therefore we must pray daily for forgiveness of sins.

"As we also have forgiven our debtors." God has promised the forgiveness of sins. Of that you must be certain and sure, in so far as you [also forgive your neighbor]. If you have someone whom you do not forgive, you pray in vain. Therefore let each one look to his neighbor, if he has been offended by him, and forgive him from the heart; then he will be certain that his sin too has been forgiven. Not

---

[34] Sermons in which greed and anxiousness for the morrow are attacked.

that you are forgiven on account of your forgiveness, but freely, without your forgiveness, your sins are forgiven. He, however, enjoins it upon you as a sign, that you may be assured that, if you forgive, you too will be forgiven.

There you have them both, the promise and the sign, that your heart may rejoice, if you can produce the sign and forgive your enemy. You must seek the sign. If you do not find it here, do you think you will find it in far-away St. James?[35] What are all the letters of indulgence[36] compared with this petition in the Lord's Prayer? Here is where indulgence should be preached. Here God promises forgiveness of sins and stamps the seal upon it. He does not say: Put five pennies in the poor-box, but only: Forgive the other person. If he will not accept it, let him go, as long as your heart is at peace. This is the way to look at all prayers. Don't mutter like the clerics, "Forgive us our sins," but pray with sure confidence, for he has added this seal in order that you may be certain.

"And lead us not into temptation"

"Into evil enticement."[37] This is very fine old German.[38] We say "trial," "temptation" [Anfechtung, Versuchung]. Here we need to know what these words mean. Sins cling [to us]. The first temptation is that of the flesh, which says: Go ahead and have illicit intercourse with another's wife, daughter, maid! That is Master Flesh [Junker Fleisch]. Or he says: I'm going to sell the grain, beer, or goods as dearly as I can. This is the temptation of the flesh. Here the greed of your flesh is seeking its own advantage. Then you should pray: Guard us, dear Lord, from temptation! Likewise, the flesh seeks to satisfy its lust in glutting, guzzling, and loafing.

Next is the world, which tempts you with envy, hatred, and pride. Your neighbor irritates you to anger when you are making a bargain and all of a sudden there is impatience, the nature of the world—up she goes, blow your top, and it's all off! Then one conforms to the world. These are worldly temptations. Therefore pray:

---

[35] St. James of Compostella, a famous shrine in Spain, much frequented by pilgrims seeking indulgences.

[36] Which were intended as signs of the forgiveness of sins.

[37] In his search for words in common usage, Luther here uses the term "böse Bekörung," evil allurement.

[38] In the Large Catechism (WA 30I, 208), Luther says, "as our Saxons called it from ancient times"; cf. also WA 30I, 16, 10 and 49, 26.

O Lord, bring it to pass that the flesh and the world shall not seduce me! Both of them, the flesh and the world, contribute much toward your feeling an inclination to spite and lechery and dislike for your neighbor. Against all this pray: "Lead us not into temptation." Dear Father, let me not fall into this or other temptations.

The third companion and tempter is Master Devil [*Junker Teufel*]. He tempts you by causing you to disregard God's Word: Oh, I have to look after the beer and malt, I can't go to hear a sermon; or if you do come to church to hear the sermon you go to sleep, you don't take it in, you have no delight, no love, no reverence for the Word. Then pray that you may not despise it! Then, too, it is Satan's temptation when you are assailed by unbelief, diffidence, by fanatics, superstition, witchcraft, and the like. When you feel such temptations, go running to the Lord's Prayer! You have the promise that God will deliver you from the temptation of the flesh, the world, and the devil. Our whole life is nothing but temptation by these three, the flesh, the world, the devil. Therefore pray: Father, let not our flesh seduce us, let not the world deceive us, let not the devil cast us down. Thus these six petitions deal with very great matters and needs. Whatever needs are in the world, they are included in the Lord's Prayer. And all the prayers in the Psalms and all the prayers which could ever be devised are in the Lord's Prayer.

"But deliver us from evil"

In the Greek it is *ponēros*.[39] We receive evil from everything which hurts us. It's whole meaning points to the devil. We can sum it up this way: Deliver us from the wicked devil, who hinders everything we have previously been talking about; from that wicked one, evil one, deliver us! Nevertheless, you must include in this "evil" everything on earth which is evil, such as sickness, poverty, death, whatever evil there is in the dominion of Satan, of which there is very much on earth. For who can count all the evils? A child becomes sick, and so forth. In short: Deliver us from the devil! Then the name of God will be hallowed, his kingdom come, and his will be done, and we shall be delivered from all things.

---

[39] Luther means to say that the correct reading is "Deliver us from the evil one," masculine (*ponēros*), not neuter (*ponēron*).

First, we are commanded to pray; second, the promise [is given]; third, there are so many and such great needs, which ought to drive us to prayer. And finally, a form and way to pray has been prescribed for us.

Prayer, then, requires first that one lay before God the needs or perils, all of which are included in the Lord's Prayer. The first three petitions deal with the most important matters of all. We do not pray the petitions like clods, who pay no heed to the magnitude of the things we pray for, who seek only food for the belly, gold, and so forth, not caring about how we may become good, how we may have the pure Word and live holy lives, not caring that the will of God is hindered by the devil, who throws himself athwart to prevent its being done. We pray, therefore, that he trample the devil under foot and subject us to himself. Likewise there is great need to pray for the bread we eat, for grain, cattle, and the like, and for all that we have, in order that we may know that all this comes to us from God. But we are always falling down and hence we have a bad conscience; therefore we pray: "Forgive us our trespasses." In these seven petitions are found all our anxieties, needs, and perils, which we ought to bring to God. They are great petitions, indeed, but God, who wills to do great things, is greater. Therefore, let us learn to pray well since God wants us to do this. Then we shall experience the power of God, through which he is able to give us great things, to make us good, to keep the Word, to give us a holy life and all else. He allows such manifold perils to come upon us in order that we may learn to pray and experience his help in our great evils. This is our great consolation.

There you have, then, the three parts, which you children and you other simple folk should learn. First, the Ten Commandments, what I should do and what I should not do. Second, what kind of a God our God is, what is his name and his nature. Third, how we are to get it [his help]. These three parts the holy apostles and fathers put together in order that they should be known by all in common. And yet there is nothing in the Creed about the sacraments, nothing about secular power, about the office of bishops, and so on. It should be an *institutio*, that is, an instruction for the children and simple Christians. What is to be taught beyond this simple instruction, this is the responsibility of the preachers, who rule Christendom, in order that they may defend and uphold the church. When you know these three parts, you still do not have an adequate defense; for you do not know the reasons why this or another article is true. A preacher, however, must be instructed in the Word of God in order that he may be able to defend the church. Therefore, we do not say that everything that Christianity must know is included in these three parts. But there is enough there for the sucklings until they grow up. There are others in the state who educate children, others go off to war. Some have food and drink, others bear arms. So it is here, when these three parts are preached, we have only taught the catechism. Later, when they are grown up, we will preach to them on how to fight. A mother does not immediately give wine, bread, and meat to her child, but milk.

Next we shall deal with the two sacraments. The catechism was the teaching by which one prepared the people for receiving the sacrament [of the altar].

On Baptism

You have heard the three parts, which we call the catechism [Kinderlehre] or common Christian teaching, set forth as simply and plainly as I can. On the two following days we shall deal with the two sacraments, which also belong here. For every Christian ought also to know these two sacraments.

Baptism is recorded in the last chapter of Mark: "Go into all the world and preach the gospel to the whole creation. He who believes and is baptized will be saved; but he who does not believe will be condemned" (Mark 16:15-16). Even if a person is baptized but is without faith, he is lost. But we shall at this time omit discussion of that which serves us in disputation and controversy with the adversaries. In connection with baptism the words themselves, which are recorded here, must be understood. These every person must know. In the first place, note the command of God, which is very stern when he says: "He who believes and is baptized will be saved; but he who does not believe will be condemned" (Mark 16:16). This is a strict command; if a person wants to be saved, let him be baptized; otherwise he is in God's disfavor. Therefore, these words are in the first place a strict, earnest divine command. Hence you cannot hold the opinion that baptism is a human invention or any kind of command or thing, such as putting a wreath on one's head; it is God's command. Consequently, you must esteem baptism as something high, glorious, and excellent; for here there is a divine word and command, which institutes and confirms baptism. If in former times you considered it a splendid and precious thing when the establishment of an altar was confirmed by a letter of the pope, then esteem baptism a thousand times more since it is instituted and ordained by God. If you look upon baptism as being only water, then you will consider it to be a paltry and ordinary thing.

Therefore, if you are asked what baptism is, you should not answer, as the fanatics do, that it is a handful of water, which is no good, that the Spirit, the Spirit must do it; the bathhouse servant, the minister, that is, effects nothing; therefore the Spirit should be present. But you should say: Baptism is water comprehended and sanctified in God's commandment and Word, that is, a divine and holy water because of God's commandment. The fanatics, the scoundrels rip off God's Word. If I skin a cow, it isn't worth much; but if I take the meat with the hide, it is worth four guldens. Therefore say that baptism is a living, saving water on account of the Word of God which is in it. The Word of God, however, is greater than heaven and earth, sun, moon, and all angels. Don't look at the water, and see that it is wet, but rather that it has with it the Word of God. It is a holy, living, heavenly, blessed water because of the Word and command of God, which is holy. You cannot sufficiently extol it; who can ever sufficiently extol God's Word? And all this comes in baptism because God's Word is in baptism. This is the way I also speak of parents and neighbors. If I look at a father, seeing only that he has a nose, that he is flesh and blood, with bones, limbs, skin and hair, or likewise a mother, if I do not look upon her otherwise than that, I am not seeing her at all, but trampling her under foot. But when the fourth commandment is added, then I see them adorned with a glorious crown and golden chain, which is the

Word of God. And that shows you why you should honor this flesh and blood of your parents for the sake of God's Word. This the fanatics do not consider, nor can they do it, because they abominate the Word. The round halo which is painted around the heads of saints is around the heads of parents too. The golden halo or diadem came from the heathen. Later it became a garland, then flowers were added, and now it has become the bishop's mitre. This Word of power is painted around the heads of parents as a diadem, just as if the majesty and the Word of God were painted about their heads.

So it is with baptism. Certainly when the devil sees baptism and hears the Word sounding, to him it is like a bright sun and he will not stay there, and when a person is baptized for the sake of the Word of God, which is in it, there is a veritable oven glow. Do you think it was a joke that the heavens were opened at Christ's baptism? [Matt. 3:16]. Say, therefore, that baptism is water and God's Word comprehended in one. Take the Word away and it is the same water with which the maid waters the cow; but with the Word, it is a living, holy, divine water. He who considers the words: "will be saved" (Mark 16:16) will find it [salvation]; for with his words, "will be saved," Christ puts salvation into baptism. Therefore it is impossible that this should be simple water when through it salvation, forgiveness of sins, and redemption from death and the devil is given.

But nobody believes what an excellent thing is in these words. The fanatics laugh at us and say: You neo-papists teach the people to trust in water. But when I ask them: What do you say about these words, "He who believes and is baptized will be saved"? they flutter away. So you say to them: We do not teach that one should trust in water, but we do teach that the water, when it becomes one thing with God's Word, is baptism. The water does not do it because of itself, but rather because of the Word, which is connected with it. But if you take away the Word, then don't go telling us that baptism is useless water. Then it is a figment of the devil, who is seeking to sow bad seed among us. You hear your Savior say: If you believe and are baptized, then salvation follows, not because of the water, but because you believe the Word. It is not for nothing that I insist so emphatically that you say that baptism is natural, physical water connected with the Word of God. When these two come together, water and the Word of God, then it is a baptism.

But, you say, can water benefit me? No. What then? Baptism. But isn't it water? No; for it is water connected with the Word of God; therefore it must be something other than water. That's why we declare that the water amounts to nothing, but baptism does. Therefore baptism is water with the Word of God, and this is the essence and whole substance of baptism. When, therefore, water and God's Word are conjoined, it must necessarily be a holy and divine water, for as the Word is, so the water becomes also.

Furthermore, the benefit of baptism must also be learned. If baptism is water with the Word of God, what is its purpose, work, fruit, and benefit? It saves those who believe, as the words say. A child is baptized, not in order that it may become a prince; it is baptized in order that it may be saved, as the words say, that is, in order that it may be redeemed from sin, death, and the devil, that it may become a member of Christ, and that it may come into Christ's kingdom and Christ become its Lord. Accordingly, baptism is useful to the end that through it we may be saved. There you have the transcendent excellence of baptism. The first honor is that it is a divine water, and when you see a baptism remember that the heavens are opened. The fruit is that it saves, redeems you from sin, liberates you from the devil, and leads you to Christ. The fanatics insist that one must first become holy. But I am not contending with them now, but teaching the simple.

Thirdly, that we may know the person who should be baptized: Who should receive baptism? The one who believes is the person to whom the blessed, divine water is to be imparted. If you believe that through this water you will be saved, it becomes a fact. The first point, therefore, is that baptism is water connected with God's Word. The second is the fruit, and the third is that the person who believes is the one who is worthy of baptism. Here some excellent things might be said; but you simple people, note these three points! The little word "believe" leaves no room for either works or monks' cowls. It does not say: he who obeys his parents, but: he who believes.

Here we meet the question whether children who are baptized believe? He who is simple, let him dismiss these questions and refer them to me or answer this way: I know that infant baptism pleases God; I know that I was baptized as a child; I know that I have the Holy Spirit, for this I have the interpretation of the Scriptures themselves. If the baptism of children were nothing, then certainly there would not be a single person on earth who would truly speak a single word about Christ [i.e., a Christian]. But since Christ most certainly bestows the Holy Spirit [and thus confirms baptism], for Bernard, Bonaventura, Gerson, and John Huss had the Spirit, because this is God's work, believe therefore that infant baptism is true. How do you know this? I see the wonderful works of God, I see that he has sanctified many and given them the Holy Spirit. Therefore you tell [the adversaries] that children are truly baptized and say: I prove it by the works [of God]. It is known by its fruit; if there is fruit, there must be a tree. Furthermore, for me the Word of God weighs a thousand times more, etc.[40] But this becomes a bit more learned.[41]

Note well, therefore, that baptism is water with the Word of God, not water and my faith. My faith does not make the baptism but rather receives the baptism, no matter whether the person being baptized believes or not; for baptism is not dependent upon my faith but upon God's Word. If today a Jew were to be baptized, who was seeking only the sponsor's christening gift,[42] and we baptized him nevertheless, the baptism would be genuine, for it is God's Word with water. And even though the Jew did not believe, the baptism would nevertheless not be false. Likewise, if I administer the sacrament to someone who cherishes anger or the like, he nevertheless receives the true body [and the true blood of Christ]. Therefore it is false to say that infants do not believe and therefore should not be baptized. You have already heard that they do believe, because the fruits follow, namely, the gifts of the Holy Spirit. The sacrament [of the Lord's Supper] does not rest upon faith but upon the Word of God, who instituted it, and so it is with baptism also. Even if the children did not believe which, however, is false, the baptism is not to be repeated. Therefore you should say: The baptism was genuine, but I, unfortunately, did not believe it.

---

[40] This sentence may probably be completed thus: than the thoughts of reason.
[41] *Das ist ein wenig scherffer*, i.e., too advanced for a sermon addressed to children. Cf. Large Catechism (WA 30I, 218; 132).
[42] *baten gelt, Paten Geld.*

These are crude spirits [i.e., the Anabaptists]. I am a learned man and a preacher and I go to the sacrament in the faith of others and in my own faith.[43] Nevertheless, I don't stand on that, I stand on [His words]: "Take; this is my body" [Mark 14:22]. Upon these words I go, and I know that Christ invites me, for he said, "Come to me, all who labor and are heavy-laden, and I will give you rest" [Matt. 11:28]; and this will not deceive me. Thus I certainly have the sacrament. Accordingly, I apply this to baptism and pray that faith may be given to it [the child]. But I do not baptize it upon its faith or someone else's faith, but upon God's Word and command. In my faith I may lie, but he who instituted baptism cannot lie. Therefore say: The children must necessarily be baptized, and their baptism is true, because God grants grace to children who are baptized immediately after their birth, namely, an excelling grace. Otherwise, if baptism were false, it would not manifest this [grace]. Secondly, even if the children did not believe, they must nevertheless not be rebaptized. You fanatics, you say that the earlier baptism was not genuine. This we by no means concede, for baptism is definitive, water with the Word. Therefore Augustine says, "The Word comes to the element, and it becomes a sacrament."[44]

These two sacraments may be received also by an unbeliever. Thus the devil would secretly teach us to build upon our works, and in order to accomplish this more easily he makes a sham of faith and says: If you do not believe then you are not baptized. But it simply does not follow that, if I do not obey my parents, therefore I have no parents; if I do not obey the government, therefore, the government is nothing. So it does not follow here: that person has not received baptism in faith, therefore, the baptism is nothing or is not genuine. Indeed, the baptism was genuine precisely because you did not rightly receive it. The abuse confirms the baptism; it does not deny it. If all of you here were to be baptized today and there were hardly three among you who were holy, the baptism would still not be false, but rather the contrary; for our work and misuse neither make nor unmake God's work. A prince remains a prince,

---

[43] *In aliena et mea fide.*
[44] *Lectures or Tractates on the Gospel According to St. John, op. cit.* Tractate 80, p. 344. Migne 35, 1839. Also cited by Luther in Smalcald Articles, Part. III, Art. V.

whether you are obedient or not. This the fanatics do not know, for they are blinded; that's why they look at the sacrament without the Word. There is rebellion concealed in this mind, because it always wants to separate God's Word from the person. It wants to tear down the Word; therefore it is a rebel, secretly.

The Lord's Supper

In the first place, every one of you should know the words with which this sacrament was instituted—for one should not administer the sacrament to those who do not know these words and what they do and perform. Here we are not going to enter into controversy with the blasphemers of this sacrament. You must deal with this sacrament in the same way that you heard with regard to baptism, namely, that the chief point is God's Word and command, just as in the Lord's Prayer, the Creed, and the Ten Commandments. Even though you never believe or keep the Ten Commandments, the Ten Commandments nevertheless exist and remain, and so baptism and the sacrament of the altar also remain baptism and the sacrament of the altar. Even though you never obey your parents, they still remain your parents.

Therefore, the primary thing in the sacrament is the Word: "Jesus took bread, etc." [Matt. 26:26-28]. If you believe it, blessed are you; if not, Christ will still remain faithful. When we die and are snatched away, these errors will come. Nobody wants to look upon it as God's Word; if one does not have regard for it, then it is nothing. In the sacraments, the Ten Commandments, and the Creed, God's Word is the chief thing. Therefore, do not look only upon the water, the bread and wine, but rather connect with them the words, "Take, eat"; "Do this in remembrance of me," and "Drink of it, all of you." Learn these words; in them the sacrament is summed up; if you have lost these words, you have lost the sacrament. The fanatics rip these words out, and the same goes for the pope, because he has concealed them. The Word of God is the chief thing in the sacrament. He who does not know them [the words of institution], let him not come to the sacrament.

Secondly: What is the sacrament of the altar? As baptism is water and God's Word conjoined, so it is here. Here the bread is not the kind of bread the baker bakes, nor is the wine the kind the vintner sells; for he does not give you God's Word with it. But the minister binds God's Word to the bread and the Word is bound to the bread and likewise to the wine, for it is said, "The Word comes to the element, and it becomes a sacrament."[45] In all his lifetime Augustine never said anything better. It is not the word of our prince or the emperor, but of God. Therefore, when you hear this word "is,"[46] then do not doubt. Thus the sacrament is bread and body, wine and blood, as the words say and to which they are connected. If, therefore, God speaks these words, then don't search any higher, but take off your hat; and if a hundred thousand devils, learned men, and spirits[47] were to come and say, How can this be?[48] you answer that one single word of God is worth more than all of these. A hundred thousand learned men are not as wise as one little hair of our God. In the first place, therefore, learn that the sacrament is not simply bread and wine, but the body and blood of Christ, as the words say. If you take away the words, you have only bread and wine. Hence the command of God is the greatest thing in the sacrament, as in the Lord's Prayer. Take hold only of the words; they tell you what the sacrament is. If a fornicator comes [to the table], he receives the true sacrament, because it does not lose power on account of his impiety and infidelity. Our unbelief does not alter God's Word. This I have often said. When a whore decks herself with gold, it is still gold. Misuse does not change God's Word. A robber abuses the light of day, the sun, and yet it remains the sun. Christ does not found his sacrament upon our use of it. What he says or ordains remains, no matter whether one uses it rightly or wrongly. The sacrament is body and blood, as the words say, whether it is received by one who is worthy or unworthy.

---

[45] Cf. p. 187 n. 44.
[46] In the words of institution.
[47] *Geister*, the allusion is to the spiritualist sectarians.
[48] I.e., how is it possible for the body to be under the bread?

What is the use or fruit of the sacrament? Listen to this: "given for you"; "shed." I go to the sacrament in order to take and use Christ's body and blood, given and shed for me. When the minister intones, "This cup is the New Testament in my blood," to whom is it sung? Not to my dog,[49] but to those who are gathered to take the sacrament. These words must be apprehended by faith. Therefore I use the sacrament for the forgiveness of my sins; I say: I will go and take the body and the blood; it is a sure sign that it was instituted for me and against my death. "Which is given for you." There is the benefit.

Now follows: Who are those who lay hold of this benefit? He who believes has baptism and he who does not believe does not have it. Likewise, he who believes that the body, which he receives, is given for him, has the fruit of this sacrament. Therefore, he who believes takes his rightful place at this sacrament. That's why I have said that these words are spoken, not to stones or a pillar, but to Christians. "For you." Who does "for you" mean? The door or the window, perhaps? No, those who today hear the words "for you." I am to believe it. If you believe, then you take the sacrament on the strength of these words "for you." Mark only those words! because the words "for you" make the devil more hostile to us. He says to us, My dear fellow, you must not believe this "for you." What is it to you? Drink at home and enjoy yourself! The sacrament doesn't concern you. It is this "you" that makes it our concern, just as in baptism: "He who believes and is baptized will be saved." So here it is: "for you." Therefore, note well and learn well these words! The benefit is: "given for you, shed for you." Why do you go to the sacrament? I go because it is a body and blood which is given and shed for me; that's why I go.

If the sacrament is rightly administered, one should preach, first, that the sacrament is the body and blood of the Lord under the bread and wine, as the words say. Secondly, the benefit: it effects the forgiveness of sins, as the words say, "which is shed for the remission of sins."

Beyond this I admonish you to prepare yourselves for it. Since it is the sacrament in which there is the forgiveness of sins, it is not to be despised. It is true that a large number of you come, and yet

---

[49] There is an untranslatable play on words here: *Cui canitur? Non cani meo.*

there are some among you who are so strong that they have not come once in five years. But you should go because you are the ones who need it most of all! And above all note these words, "for the remission of sins," as the pledge of the sacrament which assures us that we have the forgiveness of sins because it is proclaimed, not to a stone, but to you and to me. Otherwise the minister might as well keep silent. I remind you again of this small particle: "for you." Remember to include yourself in this "for you." Therefore let each one see to it that he comes to the sacrament himself and his family, if they want to be Christians. When you stay away so much, now that you have liberty to go to the sacrament, we see the attitude with which you came to it under the pope, when you came only by coercion. As only a few do good works, so only a few go to the sacrament. Formerly we were forced to go because we were driven. But now that nobody compels us we neglect it. I do not compel you to come to the preaching. But God ought to move you to come; for he requires it of you that you should hear and learn his Word. If you don't want to obey him, [then don't]. So neither do I compel you to come to the sacrament. What does it matter to me and the chaplains if you don't want to listen and receive the sacrament? You have four doors here—go on out! But he who is above says: If you want to be a Christian, if you want to have forgiveness of sins and eternal life, then come here! There stands your God; he offers you his body and blood, broken and shed for you. If you want to despise God and neglect the forgiveness of sins, then stay away. So I do not compel you, but Christ pleads with you lovingly. If you despise this, then you see to it! We are saying what your God is offering to you. Accordingly, I beg you to hold to the sacrament, for your sakes, not ours. There are now few boys and girls and women who come. I know that you are not holier than Peter. It really grieves me that you are so cold in your attitude toward it. If you will not do it for God's sake and my sake, then do it for the sake of your own necessity, which is exceedingly great, namely, your sins and death. There is the temptation of adultery, of fornication, avarice, hatred, pride, envy, of unbelief and despair, and you do not consider how you are ever going to get out of them, and you grow altogether cold in that ungodliness. But listen to what Christ says here: "for you." He did not give it to you as a poison; he did not say: Take and eat, this shall be your poison, or that this food should harm us, but rather free us from sin, devil, and death. But that's the attitude we take; as if it were poison. Here you have medicine, not poison. When a person is sick he can soon find an apothecary, a doctor. But who seeks this physician, who has given his body? Do you still not see your sickness; don't you want forgiveness of sins? Why do you avoid it as if it were poison? It is true that it is poison to those who sin, as formerly the priests committed fornication. But in itself it is not a poison but an antidote, which means salvation, blessedness, life, forgiveness of sins. Certainly you will find that you are full of envy, inclined to all kinds of villainy, to greed and the like. You fear death, you sense your unbelief. This certainly is lack enough. Then say: The sacrament is not given to those who are sick as a poison but as a remedy. See to it, then, that you seek the sacrament for your betterment when you find yourself in an hour of peril of life, when the flesh drives you, the world entices you, and Satan assails you. And beyond this it is of even greater benefit, etc.

Therefore, do not be so cold toward it. We are not forcing you, but you ought to come of your own free will. It is my duty to instruct you as to the reason why you should come, namely, your need, not a command, for you feel the infirmity of your faith and your propensity to all evil. These perils should move you without any command whatsoever. It is not the pope, not the emperor, not the duke who compels me, but my own need compels me. Therefore, take a better attitude now toward the sacrament and also keep your children to it when they come to understanding. For this is how we know which are Christians and which are not. If you will not go, then let the young people come; for us so much depends upon them. If you do not do it, we shall take action against you. For even if you adults want to go to the devil, we shall nevertheless seek after your children.

The need [which drives us to the sacrament] is that sin, devil, and death are always present. The benefit is that we receive forgiveness of sins and the Holy Spirit. Here, not poison, but a remedy and salvation is given, in so far as you acknowledge that you need it. Don't say: I am not fit today, I will wait a while. This is a trick of the devil. What will you do if you are not fit when death comes? Who will make you fit then? Say rather: Neither preacher, prince, pope, nor emperor compels me, but my great need and, beyond this, the benefit.

First, the sacrament is Christ's body and blood in bread and wine comprehended in the Word. Secondly, the benefit is forgiveness of sins. This includes the need and the benefit. Thirdly, those who believe should come.

SERMON AT COBURG ON CROSS AND SUFFERING

1530

SERMON AT COBURG ON CROSS
AND SUFFERING
1530

Sermon on Cross and Suffering, Preached at Coburg
the Saturday before Easter, Based on the
Passion History, April 16, 1530

A Harmony of Matthew 27, Luke 25, and John 19

This sermon was preached on the day after Luther's arrival at Feste Coburg where he stayed during the Diet of Augsburg at which the Augsburg Confession was presented. Among the congregation in the chapel of the castle were the Elector John, Count Albrecht of Mansfeld, Melanchthon, Justus Jonas, Veit Dietrich, John Agricola, and some thirty retainers of the Elector. Notes for the sermon were taken down by Veit Dietrich, who prepared the printed version of 1530, but the notes themselves were incorporated in Georg Rörer's collection. Another transcript by Stoltz is also extant.

Text in German; WA 32, 28-39.

Dear friends, you know that it is customary in this season to preach on the Passion, so I have no doubt that you have heard many times what kind of passion and suffering it was. You have also heard why it was that God the Father ordained it, namely, that through it he wanted to help, not the person for Christ, for Christ had no need at all for this suffering; but we and the whole human race needed this suffering. Thus it was a gift which was given and presented to us out of pure grace and mercy. But we shall not deal with these points now, for I have often spoken of them on other occasions.

But since there are many false fanatics abroad, who only distort the gospel and accuse us and say that we have nothing else to teach and preach except faith alone, that we leave out the doctrine of good works and the holy cross and suffering; and they also say that they have the true Spirit, who moves them to teach as they do, we shall at this time speak only of the example which this Passion gives to us, what kind of cross we bear and suffer, and also how we should bear and suffer it.

Therefore we must note in the first place that Christ by his suffering not only saved us from the devil, death, and sin, but also that his suffering is an example, which we are to follow in our suffering. Though our suffering and cross should never be so exalted that we think we can be saved by it or earn the least merit through it, nevertheless we should suffer after Christ, that we may be conformed to him. For God has appointed that we should not only believe in the crucified Christ, but also be crucified with him, as he clearly shows in many places in the Gospels: "He who does not take his cross and follow me," he says, "is not worthy of me" [Matt. 10:38]. And again: "If they have called the master of the house Beelzebul, how much more will they malign those of his household" [Matt. 10:25].

Therefore each one must bear a part of the holy cross; nor can it be otherwise. St. Paul too says, "In my flesh I complete what is lacking in Christ's afflictions" [Col. 1:24]. It is as if he were saying: His whole Christendom is not fully completed; we too must follow after, in order that none of the suffering of Christ may be lacking or lost, but all brought together into one. Therefore every Christian must be aware that suffering will not fail to come.

It should be, however, and must be the kind of suffering that is worthy of the name and honestly grips and hurts, such as some great danger of property, honor, body, and life. Such suffering as we really feel, which weighs us down; otherwise, if it did not hurt us badly, it would not be suffering.

Beyond this, it should be the kind of suffering which we have not chosen ourselves, as the fanatics choose their own suffering. It should be the kind of suffering which, if it were possible, we would gladly be rid of, suffering visited upon us by the devil or the world.

Then what is needed is to hold fast and submit oneself to it, as I have said, namely, that one know that we must suffer, in order that we may thus be conformed to Christ, and that it cannot be otherwise, that everyone must have his cross and suffering.

When one knows this it is the more easy and bearable, and one can comfort oneself by saying: Very well, if I want to be a Christian, I must also wear the colors of the court; the dear Christ issues no others in his court; suffering there must be.

This the fanatics, who select their own cross, cannot do; they resist it and fight against it. What a fine and admirable suffering that is! And yet they can reproach us, as if we did not teach aright concerning suffering and they alone can do it. But our teaching is this, that none should dictate or choose his own cross and suffering, but rather, when it comes, patiently bear and suffer it.

But they are wrong, not only with respect to their choosing their own cross, but also in that they flaunt their suffering and make a great merit of it and thus blaspheme God, because it is not a true suffering but a stinking, self-chosen suffering. But we say that we earn nothing by our suffering and therefore do not frame it in such beautiful monstrances as they do. It is enough that we know that it pleases God that we suffer in order that we may be conformed to Christ, as I have said.

So we see that the very ones who boast and teach so much about cross and suffering know the least either about the Cross or of Christ, because they make their own suffering meritorious. Dear friends, it isn't that kind of thing at all; nor is anybody forced or compelled to it. If you don't want to do it for nothing and without any merit, then you can let it lie and so deny Christ. The way is at hand, but you must know that if you refuse to suffer you will also not become Christ's courtier. So you may do either one of these two, either suffer or deny Christ.

If you are willing to suffer, very well, then the treasure and consolation which is promised and given to you is so great that you ought to suffer willingly and joyfully because Christ and his suffering is being bestowed upon you and made your own. And if you can believe this, then in time of great fear and trouble you will be able to say: Even though I suffer long, very well then, what is that compared with that great treasure which my God has given to me, that I shall live eternally with him?

Look what happens then: the suffering would be sweet and easy and no longer an eternal suffering, but only a modicum which lasts only a short time and soon passes away, as St. Paul [II Cor. 4:17], and St. Peter [I Pet. 1:6], and also Christ himself says in the Gospels [John 16:16-22]. For they look to that great, immeasurable gift, which is that Christ with his suffering and merit has become altogether ours. Thus the suffering of Christ has become so mighty and strong that it fills heaven and earth and breaks the power and might of the devil and hell, of death and sin. And then if you compare this treasure with your affliction and suffering, you will consider it but small loss to lose a little property, honor, health, wife, child, and even your own life. But if you refuse to regard this treasure and to suffer for it, so be it; go on and let it lie. He who does not believe will also receive none of these unspeakable goods and gifts.

Furthermore, every Christian should submit himself to this suffering that he is sure that it will work for his good and that Christ, for his Word's sake, will not only help us to bear this suffering but also turn and transform it to our advantage. And again what makes this cross more agreeable and bearable for us is the fact that our dear God is ready to pour so many refreshing aromatics and cordials into our hearts that we are able to bear all our afflictions and tribulations, just as St. Paul says in I Cor. 10 [:13], "God is faithful, and he will not let you be tempted beyond your strength, but with the temptation will also provide the way of escape, that you may be able to endure it." This is true. When the suffering and affliction is at its worst, it bears and presses down so grievously that one thinks he can endure no more and must surely perish. But then if you can think of Christ, the faithful God will come and will help you, as he has always helped his own from the beginning of the world; for he is the same God as he always has been.

Moreover, the cause of our suffering is the same as that for which all the saints have suffered from the beginning. Of course the whole world must bear witness that we are not suffering because of public scandal or vice, such as adultery, fornication, murder, etc. Rather we suffer because we hold to the Word of God, preach it, hear it, learn it, and practice it. And since this is the cause of our suffering, so let it always be; we have the same promise and the same cause for suffering which all the saints have always had. So we too can comfort ourselves with the same promise and cling to it in our suffering and tribulation, as is highly necessary.

So in our suffering we should so act that we give our greatest attention to the promise, in order that our cross and affliction may be turned to good, to something which we could never have asked or thought. And this is precisely the thing which makes a difference between the Christian's suffering and afflictions and those of all other men. For other people also have their afflictions, cross, and misfortune, just as they also have their times when they can sit in the rose garden and employ their good fortune and their goods as they please. But when they run into affliction and suffering, they have nothing to comfort them, for they do not have the mighty promises and the confidence in God which Christians have. Therefore they cannot comfort themselves with the assurance that God will help them to bear the affliction, much less can they count on it that he will turn their affliction and suffering to good.

So it is, as we see, that they cannot endure even the small afflictions. But when the big, strong afflictions occur, they despair altogether, destroy themselves, or they want to jump out of their skin because the whole world has become too cramped for them. Likewise they cannot observe moderation either in fortune or misfortune. When things go well, they are the most wanton, defiant, and arrogant people you can find. When things go wrong, they are utterly shattered and despondent, more than any woman; as we see those who are now pawing and bridling and bragging and boasting were so timid and nervous during the peasant uprising that they hardly knew where to go. So it must be when one does not have the promises and God's Word. But Christians have their consolation even in the worst of suffering and misfortune.

But in order that you may better understand this, I will give you a fine example in which the Christian's suffering is depicted. All of you are doubtless familiar with the way in which St. Christopher has at times been portrayed. But you should not think that there ever was a man who was called by that name or who actually did what is said about St. Christopher. Rather the person who devised this legend or fable was without a doubt a fine intelligent man, who wanted to portray this picture for the simple people so that they would have an example and image of a Christian life and how it should be lived. And actually he did hit it off very well; for a Christian is like a great giant, he has great strong legs and arms, as Christopher is painted, for he bears a burden which the whole world, which no emperor, king, nor prince could carry. Therefore every Christian is a Christopher, that is, a Christ-bearer,[1] because he accepts the faith.

How goes it then with him? This way: when a man accepts the faith, he does not allow himself to think of it as something burdensome. He thinks of it as being like a little child, which is beautiful and well formed and easy to carry, as Christopher found. For at first the gospel looks like a fine, pleasant, and childlike teaching; as we saw at the beginning, when it started everybody got cracking and wanted to be an Evangelical. There was such a yearning and thirst for it that no oven is as hot as the people were then. But what happened? The same thing that happened with Christopher. He did not find out how heavy the child was until he got into the deep water.

So it was with the gospel; when it began to take hold the waves rolled out and pope, bishops, princes, and the crazy rabble set themselves against it. Then we first began to feel how heavy the child is to carry. For it came so close to the good Christopher that he came very near to drowning. As you see, the same thing is happening now; on the other side which is against the Word there are so many tricks and strategems, so much deceit and cunning, everything aimed at one purpose, to drown us in the water. There is such threatening and terror that we would be frightened to death if we did not have another consolation to oppose to it.

All right then, anybody who has taken upon himself the burden of the Christ, the beloved child, must either carry him all the way across the water or drown; there is no middle way. It's no good to drown; therefore we'll go through the water with the Christ, even though it looks again as though we would have to stay in it. After all, we have the promise that he who has Christ and relies and believes on him can boldly say with David in Ps. 27 [:3], "Though a

---

[1] Christopher is derived from the Greek contraction of the name of Christ (*Christos*) and the verb *pherein* (to bear).

host encamp against me, my heart shall not fear; though war arise against me, yet will I be confident." Let them paw and stamp their feet, let them threaten and frighten as they please, were the water never so deep we shall nevertheless go through it with Christ.

So it is with all other things; when it gets going it becomes too heavy, whether it be sin, devil, hell, or even our own conscience. But how are we going to do it? Where shall we go and hide ourselves? For us it looks as if the whole thing would fall to the ground. But on the other side they are confident and proud; they think they already have won the day. I too see the good Christopher sinking; nevertheless he gets through, for he has a tree which he holds on to. This tree is the promise that Christ will do something remarkable with our suffering. "In the world," he says, "you shall have afflictions and tribulations, but in me you shall have peace" [cf. John 16:33]. And St. Paul says, "We have a faithful God who helps us out of affliction, so that we can bear it" [cf. I Cor. 10:13]. These sayings are staves, yea, trees, which we can hold on to and let the waters roar and foam as they will.

So in Christopher we have an example and a picture that can strengthen us in our suffering and teach us that fear and trembling is not as great as the comfort and the promise, and that we should therefore know that in this life we shall have no rest if we are bearing Christ, but rather that in affliction we should turn our eyes away from the present suffering to the consolation and promise. Then we will learn that what Christ says is true: "In me you shall have peace" [John 16:33].

For this is the Christian art, which we must all learn, the art of looking to the Word and looking away from all the trouble and suffering that lies upon us and weighs us down. But the flesh is utterly incapable of this art, it sees no farther than the present suffering. For this also is the way of the devil; he removes the Word far from one's eyes, so that one sees nothing but the present difficulty, just as he is doing with us now. What he wants is that we should deny and forget the Word altogether and gaze only at the danger which threatens us from the pope and the Turks. Then if he wins the play, he drowns us in the difficulty, so that we see nothing but its rush and roar. But this should not be. For this is what happens: when a person wants to be a Christian and acts according to his feelings, he soon loses Christ. Drive the suffering and cross from your heart and mind as quickly as you can; otherwise if you think about it for long the evil grows worse. If you have affliction and suffering, say: I have myself not chosen and prepared this cross; it is because of the Word of God that I am suffering and that I have and teach Christ. So let it be in God's name. I will let him take care of it and fight it out who long ago foretold that I should have this suffering and promised me his divine and gracious help.

If you give yourself to Scripture, you will feel comfort and all your concerns will be better, which otherwise you cannot control by any act or means of your own. After all, a merchant can bring himself, for the sake of gaining money and wealth, to leave house and home, wife and child, and risk his life for the sake of filthy lucre, and still have no sure promise or assurance that he will return home in health to wife and child; and yet he is foolhardy and rash enough to venture boldly into such danger without any promise whatsoever. Now, if a merchant can do that for money and riches, fie upon you, that we should not want to bear a little cross and still want to be Christians, even though besides we have in our hands the tree to which we cling against the waves, namely, the Word and the fine strong promises that we shall not be overwhelmed by the waves.

So the knight does too. He surrenders himself to battle, where innumerable spears, halberds, and firearms are directed against him. He too has no promise with which to console himself except his own mad spirit; and yet he goes on, even though his whole life is nothing but hard living and hard suffering.

And so it is with the papists too. They grudge no effort or labor to re-establish their abomination and idolatry. How often, just since the time when the gospel has been proclaimed anew, have they taken counsel together, even to this day, one deliberation after another, all of which have failed and fallen to ashes. And yet they want to imagine and are even sure they can sing this thing away and suppress the Word of God, so in sheer foolhardiness they go into it.

Now if merchants, knights, papists, and such riffraff can muster up such courage to take upon themselves and suffer such peril, effort, and labor, we should be simply ashamed that we rebel against suffering and the cross, even though we know, in the first place, that

God has appointed that we should suffer and that it cannot be otherwise. In the second place, we also know our promise and assurance, that, even though we are not such good Christians as we ought to be and are timid and weak both in life and faith, He will nevertheless defend his Word simply because it is his Word. Therefore we know that we can quite rightly bid defiance and say: Even though there were ten popes or Turkish emperors, I would like to see whether all of them together are a match for the Man who is called Christ. They may very well start a game which will grow too big for them to handle, but they will not demolish the Word. And this will happen even though we are weak in faith.

This then is the true art, that in suffering and cross we should look to the Word and the comforting assurance, and trust them, even as He said, "In me you shall have peace, but in the world, tribulation" [cf. John 16:33]. It is as if he were saying: Danger and terror will surely hit you if you accept my Word; but let it come, this will happen to you because of me. So be of good cheer; I will not forsake you, I will be with you and will help you. No matter how great the affliction may be, it will be small and light for you, if you are able to draw such thoughts from the Word of God.

Therefore in affliction every Christian should so arm himself that he may defend and guard himself with the fine, comfortable assurances which Christ, our dear Lord, has left us when we suffer for his Word's sake. But if we do not do this, if we let the comforting sayings go, then when the cross comes the same thing that happened to Eve in paradise will happen to us. She had God's commandment and with it she should have beaten down the devil's suggestions and instigations. But what did she do? She let the Word go and kept thinking what a fine apple it was and that after all such a little thing was of no great importance. So she went her way. And when one lets the Word go, there can be no other result. But when we stay with the Word and hold on to it, we shall certainly have the experience of conquering and coming out of it fine.

You see that we teach these two things when we preach on suffering and cross. And anybody who accuses us of teaching nothing about suffering is doing us an injustice. But this we do not do; we do not make our suffering meritorious before God. No, far

205

from it. Christ alone did that and nobody else, and to him alone belongs the glory.

In the third place we want also to consider why it is that our Lord God sends us such suffering. And the reason is that in this way he wants to make us conformed to the image of his dear Son, Christ, so that we may become like him here in suffering and there in that life to come in honor and glory [cf. Rom. 8:29; 8:17; II Tim. 2:11-12], as he says, "Was it not necessary that the Christ should suffer and enter into glory?" [cf. Luke 24:26]. But God cannot accomplish this in us except through suffering and affliction, which he sends to us through the devil or other wicked people.

The second reason is this, that even though God does not want to assault and torment us, the devil does, and he cannot abide the Word. He is by nature so malicious and venomous that he cannot endure anything which is good. It irks him that an apple should be growing on a tree; it pains and vexes him that you have a sound finger, and if he were able he would tear everything apart and put it out of joint.

But there is nothing to which he is so hostile as the beloved Word. And the reason is that he can conceal himself beneath every created thing; only the Word exposes him, so that he cannot hide himself, and shows everybody how black he is. Then he fights back and resists and draws together the princes and the bishops, thinking thus to conceal himself again. But it is of no avail; the Word nevertheless drags him out into the light. Therefore he too does not rest, and because the gospel cannot suffer him, so he cannot suffer the gospel, and that makes it equal. And if our dear God were not guarding us through his angels and we were able to see the devil's cunning, conspiring, and lying, we should die of the sight of it alone, so many are the cannon and guns he has ranged against us. But God prevents them from striking us.

So the two heroes meet, each doing as much as possible. The devil brews one calamity after another; for he is a mighty, malicious, and turbulent spirit. So it is time that our dear God be concerned about his honor; for the Word which we wield is a weak and miserable Word, and we who have and wield it are also weak and miserable men, bearing the treasure as Paul says [II Cor. 4:7], in earthen vessels, which can easily be shattered and broken. Therefore the evil spirit spares no effort and confidently lashes out to see if he can smash the little vessel; for there it is under his nose and he cannot stand it. So the battle really begins in earnest, with water and fire to dampen and quench the little spark. Then our Lord God looks on for a while and puts us in a tight place, so that we may learn from our own experience that the small, weak, miserable Word is stronger than the devil and the gates of hell. They are to storm the castle, the devil and his cohorts. But let them storm; they will find something there that will make them sweat, and still they will not gain it; for it is a rock, as Christ calls it, which cannot be conquered. So let us suffer what comes upon us and thus we shall learn that God will stand by us to guard and shield us against this enemy and all his adherents.

Thirdly, it is also highly necessary that we suffer not only that God may prove his honor, power, and strength against the devil, but also in order that when we are not in trouble and suffering this excellent treasure which we have may not merely make us sleepy and secure. We see so many people, unfortunately it is all too common, so misusing the gospel that it is a sin and a shame, as if now of course they have been so liberated by the gospel that there is no further need to do anything, give anything, or suffer anything.

This kind of wickedness our God cannot check except through suffering. Hence he must keep disciplining and driving us, that our faith may increase and grow stronger and thus bring the Savior more deeply into our hearts. For just as we cannot get along without eating and drinking so we cannot get along without affliction and suffering. Therefore we must necessarily be afflicted of the devil by persecution or else by a secret thorn which thrusts into the heart, as also St. Paul laments [cf. II Cor. 12:7]. Therefore, since it is better to have a cross than to be without one, nobody should dread or be afraid of it. After all, you have a good strong promise with which to comfort yourself. Besides, the gospel cannot come to the fore except through and in suffering and cross.

Lastly, Christian suffering is nobler and precious above all other human suffering because, since Christ himself suffered, he also hallowed the suffering of all his Christians. Are we not then poor, foolish people? We have run to Rome, Trier, and other places to visit the shrines; why do we not also cherish cross and suffering, which was much nearer to Christ and touched him more closely than any garment did his body. This touched not only his body but his heart. Through the suffering of Christ, the suffering of all his saints has become utterly holy, for it has been touched with Christ's suffering. Therefore we should accept all suffering as a holy thing, for it is truly holiness.

Since we know then that it is God's good pleasure that we should suffer, and that God's glory is manifested in our suffering, better than in any other way, and since we are the kind of people who cannot hold on to the Word and our faith without suffering, and moreover since we have the noble, previous promise that the cross which God sends to us is not a bad thing, but rather an utterly precious and noble holy thing, why should we not be bold to suffer? As for those who will not suffer, let them go and be cavaliers; we preach this only to the devout who want to be Christians, the others wouldn't carry it out anyhow. After all, we have so many assurances and promises that he will not allow us to stick in our suffering but will help us out of it, even though all men should doubt it. Therefore, even though it hurts, so be it, you have to go through some suffering anyhow; things cannot always go smoothly. It is just as well, nay, a thousand times better, to have suffered for the sake of Christ, who promised us comfort and help in suffering, than to suffer and despair and perish without comfort and help for the sake of the devil.

This, you see, is the way we teach concerning suffering, and you should also accustom yourself to distinguish carefully between the suffering of Christ and all other suffering and know that his is a heavenly suffering and ours is worldly, that his suffering accomplishes everything, while ours does nothing except that we become conformed to Christ, and that therefore the suffering of Christ is the suffering of a lord, whereas ours is the suffering of a servant. And those who teach otherwise know neither what Christ's suffering nor our suffering is. Why? Because reason cannot do otherwise; it likes to put on a display with its suffering, as with all other works, so that it may gain some merit. That's why we must learn to distinguish. We have said enough for this time concerning the example of the Passion and our suffering. God grant that we may understand and learn it aright. Amen.

SERMON ON THE AFTERNOON OF CHRISTMAS DAY

1530

SERMON ON THE AFTERNOON
OF CHRISTMAS DAY
1530

Sermon on the Afternoon of Christmas Day,

Luke 2:1-14, December 25, 1530

If we examine a listing of Luther's sermons we find a wealth of Christmas sermons. He preached about sixty times on Luke 2:1-20 and John 1:1-14 and only three times on the Epistles, showing the same preference for Gospel texts that he does in the Lenten season. If frequency of choice indicates preference, however, it was the story by Luke which was his favorite. In 1530 he preached five sermons on Luke 2:1-20, which together constitute a connected series on the Christmas story. Buchwald calls the sermon here translated "one of the most beautiful of the Christmas sermons." It is translated from Rörer's text, compared with the Nürnberg Codex Solger and Buchwald's reconstruction in German (op. cit., II, 54-60).

Text in macaronic Latin; WA 32, 261-270.

You have heard today the story from the Gospel of St. Luke of how it came to pass that our Lord Christ was born and then also the message of the angel, who announced who the boy was who was born.[1] Now we shall go on and take up the message of the angel. So for today you have heard only that the child was born and that he is the Lord and Savior. Thus we spoke of the story, how it unfolded, and who the persons in it were. This article is so high that even today it is believed by only a few. Nevertheless, God has preserved

---

[1] Luther is referring to the sermon he preached that morning on Luke 2:1-10 (text in WA 32, 251-261; Buchwald, *Martin Luther Predigten*, op. cit., II, 47-53).

211

it even through those who have not believed it. For at all times in the monasteries and universities there have been disputations and lectures which dealt with the fact that Christ the Lord, born of Mary, is true man and God. But it went no further than saying and hearing it.[2] But this belief is held by the devil too and the Turks and all the godless among the Christians, and is the kind of belief which everybody believes that it is true but would not die for it, as Eck[3] and many others show today. If they had as much from Christ and the teaching of the gospel as from the devil, they would also think as much of Christ. The Turk too admits that Christ was born of the Virgin Mary, that Mary was an immaculate virgin, and that Christ was more than a man; but the Word of God, as it is given in the gospel, he denies, and yet I fear that the Turk believes more of this article than does the pope. Therefore it is a high article to believe that this infant, born of Mary, is true God; for nobody's reason can ever accept the fact that he who created heaven and earth and is adored by the angels was born of a virgin. That is the article. Nobody believes it except he who also knows this faith, namely, that this child is the Lord and Savior.

But for whom was he born and whose Lord and Savior is he? The angels declare that he was born Lord and Savior. The Turks, the pope, and the scholars say the same thing, but only to the extent that it brings in money and honor. But that anyone could say, "to *you* is born," as the angel says, this is the faith which we must preach about. But we cannot preach about it as we would like to do. Indeed, who could ever grasp [the full meaning of] these words of the evangelist: "a Savior, who is the Lord," and, "to you"! I know well enough how to talk about it and what to believe about it, just as others do. So there are many who have this belief and do not doubt this first belief that Christ is the Lord, the Savior, and the virgin's Son. This I too have never doubted. But if these words are planted no higher than in my thoughts, then they have no firm roots. We are certain that this was proclaimed by the angel, but the firm faith does not follow. For the reason does not understand both sides of this faith, first that Christ is a man, but also the Savior and Lord

---

[2] This sentence supplied from Nürnberg Codex Solger.
[3] Johann Eck (1486-1543), one of Luther's earliest opponents. Cf. *The Leipzig Debate*. LW 31, 308-325.

or King. This needs to be revealed from heaven. One who really has the first faith also has the other.

Who, then, are those to whom this joyful news is to be proclaimed? Those who are faint-hearted and feel the burden of their sins, like the shepherds, to whom the angels proclaim the message, letting the great lords in Jerusalem, who do not accept it, go on sleeping. Beyond the first faith there must be the second faith, that Christ is not only the virgin's Son, but also the Lord of angels and the Savior of men. The words anyone can understand, antisacramentarians, fanatics, sectarians, and Turks; but they do not proceed from the heart, they come only from hearing and go no farther than hearing. This is not faith, however, but only a memory of what has been heard, that one knows that he has heard it. Nobody ventures upon it, so as to stake goods, life, and honor upon it. And yet we must preach it for the sake of those who are in the multitude to whom the angel preached.

This is our theology, which we preach in order that we may understand what the angel wants. Mary bore the child, took it to her breast and nursed it, and the Father in heaven has his Son, lying in the manger and the mother's lap. Why did God do all this? Why does Mary guard the child as a mother should? And reason answers: in order that we may make an idol of her, that honor may be paid to the mother. Mary becomes all this without her knowledge and consent, and all the songs and glory and honor are addressed to the mother. And yet the text does not sound forth the honor of the mother, for the angel says, "I bring to you good news of a great joy; for to you is born this day the Savior" [Luke 2:10-11]. I am to accept the child and his birth and forget the mother, as far as this is possible, although her part cannot be forgotten, for where there is a birth there must also be a mother. Nevertheless, we dare not put our faith in the mother but only in the fact that the child was born. And the angel desired that we should see nothing but the child which is born, just as the angels themselves, as though they were blind, saw nothing but the child born of the virgin, and desired that all created things should be as nothing compared with this child, that we should see nothing, be it harps, gold, goods, honor, power, and the like, which we would prefer before their message. For if I receive even the costliest and best in the world, it still does not have the name of Savior. And if the Turk were ten times stronger than he is, he could not for one moment save me from my infirmity, to say nothing of the peril of death, and even less from the smallest sin or from death itself. In my sin, my death, I must take leave of all created things. No, sun, moon, stars, all creatures, physicians, emperors, kings, wise men and potentates cannot help me. When I die I shall see nothing but black darkness, and yet that light, "To you is born this day the Savior" [Luke 2:11], remains in my eyes and fills all heaven and earth. The Savior will help me when all have forsaken me. And when the heavens and the stars and all creatures stare at me with horrible mien, I see nothing in heaven and earth but this child. So great should that light which declares that he is my Savior become in my eyes that I can say: Mary, you did not bear this child for yourself alone. The child is not yours; you did not bring him forth for yourself, but for me, even though you are his mother, even though you held him in your arms and wrapped him in swaddling clothes and picked him up and laid him down. But I have a greater honor than your honor as his mother. For your honor pertains to your motherhood of the body of the child, but my honor is this, that you have my treasure, so that I know none, neither men nor angels, who can help me except this child whom you, O Mary, hold in your arms. If a man could put out of his mind all that he is and has except this child, and if for him everything—money, goods, power, or honor—fades into darkness and he despises everything on earth compared with this child, so that heaven with its stars and earth with all its power and all its treasures becomes as nothing to him, that man would have the true gain and fruit of this message of the angel. And for us the time must come when suddenly all will be darkness and we shall know nothing but this message of the angel: "I bring to you good news of great joy; for to you is born this day the Savior" [Luke 2:10-11].

This, then, is the faith we preach, of which the Turks and the pope and all the sectarians know nothing. The fanatics do, it is true, snatch to themselves the words of the angels, but how earnest they are is plain to see. For they receive the Word only as a piece of paper, as the cup and corporal receive the body and blood of Christ. The paper does no more than contain something and pass it on to others, but yet it remains paper. Thus you copy something from one paper on another paper; from my tongue the Word sounds in your ear, but it does not go to the heart. So they receive this greatest of treasures to their great harm and still think they are Christians, just as though the paper were to say: I certainly have in me the written words, "to you is born this day the Savior"; therefore I shall be saved. But then the fire comes and burns up the paper.

Therefore this is the chief article, which separates us from all the heathen, that you, O man, may not only learn that Christ, born of the virgin, is the Lord and Savior, but also accept the fact that he is your Lord and Savior, that you may be able to boast in your heart: I hear the Word that sounds from heaven and says: This child who is born of the virgin is not only his mother's son. I have more than the mother's estate; he is more mine than Mary's, for he was born for me, for the angel said, "To you" is born the Savior. Then ought you to say, Amen, I thank thee, dear Lord.

But then reason says: Who knows? I believe that Christ, born of the virgin, is the Lord and Savior and he may perhaps help Peter and Paul, but for me, a sinner, he was not born. But even if you believed that much, it would still not be enough, unless there were added to it the faith that he was born for you. For he was not born merely in order that I should honor the mother, that she should be praised because he was born of the virgin mother. This honor belongs to none except her and it is not to be despised, for the angel said, "Blessed are you among women!" [Luke 1:28]. But it must not be too highly esteemed lest one deny what is written here: "To you is born this day the Savior." He was not merely concerned to be born of a virgin; it was infinitely more than that. It was this, as she herself sings in the Magnificat: "He has helped his servant Israel" [Luke 1:54]; not that he was born of me and my virginity, but born for you and for your benefit, not only for my honor.

Take yourself in hand, examine yourself and see whether you are a Christian! If you can sing: The Son, who is proclaimed to be a Lord and Savior, is my Savior; and if you can confirm the message of the angel and say yes to it and believe it in your heart, then your heart will be filled with assurance and joy and confidence, and you will not worry much about even the costliest and best that this world has to offer. For when I can speak to the virgin from the bottom of

215

my heart and say: O Mary, noble, tender virgin, you have borne a child; this I want more than robes and guldens, yea, more than my body and life; then you are closer to the treasure than everything else in heaven and earth, as Ps. 73 [:25] says, "There is nothing upon earth that I desire besides thee." You see how a person rejoices when he receives a robe or ten guldens. But how many are there who shout and jump for joy when they hear the message of the angel: "To you is born this day the Savior?" Indeed, the majority look upon it as a sermon that must be preached, and when they have heard it, consider it a trifling thing, and go away just as they were before. This shows that we have neither the first nor the second faith. We do not believe that the virgin mother bore a son and that he is the Lord and Savior unless, added to this, I believe the second thing, namely, that he is my Savior and Lord. When I can say: This I accept as my own, because the angel meant it for me, then, if I believe it in my heart, I shall not fail to love the mother Mary, and even more the child, and especially the Father. For, if it is true that the child was born of the virgin and is mine, then I have no angry God and I must know and feel that there is nothing but laughter and joy in the heart of the Father and no sadness in my heart. For, if what the angel says is true, that he is our Lord and Savior, what can sin do against us? "If God is for us, who is against us?" [Rom. 8:31]. Greater words than these I cannot speak, nor all the angels and even the Holy Spirit, as is sufficiently testified by the beautiful and devout songs that have been made about it. I do not trust myself to express it. I most gladly hear you sing and speak of it, but as long as no joy is there, so long is faith still weak or even non-existent, and you still do not believe the angel.

You can see what our papists and Junkers, who have chosen innumerable saviors, have felt about this faith. Indeed, the papists still want to retain the mass, the invocation of saints, and their invented works by which we are to be saved. This is as much as to say, I do not believe in the Savior and Lord whom Mary bore; and yet they sing the words of the angel, hold their triple masses [at Christmas] and play their organs. They speak the words with their tongues but their heart has another savior. And the same is true in the monasteries: if you want to be saved, remember to keep the rule

216

and regulations of Francis[4] and you will have a gracious God! And at the Diet of Augsburg they decided to stick to this. In the name of all the devils, let them stick there! It has been said sufficiently that this Savior lies in the manger. But if there is any other thing that saves me, then I rightly call it my savior. If the sun, moon, and stars save, I can call them saviors. If St. Bartholomew[5] or St. Anthony[6] or a pilgrimage to St. James[7] or good works save, then they surely are my savior. If St. Francis, then he is my savior. But then what is left of the honor of the child who was born this day, whom the angel calls Lord and Savior, and who wants to keep his name, which is Savior and Christ the Lord. If I set up any savior except this child, no matter who or what it is or is called, then he is not the Savior. But the text says that he is the Savior. And if this is true—and it is the truth—then let everything else go.

One who hears the message of the angel and believes it will be filled with fear, like the shepherds. True, it is too high for me to believe that I should come into this treasure without any merit on my part. And yet, so it must be. In the papacy this message was not preached in the pulpit, and I am afraid that it will disappear again. It was the other message that the devil initiated and has allowed to remain in the papacy. All their hymns are to this effect. Among the Turks the devil has completely wiped it out. Therefore, remember it, sing it, and learn it, while there is still time! I fear that the time will come when we shall not be allowed to hear, believe, and sing this message in public, and the time has already come when it is no longer understood; though Satan does allow it to be spoken with the mouth, as the papists do. But when it comes to declaring that he is born for you, and to singing:

> *In dulci jubilo*
> Now sing with hearts aglow!
> Our delight and pleasure

---

[4] Francis of Assisi (1182-1226), founder of the Franciscan Order, who was canonized two years after his death by Pope Gregory IX.
[5] According to Matt. 10:3, Mark 3:18, Luke 6:14, and Acts 1:13, Bartholomew is one of the twelve Apostles. His feast day is usually observed on August 24.
[6] St. Anthony (b. *ca.* 250 A.D.), a hermit who is considered the forerunner of the monastic movement.
[7] St. James of Compostella was the most frequented place of pilgrimage in Europe for many centuries.

Lies *in praesepio,*
  Like sunshine is our treasure
Matris in gremio
Alpha est et O![8]

—this he is unwilling to allow.

What we have said, then, has been about that second faith, which is not only to believe in Mary's Son, but rather that he who lies in the virgin's lap is our Savior, that you accept this and give thanks to God, who so loved you that he gave you a Savior who is yours. And for a sign he sent the angel from heaven to proclaim him, in order that nothing else should be preached except that this child is the Savior and far better than heaven and earth. Him, therefore, we should acknowledge and accept; confess him as our Savior in every need, call upon him, and never doubt that he will save us from all misfortune. Amen.

---

[8] Fourteenth century macaronic German carol. *The Oxford Book of Carols* (Oxford University Press, 1928), No. 86.

SERMON ON THE TWELFTH SUNDAY AFTER TRINITY

1531

SERMON ON THE TWELFTH
SUNDAY AFTER TRINITY
1531

Sermon on the Epistle for the Twelfth Sunday after

Trinity, II Cor. 3:4-6, Preached on the

Afternoon of August 27, 1531

*Preached in the parish church in Wittenberg, this sermon on the
bold and confident certainty of the true preacher is a bright picture
of Luther himself as a preacher. The text is preserved in two sets of
notes, Rörer's and the Nürnberg Codex Solger, and the translation
is based on these compared with Buchwald's reconstruction (op. cit.,
II, 457-463).*

Text in macaronic Latin; WA 34ᴵᴵ, 156-165.

This is the Epistle for today and it is our custom to preach on
it, but I do not like to preach on this Epistle because it is not for the
people who cannot follow it. However, in order not to disturb the
order, I shall deal with it briefly.

This was the situation at the time after Paul had preached at
Corinth: When he turned his back, other preachers had come in his
place, and everything he had planted they rooted out and did much
better. But there were also some sincere hearts there, who remained
in the doctrine which Paul had given them, though many defected.
And yet they were few and therefore the sectarians entered in force,
as we read in the First Epistle. This is what happened to Paul, and
in the very church where he himself had preached and installed
preachers. It grieved him and it was a rotten business, for he did
not know what to do. If he kept silent, this would not be good; if

221

he said nothing concerning his office, it would be regrettable; if he were to praise himself, it would not sound well. Meanwhile the godless went on extolling themselves. This is the general meaning of what he outlines in this chapter: he lauds himself but yet does not laud himself and then lashes out and gives the false apostles a slap. In short, the office of preaching is an arduous office, especially when it is like what Paul encountered here. I have often said that, if I could come down with good conscience, I would rather be stretched upon a wheel or carry stones than preach one sermon. For anyone who is in this office will always be plagued; and therefore I have often said that the damned devil and not a good man should be a preacher. But we're stuck with it now. Our Lord God was a better man than we are. And so it was with Jeremiah [Jer. 20:14-18]. If I had known I would not have let myself be drawn into it with twenty-four horses. Ingratitude is our reward; and after that we still have to bother ourselves with the sectarians and give an account to God on the last day. And for this we have let the peasants and the noblemen starve us until we feel like turning in our key and saying, "Go, preach yourselves, in the name of all the devils!"

So Paul here hardly knows what to do. "Do we need, as some do, letters of recommendation to you, or from you? You yourselves are our letter of recommendation" [II Cor. 3:1-2]. His words are kindly for the sake of the devout, who have the gospel in their hearts and have not been defected, not for those who are evangelical in name but are devils nevertheless. But he says, "Such is the confidence that we have through Christ toward God" [II Cor. 3:4]. And that we can set down and let stand. If I can't convert the whole crowd, then I'll gain one or two. This is our confidence: when we have preached, it will not have been in vain. If the townsmen, peasants, and the big fellows don't want it, let them leave it; let them go; they will see for themselves that they will regret it. And then there are some who always know better, like the sectarians and our young noblemen, who can handle it better than we can. But when it comes to a showdown, they turn out to be scamps and traitors. The townsmen, the fellows who, when they have read one book are full of the Holy Spirit, are the worst. If I were to follow my own impulse I would say, "Let the damned devil be your preacher!" So I have often thought, but I cannot bring myself to do it. But then confidence returns and we say, let happen what may, we still have our confidence through Christ.

"Not that we are sufficient of ourselves" [II Cor. 3:5]. We have something else in which we put our confidence and that's the end of it. I cannot boast of anything higher except that I am preaching by God's command and will; it is his will and I know that it is not fruitless. Nevertheless, it is disgusting for me to have to look at the pope, the sectarians, and our own people chewing up the gospel. But we must shut our eyes and look to Him and remember that I did not invent this Word of God and this office. It is God's Word, God's work, his office. There we two [i.e., God and I] are at one in the cause. It didn't grow in my garden. If he that is above is pleased, what can the world do to me? And I lump them all together: the wise, the powerful, and the hypocrites. It is our confidence, no matter how much the world may boast, that God has qualified us to be ministers, and, secondly, that it is not only pleasing to the heart of God but also that we shall not preach in vain and that this ministry will lift to heaven some few who receive the Word. So Paul comforted himself, since he was having the same trouble that we are. All of Asia defected from Paul to the false apostles, as most of Germany now. What should he do? Should he fall into desperation and disputation as to whether God had really sent him? No, he says, "Fall away who will, be wise who will, we have confidence through Christ toward God." But quickly he turns and says, "Not that we are sufficient of ourselves." Before he says, "Such confidence have we," he says, "It has pleased God to call me to the ministry. I have taught the Corinthians rightly and God sent me and qualified me. But they do not consider me qualified. Therefore we have confidence that God has qualified us. If he does so, that's all that matters. If the world does not consider us qualified, so be it!" So Paul lays about him. "Not that we are sufficient of ourselves." As if he were saying: This is what the others, the noblemen, are doing; they qualify themselves, just like my little squires, the dunces who do not even have one little spark of faith and haven't even begun with works. We can't do things right for them; they can do much better, these fellows who know nothing and yet dispute our preaching. And it is true, when they come to make a speech they can talk a lot, but when you examine it by daylight it's nothing

223

but chaff. So they are sufficient of themselves. And Paul says: These godless people, whom God did not send and who are not qualified by God and do not have the Holy Spirit, are self-qualified and what they preach, they think is right. So he gives them a slap. The truth is that no matter how learned a man may be, if he has no sure call and does not rightly teach the Scriptures, he may talk as he will but there is nothing behind it. And the same is true of those who want to judge others; if they understand a single word, then the devil take me!

So there you have two kinds of preachers. First those who qualify themselves and preach whatever they please. But Paul says: Such we do not want to be. We are not sufficient of ourselves, but God has made us sufficient, so that we know what the whole world does not know. So poor Paul is obliged to praise himself and rebuke others, even though it is courteously spoken. They speak as they please. That is politely said but nevertheless it is a rough slap. And this is high praise to say, God has qualified me; nor can I be censured by those who say God does not praise me and has not qualified me. Therefore anybody who wants to be a preacher, and especially one who is going to fight the battle, must learn this. We shall have these two kinds, Mr. Wiseacre and the good preachers, if not here, then outside. If they dared to do it, they would stop my mouth and that of all the learned men here. So it's a rotten office to have to deal with these people, not to speak of having to suffer such physical misery and give an accounting on the last day, that a man would rather be a swineherd. But this is our consolation, I can boast to them: if it pleases God, good enough; if it does not please him, let it fall. I wouldn't risk a hair of my head to uphold my office. But if it pleases God, I'd like to see the fellow who would knock it down.

"Our sufficiency is from God" [II Cor. 3:5]. What Paul means is that whatever good we do in preaching is done by God; when we preach it is God's work if it has power and accomplishes something among men. Therefore if I am a good preacher who does some good, it isn't necessary for me to boast. It's not my mind, my wisdom, my ability. Otherwise at this hour all of you would be converted and the godless would be damned and all the wiseacres, anti-sacramentalists, sectarians, and Anabaptists who say, "The gospel in Wittenberg is nothing, because it does not make people holy," would be checked. Let Paul give the answer here! "If I were the one who could make people holy, I would begin with myself and make everybody else holy. I do not ascribe this to myself but to God. If my ministry is profitable, I ascribe it to God. If it produces fruit, I do not glory in myself; this is not my work, but the mercy of God, who has used me as his instrument. This the false scholars, wiseacres, and fanatics cannot do." These are real blows, thunder and lightning hurled against the false apostles, who also were boasting that they would make the people holy and who today are saying, "A good beginning has been made but we're going to do better." But the answer to that is that what we have done was done by God. If anybody can do it better, then by God's grace I have the humility to say: If somebody else can do better, we will follow him. There are many who want to do it, but how many are able? I would help to pay him myself, if there were such a person. I know what preaching is.

"Who has qualified us to be ministers of a new covenant, not in a written code but in the Spirit; for the written code kills, but the Spirit gives life" [II Cor. 3:6]. These are all words of attack and they are all aimed at vile preaching. We know nothing; you know everything, as he says in I Cor. 4 [:10], "We are fools for Christ's sake, but you are wise in Christ." If I say, I am more learned than you, I am a proud dunce. If I humble myself, then nobody will want to learn from me. Therefore I say, I am utterly nothing, God knows it. But when I accomplish anything through God, I do it not for the sake of the crowd but to commend our office, that is, good luck to you,[1] but we still preach better than you; we preach the New Testament. Here he sets up a mark for them. Emulate me in this! You are preachers and learned men. We know the New Testament and preach it; you preach the Old Testament.

"Not in a written code but in the Spirit." These are Pauline words. You have heard that Paul exalted his office over against those who have put themselves forward and gloried in its fruits over against the sectarians. Now he also glories in the doctrine. And this is the controversy: We preach the Spirit and the New Testament, you the letter and the Old Testament. None of you preach the Spirit and no wiseacre teaches the New Testament; you all preach

---

[1] Irony.

the letter and the Old Testament, that is, the law. Nobody preaches the New Testament except those whom God has qualified. In all the apostles who taught at that time you can see how they fought against the false apostles who taught the Old Testament. And look at the Anabaptists today. When they rise up they say, We must follow Christ's example, leave wife and child. That has a fine shine on it, but if you examine it you see that this is only preaching about what I should do. Likewise the anti-sacramental fanatics will not admit that there is forgiveness of sins in the sacrament and insist that it is only a work. The pope, too, says the mass is a good work. One who makes himself wise can never preach the New Testament, no matter how he preaches. In short, it is impossible for a sectarian to preach the New Testament. Therefore we can boast that we have not only the ministry and the fruits which proceed from it but also the doctrine; for I know that nobody except us proclaims this doctrine. They do not know what the New Testament is. Even though they talk about it they still run out into juridical legalism. They preach what magistrates and kings should be preaching. But Paul calls all this the "letter" which "kills." All doctrine which does not preach the New Testament, the Spirit, he calls the "letter." Ah, dear Paul, you are a vexing preacher when you hurl back these fellows and say that when they preach long sermons it still is nothing but words in a man's mouth and letters in a book. All their blabbering is like a letter in a book; it produces nothing. He who lacks the New Testament loves not God, believes not, hears and teaches not God's Word, and there is nothing there but what is written in a book. It is letter and remains letter, it produces nothing, and a man remains an angry, envious man, a thief, rascal, backbiter, adulterer. That's what it means to preach the letter, which teaches nothing more than what I should do. Then I and the preacher have nothing but letters and a book has just as many of them as we do. It lies like a dead letter in the heart, but I do not accept it for myself; it is a dead letter in a book. Therefore where the only preaching is, "Do this," it remains only a letter. So Paul is against the false apostles who disparaged and reviled him. He could not please anybody. In short, they preach the letter, but they themselves neither hear nor perform what they preach, they remain without

God and with the Spirit. Hence there is no fear, no faith, no obedience to God, no chaste hearts, no humility.

Therefore we preach something better: the Spirit and the New Testament, which is that Jesus Christ has come for your sake and taken your sins upon himself. There you hear, not what you should do, but what God is doing through Christ, which means, of course, that he works faith and bestows the Holy Spirit. This is what it means to preach the New Testament and the Holy Spirit. But nobody who wants to make people good through laws is practicing this preaching. That's Moses' and the hangman's business. Otherwise all people would long since have been good; for I preach daily that you should be good and not steal, but the more you hear it the worse you become; you remain the same rascals you were before. Therefore it remains merely letter. When the hangman comes he can chop off a finger, but the heart remains a rogue. I don't want to talk in subtleties about the law and how it frightens people, but only crassly. We have the confidence to say that we preach rightly, that we are sufficient and the fruit follows, that our doctrine is true, and that our ministry is pleasing to God. If we have these three things, then I who preach and you who hear have enough. If the vulgar crowd departs, what is that to me? I might well be angry on account of ingratitude and the fanatics, but I must let it be, as Paul did. If it does not please the world, it is enough that it pleases God. If it does not produce fruit in all, it is enough that it produces fruit in some. If the doctrine be true, let those who preach falsely go. There I can defend myself against spite and vexation. But that I should wish to stop their mouths and persuade the people not to despise me and to be grateful, this confidence we must not have. God is my Lord, the world is my enemy. The fruit will come and the third[2] will come too. So in the fourth chapter also, Paul comforts himself and his followers, admonishing them not to be offended when it appears that our doctrine is lost, if only it please the One who is above.

---

[2] I.e., that my ministry shall please God.

TWO FUNERAL SERMONS

1532

TWO FUNERAL SERMONS, 1532

Elector John of Saxony died on August 15, 1532 and the funeral was held in the Castle Church at 7 a.m. on Sunday, August 18, with Luther preaching the sermon. At the request of the new Elector John Frederick, he preached again in the Castle Church at 9 a.m. on the following Thursday, continuing his treatment of the same text. Two versions of these sermons are given in the Weimar edition: Rörer's transcript and the printed version of 1532 (probably prepared on the basis of Rörer's stenographic notes by an unknown person). The present translation is based on the printed version compared with Rörer's text.

Text in German; WA 36, 237-270.

Sermon at the Funeral of the Elector, Duke John of Saxony, I Thess. 4:13-14, August 18, 1532

My dear friends, since this misfortune has happened to our beloved sovereign prince, and the habit and custom of holding masses for the dead and funeral processions when they are buried has ceased, we nevertheless do not wish to allow this service of worship to be omitted, in order that we may preach God's Word to the praise of God and the betterment of the people. For we must deal with the subject and also do what is right on this occasion, since the Lord our God has again[1] taken unto himself and graciously summoned our beloved head. Therefore we shall take as our text what St. Paul says to the Thessalonians in the fourth chapter:

"But we would not have you ignorant, brethren, concerning those who are asleep, that you may not grieve as others do who

---

[1] Duke John's brother and predecessor as elector, Frederick the Wise, died on May 5, 1525 and Luther preached two funeral sermons on I Thess. 4:13-18, May 10 and 11, 1525; see WA 17^I, 196-227.

have no hope. For since we believe that Jesus died and rose again, even so, through Jesus, God will bring with him those who have fallen asleep" [I Thess. 4:13-14].

So much we shall take up for now, in order that I may not overburden myself and you. You know that the greatest divine service is the preaching [of the Word of God], and not only the greatest divine service, but also the best we can have in every situation; but especially on these solemn occasions of sorrow [there is nothing better we can do than to preach]. Now St. Paul writes to the Thessalonians that they are not to sorrow as others do who have no hope. For there were some pagans who held that it was a manly virtue not to grieve or weep when a good and loved friend died, just as in our times the sectarians began to try and make sticks and stones of us by alleging that one must eliminate the creature altogether and not accept anything that is natural; even though father, mother, son, daughter, [or prince] should die, one must simply go on with dry eyes and a serene heart. Thus these heathens were trying to re-establish virtue. But at bottom it is an artificial virtue and a fabricated strength, which God did not create and also does not please him at all. And the reason is that such a hard heart, which is not softened when a good friend dies, shows that he never did have any real liking or love for him, or he wants to be a hypocrite and appear to be so firm before men that they will praise him and say: Ah, there's a man who has a firm hold on himself!

This fabricated sectarian and heathen virtue we condemn and say that it is not right. For not only examples from the holy fathers but also the Word of God in the Scriptures declare that it is right and fitting, even godly, to mourn a good friend who has died, as Paul himself indicates in these words which he utters at the end of this chapter: "Therefore comfort one another" [I Thess. 4:18]. If one is to comfort oneself, then there must have been sorrow, grief, and mourning. Now obviously those to whom Paul is here writing were Christian people, who were pleasing to God and possessed of the Holy Spirit, and yet Paul does not disapprove of their grief but only that it must be Christian and in moderation.

Since this is so, why should not we too properly mourn and grieve because our head, the beloved sovereign, lies here dead? For the steadfast man is not the one who thinks himself so strong that he refuses to be touched when a good friend has slipped away; rather the Christian is one who is hurt but yet endures it in such a way that the spirit rules the flesh. For God has not created man to be a stick or a stone. He has given him five senses and a heart of flesh in order that he may love his friends, be angry with his enemies, and to lament and grieve when his dear friends suffer evil. Thus St. Paul also says in Phil. 2 [:27] that his heart was grieved for his servant Epaphroditus and that God had had mercy not only on Epaphroditus but on him and permitted him to be restored, lest he should have sorrow upon sorrow. Christ also was deeply moved at the death of Lazarus in John 11 [:33]. These and similar examples are far more sure and better than this unprofitable chatter which would make sticks and stones of us and forbid us to weep or sorrow over the deceased.

Let this suffice as a preface and introduction to this sermon. Now let us listen to the text as it comforts us. This is what the beloved Paul says:

"But we would not have you ignorant, brethren, concerning those who are asleep, that you may not grieve as others do who have no hope" [I Thess. 4:13].

Here St. Paul puts in some good sugar, mixing the bitterness which is here with sweetness, and saying: You are sorrowful and grieving over those who have died. It is true that it hurts to lose a good friend. I do not reproach you for this; I praise it, for it is a sign that these are good hearts which are thus concerned about the deceased. But you must discriminate between your death and the death of the heathen, between your sorrow and that of the heathen. They have no hope after this life, but you know that you do not die but only fall asleep. For "since we believe," he goes on, "that Jesus died and rose again" [I Thess. 4:14], it is also certain that God will bring with him those who have died in Christ and will not let them simply remain where we think they remain, but will bring them to himself.

Note particularly that he does not say: Since you believe that Christ fell asleep. He rather speaks more sternly of Christ's death than ours and says: Since we believe that Christ died. But of us he says that we do not die, but only fall asleep. He calls our death not a death, but a sleep, and Christ's death he calls a real death.

Thus he attributes to the death of Christ such exceeding power that by comparison we should consider our death a sleep. For this is the right way to give comfort, to take the death which we suffer as far as possible from our eyes, at least according to the spirit, and look straight at the death of Christ. Therefore St. Paul in these words is saying: Why do you think so much about your death? Look at him who is really dead, compared with whom all the other dead are as nothing. They did not die, but he died. Therefore, if we are going to grieve, we should also grieve over Christ's death. That was a real death, not only in itself, because it was so bitter, ignominious, and grandiose, but also because it is so potent that it has baptized all the other dead, so that now they are called, not dead, but sleepers. And this is true, for we see in the Passion that Christ died as no one else dies or ever will die.

Therefore, says St. Paul, if you are assailed by sorrow and grief on account of your good friends whom you have lost, then look to this death and mingle, yea, cover with the death of Christ all other human deaths, and so magnify this death that other deaths are only a sleep compared with it. If this is true, why should we sorrow much over the death of others or even our own death and burial? After all, it is only a man that dies, and not even the whole man, but only a part, the body, but here is God's Son himself, here the Lord of creation dies. My death and your death will not have the bitterness which Christ's death had because he is immeasurably different from all other dead, in himself and by reason of his person.

Thus St. Paul is trying to turn us around and draw us into the death of Christ, that we may see how immeasurably great it is, in order that when your heart is grieved over a good friend who has died you may learn to say: Here you are grieving so much over your friend, who would have to die some day anyhow; why don't you also grieve over this death? Why aren't you also weeping and lamenting over Christ your Lord, whose death was so much greater and more horrible than that of all other men? As the beloved apostles [cf. Luke 24:17-24] had to do when they were present at his passing and also thought he would remain dead; as we think when we judge according to our five senses. No better comfort can be found than to contemplate this death and see how mighty and glorious it has become and how it has devoured all other deaths, so that, by comparison, this death is the most grievous and cruel of all. Therefore he goes on to say:

"For since we believe that Jesus died and rose again, even so, through Jesus, God will bring with him those who have fallen asleep" [I Thess. 4:14].

It is as if he were saying: Be of good courage and cheer up, for if this is true there is no need to sorrow over those who have fallen asleep. The only important thing here is that we lay hold of this article that Christ died and rose again, when we are in distress and there is sorrow and grief. Just as now, when our sovereign prince, our beloved lord and father has fallen, under whose protection we have lived in peace till now and from whose hands we have eaten our dear bread, and now there will be another ruler and government, and nobody knows how it will turn out. The only one who knows is God, who has now taken from us our head and has not revealed what he proposes to do with us henceforth. Therefore in this case we may well be afraid and distressed; although I do not doubt that there are some among you who are not particularly concerned about it and think that it is an easy matter to take hold of government. But changing and improving are two different things. Changing the government we will leave to men, but improving it is in God's hands alone.

Now, because all this is so, the best consolation is to say with St. Paul: Beloved, look not at this dead body; you have something higher and better to contemplate, namely, the death and resurrection of Jesus Christ. If you gaze steadfastly at this mirror and image, at Christ the Lord, who died and rose again, you will see where you will go and where those will go who have not fallen asleep in Christ, namely, that God intends to bring with him you and all others who have been baptized and have fallen asleep in Christ, because he has wrapped them in Christ's death and included them in his resurrection and does not intend to leave them lying under the ground, even though for our reason and five senses there is no reason why this should be so, in order that faith may find room and we learn to trust God even in that which we do not see.

Therefore, even though it is hard, we must learn to look at the death of Christ, through which our death is destroyed, and even though it seems otherwise to our eyes, the Holy Spirit nevertheless mingles this sour vinegar with honey and sugar, that our faith may soar up to God and learn to see the dead, not lying in the grave and coffin, but in Christ. When you see him there, then the dead body is no longer in the coffin. Even though the carcass be foul and stinking it makes no difference; turn your eyes and nose and all five senses away and remember what St. Paul says in the fifteenth chapter of I Corinthians [I Cor. 15:42-50]: One buries the body in all dishonor; this is true, but don't look at that, for it will rise again in all glory. It is buried and sown as something perishable and it will rise up imperishable. It is sown in weakness and will rise in power. It is sown a natural body and will rise a spiritual body, etc. Thus he is constantly turning our hearts, because he cannot turn our eyes, away from that which the eyes see to that which God is saying and to Christ, so that we may have no doubt that he will bring us with Christ. So anyone who can believe this will have good comfort in his own death and the death of other people.

Since St. Paul so extols the dead, as you have heard, we ought to thank God unceasingly for his grace in also including our beloved elector in the death of Christ and embracing him in his resurrection. For you know what a death he suffered in Augsburg at the Diet.[2] I shall not praise him now for his great virtues, but rather let him remain a sinner like all the rest of us, who also purpose to go to the judgment and hand over to our Lord God many a grievous sin, as we too hold steadfast to that article which is called "the forgiveness of sins." Therefore I am not going to make out that our beloved lord was altogether pure, though he was a very devout, kindly man, free of all guile, in whom never in my lifetime have I seen the slightest pride, anger, or envy, who was able to bear and forgive all things readily and was more than mild. I shall say no more of this virtue now.

If along with this he sometimes failed in government, what can be said against that? A prince is also a human being and always has ten devils around him where another man has only one, so that God must give him special guidance and set his angels about him. When we see them sometimes make a false step in government we are quick to say, Ah, I would have done so and so, but if we were to govern we would probably drive the cart into the mire or even

---

[2] This is explained in the next paragraph but one.

turn it upside down. So nobody can do right as far as we are concerned, and if we look at ourselves we have never yet been right.
All this we shall pass over now and we shall stick to praising him,
as St. Paul praises his Christians, saying that God will bring with
him those who are in Christ, and we shall not look upon him according to his temporal death, but according to Christ's death and
his spiritual death, which he died in accord with Christ.

For you all know how, following Christ, he died two years ago
in Augsburg and suffered the real death,[3] not only for himself, but
for us all, when he was obliged to swallow all kinds of bitter broth
and venom which the devil had poured out for him. This is the
real, horrible death, when the devil wears a man down. There our
beloved elector openly confessed Christ's death and resurrection
before the whole world and he stuck to it, staking his land and
people, indeed his own body and life, upon it. There can be no
doubt that he felt this death and its severity in his heart. And since
this confession is publicly known, we are ready to praise him for it
as a Christian. If along with this there should be something lacking
in his personal life [in government], we shall let this pass, for we
will not consider such insignificant sins in such a great person, but
rather, over against this, praise the fact that he confessed Christ's
death and resurrection, by which He swallowed up death and hell
and all sins, and remained steadfast in this confession. This covers
and swallows up the multitude of sins as the great ocean swallows
a spark of fire. Therefore all other sins are as nothing compared
with this one thing, that Christ's death and resurrection be not
denied, but openly confessed.

We should therefore take comfort in the fact that Christ died
and our beloved prince is caught up and fallen asleep in Christ's
death and that he suffered a far more bitter death at Augsburg than
now, a death which we are still obliged to suffer daily and in-
cessantly from the tyrants and sectarians, and, indeed, also from our
own conscience and the devil. This is the real death. The other
physical death, when we pass away in bed, is only a childish death

---

[3] Luther frequently spoke of himself as suffering death, by which he meant
severe trial (*Anfechtung*); cf. WA 30[II], 583. Cf. Luther's letters to Elector
John, Theodore G. Tappert (ed.), *Luther: Letters of Spiritual Counsel*,
pp. 140-144, 151-152.

[*Kindersterben*] or an animal death. The other, however, is the real, manly death, which still faces us, the death in which we would rather risk our neck, if this were possible, before we would deny the man who is called Jesus Christ. This may be called a manly, real death, and St. Paul also speaks of it in the eleventh chapter of I Corinthians [I Cor. 15:31]: "I protest, brethren, by my pride in you which I have in Christ Jesus our Lord, I die every day!" The other death is only when the reason and the five senses die, the eyes no longer see, the ears do not hear, and the hands no longer feel, etc. So a cow also dies; it is only an outward dying away of the body, the poor bag [of worms];[4] it is only a childish death compared with the other death.

As far as that death is concerned, our beloved prince has now passed away and one could feel that it was only a childish death; for our Lord God had so caught him up in His death that he suffered no buffeting at all nor disputed much with the devil, as some do, who fall into despair over the grievous thought of sin, the last judgment, hell, and the like, which the devil inspires in them, and labor over it so that the cold sweat breaks out and they are almost paralyzed. This is a real death, not a baby death. But when it happens, as it did with our beloved prince, that the body merely lies upon the bed and there is no fright and trembling, because he was called into Christ's kingdom through baptism and afterwards openly confessed Christ and listened with all diligence and his whole heart to God's Word, and thus only the five sense died away—then this is the least of death and only half of death, when a man struggles only with physical death, even though we untempted folk think it the greatest. [It is not the real death, which one should struggle with in the heart.]

Therefore, the person whom God takes away in such a way that he does not feel the posioned darts of the devil dies truly and well. So God took this man away. There was nothing there, as I saw it, except a real childish death. Our dear Lord God was thinking: The good prince has already gone through his real death at Augsburg; therefore I have included him in my death and henceforth he shall nevermore die, except physically. So that he passed away as in a sleep, as children and irrational animals die, except that animals

---

[4] *Sack;* Luther usually uses the term *Madensack.*

have no hope of another life. Therefore it is a comforting death when a person dies so gently, his five senses simply dying away, if only the person looks upon it rightly; when he passes on so wrapped in our Lord Christ's suffering that our Lord God says: I will allow the devil to destroy you only physically; therefore do not look so steadily at your death, but look at the fact that my Son died for you and the fact that you have already been spiritually killed. So now I will send death to you only in the sense that you will die as far as your five senses are concerned, as in a sleep.

For this reason we shall reckon our beloved sovereign among those who sleep in Jesus Christ, but especially because he did not depart from the confession of the death and resurrection of Christ, but suffered all manner of injury and affront for it. We therefore are not going to make him a living saint. If some sin crept in,[5] let it go, we shall let him remain a human being, but will so cloak it over that the devil will not see such small sins and emphasize the great works which the angels in heaven will extol. For what can the devil bring up against his personal righteousness, since Christ is standing there alongside him and for him with His death and resurrection, which is more than the sin of the whole world?

It is my hope that we too shall die this way and carry with us to heaven a poor sinner, if only we hold on to this cloak and wrap ourselves in the death of the Son of God and cover and veil ourselves with his resurrection. If we stand firmly upon this and never depart from it, then our righteousness will be so great that all our sins, no matter what they are, will be as a tiny spark and our righteousness as a great ocean, and our death will be far less than a sleep and a dream. Moreover, the shame of our being buried so nastily is covered with a dignity which is called the resurrection of Jesus Christ, by which it is so adorned that the sun is put to shame when it looks upon it and the beloved angels cannot gaze upon it sufficiently. We are graced and adorned with such beauty that all the other uncleanness of our poor body, such as death and the like, are as nothing.

Hence, one must look upon a Christian death with different eyes, not the way a cow stares at a new gate, and smells it in a

---

[5] The macaronic Rörer version reads: *Si quid mali cum monasteriis,* in connection with the secularization of monasteries.

different way, not as a cow sniffs grass, by learning to speak and think of it as the Scriptures do and not considering deceased Christians to be dead and buried people. To the five senses that is the way it appears. As far as they can lead us, it brings only woe. Therefore go beyond them and listen to what St. Paul says here, that they are sleeping in Christ and God will bring them with Christ [as he brought with him the Savior, the devourer of death, the destroyer of the devil]. Learn to comfort yourselves with these words and instil in your hearts the fact that it is far more certain that Duke John of Saxony will come out of the grave and be far more splendid than the sun is now [cf. Dan. 12:3; Isa. 60:19] than that he is lying here before our eyes. This is not so certain as the fact that he will live again and go forth with Christ because God cannot lie. But take it to heart! For he who does not have this comfort can neither comfort himself nor be happy, but the more the Word escapes him the more the consolation also escapes him.

Therefore, let us comfort ourselves now in this sorrow with the fact that we know with certainty that he will rise again with Christ. For here the words of Christ stood sure: "Every one who acknowledges me before men, I also will acknowledge before my Father" [Matt. 10:32]. Otherwise, if that Man had not ascended into heaven, we could have little hope indeed.

But when some keep coming with the law and arguing: Now my dear, who knows whether God will consider you to be good? This is the dismal devil himself, who is always pointing us to personal righteousness,[6] how good I am and how bad I am; for his whole skill consists in using this image of our goodness to snatch from our eyes the image of the Man who died and rose again. Therefore, it was a very good thing that happened with our prince, that he was not drawn into this disputation,[7] otherwise the devil would doubtless have assailed him: Listen to me; how have you lived, how have you reigned? and so on; and would have presented him with a record which would have terrified him and subjected him to a hard struggle. This is the devil's strategy and he often tries it on me. He asks me how good and how evil I am, and, what

---

[6] As opposed to the righteousness we have in Christ.

[7] In argument with the devil, that is, struggle of conscience as to how he would stand before the judgment of God.

is more, he makes a very masterful use of the Scriptures and the law. You must do this and that. You must be good and keep the law. But you have not kept it? How are you going to get out of that?

And with that thought he brings one into such anxiety that one is ready to despair. And again when occasionally I have done something good, he is nevertheless able to turn it around in such a way that my holiness is reduced to nothingness. Then I make haste to seize hold of the article of the forgiveness of sins through Jesus Christ, who died and rose again for my sins [cf. I Cor. 15:31]; and this is precisely what he does not want to let into my heart. But what does go into the heart is that I have done this and not done that, that I have given alms, been good, etc., just as I can say of our beloved prince that he had a faithful heart, devoid of malice and envy.

But by all means take care not to let anybody persuade you of this on your deathbed; for then the devil is not far away; he can throw in your face a little sin which reduces all such fine virtues to nothing, so that finally you come to such a pass that you say: Devil, rage as much as you please, I do not boast of my good works and virtues before our Lord God at all, nor shall I despair on account of my sins, but I comfort myself with the fact that Jesus Christ died and rose again, as the text here says.

Lo, when I believe this with my whole heart, then I have the greatest treasure, namely, the death of Christ and the power which it has wrought, and I am more concerned with that than with what I have done. Therefore, devil, begone with both my righteousness and my sin. If I have committed some sin, go eat the dung; it's yours. I'm not worrying about it, for Jesus Christ died. St. Paul bids me comfort myself with this, that I may learn to defend myself from the devil and say: Even though I have sinned, it doesn't matter; I will not argue with you about what evil or good I have done. There is no time to talk of that now; go away and do it some other time when I have been a bad boy, or go to the impenitent and scare them all you please. But with me, who have already been through the anguish and throes of death, you'll find no place now. This is not the time for arguing, but for comforting myself with the words that Jesus Christ died and rose for me. Thus I am sure that God will bring me, along with other Christians, with Christ to his right hand and carry me through death and hell. Therefore, they should not be called dead people but sleeping and henceforth death should not be called death but a sleep, and such a deep sleep that one will not even dream; as without doubt our beloved lord and prince lies in a sweet sleep and has become one of the holy sleepers. And all this, not because he was a mild, merciful, kindly master, but because he confessed Christ's death and clung to it and stuck to it.

This, then, is the devil's real strategy, as I have said, to tear us away from this comfort and meanwhile lead us into an argument about how good we are. On the other hand you have now heard that you should tell him to go to those who have such thoughts, who care nothing for Christ's suffering and death and live their lives away in reveling and let him argue with them. But this he will not do, he's got them already, they are already his. Therefore he also wants these others, the discouraged, timid, and terrified consciences. The others he has because they go on living in insolence and security and without any fear of God. These he tries to get through despondence and despair. But you must learn to say: Devil, you're coming at the wrong time. No devil is going to argue with me now, but rather I shall talk with my Lord Jesus Christ, that I may learn that he suffered for me and died and rose again for my sins, and that God will bring me with him on the last day.

And for a sign of all this I have his dear baptism, his gospel, his Word and sacraments, to which I have been called and which I have confessed before the whole world. These seals and letters cannot fail me, any more than God himself can fail me. If some few sins should occur, such as living and doing wrongly, these nevertheless will not count, in order that Christ's death and resurrection may be prized beyond my sin and the sin of the whole world. Speak out freely and say: No matter how much sin I have committed, even more than ten worlds can commit, I still know that Christ's death and resurrection is far greater. Swiftly fling out that defiance and boast, not of yourself or your righteousness, but of the fact that Jesus Christ died and rose again for you. If you believe this, then be bold and assured that he will bring you with Christ, and as you have heard that Christ is risen, so you too will rise again.

You see, dear friends, this is the meaning of this text [which I have wanted to speak on this morning]: that we should sorrow over our beloved ruler according to the outward man. For who knows why our dear Lord God has taken him away? You know that we are all wicked, ungrateful villains and that the people, young and old, are so utterly wanton that there is no longer any discipline or fear. If now our Lord God so manifests himself and takes away the head, not even sparing a prince, he is surely giving you to understand that this means you. Therefore humble yourself and improve your life, that you, like him, may be among those who suffer and die with Christ. I hope that there are many of you who have died and suffered as my ruler did at Augsburg, for then you too will attain to such a gentle death that it will come as softly and easily as sleep. This will be the end of all who believe in the death and resurrection of Christ and confess the same; they will finally rise with him and be brought with Christ. May God grant this to us. Amen.[8]

Second Sermon at the Funeral of the Elector, Duke John of Saxony, I Thess. 4:13-18, August 22, 1532

Since we are still in the week of mourning and have begun to comfort ourselves with God's Word from St. Paul's Epistle, we shall now speak somewhat further about it for further comfort and expound the chosen text fully.

In the first part of this Epistle of St. Paul we have heard how he admonishes and comforts the Christians, telling them that they should not act so dreadfully by weeping and wailing over the deceased, but rather show that there is a difference between those who have no hope, that is, the unbelievers and pagans, and us, who believe in Christ and have far different minds, hearts, and thoughts from theirs. For a Christian should be a new creature or a newly created work of God, who in all things speaks and thinks and judges differently from the way the world speaks or judges. And

---

[8] The printed text ends with the words: "The second sermon follows."

because he is a new man, everything here in this life should and must become new through faith, as it will become new in the life to come through manifest revelation itself. Now the world cannot do anything else but think of death according to its ancient custom and nature, that it is the most abominable and horrible thing on earth, the end of life and all joy, just as it also follows that ancient delusion in looking upon all other misery and misfortune as something which is evil and intolerable, from which it should flee, and when it happens, it is terrified and is ready to give up in despair.

But a Christian, on the contrary, as a new man, should be so constituted that he can have far different, even completely opposite thoughts and, as St. Paul says in Rom. 5 [:3], can even boast and glory and rejoice when things go wrong, and his heart should seize only upon such thoughts as that he possesses great wealth when he is poor, that he is a mighty prince and lord when he lies in prison and superlatively strong when he is weak and sick, and that he is floating in honors when he is being covered with shame and ignominy. He should know that he only becomes a new, living man when he dies here and now; in short, he must gain a completely new heart and mind and thereby make all things on earth new, and thus begin here a prelude to the life to come, when all things will become as new, manifestly and visibly, as he now imagines and conceives them by faith according to his new nature.

And all this, not in us, but in Christ, as St. Paul here shows us; for he alone accomplished the deed of having all things new already in this manifest and visible life and, as St. Paul says in Rom. 6 [:9], will never die again and death has no power or dominion over him, but rather everything that it was able to do, even physically, was stripped away, so that it was no longer able to bind, or imprison or torment him with hunger, thirst, and wounds. In short, death lost all its venom, cords, spear, sword, and whatever evil it possesses to Christ. In this Man we too should allow ourselves to think even now that all things have become new and accustom ourselves to the strong thoughts of faith, keeping ever before our eyes the beloved image of the dead and risen Christ and carrying it with us against the old nature, which still assails and confronts us and tries to frighten us with misery, distress, misfortune, poverty, death, and whatever else there may be.

244

You see why the Apostle uses these particular words: you should be different from the other people, who have no hope, simply because you believe that Christ rose from the dead and that through him death has been conquered. It is as if he were saying: In this way you have become people who are altogether different from what you were as you came from your father and mother and earthly being. Since you have been baptized in His name, as well as into His nature and kingdom, death and resurrection, you must remember that your whole attitude toward those things of which the world is terrified should be different, and that you should have eyes, ears, senses, and thoughts which are different from those you had before from Adam, when you were frightened and sorrowful, as those who had no hope. But now you no longer act this way, but think and speak just the opposite, confident that, because he has overcome death, he will also snatch us from death and bring us with him. For he rose again in order that he take us with him out of death into life and eternal glory [cf. Eph. 2:6].

This, after all, is what had to be done by the dear patriarchs, who had not yet seen the work and image of Christ's rising from the dead which has been presented to us, but saw it only in faith and from afar, as through dark blue clouds, whereas for us the clear, bright sun is shining. Nevertheless, they had to depend on Christ, who was still far away, and also soar up to the comforting thought that through his resurrection they too would rise up from death and live with him. That is why they sang such comforting songs: "Precious in the sight of the Lord is the death of his saints" (Ps. 116 [:15]).[9] Again in Ps. 72 [:14]: "Precious is their blood in his sight." And again in Ps. 9 [:12]: "He who avenges blood is mindful of them."

So they go on speaking, those devout hearts, and from such words they must have spun many a strong sermon—though they were doubtless briefly expressed and written only as a theme or conclusion of their sermons—for they have provided mighty and rich consolation, with which one can lift up a man's heart, because they argue so powerfully. [This is their argument:] Dear friend, you may well think otherwise and to your eyes it looks as if the death of the saints is pure defeat and destruction and it appears as if they now

---

[9] Cited first in Latin and then in German.

were utterly forgotten and silenced, as if they had no God to befriend them, because he did not befriend them while they were
living and allowed them to perish so miserably as those who are
torn and devoured and burned and pulverized. So no rational mind
can say anything else but that their death was a pitiful, miserable,
shameful thing. But before God, say the dear patriarchs, you must
take it as sure truth that when a saint (which means every Christian) dies, then there is offered to him excellent, costly, precious
sacrifice, the loveliest and sweetest odor of incense and the best and
highest worship [Gottesdienst] that can ever be given to him.

For he does not care so much for the living saints as the dead.
Indeed, while they are living he allows them to go their way, so
weak and miserable and tormenting themselves with sin, the world,
the devil, and death, as if he did not even see it and would not help
them. But no sooner are they out of the sight of men and have become a foul, stinking carcass, which nobody can abide, or powder
and dust, so that nobody knows where they are, cut off and forgotten by all the world as those who have nothing more to hope for,
then, and precisely then, do they begin to become a precious thing
in the sight of God. Then they not only begin really to live but also
become a precious treasure which God himself holds dear and precious and glories in beyond all else. And the more they are forgotten in the eyes of the world the more he honors and glorifies
them.

You have a beautiful example of this in the first two brothers in
Gen. 4 [:8-16]. When the rascal Cain had secretly murdered and
buried his brother he walked away and wiped his mouth as if he
had done nothing wrong,[10] thinking that nobody would know and
it would remain secret, since Abel had nobody to take his part, etc.
And when God asked him, "Where is Abel your brother?" he acted
so holy and pure that he even boasted that he was not responsible
for him and said, "I do not know; am I my brother's keeper?" But
then came "he who avenges blood" [Ps. 9:12],[11] who requires and
avenges the blood of his saints [cf. Ezek. 3:18-20; Rev. 6:10; 19:2],
and said, "The voice of your brother's blood is crying to me from

---

[10] Wischet das maul. Cf. Ernst Thiele, Luthers Sprichwörtersammlung (Weimar, 1900), p. 315.
[11] Cited in Latin.

the ground" [Gen. 4:10]. Who tells God to speak so? He cannot forget it, now that he is dead and gone, but must call out from heaven and cry over this blood which troubles him so greatly that he can neither bear it nor keep silent, even though he could have averted it and prevented Cain's now being alone without a brother or heir, but punishes him so severely that he must be cast out by his parents and even the earth is cursed on his account. That means that he really cares for this blood which was now corrupted. He did not show such care and concern while Abel was living, except that he was pleased with his sacrifice. But now that he is gone and lying under the ground, he forthwith becomes alive and speaks in heaven, so that God himself speaks for him and makes such an outcry in all the world that both he and his murderer must stand eternally as an example in the Scriptures which will never be extinguished.

You see, this is how the dear patriarchs looked upon such an example and drew from it their sayings that the dead saints most certainly live in the sight of God and will rise again more glorious than before. For he does not concern himself in this way with any living beasts or cattle and whatever has no hope, nor with the tyrants and the godless, who die in the devil's name. But he is concerned with his poor saints, who perish so miserably and shamefully, and consider their deaths more precious than their whole lives. For their lives cannot be without sin, even though they too are subject to forgiveness and to Christ; but it is as nothing compared to a man's leaving this life and dying to sin and the world; for then God opens both his eyes and all the angels must be there to wait upon him, below and above and round about him, if it so be that he is clothed with the baptism of Christ and with faith and God's Word that he may be counted among those who are called God's saints.

For surely you know, thank God, who God's saints are; that the Scriptures do not mean the saints in heaven above, as the pope creates saints, whom one should invoke, whose days one should observe with fasting, and whom one should choose as mediators. Nor does it mean those who have sanctified themselves, like the Carthusians, the barefooted friars, and other monks or [pilgrims]¹²

---

¹² So in Rörer's version, *Walbrüder*; in printed text, *Waldbrüder*, hermits.

and such like devils who want to make themselves holy through their works. It means rather those whom God has sanctified, without any of their works or co-operation whatsoever, by reason of the fact that they are baptized in Christ's name, sprinkled and washed clean with his blood, and endowed and adorned with his dear Word and gifts of the Holy Spirit. All of which we have not engendered and cannot engender, but must receive from him by pure grace. But he who does not have this and seeks some other holiness is a stench and abomination to the Lord, because he denies that this bath of the blood of the innocent Lamb does not make one holy and clean.

Now those who are such baptized Christians, who love his Word, hold fast to it, and die in the same, no matter whether they are hanged, broken on the wheel, burned, drowned, or perish of pestilence, fever, or the like, simply include them in Christ's death and resurrection and without a moment's hesitation speak this text over them: "Precious in the sight of the Lord is the death of his saints" [Ps. 116:15]; for he deems it [i.e., their dying] an excellent and beautiful treasure, the most precious jewel on earth. Whether the devil strangle you in your bed or the hangman on the gallows, it is settled that such a death is a holy death and so highly esteemed by him that he will not leave it unavenged, but will hale the devil who kills you before the judgment and torture him with eternal punishment, strike off the head of sin, bury death in hell, and avenge everything that has caused his saint to die.

And because he so greatly cares for them, he certainly will not allow them to remain in death, perishing and decaying in the earth, but will raise them again, so that their death shall not be a death, but a completely new life with Christ in everlasting light and glory, as we confidently and without all doubt hope in the case of our beloved head [the deceased Elector John]. Though we have lost him according to the body and the old nature, he is not lost and not forgotten before God in Christ, who has received him and brought him to rest, so that now he is safe from the devil and all enemies, and will bring him and all the saints with him on the last day before our eyes and the eyes of the whole world.

Behold, this is what St. Paul is trying to do with this text, with which he bids his Thessalonians to comfort one another, and with

which we also ought to comfort ourselves as they did and thank God
when we see him taking away a person in the knowledge of his
Word, even though it is true that as far as the outward man is concerned it is not altogether without grief and sorrow. For not yet
do we have holiness entire, but only in our hearts by faith. We
still do not lay hold of it in our outward being; we are still stuck
in the muck and mire of our old Adam, who still befouls himself
and hawks and snuffles. We must let him have his clinging muck,
infirmities, and sins until he is completely buried; then there will
be an end to all grief and suffering.

Nevertheless, beyond and above this grief there should be the
faith that Christ died and rose again for the sake of his Christians
and that their death is a noble, precious treasure, in order that we
may learn to distinguish between the world's eyes and God's eyes,
between reason, according to which the old man remains in the
grave, and faith, by which we are new, heavenly men and receive
totally new hearts and thoughts about death and all misfortune.
And we must on no account judge as the world sees it, but as it
appears before God in the new being, which we do not see but only
hear spoken of in the Word. We should lay hold of this example,
which the Scriptures provide, that he was so greatly and earnestly
concerned about the dead Abel, and realize that it was written for
us and set before us as a fine mirror, yea, as a sun, for all who die, as
he died, in God's Word, and that as he looked upon him after his
death so he will most certainly look upon all who live and die in
faith in him.

This, then, was St. Paul's conclusion: If you have believed
and understood that Christ died and rose again, then there can be
no doubt that he will also raise up with him those who have fallen
asleep, if they have remained in him and therefore have died in
him and through him and, indeed, also for his sake. For if we are
baptized and believe in Christ, we shall certainly not die for our
sake but for Christ's sake, as he too did not die for his own sake, for
there was no death in him. But the devil kills the Christians and
destroys them with all manner of torments, and this he does solely
because they believe and are Christians. For he cannot abide anybody on earth who believes in Christ, though he also gives the others
their due. But to these he is especially hostile and he means to

destroy them, the sooner the better. He slinks about day and night and will not rest until he kills and exterminates them. And to accomplish this he employs all kinds of plagues, war, sword, fire, water, pestilence, syphilis, apoplexy, dysentery, etc., which, as the Scripture says, are all his weapons, his arrows, armor, and equipment, by which he accomplishes nothing less than to kill the Christians. For he is the master and author of death, who first introduced death, says the Epistle to the Hebrews [Heb. 2:14], and the chief hangman to destroy the believers. And he also honestly pursues his craft throughout the whole world and kills us all in the end, as he also killed Christ, so that every Christian owes his death to him.

But Christ, on the other hand, is a lord and prince[13] of life beyond all the power of the devil. Therefore he leads out his own and brings them with him to heaven, because they are in him, and they live and die and lie in his bosom and arms, not in the grave or in the power of the devil, except in the old being. Just as Christ also, though he lay in the grave, yet in a moment he was both dead and alive and rose again like a lightning flash from heaven. So he will raise us too in an instant, in the twinkling of an eye, out of the grave, the dust, the water, and we shall stand in full view, utterly pure and clean as the bright sun. This is what St. Paul certainly wants us to conclude and believe (though it is incredible and ridiculous to reason) as a sure consequence of the fact that Christ died and rose again. Then he goes on and proceeds to explain how this will happen, saying:

"For this we declare to you by the word of the Lord, that we who are alive, who are left until the coming of the Lord, shall not precede those who have fallen asleep" [I Thess. 4:15].

With these words he provides a preface, the more to strengthen their faith. For he is concerned, the dear Apostle, lest this message be considered too slightly and not be taken as the Word of God, this message which speaks of such glorious, incomprehensible things. For God himself had not let it ring forth from heaven with glorious splendor by thousands of angels, in which case we should all have had to fall on our knees and accept it and believe it with trembling, but rather committed it to an insignificant, poor man like Paul, who

---

[13] *Hertzog*, literally, "duke."

was a poor, plain person. He himself says that the Corinthians were saying of him that he preached and wrote as if he were a god and yet was such a small, insignificant person with a thin, dried-up body, which was the reason why the false apostles proudly despised and belittled him [II Cor. 10:7-12].

So he says: I know very well that I am speaking of things so high that the world and reason is offended. Therefore I beg and admonish you not to look upon us, nor to accept as our word what we are saying, but rather to forget our person and listen to it as the word of the divine Majesty spoken from heaven. For it is a great hindrance to faith to stare at the masks and persons with one's eyes, as flesh and reason does, so that one cannot see and esteem the Word as greatly as it should be. This also happens with baptism, where one sees nothing but the finger of the man who is baptizing and the water which he pours over the child, a mere creature, and hears nothing but the poor voice from the lips of the baptizer, so that for us men it seems all too insignificant.

Therefore, see to it, he is saying, that you pay no heed to how insignificant the person or creature may be, but rather be assured that the word which I speak is God's Word, which he himself is speaking. But if it is God's Word, then it must be mightier than heaven and earth and all angels and the devil besides. For what is all power in heaven and earth compared with what God says? If, then, you believe that what I preach to you is God's Word, then you will easily believe what is says. That's the only effort that's necessary, positively to believe that it is God's Word; after that there is no trouble. For with one word he created heaven and earth and all that is in them when everywhere there was still nothing and every year creates new fruits and what lovely summer brings. So it is here; though you see that everything dies away and less remains of man than summer in coldest winter, when neither foliage nor grass remains and no leaf or fruit is to be found upon a tree, here there is even less life, since what the person has been becomes altogether powder and dust, burned to powder by fire or wasted in water or eaten by birds and animals and worms in the ground. And yet, as surely as God's Word is true, you must firmly believe that he will bring us forth again as a whole transformed body, just as he now does every year as a symbol, bringing back from dead winter a beautiful, green summer, and as he made everything out of nothing. Therefore, by all means remember to accept it, not as man's word, but as God's Word.

This is what will happen, he says: "We who are alive, who are left until the coming of the Lord, shall not precede those who have fallen asleep" [I Thess. 4:17]. This is a paraphrase, spoken in a roundabout way, but, briefly, what it says is that we shall all go thither together at the same time, both those who have died previously and those who have lived until Christ's coming and that thus all will soar up together in an instant and see one another again. It says, therefore, that we who may still be living will not see the Lord Christ any sooner than those who have died, even though we shall be drawn upward with open eyes and still be living in the body, whereas the others have long since decayed and, to our minds, become nothing, and even though it would seem that we, who are still living, would be the first and would see the Lord much sooner than the dead. But he would have it that the dead would all rise with us in the same moment and have eyes as pure and fine as ours to see as well as we do. (Reason calls this ridiculous, but he tells me that he is speaking the Word of God.)

He therefore will do the same with Christians that he did with Christ, whom he raised up from the locked and sealed grave in the twinkling of an eye, so that in the selfsame moment he was in it and out of it. So in the last moment he will bring together both us who are still living in our five senses, and all who are decomposed, pulverized, and scattered throughout the world, and we and they together will be caught up to heaven, soaring in the clouds (as he says later), lighter than the birds [cf. I Cor. 15:39] and more beautiful than the sun [cf. I Cor. 15:41], and the heavens will be so full of light and splendor that all the light and splendor of the sun and all the stars will be as nothing compared with it, and we shall see neither sun nor stars for the light and splendor of Christ and his angels and saints. Now I know that this sounds as false as a sweet idea and human dream, but I have declared that it is God's Word. He who will not believe this cannot believe us either. It's one and the same thing.

Then he goes on to tell how the Lord Christ will come, by what means he will perform it, and what power he will employ to accomplish it.

"For the Lord himself will descend from heaven with a cry of command, with the archangel's call, and with the sound of the trumpet of God. And the dead in Christ will rise first; then we who are alive, who are left, shall be caught up together with them in the clouds to meet the Lord in the air; and so we shall always be with the Lord. Therefore comfort one another with these words" [I Thess. 4:16-18].

This is the meaning we have just explained, namely, that everything will happen at once, that we are not to think that we who are living will arrive and see Christ sooner, but will be caught up together with him, all in one moment, that we shall be changed and they be made alive again out of the grave and the dust in the selfsame moment, and, wherever we may be found, fly straightway into the air, most beautifully clothed. And this he, the Lord, will do. He will no longer send an apostle or preacher or John the Baptist, but will come down in his own person as a Lord in his majesty, with a great shout of command and the voice and trumpet of the archangel.

These words are purely allegorical. He was trying to paint a picture, as we must use pictures with children and simple people, and use words which we are accustomed to use in describing a grand, magnificent march of an army, when a lord takes the field in great triumph with his lifeguards, banners, trumpets, and canisters, so that everyone hears that he is coming. So Christ too will go forth with a shout of command and cause a trumpet to sound which is called the trumpet of God. This will be done by the archangel with his innumerable host of angels, who will be his vanguard or forerunners and set up such a tumult that heaven and earth will be burned in an instant and lie in a heap, transformed, and the dead will be brought together from everywhere. That will be quite a different trumpet and it will sound quite different from our trumpets and canisters on earth. But it will be his own voice and language, perhaps Hebrew, but even if it is not a particular language, it will be a voice which will wake all the dead.

I like to think that it will be a voice which says: Rise up, ye dead! as Christ called the dead Lazarus from the grave, "Lazarus, come out," (John 11 [:43]) and as he said to the girl and the young man in Matt. 9 [:25] and Luke 7 [:14], "I say to you, arise," accomplishing it with one word, as he spoke to the blind and the lepers: Receive your sight, be clean, etc. Here Paul calls this a cry of command or the voice of the archangel, that is to say, the voice of the archangel will shout so that it will be heard with our ears. And yet it is called a trumpet of God, that is, a trumpet by which God will wake up the dead through his divine power, just as he said in John 5 [:28-29], "The hour is coming when all who are in the tombs will hear his voice and come forth, those who have done good, to the resurrection of life," etc. Here he means, not the voice which Christ himself will utter, but the voice of the archangel and the trumpet, which is God's voice or trumpet. Just as here on earth the preacher's voice which proclaims God's Word is not called man's word but God's Word, so here the voice is the voice of the archangel and yet the voice of the Lord Christ, as being spoken by his command and power.

You see, he portrayed how it will happen in such grand terms in order that we should be confident and bold and not be so frightened over those who die, especially those who die in faith in and through Christ, and that we should hope that Christ himself may come and take them, and us with them. That we should hope that the archangel will come first with his trumpets and thousands of angels (like the angel in Luke 2 [:13] who appeared to the shepherds at Christ's birth with the multitude of the heavenly host) and strike up the cry of command, with Christ suddenly striding forth, and afterwards, when we have been raised and caught up into heaven, sing everlastingly: *Gloria in excelsis Deo,* "Glory to God in the highest" [Luke 2:14].

This, concludes St. Paul, we should most certainly expect, and comfort one another with these words. And he describes it so confidently, as if it had already happened. He prophesies of future things still not experienced as if they were history, in order that he may make us as certain as he is, that we may not be frightened of death and disdain all plague, pestilence, and disease, and keep our eyes fixed upon that beautiful picture of what is to come, when out of this present winter in which everything is dead and buried he will make a beautiful, eternal summer and bring forth the flesh, which lies buried and decayed, far more beautiful and glorious than it ever was before, as St. Paul says in I Cor. 15 [:43], "It is sown in dishonor, it is raised in glory. It is sown in weakness, it is raised in power." For dishonor and weakness means that miserable, shameful form of man, than which there is no more shameful, insufferable carcass on earth, which is a great dishonor and shame to this noble creature. But this does not matter, for it will be raised again in honor and in a glorious form, just as a seed which is cast into the ground must decay and become nothing, but when summer comes it comes forth again with beautiful blades and ears of corn.

So we too should hope and shall hope that the merciful God has thus taken our beloved, deceased elector and will raise him up again with Christ, because, after all, we know that he was baptized into Christ, and that he so confessed the gospel and remained steadfast in the Christian confession and died in the same, that I have no doubt that when the trumpet of the archangel is sounded he will joyfully rise in an instant from this crypt and, with us and all Christians, go to meet Christ, shining more brightly than the sun and all the stars. To this end help us, God the Father, Son, and Holy Spirit. Amen.

SERMON ON THE SUM OF THE CHRISTIAN LIFE

1532

SERMON ON THE SUM OF
THE CHRISTIAN LIFE
1532

Sermon on the Sum of the Christian Life, I Tim. 1:5-7,

Preached in Wörlitz, November 24, 1532

In November 1532, Luther was invited by the princes of Anhalt, Johann, Joachim, and Georg, who had recently introduced the Reformation in their territories, to visit them in Wörlitz, where the Elector Prince Joachim of Brandenburg was their guest at a great hunting party. Luther made the journey with Melanchthon and Cruciger, and the latter, one of the best recorders of Luther's sermons, took notes and prepared the transcript for the sermon here translated. A contemporary says that when Luther read the printed sermon he "was amazed at how he had spoken and praised the skill of Magister Caspar Cruciger who was so adept at catching his words and understanding his way of speaking, saying, 'I think he made it a better sermon than the one I preached.'" The hand of the editor is apparent not least in the length of the sermon but its excellence is such that it could not well be omitted from any collection of Luther's sermons.

Text in German; WA 36, 352-375.

Here in a few words St. Paul has expressed the sum of the whole Christian life (I Tim. 1 [:5-7]): "The aim of our charge[1] is love that issues from a pure heart and a good conscience and sincere faith. Certain persons by swerving from these have wandered away

---

[1] Luther's translation: "The sum (*Heubt summa*) of the commandment" provides the key word of the title of the sermon.

259

into vain discussion, desiring to be teachers of the law, without understanding either what they are saying or the things about which they make assertions."

Foreword

Dear friends, you know how earnestly God has commanded everyone to hear and to learn his precious Word, for it cost him much to bring it to the world. He hazarded his prophets for this purpose, indeed, he even sent his own Son into the world and allowed him to be crucified and to die for this. He permitted all the apostles to be persecuted and all Christians to be afflicted for this purpose, and commanded the former faithfully to administer it and the others diligently to hear it. And if there were no other reason for doing this except that it is God's good pleasure and will and strict command, this one reason would be sufficient, for as creatures we owe it to our Lord and Creator to be obedient to him and do this with all willingness as to him who has given us and every day continues to give us so many good things that we shall never be able to thank him sufficiently.

But he does not leave it at that; he does not wish that it be imposed upon us only as a command or to demand it of us as bound in duty, but also promises that great fruits and benefits shall redound to us thereby and causes it to be proclaimed that in doing this one gives to him his greatest and highest service [*Gottesdienst*]. For he is a great Lord, whom we serve, who has many and various kinds of service, and we can serve him in many ways; but this one way excels all the rest, for wherever a devout farmer or citizen or subject serves his master, he is also serving God. The same applies to a child, a servant, or a maidservant in the house, if they are obedient and faithfully do that which they should, likewise princes and masters, fathers and mothers, when they govern well and attend to their office. All this means to serve God, for this is his will and command, which he requires of us.

Now, the whole world is full of such service, if only they [i.e., the persons just mentioned] would perform it, for everyone in his station has his work laid upon him by God, in which he not only should but can serve him daily and constantly. For we are his own people and he has so ordered things that his service should go on everywhere, and nobody can excuse himself by saying that he does not know how or wherewith he should serve God, or pursue other trumpery stuff and seek in his own way to serve God, a way which he has neither ordained nor commanded, and meantime neglect what he has been commanded to do, as we in our blindness have done hitherto.

But far beyond and above all these services He has especially exalted and extolled this service, both of those who hear and those who preach his Word, and so he has this chosen service above all others on earth to be his special service, for the other services are done unto men. Therefore he also ordained a special day of the week on which we are to attend only upon this service, even though we also serve God throughout the week in other labors which he has not bound to any particular time or special day. But this day he has specially marked out and strictly commanded that it be kept, in order that men may have time and leisure for this service, lest anyone should complain that he cannot perform it or come to it because of his work. Moreover, he has also appointed special places, such as, among us, churches or houses, where we come together. Indeed, he has instituted and preserved the whole priesthood for this purpose, and furnishes and gives besides what is needed for the performance of this office, such as all sorts of arts and languages and diverse gifts. In short, he has given to all the world a special commandment to keep this [day] holy and high and so observe it that it may be understood how highly he esteems it and how precious and acceptable to him is the service in which his Word is handled.

It would be well if we were able to accustom people to understand that when they say they are "going to sermon"[2] this means "going to divine service,"[3] and that preaching means serving God, and that all who are assembled together are assembled in real and high service of God. Just as in former times the beloved apostles and ancient fathers expressed it—and it is from them the expression came and remained to this day—we say "go to mass" and "hear mass," as the pope himself strictly commanded in his decree that everyone should "hear" mass every Sunday. Nobody is accus-

---

[2] *zur predigt gehen.*
[3] *zu Gottes dienst gehen.*

tomed to say "I am going to see a mass," but rather "I am going to hear a mass," and this really means the same as to go to divine service and hear preaching or God's Word, which is the best and most necessary part of the mass, not as the pope does with his secret sacrificial masses in which there is no preaching nor hearing of God's Word, especially in that part which they consider the greatest and is called the canon of the mass [*Stillemesse*]. For the little word "mass,"[4] which appears to have been taken from the apostles, means in Hebrew the equivalent of a tribute or statute labor, as a peasant or tenant brings his lord his portion [*Mess*], that is, his due tribute or service, or serves his lord, thus acknowledging him to be his lord and rendering his obedience. So here too they said, "I am going to mass," or "to hear mass," as much as to say, "I am going to give or pay God his tribute and present and perform his service in the highest and most acceptable service." Thus, to hear mass means nothing else but to hear God's Word and thereby serve God.

I say this to you in order to admonish you and show you why we should willingly hear God's Word and come to church [*zur predigt gehen*], not only because it is God's stern commandment, but also because it carries with it the highest promise that it is acceptable to God and the greatest and most loving service we can perform for him, and far excels all other service as the sun exceeds all the stars and the sabbath day or Sunday excels all other common days, in short, as much as God's kingdom surpasses the kingdoms of the world. For here all things are hallowed and especially chosen—the time, the person, the place and the churches—all for the sake of the Word, which makes all things holy to us. [I say this to you] in order that we may take heed and not become so slothful and sluggish, like those shameful, satiated spirits who allow themselves to think that now they have the whole thing and know it all too well and even better than anyone can preach it to them, or like those others also who are soon fed up and think, "Oh, I've heard that often, why should I have to listen to the same thing over and over again?" They do not know and consider what a great and excellent thing it is and what a sublime service of God this is, which they so shamefully despise or so foully forsake and neglect, and thus pro-

---

[4] Cf. Luther's discussion of the meaning of mass in *Against the Heavenly Prophets*, LW 40, 120-130.

voke God to wrath because they so cocksurely cast his earnest command to the winds and allow his promise to be made void in them, and as much as in them is,[5] impair or even hinder by their example this laudable service of God.

For even if it were true, which, God be praised, it is not, that you did know all things perfectly, as well as the Lord Christ himself, you still must see how diligently he applied himself to preaching and carrying on this work, which, he knew so perfectly beyond all measure and had no need of whatsoever, as we so greatly need it. Likewise, St. Paul, the great apostle, even though he was highly learned and a great and excellent doctor, nevertheless went about from place to place and preached day and night, never becoming weary or fed up, as if he knew it all too well. And God himself, who gave it, takes such pleasure in hearing and seeing it that he can never grow weary of it, and therefore devotes so much to it and so earnestly ordains and commands that it should be carried on and practiced in all the world until the last day. Therefore you, after all, should be far less weary of it, since, even apart from this, you so badly need it to fight against the devil and all temptations.

And even though you do not need it for yourself in every respect, you ought not to grow weary or surfeited with going to divine service for an hour of the day or week, considering that before you did not grow weary of attending false worship in the churches every day, even running from one church and altar to another, and still you did not say, as you do now, "Oh, it's nothing new, I've seen it every day." What you thought was rather, "Yes, I went to mass yesterday and today and every day, yet tomorrow I will go again." So now you ought to do this even more, because now you know that this is the only right mass and service of God, and say, "Even though I knew it all perfectly, which is not the case, I will nevertheless perform my service to honor God and in obedience to him and hear the preaching for love and in praise of him; that he, my dear Lord, may see that I am willing to serve him in this high service, which he esteems so highly and to which he devotes so much; that, even though I derive no other benefit from it, I may at least take comfort in the fact that I have done the holiest work for him and performed

---

[5] "To do what is in one" is a scholastic phrase which implies that a Christian can do meritorious works agreeable to God. Cf. *LW* 31, 10 n. 5.

the most acceptable service of God, and that all other service is to be counted as insignificant and common everyday work compared with this high feast."

Now, as for him who will neither heed this nor be moved to hold God's Word in honor and esteem and gladly hear and learn it whenever he can, I do not know how to advise him, for I neither can nor will drag anybody in by the hair. Anybody who despises it, let him go on despising it and remain the pot-bellied sow that he is until the day when God will slaughter him and prepare a roast for the devil in the eternal fires of hell. For such a person cannot be a good man, nor is it a human sin, but rather the devil's obstinacy, when a man can so despise that for which God himself has appointed a place, person, time, and day, and besides admonishes and pleads with him so solemnly through his command and promise, and lays all this at our doorstep free of charge. This is something for which you ought to run to the ends of the world, something you cannot pay for with any gold or silver. And yet it is such an easy service that it costs you no labor or work, no money or goods, only to lend your ears to hear, or your mouth to speak and read, and surely there is no easier work than this. For even though this may bring with it the peril that you will have to bear the cross and suffer for it, yet the work in itself is easier than even the easiest of labors. If you can sit day and night in a tavern or somewhere else with good companions, gossiping, talking, singing, and bawling, and not grow tired or feel that it is work, then you can also sit in church for an hour and listen in the services of God and his will. What would you do if he commanded you to carry stones or to go on a pilgrimage or imposed some other heavy work upon you, as was imposed upon us formerly, when we willingly performed everything we were told to do and into the bargain were fleeced of money, goods, and body with silly lies and frauds?

But now we have the damnable devil, who makes the people so blind and so surfeited and sated that we do not realize what a treasure we have in the dear Word and go on living so rudely that we become like wild beasts. Let us take it to heart then and remember, whenever we preach, read, or hear God's Word, whether it be in the churches or at home through father, mother, master, or mistress, and gladly believe that wherever we can obtain it we are in the right, high, holy service of God, which pleases him beyond all measure. Thus you will be warmed and stirred to love hearing it all the more and God will also grant that it bear fruit, more than anybody can tell. For the Word never goes out without bringing forth much fruit whenever it is earnestly heard, without your being the better for it. Even though you do not see it now, in time it will appear. But it would take too long to tell all the fruits now, nor, indeed, can they all be numbered.

Let this suffice as a foreword to St. Paul's message, to stir us to listen more diligently to God's Word, as indeed it is necessary to be reminded of this every day and in every sermon. And it also is pertinent to this text we have taken from St. Paul, for in it he reproaches these same shameful spirits who take hold of God's Word with their own wisdom and likewise soon allow themselves to think they know it well and that they no longer need to listen to it or learn from anybody else. They turn to unprofitable talk about whatever is new or strange and the mob likes to hear. They presume to be masters of the Scripture and everyone's master; they want to teach the whole world and still they do not know what they are saying or asserting. For this is precisely the plague that results; when the Word of God is not proclaimed with earnestness and diligence, the listeners become listless and the preachers become lazy; there the concern must soon collapse and the churches become desolate. Then inevitably there appear these false spirits, who offer something new, attract the rabble to themselves, and boast that they are masters of the Scriptures, and yet are always the kind of people who themselves have neither known nor ever experienced what they are teaching. This is already gaining ground among us and God's wrath and punishment for our weariness and ingratitude is coming down upon us.

Therefore he begins his epistle to his disciple Timothy by urging him to see to it that such teachers do not arise, who can blab and babble a lot about the law and bring up many new questions and doctrines of what one must do and how to be religious, in order that they may be seen and praised as being more learned than others. And yet they never get to the point where they teach anything that is sure and right; they never get hold of the middle, the beginning, or the end of anything, but just go on talking about how to be religious, how to do good works, how to serve God, and so on. But they themselves do not understand what this means. And if you ask them how to do this, they begin to mince and drip words, here a piece and there a drop, here a work and there a work; this one says, be circumcised, another says, offer so much at the altar, go to a monastery, go on a pilgrimage, endow masses, and so on. And when this has been taught and performed they bring up something else; always something new. And yet they are incapable of instructing anybody with constancy and certainty or of saying: This is it or this is what it consists of! And meanwhile what they teach is supposed to be an excellent thing, and they can go on boasting and promising that they alone are the right teachers and criticizing and finding fault with others.

But the right master, Paul says, would be the one who grasps the main point and can rightly seize and put his finger on the sum total, that is, the state of the heart and conscience and the whole man. But they know nothing about this; they say the words all right, but the sum and the ultimate meaning of the law they corrupt altogether and meanwhile they go on preaching and babbling, out of the church window and in through the door, so that nobody knows where to stop or where to begin, what purpose it serves, or how he is to better and console himself, as we have jolly well seen and suffered from our dream-preachers under the papacy.

What, then, is the sum total of what should be preached? St. Paul's answer is: "The aim of our charge is love that issues from a pure heart and a good conscience and sincere faith."

There it is; there you have everything in a nutshell, expressed in the finest and fullest way and yet briefly and quickly said and easily retained. This is how you must perform the law if you are going to take hold of it right and seize it by the head, so that you will know what you are to do and not to do, how to submit yourself to it, and not go looking and begging elsewhere and everywhere: You must have the love that flows and issues from a pure heart and a good conscience and sincere faith. You just stick to that! All right preaching starts from there and remains there, which is something none of these rabblerousers and sated spirits can do. He does not do it, Paul is saying, with a doctrine of all kinds of works, in which everything is cut into pieces and peddled. What must be there is what the law really requires, and that is love, and the kind of love that flows like a rivulet, a stream, or a spring from a heart which is pure and a good conscience and sincere, unfeigned faith. If that's the way it goes, it's right; if not, then the meaning and sense of the whole law is missed.

Now these are deep and genuinely Pauline words, and besides they are very rich, so we must explain them somewhat in order that we may understand it a little and become accustomed to his language. In the first place, he says that the sum of the whole law, that in which it consists and is wholly comprehended is love. But "love" in German, as everyone knows, means nothing else except to be favorably and affectionately disposed toward a person from the heart and to offer and show him all kindness and friendship.

Now these other teachers also use this word. They preach and puff a lot about love. But they do so only from their own angle and turn it to their own advantage, just as the heretics, the godless, and the rascals also have love, but only among themselves and for those who are like them, but meanwhile they hate and persecute all good Christians and would gladly murder them if they could. But it is still a long way from being love when I select a person or two who please me and do what I wish and treat them kindly and favorably and nobody else. This is a crummy love [parteken liebe] which does not issue from a pure heart but is nothing but a filthy mess.

True love flows from a pure heart. God has commanded me to let my love go out to my neighbor and be kindly disposed to all, whether they be my friends or enemies, just as our heavenly Father himself does. He allows his sun to rise and shine on the good and evil and is most kind to those who are constantly dishonoring him and misusing his goods through disobedience, blasphemy, sin, and shame. He sends rain on the grateful and the selfish [Matt. 5:45; Luke 6:35] and gives even to the worst rascals on earth many good things from the earth, and money and possessions besides. Why does he do this? Out of sheer, pure love, of which his heart is full to overflowing, and which he pours out freely over every one without exception, be he good or bad, worthy or unworthy. This is a real, divine, total, and perfect love, which does not single out one person nor cut and divide itself, but goes out freely to all.

The other kind of love—when I am a good friend to one who

can serve and help me and who esteems me, and hate the one who disregards me and is not on my side—is false love. For it does not issue from a heart which is basically good and pure, the same toward all alike, but which rather seeks only its own and is stuffed full with love for itself and not for others; for he[6] loves nobody except for his own advantage, regards only what will serve him, and seeks in everyone his own profit, not the neighbor's. If you praise and honor that kind of a person, he smiles; but if you make a sour face at him or say something he doesn't like to hear, he flares up, begins to scold and curse, and the friendship is over.

On the contrary, he who has a pure heart should be so in accord with God's Word and his example that he will wish everyone well and do good to all, as God wishes him well and gives his divine love to him. If God can bestow all good upon Judas the traitor or Caiaphas, as well as upon his good children, why should I not also do the same? For what can we give to him which he has not more richly given to us?

Yes, you say, but he is my enemy and he does nothing but evil to me. Yes, my dear man, he is God's enemy too and he does far more evil to him than he can do to you or to me. But my love should not grow dim or cease because he is evil and unworthy of it. If he is evil, he will find it out; but his wickedness must not overcome me. On the contrary, if through love I can rebuke and admonish him or pray for him, that he may amend his ways and escape punishment, this I should do and do gladly. But to want to fly out at him and become his enemy and do evil to him besides, this will not do; for what good will it do me? It will not make me any better and it only makes him worse. But it will help me if I grant and show him all goodness (provided he will tolerate and accept it) and pray for him and so on. Then I shall have peace and will not be bickering and biting at anybody, and perhaps he too will thus be helped to improve. Otherwise, when I take love and make it separative and selective, I receive as much ill will from those I hate as joy and benefit from the others whom I favor. This means then that the source or water has been muddied and made impure, so that love does not remain pure, just as did the Jews, against whom Paul is

---

[6] The change in gender occurs in the original.

here speaking. They chose and selected those whom they loved and concocted a filthy, false love; therefore their hearts also could not be pure.

But what is it that makes the heart pure? The answer is that there is no better way of making it pure than through the highest purity, which is God's Word. Get that into your heart and order your life by it, and your heart will become pure. For example, take this saying: "You shall love your neighbor as yourself" [Matt. 19:19], and order your life by that, and you will see very well whether it will not wash it clean and scour out the selfishness and self-love which is there. For when he commands you to love your neighbor he excludes nobody, be he friend or enemy, good or evil. For even though he be a bad man and one who does evil to you, he does not on that account lose the name of neighbor but remains your flesh and blood and is included in the words: Love your neighbor. Therefore I say to you, if you look at him in the way the Word teaches and directs you, your heart will become pure and your love true, so that you will make no false distinction between persons nor will you look upon him as anything but another person who is good and does good to you.

It is true, of course, that the good man is more likeable and everybody naturally is glad to associate with him, whereas one shies away from rough, evil people. But this is still flesh and blood and not yet the true Christian love, for a Christian must not derive his love from the person, as the world does, as a young man is attracted by a good looking wench, a skinflint by money and property, or a lord or prince by honor and power. All this is a derived or borrowed love, which cleaves outwardly to the good it sees in a person and lasts no longer than this good lasts and can be enjoyed. This love, however, should be a flowing love, which flows from the inside of the heart like a fresh stream that goes on flowing and cannot be stopped or dried up. This love says: I love you, not because you are good or bad; for I draw my love, not from your goodness, as from another's fountain, but from my own little spring, from the Word, which is grafted in my heart and which bids me to love my neighbor. Then it flows out abundantly and is there for all who need it, touching both the good and the bad, friend and foe. Indeed, it is ready most of all for enemies, because they are the ones who have more need that I should help them out of their misery and sins and especially for the greatest good I can do them, namely, to pray for them and do whatever I can that they too may become good and be delivered from sins and the devil. Look! this is a love that flows out of the heart, not into it; for it finds nothing in it from which it can draw this love, but because he is a Christian and lays hold of the Word, which in itself is altogether pure, it also makes his heart so pure and full of genuine love that he lets his love flow out to every man and does not stop at anybody, no matter who the person is.

Look! this is the way to preach if you want to teach rightly concerning love, which is required by the law and of which these others know nothing and for which they have no regard, even though they talk a lot about the law and dispute at length about love. They do not see, it does not even occur to them, that this is the way we must love, that it must flow outward from the inside, that a man must have a pure heart. This never occurs to them, even though they hear and read much about it and even preach about it. They operate with nothing but rambling and useless ideas, with purely dead dreams. Therefore, let everything else go for what it is worth, everything that is preached about works and the good life, whether it be circumcision, sacrifice, fasting, or whatever else. It is right only when it issues from God's Word, from a pure heart and sincere faith. This must be the source and spring, which must be there before all these other things.

You can see in every station of life how each person in his calling should do the work committed to him and practice the work of love. A servant, for example, who works and neither sees nor thinks any farther than this: My master gives me my wages and that's why I serve him; otherwise I have no regard for him. He does not have a pure heart or intention, for he works only to obtain a bit of bread. When this ceases his service also ceases. But if he were good and a Christian, this is what he would say: I'm not going to work because my master pays me or does not pay me, or because he is good or bad; but rather because the Word of God is there and it tells me: Servants, be obedient to your masters, as to Christ [Eph. 6:5]. Then it issues of itself from the heart, which has laid hold on the Word and esteems it, and he says: All right, I will serve my master and take my wages, but the chief reason why I do so will be that in this way I shall be serving my dear God and Lord Christ, who has commanded me to do this and I know that this is well pleasing to him. There you see a true work performed out of a pure heart.

Or take a lord or prince or one who must govern, who reasons thus: God has committed the government to me that I should be the ruler; but if I am concerned only to hold on to my dignity, riches, and power, then my heart is not pure, even though I do the work of a prince in such a way that the world cannot complain of me nor the emperor and the lawyers criticize or rebuke me according to their laws, any more than they can rebuke a servant who serves for pay, no matter whether he is selfish or not. But in the sight of God his heart is impure, the work of no man pleases him, for the Word of God is not in it, but rather his own idol, his own glory, money, and power. But when he says in his heart: Because I am in the office to which God has appointed me and the Word has declared that he who rules or has an office should do so with diligence [cf. Rom. 12:8], therefore I shall administer the same with all faithfulness to the service and glory of God; then his governing issues and flows from a fine, pure, true heart, which delights both God and the world. And it is also a love which does not cleave to the person or to wealth and honor, but rather grows out of the heart and keeps in view God's Word, which, because it is true and pure, makes the heart pure also. Thus his government and all his works become nothing but service of God and acceptable sacrifice because they are performed according to the Word and solely for God's sake. This those windbags[7] can neither teach nor demonstrate; all they know is to rant that one should be good, when they do teach their best, and produce only a legalistic sermon out of the laws of men like those which the emperor and his scholars preach. But how the heart is made pure, this is something they have never tasted nor have they ever thought of how God's Word is to be applied to all states and conditions of men.

Further, if you are in the spiritual estate and office, you will say: If I or any other preach in order to get a good fat parish, when I would otherwise just as soon let it go, I may very well be preaching the gospel, but my heart is not pure, but nothing but a nasty mess. And therefore, even though I preach at length and call it a good

---

[7] *Lumpenwescher.*

271

work and a precious office, I still do not understand it myself, for it does not come from the heart. On the other hand, however, the heart is right when a man says: Even though I should receive a living from it, I have not let it go at that, but rather, because God has called and commended me to this office in order to administer it faithfully and diligently to his praise and the salvation of souls, I do this gladly from the heart for the sake of the Word. In doing this I do not seek love, friendship, honor, and thanks from the people; it rather issues from the heart and performs this before it receives honor, money, or favor, although if these come and follow, I may have and receive them without sin.

You see, then, that the Word is the cause, foundation, ground, fountain, and spring of love from the heart and of all good works, if they are to please God, for they cannot do so unless the heart first be pure. Even among men works are not acceptable when they are done without the heart in pure hypocrisy. So, if even the emperor and men require the heart, although they cannot see it, how much more does God require a heart which does everything for the sake of the Word? That is why he causes his Word to be preached, in order that we conform ourselves to it in all our life and action. Let us allow nothing to hinder or trouble us or make us weak or weary, even though we suffer loss, ingratitude, and contempt because of it, but rather go boldly on and say: I did not begin this for any man's sake and therefore I will not cease because of men; I shall do it rather for God's sake, let happen what may. This will produce fine people, masters, princes, subjects, preachers, etc., ready to do all good works and to serve and please God with good will and love, for then the fountain and spring is good, not drawn and carried in from the outside.

Let this suffice for now as a brief treatment of the first point, namely, that the heart is made pure only through the Word and not, as the monks have dreamed, by doing battle oneself with evil or impure thoughts and thinking other thoughts, for whatever the thoughts are, the heart still remains impure if the Word of God is not in it, even though they put on a great show of a godly life, as Paul himself says of them. But this purity of which he speaks goes further than that outward, bodily purity, which the Jewish holy men practiced, through their many ablutions, washings, foods and drink, and that of our spirituals, with their fasting, garb, orders, and so on. It means rather a purity of the spirit, that a man knows through God's Word how to serve him in every calling.

Now comes the second part, concerning a "good conscience," namely, that love should issue from a heart which has a joyful, quiet conscience both toward men and toward God: Toward men in the sense in which St. Paul boasted that he had so lived that he had neither offended nor grieved anybody nor given a bad example, but that all who saw and heard him were compelled to bear witness that he had served, helped, counselled, and done good to all men. Moses, too, gloried in such a conscience over against his rebellious people in Num. 16 [:15], "I have not taken one ass from them, and I have not harmed one of them." Likewise, Jer. 18 [:20], "Remember how I stood before thee to speak good for them, to turn away thy wrath from them." And likewise Samuel in I Kings [I Sam. 12:2-3], "I have walked before you from my youth until this day. Here I am; testify against me before the Lord . . . Whose ox have I taken? Or whose ass have I taken? Or whom have I defrauded? Whom have I oppressed? Or from whose hand have I taken a bribe to blind my eyes with it? Testify against me and I will restore it to you."

Look, this is the kind of glory and confidence every Christian should possess, that he may so live before every man and practice and prove his love, that none may bring any complaint against him to terrify and dismay his conscience, but rather that every man will be compelled to say, if he is going to speak the truth, that he has so conducted himself that nothing but improvement has resulted for those who would accept it, and can declare this before God against every man. This is what it means to have a good conscience toward men or against men.

Even though such a conscience will not be able to stand before God's judgment, any more than the purity of heart which consists in outward life and works of love can stand before him, for before God we still remain sinners, nevertheless we should have this kind of a heart in order that we may comfort ourselves before him and say: This God has enjoined and commanded, therefore I do it out of a pure heart and a good conscience, and I would not willingly do otherwise nor offend and hurt anybody; but rather what I say and do is what God has ordered and commanded me to do. No Christian must ever allow to be taken away from him this confidence of being able to boast and appeal to God's Word against the whole world. For any man who does not pay any attention to living his life in such a way that he can put everyone to silence and defend himself and prove before men that he has lived, spoken, and done well, that man is not yet a Christian and has neither a pure heart nor love within him. For if a person is thus inclined to rely on the doctrine of faith, as if when he has it he can do whatever he likes, whether it harms or helps his neighbor, this will do him no good. Otherwise this doctrine will get the reputation of giving license to every kind of excess and villainy. It is rather love from a pure heart and a good conscience, that no man can blame or accuse him of anything evil.

Even though these things are said about our life and our acts, and even though a Christian is quite another man before God, as we shall hear later, nevertheless he must earnestly endeavor to be blameless before the world. And when he fails to do this, he must interpose the Lord's Prayer and say, both to God and to men, "Forgive us our trespasses, as we forgive those who trespass against us," that so his life may remain blameless at least before men and retain a good conscience, if not through perfect love and purity of heart, then at least through the humility which begs and asks forgiveness of men whenever he has not acted purely and perfectly enough toward them or has not been able to do so. Then your neighbor will be compelled to say: Very well, even though you have harmed me or failed to serve me as you should, yet because you have so humbled yourself before me, I will gladly forgive and pardon you, for I too am guilty and I want you to treat me in the same way. For humility's sake, I must admit that you are a good man, for you do not stubbornly and willfully insist upon offending me, but rather turn to love. So it can still be called blameless, because it has been covered by humility and what was blameworthy has been set right, so that none can complain. This is the way the law should be interpreted and preached, in order both that love for every man may rightly proceed from a pure heart for God's sake and that the conscience may stand before the world. This is what those vain talkers should be preaching instead of their loose, lazy, and cold gibblegabble.

But, in order that all this may be acceptable and stand before

God, there is still one other thing that must be added, which is as follows: "and sincere faith."

For, as I have said, even though I have a good conscience before men and practice love from a pure heart, nevertheless there still remains in me the old Adam, the sinful flesh and blood, so that I am not altogether holy and pure and, Paul says in Gal. 6 [Gal. 5:17], "The desires of the Spirit are against the flesh; for these are opposed to each other, to prevent you from doing what you would." And in Rom. 7 [:17-24] he says of himself that he must constantly battle and struggle with himself and that he cannot do the good which he would. The Spirit is willing to live purely and perfectly according to God's Word, but the flesh remains and resists and tempts us, so that we continue to pursue our own honor, greed, and good days and become slothful, fed up, and weary in our calling.

Thus there remains in us an everlasting strife and resistance, so that much impurity is always creeping in and thus dividing our person, and there can be no flawless purity, or a good conscience, or perfect love, except perhaps what may appear to be so to men. But before God there is still much in us which is faulty and culpable, even though for men everything were altogether perfect. For example, even though David can boast before men that nobody can reproach him and the holy prophets, Isaiah, Jeremiah, etc. boast and are confident that what they have done in pursuance of their divine office was right and well done, because it was God's Word and command, and that in doing so they acted with a pure heart and conscience; nevertheless, they could not glory in this before God's judgment. Rather they are compelled to say: If we are to strive in judgment before thee, then no man has such a good conscience or pure heart that he need not dread thy judgment and acknowledge his guilt. For God has reserved to himself the prerogative of having cause and claim upon every saint, so that no man is so holy that he cannot rightly condemn him as worthy of damnation. Therefore, even though before men both heart and conscience are pure and good, you must still remember that the heart must be pure and the conscience good before God, that he may not condemn them and they be as safe from his judgment as that of men.

And here the third part must be added, that is, faith. This is really the chief article and the highest commandment of all, which contains within it all the rest, in order that we may realize that when love is not perfect, the heart not sufficiently pure, and the conscience not at peace, and though the world cannot reproach us, God still finds in us that which is culpable, then faith must be added. And it must be a faith which is not hypocritical and mixed with confidence in our own holiness. For wherever this faith is not present the heart does not become pure before God and the conscience cannot stand when the searching judgment and reckoning begins. Then men will probably let me go in peace and, as far as they are concerned, I may be able to boast that I have served them, preached to them, helped, ruled, and directed them with all faithfulness. And I may say that if I have done too much or too little, I am sorry, for I wanted to do everything I should. Then I shall be safe and excused and they will have nothing more to require of me and will have to wipe the record clean. But here it says bluntly that I must have a pure heart and a good conscience before God, that he may not be able to accuse and condemn me. And this we do not find in ourselves, even though we may have something to boast of before the world.

Here, therefore I must have something else, something I can hold on to when it comes to the last gasp and my abashed and terrified conscience cries out: I may very well have done what I could, but who knows how often I have done too little, for I can not see and mark all things, as Ps. 19 [:12] says, "Who can discern his errors?" Therefore I can put no trust whatsoever in my own holiness or purity. I have the Word all right and it says: This is the way you must live and love and have a good conscience, and this is pure and holy; but what is lacking is that I can never conclude that this is the way my heart is and I never find within me a conscience which is as pure and good as the Word requires. For there is no man on earth who can say: I know that I have done everything and before God I owe nothing. Even the holiest of saints must confess: I have done what I could, perhaps, but I have failed far oftener than I know. So our conscience stands against us all, accusing us and declaring us unclean, even though we have passed with highest honors before the world or even now are passing. For the conscience must judge itself according to the Word, which declares:

This you should have done or this you should not have done. This it can neither avoid nor answer; the most it can do is to doubt. But when it doubts it is already impure, for it does not stand up before God but rather flounders and flees.

Here, therefore, the chief article of our doctrine must come to our help, namely, that our Lord Jesus Christ, who was sent into the world by the Father, suffered and died for us and thereby reconciled and moved the Father to grace, and now sits at the right hand of the Father, pleading our cause as our Savior and as our constant mediator and intercessor interceding for us who can not of ourselves have or obtain this perfect purity and good conscience. Therefore through him we can say before God: Although I am not pure and cannot have a good conscience, yet I cleave to him who possesses perfect purity and good conscience and offers them for me, indeed, gives them to me. For of him alone is it written, as St. Peter [I Pet. 2:22] quotes from Isa. 53 [:9], "He committed no sin; no guile was found on his lips." He bears with great honor the distinction of having no need of that part of the Lord's Prayer which says, "Forgive us our debts" nor of that article of the Creed, "I believe in the forgiveness of sins," but is free and secure in perpetual, pure, and perfect righteousness and purity, whom none, neither man nor devil nor God himself, can accuse or lay anything upon his conscience, for he himself is God and can not accuse himself.

This, then, is the faith which is neither feigned nor hypocritical, but which dares to come before God in the midst of this struggle and trembling of conscience and say: Dear Lord, before the world I may be innocent and safe, so that it cannot punish or accuse me; for even though I have not performed all things, I nevertheless beg every man to forgive me for God's sake as I in turn forgive every man. Thus I have satisfied them, so that they have no further just claim against me. But before thee I must verily down my peacock's plumes and confess that I am guilty of all things, and say as David said in Ps. 43 [Ps. 143:2], "Enter not into judgment with thy servant; for no man living is righteous before thee." Therefore, if the law is to obtain, I cannot bargain with thee, but must straightway appeal from thy judgment seat to thy mercy seat. Before the judgment seat of the world I am content to be dealt with according to the law; there I will answer and do what I ought. But before thee I would appeal to no law, but rather flee to the Cross and plead for grace and accept it as I am able.

For the Scriptures teach me that God established two seats for men, a judgment seat for those who are still secure and proud and will neither acknowledge nor confess their sin, and a mercy seat for those whose conscience is poor and needy, who feel and confess their sin, dread his judgment, and yearn for his grace. And this mercy seat is Christ himself, as St. Paul says in Rom. 3 [:25],[8] whom God has established for us, that we might have refuge there, since by ourselves we cannot stand before God. There shall I take my refuge when I have done or still do less than is meet and done much more of sin according to the law, both before and after my sanctification and justification. There my heart and conscience, regardless of how pure and good they are or can be in the sight of men, shall be as nothing, and they shall be covered over as it were with a vault, yea, with a fair heaven, which will mightily protect and defend them, the name of which is *grace and the forgiveness of sins*. Thereunder shall my heart and conscience creep and be safe.

For he himself caused it to be preached and proclaimed through his apostles [Acts 10:43], that through his name every one who believes shall receive the forgiveness of sins. Again, "He who believes and is baptized will be saved" [Mark 16:16]. And he himself says in John 3 [:16], "God so loved the world that he gave his only Son, that whoever believes in him should not perish but have eternal life." Therefore God himself has established the mercy seat and is pointing us from the judgment seat to the mercy seat. Others, such as the proud holy ones, the despisers and persecutors of God's Word, we may leave before the judgment seat; there they shall hear their sentence. Let them remain in their vicious circle until they too humble themselves; we, however, will not remain in that circle, but step out of it as far as ever we can, into that free circle and place where stands the mercy seat. And we appeal to it with full right, because we did not invent it with our own brain. It is rather his own Word which declares it and threatens stern, terrible judgment upon them who come with their own holiness, as if they could stand before God with that, and pay no regard to the mercy seat of Christ. For the sentence has already been pronounced, that they must come

---

[8] Luther translates *hilasterion* as "mercy seat"; RSV: "expiation."

before the judgment seat, as Christ says in John 3 [:18], "He who does not believe is condemned already, because he has not believed in the name of the only Son of God" but "he who believes in him is not condemned." That is, he will not come before the judgment seat but before the mercy seat, where there shall be no wrath, where rather he shall be called a beloved child and everything that is not pure within him shall be forgiven, yea, blotted out as a drop of water is consumed by the heat of the sun. For where the mercy seat reigns there is nothing else but utter forgiveness and remission of all sin.

Consequently, we must now learn to distinguish between the two parts which are called the law and the gospel, which is something that we are always teaching. The law brings us before the judgment seat, for it demands that we must be good and love out of a pure heart and a good conscience. Its purpose is to make us exercise ourselves in this; so far it must go and then stop. But when it comes and demands that you settle accounts and pay what it requires, there it cancels itself. For even if you have performed what it requires, this still will not stand before God, since before him there will still be much which is lacking and failing, which you have not done and which you do not even realize you have not done. Where will you turn then? The law keeps harrying you and accusing you through your own conscience, which testifies against you, and absolutely demanding the judgment upon you. Then you must simply despair and there is no help or counsel for you unless you know that you can flee from the judgment seat to the mercy seat. For example take a bishop who has been pious and led a good life. He dies in his holiness, not knowing Christ except as a stern judge, as he has hitherto been preached and portrayed and as he actually is to such people, not because he wants to be, for in actuality he is nothing but pure grace and comfort, but because in their hearts they neither feel nor consider him to be anything else. Behold, that man is hindering and preventing himself from receiving any grace, and there is no one to help him on account of his ignorance. He does not know the difference between the judgment seat and the mercy seat; in fact, he does not know about the mercy seat at all, and therefore must necessarily miss it and remain under the judgment seat.

But we teach that one should know and look upon Christ as the one who sits there as the advocate of the poor, terrified conscience, believe in him, not as a judge, who is angry and ready to punish, but as a gracious, kindly, comforting mediator between my fearful conscience and God, and says to me: If you are a sinner and are terrified, and the devil is drawing you to the judgment seat through the law, then come unto me and have no fear of any wrath. Why? Because, if you believe in me, I am sitting here in order that I may step between you and God, so that no wrath or displeasure can touch you; for should wrath and punishment befall you it must first come upon me. But this is impossible; for he is the beloved Son, in whom all grace dwells, so that when the Father looks upon him everything in heaven and earth becomes pure love and favor and all wrath disappears and vanishes away. And whatever he desires and asks of the Father must all be granted without a single doubt or denial. Thus through faith we are made wholly safe and secure, so that we shall not be condemned, not because of our holiness or purity, but because of Christ, because through this faith we cleave to him as our mercy seat, sure that in and with him no wrath can remain, but only love, pardon, and forgiveness. Thus the heart is made pure and the conscience good and secure before God, not out of regard for my own purity or life before the world, but for that lovely treasure which my heart takes hold of, which is my surety and rich store when I am lacking and cannot pay God.

But here is where the emphasis lies—that we must see to it that our faith is not false or, as Paul says, feigned, but rather sincere. For if this fails or proves to be false, then everything fails. For there have always been many, as there still are, who talk a lot about faith and pretend to be masters not only of the law but also the gospel, and say, as we also say: Faith is what does it, [but then they go on and say] but yet the law and good works must be added to it, otherwise faith does not avail. Thus they mingle together our life and works and Christ. This is not to teach faith purely and sincerely, but is rather faith so colored, feigned, and falsified that it is not faith at all, but a false semblance and shade of faith, because the confidence of the heart does not rest purely upon Christ as the only mercy seat, but is placed rather in our own holiness, as if this could stand before the judgment seat; wherefore before God it is quite rightly condemned and rejected, which is where it belongs.

For if faith is to be pure, unalloyed, and unfeigned, these two, Christ and my works, must be rightly distinguished. For, after all, everyone must realize that Christ and his work is not my work and life, but something separated from the law and all men's work, far more than one man is different from another. I cannot say that I and the emperor or the pope in Rome are the same thing, and yet I am much nearer and more like them as one mortal, sinful man is to another than to the Lord Christ, who is not only a pure, holy man without any sin whatsoever but also is the one God himself. Therefore let the law and your pure heart and good conscience suffice before men here on earth, but there where the mercy seat stands at the right hand of the Father and is the mediator between you and God, there no human work or merit shall have any access or count for anything at all. For what have I or any other man contributed toward his sitting at the right hand of the Father? He was seated there without any of my work or thought whatsoever and without any co-operation of the law, for there is not a single letter about this in the law. Therefore he must be cleanly separated from all my being, life, and works and it must be inflexibly concluded that he is something other than our life led before men with a pure heart and good conscience, no matter how good it is. For when that life appears before God and I come before the judgment seat to which the law relegates me, I am condemned and lost. But Christ the mercy seat and those who cleave to him cannot be condemned or convicted.

Thus the judgment seat, the law, and all my life is separated and put on one side; there I and all the saints remain and let it all be judged and condemned in God's name. But my faith must flee to the other side and as a poor condemned man who acknowledges his sin leap over to the blessed mercy seat and cling to him who is pure and has no sin, of whom the Scriptures say, "He who believes in him will not be put to shame" [Rom. 9:33; Isa. 28:16], because he is standing there and interceding for me. And besides, he gives me all his purity and holiness, so that, clothed and adorned with it, I may be able to stand before God, and all wrath will be removed and instead pure love and grace will hover above me.

You see, that's the way faith remains pure and sincere. For it does not rest upon me and is not founded upon my works, as if that were why God should be gracious to me, as the false, feigned faith does by mingling together God's grace and my merit. Even though this false faith does talk about Christ, it still puts the heart's confidence in itself. Therefore it is only a painted color, which cannot endure, for in the end, if you go on believing that God should be gracious to you because of the life you have led, you will still come to the point where you must doubt and say: Who knows how well you have done? How can you be certain that nothing has been neglected or omitted? Then the foundation falls and slides from under you like sinking sand, and faith lies in utter ruin.

This is why it is aptly called a colored or painted faith, through which the heart looks, as it were, through a painted glass, through which a thing appears to be red or blue, as the glass is, and yet is not. Thus they believe God is disposed to regard our works and merits and so they paint him according to their own opinion and dream, which in itself is false, and thus see both God and everything else to which they turn through a painted glass. But you will see him with pure and unclouded eyes if you clearly distinguish between these two seats, that heaven with its stars (grace and forgiveness through the Mediator), where Christ reigns with his works, may remain pure [and clearly separated from] the earth with its trees and grass, where we and all our works belong.

I say that, if we are ever to stand before God with a right and uncolored faith, we must come to the point where we learn clearly to distinguish and separate between ourselves, our life, and Christ the mercy seat. But he who will not do this, but immediately runs headlong to the judgment seat, will find it all right and get a good knock on the head. I have been there myself and was so burnt that I was glad I was able to come to the mercy seat. And now I am compelled to say: Even though I may have lived a good life before men, let everything I have done or failed to do remain there under the judgment seat as God sees fit, but, as for me, I know of no other comfort, help, or counsel for my salvation except that Christ is my mercy seat, who did no sin or evil and both died and rose again for me, and now sits at the right hand of the Father and takes me to himself under his shadow and protection, so that I need have no doubt that through him I am safe before God from all wrath and terror. Thus faith remains pure and unalloyed, because then it makes no pretensions and seeks no glory or comfort save in the Lord Christ alone.

The man who can do this will be the justified man. All the others operate with a feigned faith. They talk a lot about faith but they mix things together, as a barkeeper mixes water and wine, by saying if you live in such and such a way God will be gracious to you, and they turn the mercy seat into a judgment seat and the judgment seat into a mercy seat. But nothing comes of it, for it will still remain the judgment seat. Therefore, keep these two widely separated from each other, as widely as ever you can, so that neither can approach the other: on one side your life and holiness and the judgment seat, which demands and drives you to have a good conscience and live rightly toward men, but on the other side your sin before the mercy seat, where God will lovingly welcome you and take you into his arms like a beloved child with all your sins and frightened conscience and will no more remember any wrath.

See, if that is the way faith were preached, men would be justified and all the rest; a pure heart and good conscience through genuine, perfect love, would follow. For the man who through faith is sure in his heart that he has a gracious God, who is not angry with him, though he deserves wrath, that man goes out and does everything joyfully. Moreover, he can live this way before men also, loving and doing good to all, even though they are not worthy of love. Toward God, therefore, he stands in a relationship of certainty that he is secure for Christ the Mediator's sake, that he does not wish to cast him into hell, but rather lovingly smiles upon him and opens heaven for him.

This is the highest security, the head and foundation of our salvation. Accordingly, I go out toward my neighbor with my life and do the best I can for him as my office or station requires and commands. And when I do less than is right, I go to him first and ask him to forgive me. Thus I have a good, sure conscience both before God and before men, so that henceforth neither he nor the world can punish me, nor hell swallow me up, nor the devil devour me. So a man is made wholly perfect toward men through love, but before God, not through the law, but through Christ, whom he apprehends by his faith as the mercy seat, who lays down his holiness and gives it to me, so that in him I have what I need for salvation.

This, then, is the right, pure doctrine, which should be cultivated and in which the people should be instructed so they can tell how they are to be justified both before God and before men, and so that they will not interchange and mix up faith and love or life toward God and life toward men. This is what those vainglorious preachers should be doing, since they want to be regarded as masters of the law, in order that it may be well known and observed in Christendom. For even when it is taught in the best possible way it is difficult enough to learn it well, especially for us, who have been so habituated and trained in the doctrine of works and pointed only to the law and ourselves. And besides this add our own nature, which is itself inclined in this direction. It is thus so rooted and strengthened by habit and the heart so strongly influenced that we cannot get away from it or think anything except that, if I have lived a holy life and done many great works, God will be gracious to me. Thus we must contend both with our nature and with strong habit. And it will be exceedingly difficult to get into another habit of thinking in which we clearly separate faith and love, for the muck still sticks and clings to us, even though we are now in faith, so that the heart is always ready to boast of itself before God and say: After all, I have preached so long and lived so well and done so much, surely he will take this into account. We even want to haggle with God to make him regard our life and for our sake turn his judgment seat into a mercy seat. But it cannot be done. With men you may boast: I have done the best I could toward everyone, and if anything is lacking I will still try to make recompense. But when you come before God, leave all that boasting at home and remember to appeal from justice to grace.

Let anybody try this and he will see and experience how exceedingly hard and bitter a thing it is for a man, who all his life has been mired in his work righteousness, to pull himself out of it and with all his heart rise up through faith in this one Mediator. I myself have now been preaching and cultivating it through reading and writing for almost twenty years and still I feel the old clinging dirt of wanting to deal so with God that I may contribute something, so that he will have to give me his grace in exchange for my holiness. And still I cannot get it into my head that I should surrender myself completely to sheer grace; yet this is what I should and must do. The mercy seat alone must prevail and remain, because he himself has established it; otherwise no man can come before God.

So it is no wonder that others find it hard to grasp faith thus purely, especially when the situation is made worse by these devil's preachers, of whom St. Paul speaks, who cry out against it and keep emphasizing the law by quoting such texts as, "Do this, and you will live" [Luke 10:28] and "If you would enter life, keep the commandments" [Matt. 19:17], etc. Which, of course, is right and true, if you understand it rightly. You must tell me the true meaning of these words. Otherwise I know well enough already that I must be good and keep the commandments. But how am I going to do this? Or what does it mean to be good? If you say it means to have a good conscience and a pure heart and to do all that God has commanded, this is right. But go ahead and do it or show me one man who can say he has. It will be a long time before you can produce for me a heart or conscience which God cannot reproach and condemn. But the law demands, as has been sufficiently said, a heart which has a good conscience before God. Where are you going to get it? This is the question and the point we are dealing with. Certainly not by preaching the judgment seat, but rather by having pure, unfeigned faith, which takes hold of Christ and in him finds and obtains all the law requires. Then everything is pure and of good conscience and is counted good and just before God, for though much is lacking in me, he stands there for me and has so much goodness that he can make up for my and all men's deficiencies.

So we show the way a man becomes good before God. But they, even if they do well in other matters, show only the way a man becomes good before men. And yet they want to elevate this and make it count before God. Thus they mix it all up in one brew, like those who neither know nor have experienced anything of "what they are saying or the things about which they make assertions." What good is all this shrieking: If you want to get to heaven, you must keep the commandments? You won't accomplish it that way, not by a long shot! For just look into yourself and search out the evil within you and you will find that you were born in sin and have lived in sin and are unable to produce what the law demands. Why then do you go on making the people gape by repeating these words:

You must be good, then you will be saved; when nothing comes of it and you never show anybody how to achieve it? I hear well enough what the law demands, but how am I going to accomplish it? Then you point me back to myself again and say: You must do good works. But how can I stand before God after I have long performed good works and been good before men, as you teach me, and be sure that God also considers me good? For there my own heart and conscience are against me and they say No.

You, however, should be teaching me what Paul teaches here and everywhere, that it must issue from pure, unfeigned faith, that before everything else one must come to the mercy seat and there secure and complete what we lack. This is the right understanding of the words: Keep the commandments. For what the law demands is that you be wholly good, before God as well as before men. When you have this, then go out among men and practice love and do good works. Then you get to the point of the matter and all such commandments are fulfilled. For when a man does this he gives and does what the law requires: first, before God, though not through what he does of himself, but through Christ, without whom we can do nothing before God, and secondly, through what he himself does before men. Then he is wholly good, inwardly, through faith or Christ, and afterwards outwardly, through his works; but yet in such a way that there is also mutual forgiveness of sins. So the Christian's righteousness consists far more in forgiveness than in his own works, which those loose talkers turn upside down and, without preaching forgiveness, emphasize only our works.

You see, then, that Paul is rebuking the error and ignorance of those who were extolling and preaching the law and yet neither understanding it themselves nor showing how what one can do about it or how it can be performed. They could do no more than babble the words: Keep the law, keep the commandments and be saved, do good works, and so on. Just as to this day they are scribbling books and spewing the churches full of this idle wish-wash, which they do not understand themselves. But never a word do they say about Paul's teaching here that the chief thing is that love should issue from a pure heart, a good conscience, and sincere faith. All they say is: Keep the commandments, but never penetrate the central meaning of Paul's teaching. Therefore they make it all wrong and false, both love and heart and conscience. For the main source is lacking, namely, sincere faith. But when this is not right then everything that should grow out of it will be wrong. And what they hand out is pure delusion and deception before your eyes, seen through painted glass, which looks like the real thing, but isn't. They think that because of the way they have lived before men, God should see it the same way they see it in their blind conceit. But if that were God's opinion, he might just as well have kept Christ and the whole message of the gospel to himself. What need would there be for him to set up such things, to send his Son down from heaven, and allow him to shed his precious blood in order to gain and give something which we ourselves already have? It would only be a fool who would bestow such treasure on something that nobody needs.

So you see that they are only teaching their own dreams, which they do not understand and which only confuse the people, because they cannot show how one can achieve what they set forth, but only point to ourselves, and thus men are strengthened in their old nature and habit, whereas they ought to lead people away from it. These are indeed disgusting, malevolent people, so that Paul not unreasonably rebukes and denounces them. And they must not have been ordinary people, for he himself says that they were teachers of the law and wanted to be praised and commended, even more highly than the apostles themselves.

Therefore let us hold on to this text, for it is excellently expressed and a pure, perfect teaching of how we are to be righteous both before God and before men, as the law requires, and how these three are to be brought together, a pure heart, a good conscience, and sincere faith, and out of them all our life should flow and continue. Then we shall have found and fulfilled the meaning of the law. But above all, it teaches us that we must look to Christ and bring him into it, who "is the end of the law" [Rom. 10:4] and of everything else and our whole righteousness before God, which we do not find in ourselves and without faith never will find, no matter how long and repeatedly one blabbers and pushes the law, though without understanding and knowledge. Let this suffice for this time on this text, wherewith we have served God and brought a thank offering to the praise and honor of his grace. Amen.

SERMON ON SOBERNESS
AND MODERATION

1539

SERMON ON SOBERNESS
AND MODERATION
1539

Sermon on Soberness and Moderation against Gluttony

and Drunkenness, I Pet. 4:7-11, May 18, 1539

This sermon, preached in the parish church of Wittenberg on the Epistle for Exaudi Sunday, in which Luther deals head-on with a social question of his day, is remarkable for its non-legalistic treatment of the subject. The title given above is that of the printed version which appeared in Augsburg (without date, but not before 1542). Three texts are given in the Weimar edition: Rörer's transcript, Stoltz's transcript, and the printed version which is Aurifaber's based on Rörer's notes. The Rörer transcript forms the basis of this translation, with occasional references to the other two versions.

Text in Latin and German; WA 47, 757-772.

This part of [the first] Epistle [of Peter] is an exhortation to good conduct. Those who are Christians are to see to it that they are grateful for grace and redemption and conduct themselves modestly, moderately, and soberly, so that one does not go on living the swinish life that goes on in the filthy world. For this Epistle was written to the Greeks, who were great high livers. In those regions there was gluttony just as in Germany today.

Where one can find sermons which will stop the Germans from swilling I do not know. We might just as well have kept silent altogether. Christ says that the coming last day will come upon men unawares and snatch them away (Luke 21 [:35]), and Paul says the same thing in I Thess. 5 [:2], and also the prophets likewise. The

Italians call us gluttonous, drunken Germans and pigs because they live decently and do not drink until they are drunk. Like the Spaniards, they have escaped this vice. Among the Turks it is really the worst sin for a man to be drunk. So temperate are they that they do not even drink anything which inebriates. That is why they can make war and win; while we drunken sows sleep they keep awake, and thus can consider their strategy and then attack and conquer. When the time comes for us to defend ourselves and be prepared, we get drunk. This has become so widespread that there is no help for it; it has become a settled custom.

At first it was the peasants who drank to excess, then it spread to the citizens. In my time it was considered a great shame among the nobility. Now they are worse than the citizens and peasants; now those who are the greatest and best are beginning to fall, indeed, even the princes; and among those who are the ablest it has become a noble and princely virtue. Now the ten-year-old milksops, and the students, too, are beginning, and ruining themselves in their flower; when the corn should be growing and flourishing it is beaten down by a storm. We preach, but who stops it? Those who should stop it do it themselves; the princes even more. Therefore Germany is a land of hogs and a filthy people which debauches its body and its life. If you were going to paint it, you would have to paint a pig.

Some spark of sobriety may remain among young children, virgins, and women, though underneath one finds pigs among them too. However, there remains some bit of decency, for it is still said that it is especially shameful for a woman to be drunken. The Turks have this teaching, which is a fine thing, and the Italians too. Among us it is considered most shameful. But if it ill becomes the children and young women, so that we say that such should be trampled under foot, how much more should not this be so of married women and particularly men, who should be wiser and more virtuous, since the woman is the weaker vessel [I Pet. 3:7] and the man has more strength and reason? Therefore they should do this even less, and therefore, according to reason, it is a far more shameful thing for men to drink to excess than for women. It might be said in defense of woman that she is foolish and has not such a strong body, and therefore drink affects her more quickly. But this is not so of the man, who is stronger than the woman.

This gluttony and swilling is inundating us like an ocean and among the Spaniards, Italians, and English it is reprehended. We are the laughingstock of all other countries, who look upon us as filthy pigs; and not only upon private persons, but upon nobles and princes also, as if that were the reason why they bear the coat of arms. We would not forbid this; it is possible to tolerate a little elevation, when a man takes a drink or two too much after working hard and when he is feeling low. This must be called a frolic. But to sit day and night, pouring it in and pouring it out again, is piggish. This is not a human way of living, not to say Christian, but rather a pig's life.

What, therefore, shall we do? The secular government does not forbid it, the princes do nothing about it, and the rulers in the cities do nothing at all but wink at it and do the same themselves. We preach and the Holy Scriptures teach us otherwise; but you want to evade what is taught. Eating and drinking are not forbidden, but rather all food is a matter of freedom, even a modest drink for one's pleasure. If you do not wish to conduct yourself this way, if you are going to go beyond this and be a born pig and guzzle beer and wine, then, if this cannot be stopped by the rulers, you must know that you cannot be saved. For God will not admit such piggish drinkers into the kingdom of heaven [cf. Gal. 5:19-21]. It is no wonder that all of you are beggars. How much money might not be saved![1] Twenty years ago this was considered among the princes to be a shameful vice. If we do not watch out, it will become common among virgins and women. Therefore I am utterly terrified by that word of the Lord concerning gluttony: ["Take heed to yourselves lest your hearts be weighed down with dissipation and drunkenness and cares of this life, and that day come upon you suddenly like a snare" (Luke 21:34)].

Listen to the Word of God, which says, "Keep sane and sober," that it may not be said to you in vain. You must not be pigs; neither do such belong among Christians. So also in I Cor. 6 [:9-10]: No drunkard, whoremonger, or adulterer can be saved. Do not think that you are saved if you are a drunken pig day and night. This is a great sin, and everybody should know that this is such a great iniquity, that it makes you guilty and excludes you from eternal life.

---

[1] I.e., if excessive drinking were stopped.

Everybody should know that such a sin is contrary to his baptism and hinders his faith and his salvation.

Therefore, if you wish to be a Christian, take care that you control yourself. If you do not wish to be saved, go ahead and steal, rob, profiteer as long as you can, but fear Jack Ketch[2] and the magistrates. But if you do want to be saved, then listen to this: just as adultery and idolatry close up heaven, so does gluttony; for Christ says very clearly: Take heed "lest your hearts be weighed down with dissipation and drunkenness and cares of this life, and that day come upon you suddenly" [Luke 21:34], "as the lightning comes from the east and shines as far as the west" [Matt. 24:27]. Therefore be watchful and sober. That is what is preached to us, who want to be Christians.

You parents must help to see to it that your children do not begin too early to fall into this vice. Reason, which God gives to princes and nobles [as an instrument by which to rule, will not accomplish this]; it leads a person downwards; it is a pig. A drunkard is not dissuaded from his drinking by reason any more than a murderer, an adulterer, whoremonger, or usurer; therefore you will not be moved by the reasons that excessive drinking weakens the constitution, consumes money and goods, and causes the Italians, Turks, and the English to spit upon us. What should move you is that God forbids it on pain of damnation and loss of the kingdom of heaven. A ruler cannot punish a greedy-gut, so the whole world is greedy and thus is entangled in the cares of this life [Luke 8:14; 12:34], simply because it goes unpunished; in fact, is even praised. People say it should not be called a sin because it is not punished; they say it is like greed, usury,[3] etc. Very well, go ahead and drink yourself full as a hog, nobody will punish you. If I were not so ill I would like to write a treatise on this matter; perhaps it would move a few people anyhow.[4]

We ought to give thanks to God for providing us with food and drink and then besides, liberating us from the papacy, and feeding us with food and drink. If you are tired and downhearted, take

---

[2] Cf. p. 140 n. 4.

[3] Luther preached on usury in the preceding month, April 13, 1539. WA 47, 721-730.

[4] This may indicate that it was Luther's own prompting which caused the later publication of this sermon.

a drink; but this does not mean being a pig and doing nothing but gorging and swilling. It is now becoming a custom even in evangelical cities to establish taprooms;[5] a donkey goes in, pays a penny [*Groschen*], and drinks the whole day long; and the government does nothing about it. These taverns are necessary, of course, even a pious custom.[6] They might better have built money changers' shops. Just because the magistrates and princes do not denounce and punish these vices, we shall not fail to perform our office and remind each one of his office. If we are aware of what is going on we know that such persons should be excluded from all the sacraments and will make it public, just as we would in the case of a murderer. You should be moderate and sober; this means that we should not be drunken, though we may be exhilarated.

Further on in chapter five, Peter states the reason why it is necessary for us to be sober. Why? In order to be able to pray; and this is necessary because we have an adversary, the devil, "who prowls around like a roaring lion, seeking someone to devour" [I Pet. 5:8]. He seeks, but how does he do so? He is like a wolf circling a sheepfold. What Peter is saying is this: because you are a people who have been called to the post in which you must be on the watch against sin and against the devil and his messengers, who are seeking our souls more greedily than that wolf, therefore you must defend yourself with the Word and with prayer, not only for yourselves but the whole world. You are priests, etc.[7] But when a man is drunk his reason is buried, his tongue and all his members are incapable of praying; he is a drunken pig and the devil has devoured him. Then the devil is occupying his members.

The early Christians went almost too far in this matter of prayer. In the time after the apostles the bishops with great diligence instituted the morning and evening prayers which are called matins and compline. They practiced this custom steadily and rigorously, some of them so strenuously as Augustine says, that they did not eat for three or four days. They were overdoing it. Nevertheless, they went to prayer morning and evening. But later,

---

[5] Luther is referring particularly to Torgau. Cf. Julius Köstlin and Gustav Kawerau, *Martin Luther* (2 vols.; Berlin, 1903), II, 473. WA 47, 766 n. 1.
[6] Irony.
[7] Therefore you must pray; cf. I Pet. 2:5, 9. This sentence and the one following may be susceptible to another interpretation.

abuse corrupted this custom; later came the monks, who do not pray but only babble prayers. But we have established the schools in order that morning and evening prayers may be held morning and evening. This we are obliged to do.

God does not forbid you to drink, as do the Turks; he permits you to drink wine and beer: he does not make a law of it. But do not make a pig of yourself; remain a human being. If you are a human being, then keep your human self-control. Even though we do not have a command of God, we should nevertheless be ashamed that we are thus spit upon by other peoples. If you want to be a Christian, do not argue in this way: Nobody reproaches me, therefore God does not reproach me. So it has been from the time of Noah [Gen. 9:21]. And so it was with the Sodomites, who wanted to rape the angels; they were all so drunk they could not find the door [Gen. 19:11]. Sodom and Gomorrah perished because of a flood of drunkenness; this vice was punished. God does not tolerate such confusion and inordinate use of his creatures [i.e., food and drink].

The mind will tolerate a certain degree of elevation, but this must be moderate, not indecent. Here sobriety signifies not merely abstaining from drunkenness, but also moderation in all things, respectability in dress, ornamentation, gait, and conduct in the whole of life in general.

If you have been a pig, then stop being one. Augustine said: I have known many who were drunkards and then ceased being drunkards. But you are today just as you were yesterday and you go on thinking that it is not a sin.

"Sane" means that we should be alert and sensible, in order that we may be enlightened by the Word of God and not be drunken pigs, in order that we may be ready for prayer. "Sober" means that we should not overload the body, and it applies to excess in outward gestures, clothing, ornament, or whatever kind of pomp it may be, such as we have at baptisms and the churching of women. There is no moderation in these things. When there is a wedding or a dance you always have to go to excess. Christmas and Pentecost mean nothing but beer. Christians should not walk around so bedizened that one hardly knows whether one is looking at a man or a beast. We Christians ought to be examples. We Germans are especially swamped in this vice. The Italians and the Turks far surpass us in moderation. The Turk should be put to shame by us and he should be the one to say: They do not overeat, overdrink, and overdress. But actually the tables are turned; they are the ones who give us an example in clothing, etc. They have their peculiar vices, too, of course; and they are really abominable; but in this they are far more temperate than we are. We are a shame to heaven and earth; we do harm to both body and mind.

"Above all." This could well be a sermon in itself. You have been called to love one another. People today, peasants, citizens, and nobles, go on living in hatred and envy, so that none will give another even a piece of bread; they will commit any kind of rascality so long as they can deny it. If you want to be saved, you must possess the red dress which is here described. You have put on the vestment. You are white as snow [Isa. 1:18], pure from all sins. But you must wear this red dress and color now, and remember to love your neighbor. Moreover, it should be a fervent love, not a pale-red love, not the love which is easily provoked to revenge [I Cor. 13:5]. It should be a strong color, a brown-red love, which is capable not only of doing good toward your neighbor but is also able to bear all malice from him [I Cor. 13:4, 7]. For this is the way sins are covered, even a multitude, a heap, a sea, a forest of sins. How does it do this? It does not mean my sin in the way the pope interprets this, i.e., whenever I love God and my neighbor then I blot out my sins.[8] No. It is another's love, namely, Christ's love, which has covered my sins, as Peter says in chapter two: He bore them in his body on the cross and erased them completely [I Pet. 2:24]. This is said with regard to your sins, the sins you commit against me and I against you.

In Christianity it must not happen that one person should hurt another, in the same way that the members of the body, the teeth, tongue, toes, fingers, hands, eyes, touch each other without hurting each other. It is true, of course, that even among Christians life does not go on without offenses being committed. You have only to look at husband and wife in the family. Some times a word is

---

[8] The Stoltz version reads: "Not, however, as the pope expounds the understanding of our sins, which is that my love is that garment; rather Christ erased our sin by his death."

uttered or something is done which angers the husband or the wife. But when this is done to a neighbor, then gestures are made which make people angry and the man's relatives come seeking revenge and are not satisfied until the offense has been repaid tenfold. So you must have a strong love, which is best able to cover up sins.

Also consider what Solomon said: "Hatred stirs up strife, but love covers all offenses" [Prov. 10:12]. This is how you should deal with your neighbor. If you do not do this, He will remove his cover. This is what Paul means when he says, "Bear one another's burdens, and so fulfil the law of Christ" [Gal. 6:2]. It is a grievous thing whenever a neighbor has a wife who quarrels. But the Holy Spirit has sanctified you through faith and given you love, in order that you may bear with others. Christ has borne your sins, in order that you may bear with the sins of others.

So in worldly affairs, too; one rubs against the other. Here, too, you must not become angry and be ready to do harm. Rather be content if someone possesses the same thing you have and do not be envious. If anybody speaks against you, you say: May God forgive him. If you are a Christian, your neighbor will not make you so angry that you would do him injury. If you do, then there is no love.

The head of a household must punish and should not tolerate evil. But he must not be hateful and vengeful, lest in this way he corrupt the other person. A father does not punish his son in order to make him spiteful and ruin him in body and soul, but rather to ward off his vice; he wants to purify him and wipe away his faults. He hates, not the person, but the vice. This is a wrathful love which is kind and good toward the person; hence it cannot tolerate the nastiness in him. So, too, a woman cannot bear it when there is dirt on her child's nose, but must wipe it away; she does not do this in order to hurt the child. Magistrates, teachers, and parents must chastise, but this chastisement is fatherly and kindly.

Solomon said, "Faithful are the wounds of a friend; profuse are the kisses of an enemy" [Prov. 27:6]. When an enemy speaks kindly to you, this is not affection, but rather the devil, who is out to destroy you in your sins. Ah, he says, you're doing fine; go ahead! But a friend will be willing to hurt you. This is a rod, but it comes from the heart of a friend.

Up to this point he has been speaking of being patient and

bearing with our neighbor. He now goes on to speak of whoever receives a gift. ["As each has received a gift, employ it for one another, as good stewards of God's varied grace" (I Pet. 4:10)]. If you speak, do so as one who speaks the Word of God. If you have an office, perform it as one who knows that it is of God. There is no nobler work than that of being a parent, a preacher, or a magistrate. If you are a husband, a preacher, or a magistrate, learn not so say: Oh, if I were that fellow; he has the silver chain.[9] Rather look to the station to which you have been called. If you are a preacher, a husband, a magistrate, you do not do what you do as a human work. There Peter has nailed the pope's hands to the cross, so that I need preach nothing but the Word of God. The preacher teaches the church and parents teach their children; they guide the family in upright conduct and command that which is God's commandment. A master does not say: Commit adultery, etc., but rather: Do no injury to me or to others, in order that all things may be governed as of God. Likewise a magistrate does not command stealing, but what is beneficial to the city and the common welfare. Thus we may know with certainty that it is a divine work and that this is God's Word. And nobody should undertake to do anything unless he knows with certainty that he can say: Here is the Word of God. A servant should think in this way: I am not obeying a man, but God. It is not the parents who are honored by their children, but God, Christ. Likewise, if you despise parents, magistrates, preaching, you are really despising God. The pope preached the opposite; he preached that children should leave the parental home and go into the monastery; husbands even deserted their wives. The Anabaptists are also preaching something different and new. Whenever you hear me, you hear not me, but Christ. I do not give you my baptism, my body and blood; I do not absolve you. But he that has an office, let him administer that office in such a way that he is certain that it comes from God and does everything according to the Word of God, not according to our free will. Very much needs to be preached concerning this to check the abuses which the devil has introduced. When everything that is said and done is said and done in accord with God's Word, then the glory of Christ and God will be done to all eternity.

---

[9] A necklace, sometimes of gold, the symbol of office and authority.

SERMON IN CASTLE PLEISSENBURG, LEIPZIG

LEIPZIG

1539

SERMON IN CASTLE PLEISSENBURG, LEIPZIG
1539

Sermon Preached in Castle Pleissenburg on the Occasion of the Inauguration of the Reformation in Leipzig, John 14:23-31, May 24, 1539

This sermon has historical importance because of the occasion on which it was preached. It was delivered on Saturday afternoon before Pentecost, the day before the formal introduction of the Reformation in the city where twenty years before Luther had debated so fervently and effectively and the seat of the university which opposed Wittenberg. Luther was ill but nevertheless preached to a crowded chapel in the presence of Duke Henry of Saxony, who had recently succeeded upon the death of Duke George, the champion of Rome and most bitter opponent of the Reformation. He preached again the next afternoon in St. Thomas' Church, but only the first sermon has been preserved. Luther was accompanied to Leipzig by Melanchthon, Jonas, and Cruciger, and the conjecture is that it was the latter who prepared the transcript. The sermon was not published until 1618.

Text in German; WA 47, 772-779.

Because I cannot depend upon my head, owing to physical infirmity, to venture upon expounding the doctrine in its entirety, I shall adhere by God's grace to the text of the Gospel which is customarily dealt with in the churches on the morrow.

These words of the Lord Christ, "If a man loves me, he will keep my word, etc." [John 14:23], were occasioned by the fact that shortly before this the Lord Christ had expressed himself in almost the same way: "He who has my commandments and keeps them, he it is who loves me . . . and I will love him and manifest myself to him" [John 14:21]. For this reason the good Judas (not Iscariot) asked, "Lord, how is it that you will manifest yourself to us, and not to the world?" [John 14:22]. It is to this question that the Lord Christ is replying here. And here one sees the fleshly and Jewish notions which the apostles held; they were hoping for a worldly kingdom of the Lord Christ and they wanted to be the chief ones in that kingdom. Already they had disputed about who should be the greatest in that kingdom [Mark 9:34] and had divided it up into provinces. To this day the Jews have this same attitude and they hope for an earthly messiah.

Thus since the Lord Christ said here, "He who has my commandments and keeps them, him will I love and manifest myself to him" [John 14:21], Judas says: Are we to be the only ones? Is it to be such a meager revelation and manifestation? Will it not be manifest to the whole world, including the Jews and the Gentiles? What is it going to be? Are we to be the only ones to inherit you, and the Gentiles know nothing? This false Jewish delusion was in the apostles and that is why this Gospel here describes the kingdom of the Lord Christ and paints a far different picture of it for the disciples. It is if he were saying: No, the world has a different kingdom, my dear Judas; that's why I say: If a man loves me, he will keep my word, and I will be with him along with my Father and the Holy Spirit and make our home with him. This home is God's dwelling, as Jerusalem was called the dwelling of God, which he himself chose as his own: Here is my hearth, my house and dwelling [Isa. 31:9]; just as today the churches are called God's dwellings on account of the Word and sacraments. Here I think that Christ is pronouncing a severe judgment, here he is prophesying and forgetting the dwelling of Jerusalem, of which all the prophets said: Here will I dwell forever. This dwelling the Lord Christ pulls down and erects and builds a new dwelling, a new Jerusalem, not made of stones and wood, but rather: If a man loves me and keeps my Word, there shall be my castle, my chamber, my dwelling.

In saying this Christ gave the answer to the argument concerning the true church; for to this day you hear our papists boasting and saying: the church, the church! It is true that Christ wants to have his home where the Father and the Holy Spirit want to be and to dwell. The entire Trinity dwells in the true church; what the true church does and directs is done and directed by God. Now the new church is a different dwelling from that of Jerusalem; he tears down all the prophecies concerning Jerusalem, as if Jerusalem were nothing in his eyes, and he builds another dwelling, the Christian church. Here we agree with the papists that there is one Christian church; but Christ wants to be everywhere in the land. These are fine, heart-warming words—that God wants to come down to us, God wants to come to us and we do not need to clamber up to him, he wants to be with us to the end of the world: Here dwells the Holy Spirit, effecting and creating everything in the Christian church.

But what is the dissension about between the papists and us? The answer is: about the true Christian church. Should one then be obedient to the Christian church? Yes, certainly, all believers owe this obedience; for St. Peter commands in the fourth chapter of his first Epistle: "Whoever speaks" should speak "as one who utters oracles of God" [I Pet. 4:11]. If anybody wants to preach, let him suppress his own words and let them prevail in worldly and domestic affairs; here in the church he should speak nothing but the Word of this rich Householder; otherwise it is not the true church. This is why it must always be said that it is God who is speaking. After all, this is the way it must be in this world; if a prince wants to rule, his voice must be heard in his country and his house. And if this happens in this miserable life, so much the more must we let God's Word resound in the church and in eternal life. All subjects and governments must be obedient to the Word of their Lord. This is called administration.[1] Therefore a preacher conducts the household of God by virtue and on the strength of his commission and office, and he dare not say anything different from what God says and commands. And even though there may be a lot of talk which is not the Word of God, the church is not in all this talk, even though they begin to yell like mad. All they do is to shriek: church, church! Listen to the pope and the bishops!

But when they are asked: What is the Christian church?

---

[1] Administratio, stewardship; cf. I Cor. 4:1.

What does it say and do? they reply: The church looks to the pope, cardinals, and bishops. This is not true! Therefore we must look to Christ and listen to him as he describes the true Christian church in contrast to their phony shrieking. For one should and one must rather believe Christ and the apostles, that one must speak God's Word and do as St. Peter and here the Lord Christ says: He who keeps my Word, there is my dwelling, there is the Builder, my Word must remain in it; otherwise it shall not be my house. Our papists want to improve on this, and therefore they may be in peril.[2] Christ says: "We will make our home with him"; there the Holy Spirit will be at work. There must be a people that loves me and keeps my commandments. Quite bluntly, this is what he wants.

Here Christ is not speaking of how the church is built, as he spoke above concerning the dwelling. But when it has been built, then the Word must certainly be there, and a Christian should listen to nothing but God's Word. Elsewhere, in worldly affairs, he hears other things, how the wicked should be punished and the good protected, and about the economy. But here in the Christian church it should be a house in which only the Word of God resounds. Therefore let them shriek themselves crazy with their cry: church, church! Without the Word of God it is nothing. My dear Christians are steadfast confessors of the Word, in life and in death. They will not forsake this dwelling, so dearly do they love this Prince. Whether in favor or not, for this they will leave country and people, body and life. Thus we read of a Roman centurion, a martyr,[3] who, when he was stripped of everything, said, "This I know; they cannot take away from me my Lord Christ." Therefore a Christian says: This Christ I must have, though it cost me everything else; what I cannot take with me can go; Christ alone is enough for me. Therefore all Christians should stand strong and steadfast upon the Word alone, as St. Peter says, "by the strength which God supplies" [I Pet. 4:11].

Behold, how it all happens in weakness. Look at baptism, it is water; where does the hallowing and the power come from? From the pope? No, it comes from God, who says, "He who be-

---

[2] I.e., in danger that Christ may say that his dwelling is not among them.
[3] The reference is to Martin, Roman citizen and martyr. Cf. Ernst Schäfer, *Luther als Kirchenhistoriker* (Gütersloh, 1897), pp. 235-236.

lieves and is baptized" [Mark 16:16]. For the pope puts trust in the consecrated water. Why, pope? Who gave you the power? The *ecclesia,* the church? Yes, indeed, where is it written? Nowhere![4] Therefore the consecrated water is Satan's goblin bath [*Kobelbad*], which cripples, blinds, and consecrates the people without the Word. But in the church one should teach and preach nothing besides or apart from the Word of God. For the pastor who does the baptizing says: It is not I who baptize you; I am only the instrument of the Father, Son, and Holy Spirit; this is not my work.

Likewise, the blessed sacrament is not administered by men, but rather by God's command; we only lend our hands to it. Do you think this is an insignificant meal, which feeds not only the soul but also the mortal body of a poor, condemned sinner for the forgiveness of sins in order that the body too may live? This is God's power, this Householder's power, not men's.

So also in the absolution, when a distressed sinner is pardoned. By what authority and command is he pardoned? Not by human command, but by God's command. Behold, here by God's power I deliver you from the kingdom of the devil and transfer you to the kingdom of God [Col. 1:13]. So it is too with our prayer, which gains all things from God, not through its own power, or because it is able to do this, but because it trusts in God's promise. In the world you see how hard it is to approach the Roman emperor and gain help; but a devout Christian can always come to God with a humble, believing prayer and be heard.

In short, the Word and the Holy Spirit, who prepares us for prayer, are in God's power. It is the Word which we believe—this is what makes our hearts so bold that we dare to call ourselves the children of the Father. Where does this come from? The answer is: From God, who teaches us to pray in the Lord's Prayer and puts into our hands the book of Psalms. For if we prayed without faith, this would be to curse twice over, as we learned in our nasty papistical holiness. But where there is a believing heart and that heart has before it the promise of God it quite simply and artlessly prays its "Our Father" and is heard. Outside of this church of God you may present your prayers and supplications to great lords and

---

[4] Luther's phrase is *Im Rauchloch,* i.e., in the chimney pot; written black on black and therefore invisible.

potentates to the best of your ability, but here you have no ability to pray except in Christ Jesus, in order that we may not boast that we are holy as they do in the papacy, who protest, of course, and say: Oh, it would be a presumption for anybody to call himself holy and fit; and yet they teach that man of himself has a "certain preparation"[5] for prayer.

They also teach prayer according to this doctrine in their chants and say: I have prayed in despair as a poor sinner. Oh, stop that kind of praying! It would be better to drop such praying altogether if you despair. For despair ruins everything and if you go to baptism, prayer, and the sacrament without faith and in despair, you are actually mocking God. What you should quickly say, however, is this: I am certain that my dear God has so commanded and that he has assured me of the forgiveness of sins; therefore I will baptize, absolve, and pray. And immediately you will receive this treasure in your heart. It does not depend on our worthiness or unworthiness, for both of these can only make us despair. Therefore do not allow yourself by any means to be driven to despair. For it is a mockery of God when we do not believe the words, "Go and baptize" [Matt. 28:19], that is, baptize those who repent and are sorry for their sins. Here you hear that this is not human work, but the work of God the Father; he is the Householder who wills to dwell here. But if we despair, then we should stay away from the sacrament and from prayer, and first learn to say: All right, it makes no difference that I am unworthy, God is truthful nevertheless, and he has most certainly promised and assured us; I'll stake my life on this.

And this we did not know under the papacy. Indeed, I, Martin Luther, for a long time could not find my way out of this papistical dream, because they were constantly blathering to me about my worthiness and unworthiness. Therefore, you young people, learn to know the church rightly.

Concerning penitence or penance we teach that it consists in the acknowledgment of sins and genuine trust in God, who forgives them all for Christ's sake. The pope, on the contrary, does nothing but scold and devise intolerable burdens; and besides he knows

---

[5] Latin: *praeparationem quandam.*

nothing of grace and faith, much less does he teach what the Christian church really is.

But don't you forget the main point here, namely, that God wants to make his dwelling here. Therefore, when the hand is laid upon your head and the forgiveness of sins is proclaimed to you in the words: "I absolve you from all your sins in the name of Christ," you should take hold of this Word with a sure faith and be strengthened out of the mouth of the preacher. And this is what Christ and St. Peter are saying: He, the Lord, wants to dwell in this church; the Word alone must resound in it.

In short, the church is a dwelling, in order that God may be loved and heard. Not wood or stones, not dumb animals, it should be people, who know, love, and praise God. And that you may be able to trust God with certainty in all things, including cross and suffering, you should know that it is the true church, even though it be made up of scarcely two believing persons. That's why Christ says: He who loves me keeps my Word; there I will dwell, there you have my church.

So now you must guard yourselves against the pope's church, bedaubed and bedizened with gold and pearls; for here Christ teaches us the opposite. To love God and keep his Word is not the pope's long robe and crown, nor even his decretals. There is a great difference between what God commands and what men command. Look how the pope brazenly announces—we should invoke the saints and conduct ourselves according to his human precepts. Does God's Word command this too? I still do not see it. But this I know very well, that God's Word says: I, Christ, go to the Father, and he who believes in me will be saved. For I, I have suffered for him and I also give him the Holy Spirit from on high.

So the Lord Christ and the pope each have their own church, but with this mighty difference, which Christ himself, the best dialectitian [*der beste Dialecticus*], here describes, telling us what it is and where it is, namely, where his Word is purely preached. So where you hear this, there you may know that this is the true church. For where the Word of God is not present, there also are no true-believing[6] confessors and martyrs. And if the Word of God

---

[6] This awkward word is a better translation of the sense of *"rechtgleubige"* than "orthodox."

were lacking, then we would have been deceived by Christ; then he really would have betrayed us!

Oh, if we could only stake it all on Christ and mock and laugh at the pope, since Christ clearly says here, not "he who has my Word," but "he who keeps it loves me" and is also my disciple. There are many of you who have the Word, true enough, but do not keep it, and in time of trouble and trial fall away altogether and deny Christ.

It would, of course, be desirable if we could always have both: the Word and our temporal crumbs,[7] but the good venison, peace, is very scarce in the kingdom of heaven.[8] It is therefore something which must be recognized as a great blessing of God when there is peace among temporal lords and mutual understanding. But if not, then let them all go—goods, fame, wife, and child—if only this treasure remain with us.[9]

I fear, however, that unfortunately there will be among us many weathercocks, false brethren, and suchlike weeds; and yet I am not going to be a prophet, because I must prophesy nothing but evil, and who would presume to be able to fathom it all? It will turn out all right; now we have it, let us see to it that we hold on to it. But let us be valiant against Satan, who intends to sift us like wheat [cf. Luke 22:31]. For it may well be that you will have your bit of bread under a good government and then the devil will soon set a snare for you in your security and presumption, so that you will no longer trust and give place to the Word of God as much as you did before. That's why Christ says: My sheep not only hear me, they also obey and follow me [John 10:3-5]; they increase in faith daily through hearing the Word of God and the right and perfect use of the blessed sacraments. There is strengthening and comfort in this church. And it is also the true church, not cowls, tonsures, and long robes, of which the Word of God knows nothing, but rather wherever two or three are gathered together [Matt. 18:20], no matter

---

[7] zeitliche Partecke: our poor, beggarly possessions, temporal bread and well-being. See the phrase, "bit of bread," in the next paragraph.

[8] Es ist der liebe Wilpret (der Friede) im Himmelreich gar seltsam. This is a double-edged use of a proverbial saying applied to princes (Luther is addressing princes in this sermon), who were obsessed with hunting: there is no game in heaven, what would a prince do with himself there?

[9] Note the echo of "A mighty fortress is our God."

whether it be on the ocean or in the depths of the earth, if only they have before them the Word of God and believe and trust in the same, there is most certainly the real, ancient, true, apostolic church.

But we were so blinded in the papacy that, even though St. Peter tells us that "we have the prophetic word made more sure" and that we "do well to pay attention to this as to a lamp shining in a dark place" [II Pet. 1:19], we still cannot see what a bright light we have in the gospel. Therefore we must note here once again the description of the Christian church which Christ gives us, namely, that it is a group of people who not only have his Word but also love and keep it and forsake everything for the sake of love.

From this then you can answer the screamers and spitters who have nothing in their gabs but "church! church!": Tell me, dear pope, what is the church? Answer: the pope and his cardinals. Oh, listen to that; you dunce, where is it written in God's Word that Father Pope and Brother Cardinal are the true church? Was it because that was what the fine parrot bird said to the black jackdaw?

But Christ tells you and me something far different. He says: My church is where my Word is preached purely and is unadulterated and kept. Therefore St. Paul warns that we should flee and avoid those who would lead us away from God's Word, for if anyone defiles God's temple, which we are, God will destroy him [I Cor. 3:17]. And St. Peter also says: Take heed, if you are going to preach, then you should preach nothing but God's Word [I Pet. 4:11], otherwise you will defile God's church.

Hence it is again to be diligently noted how Christ described his church for us; for this description is a strong thunderbolt against the miserable pope and his decretals by which he has made of the church of God a filthy privy.[10]

If anybody wants to teach human precepts, let him do so in secular and domestic affairs and leave the church alone. After all, the papists are really empty spewers and talkers, since Christ himself here says: He who hears my Word and keeps it, to him will I and my Father come and make our home with him. This is the end of Jerusalem and Moses; here there is to be a little band of Christ,

---

[10] The original repeats this in Latin: *contra Papam, qui fecit ex Ecclesia cloacam,* and also includes an untranslatable play on words: *Decret* and *Secret* (privy).

[*Heufflein Christi*], who hear God's Word and keep the same and rely upon it in every misfortune. This is my church. This Lord we shall believe, even though the pope blow his top over it.

But in these words Christ was also answering the apostle Judas, who also allowed himself to imagine that Christ would become a great secular emperor and that they, the apostles, would become great lords in the nations when he should manifest himself. But how wrong he was! Here Christ tells them straight out that his kingdom is not of this world, but that they and all believers should be that kingdom of heaven in which God the Father, Son, and Holy Spirit himself dwells. He does not install angels, emperors, kings, princes, and lords in that church. He himself wants to be the householder and be the only one to speak and act; there I will dwell, he says, and with me all believers from everlasting to everlasting.

But Judas, the good man, still cannot understand this and therefore the Holy Spirit must come and teach it to him. Of this future and this ministry, dear Christians, you will hear tomorrow, God willing. If I cannot do it, then it will be done by others who can do it better than I, though they will not admit it.[11] Let this today serve as an introduction or the morning sermon. May the Lord help us, I cannot go on further now.

---

[11] The next day Paul Lindenau, Justus Jonas, and Frederick Myconius preached in Leipzig churches in the morning. Luther preached in St. Thomas' Church in the afternoon.

SERMON AT THE BAPTISM OF BERNHARD VON ANHALT

1540

SERMON AT THE BAPTISM OF BERNHARD VON ANHALT
1540

Sermon on Matt. 3:13-17 at the Baptism of Bernhard von Anhalt, Preached in Dessau, April 2, 1540

Luther preached three sermons in Dessau at Easter, 1540, at the invitation of the princes of Anhalt with whom he enjoyed warm personal relations. The occasion for the invitation was the baptism of Prince Bernhard, the three-week-old son of Prince John of Anhalt. Luther stood sponsor for the child at the baptism on Thursday, April 1, and preached on repentance, John the Baptist, and the baptism of Jesus, Matt. 3:12; and on the next day preached this sermon on baptism, continuing his exposition of Matthew 3. These two sermons, along with the Easter sermon on John 20:19-31 preached on Sunday, were printed in Wittenberg in 1540. Who the transcriber was is not known, though the third sermon is preserved in Poach's copy of Rörer's notes.

Text in German; WA 49, 124-135.

Yesterday we began to speak about the baptism of Christ and said that he accepted it from John for the reason that he was entering into our stead, indeed, our person, that is, becoming a sinner for us, taking upon himself the sins which he had not committed, and wiping them out and drowning them in his holy baptism. And that he did this in accord with the will of God, the heavenly Father, who cast all our sins upon him that he might bear them and not only cleanse us from them through his baptism and make satisfaction for them on the Cross, but also clothe us in his holiness and adorn us with his innocence.

Is not this a beautiful, glorious exchange, by which Christ, who is wholly innocent and holy, not only takes upon himself another's sin, that is, my sin and guilt, but also clothes and adorns me, who am nothing but sin, with his own innocence and purity? And then besides dies the shameful death of the Cross for the sake of my sins, through which I have deserved death and condemnation, and grants to me his righteousness, in order that I may live with him eternally in glorious and unspeakable joy. Through this blessed exchange, in which Christ changes places with us (something the heart can grasp only in faith), and through nothing else, are we freed from sin and death and given his righteousness and life as our own.

Now, wherever this is preached and known one can most certainly judge and conclude that all, no matter who they are or what they are called, who teach or do otherwise than what is here said in order to be rid of sin and gain God's grace, are wrong, and that they are lost and condemned with all their devotions, good intentions, rigorous living, onerous and great works, even if they performed more of them. For they insist that they can propitiate God's wrath and acquire grace and salvation through their own righteousness and merit, which adequately shows that they know nothing at all of this blessed exchange. On the contrary, what they think is: Even though I am a sinner, there is no need to worry, I can take care of the matter; I will do this or that to the praise of God and he will accept it, and so on.

What it means, however, is that which is our own, no matter how good and holy it may seem, is nothing in the sight of God; it must become nothing and be utterly dead. For if we could atone for sin and drive out death by human powers, it would not have been necessary for Christ to become man and be baptized and die for our sins. Therefore if you would not fail and be lost, believe the Scriptures, which testify that all men are sinners, that before God no man living is righteous [Ps. 143:2; Rom. 3:20]. But if they are to become righteous, this must come to pass through Christ, the blessed Seed of whom it was promised to Adam, Abraham, etc., that he would crush the serpent's head and redeem the whole world from its curse. This he did; he took the sin of the whole world upon himself; he became a curse for us, and thus redeemed from the curse all those who believe in him (Gal. 3 [:13]).

Such knowledge and faith produces a joyful heart, which is certain and can say: I know of no more sins, for they are all lying on Christ's back. Now, they can never lie both upon him and upon us. Therefore no one can say that he makes satisfaction for sin through his own righteousness or discipline; for atonement and redemption of sin belongs to Christ alone. But Christ is neither my work nor yours nor any man's works. Nor are they his body and blood, which he sacrificed for our sins; he is true God, true man, who bears the sins of the whole world. But he takes them and drowns and smothers them in baptism and the Cross, and lets you proclaim that he has given his body for you and poured out his blood for the forgiveness of your sins. And if you believe this, then they are forgiven, you are good and righteous, you receive the Holy Spirit, in order that henceforth you may be able to resist sin. And when through weakness you are overtaken by it, it shall not be imputed to you, as long as you otherwise remain in this faith.

This is the forgiveness of sins; it does not occur without payment or satisfaction; but this payment is not yours. It cost Christ his body, life, and blood. It will be of no use even if you, indeed, the whole world, were to offer up your body and blood, for no offering is acceptable to God to pay for sin, says the Scripture, except the one sacrifice of Christ. It is his sacrifice of himself for your sin and the whole world's sin and his giving to you his innocence and righteousness that comes to your help and drowns your sin and death. And when you are baptized in this faith you are putting on Christ, who washes away your sins in baptism and gives you the Holy Spirit, etc. So you see, do you not, that this forgiveness is not brought about through your penance, but rather that Christ bears the sins of us all and kills them in his body, and that we take hold of this by faith and let ourselves be baptized according to his command.

This is what John also means when he says to the Lord, "I need to be baptized by you, and do you come to me?" It is as if he were saying: I am a sinner, so I should rightly be receiving baptism from you, Lord, and thus be cleansed and absolved of sins by you. For he well knew that Christ had no sin and yet it was He who was bearing the sins of the whole world, the only one to bring forgiveness and impart the Holy Spirit. That's why he says: I need to be baptized by you.

But Christ says, "Let it be so now; for thus it is fitting for us to fulfil all righteousness" [Matt. 3:15]; as much as to say: The purpose of my baptism is to wash away and drown the sins of all the world, that through it all righteousness and salvation may be accomplished. Therefore baptism was instituted by God primarily for Christ's sake and then afterwards also for the sake of all men. For first he must sanctify baptism through his own body and thereby take away the sin, in order that afterwards those who believe in him may have the forgiveness of sins. Therefore baptism is not a useless, empty thing, as the sectarians blasphemously say, but in it all righteousness is fulfilled.

Then repentance, as John preaches it for the forgiveness of sins, consists mostly in your acknowledging that God is right and confessing that his judgment is true when he says that we are all sinners and all condemned. When you do this from the heart, then repentance has begun. What more must I do then? Bow down and be baptized. For, says Christ, by my baptism I have accomplished it, that whoever believes in me and accepts this baptism receives the forgiveness of sins, and my Father and I and the Holy Spirit will dwell in him.

For here you see, as we said yesterday, that after he was baptized from that hour the heavens were opened above Christ (something never seen before at St. John's baptisms) and later the earth, the graves, hell, and everything were opened, and the Holy Spirit was seen in the form of a dove, and the Father's voice was heard above this baptism, saying that he was deeply pleased with it. For this Son, who stood there and allowed himself to be baptized by John, pleased him so well that even though he were bearing the sins of a thousand worlds, they would all be drowned and destroyed in his baptism. But because he is well pleased with him, he is also well pleased with those who believe in him and suffer themselves to be baptized according to his command.

Hence, not only are sins forgiven in baptism, but we are also made sure and certain that God is so well pleased with it that he, together with Christ and his Holy Spirit, proposes to be present when it is administered and he himself will be the baptizer; although this glorious revelation of the divine majesty does not now occur visibly, as it did at that time on the Jordan, since it is sufficient that it occurred once as a witness and a sign.

Therefore we should diligently accustom ourselves to look upon these things with eyes of faith and to interpret this glorious revelation and divine radiance and splendor which shone forth above the baptism of Christ as happening to us; for all this did not happen and all this was not recorded for Christ's sake, for he himself did not baptize [John 4:2], but rather for our comfort and the strengthening of our faith, for the sake of which he also accepted baptism. Therefore wherever anybody is being baptized according to Christ's command we should be confidently convinced that God the Father, Son, and Holy Spirit is present there, and that there is pure delight, pleasure, and joy in heaven over the fact that sin is forgiven, the heavens opened forever, and that now there is no more wrath but only grace unalloyed.

Not that we can gain this by our penitence or satisfaction, but rather we receive this grace on account of this Son, who bears the sins of us all upon his back and of whom the Father declares, "This is my beloved Son, etc." He is exceedingly pleased because he allowed himself to be baptized and thus drowned sin in the water and then afterwards allowed himself to be killed upon the cross. Then sin, death, damnation must needs perish and cease on account of him, and righteousness, life, and salvation break forth in their place. And that which in us was previously condemned in the sight of God is now altogether pleasing in Christ, and because of him, even the faults and failings which remain can not hurt us.

Then there is something else which should be noted, and that is that here above the baptism of Christ no such terrifying spectacle was to be seen as that which occurred on Mount Sinai when the people of Israel received the Law, when there was a great, thick, black cloud and terrible thunder and lightning and a ghastly, loud blast of a trumpet. The whole mountain smoked and flamed up to the heavens, so that the people retreated and thus could not hear God's voice speaking out of the fire. Here, by contrast, everything was lovely, comforting, and joyful; the Father most kindly allows his voice to be heard, saying that he is well pleased with the Son, the Son standing there in his manhood and allowing himself to be baptized for our benefit, and the Holy Spirit descending like a dove. Here no terrifying or majestic figure is to be seen, nor was there heard any stern, unbearable proclamation in which God showed himself and made himself heard. Rather everything was lovely and comforting to behold. Now let us speak a bit also about our baptism.

First, we should learn from God's Word in order that every Christian may know what baptism is; for hitherto there have been many sectarians and heretics, and they will always be present, who attack holy baptism. This comes from the fact that they view baptism as being only water, as our eyes tell us it is. With such a stupid view a man can never judge any differently of baptism or know any more about it than a cow. Therefore a Christian must be differently and better instructed in this matter.

Now, as I have often said, God's Word teaches us that the sacrament of baptism has three parts. The first is just natural water, which is the only thing the sectarians look at and then say: Water cannot wash the soul. Then they proceed to make of it only a sign, in the same way that we brand sheep, etc. But this is far too little to say about holy baptism, since it is only one part and the least part of it. We too say that it is water, but there is something more which is added to it, which makes this water glorious and holy, makes it in fact the real baptism, namely:

The second part, God's Word beside and with the water, which is not something we have invented or dreamed up, but is rather the Word of Christ, who said, "Go into all the world and baptize them in the name of the Father and of the Son and of the Holy Spirit" [Matt. 28:19]. When these words are added to the water, then it is no longer simple water like other water, but a holy, divine, blessed water. For where the Word of God, by which he created heaven and earth and all things, is present, there God himself is present with his power and might. What this Word with the water creates and effects, however, we shall hear about later.

And this must be noted above all things—we must not look upon the water as simply water without the Word, but rather know that the Word with and beside the water constitutes the substance of baptism, as St. Paul says clearly in Eph. 5 [:26] that Christ washed and cleansed his bride, the church, by the washing of water with the Word, which is quite a different bath and washing than that which occurs through natural water or human washing and bathing in a tub. For here, says St. Paul, is the Word of the living God which says, I baptize you in the name of the Father and of the Son and of the Holy Spirit; in other words, here not a man, but God himself is baptizing. For when it is done in his name it is done indeed by the holy Trinity.

Then there is a third part which is necessary to make it a sacrament, namely, institution or the Word which institutes and ordains baptism; for two kinds of Word must be present in order that it be a baptism. One which is spoken with the water or baptizing, the second that which orders and commands us to baptize in this way, that is, to immerse in water and to speak these words. When these two come together, namely, the command and institution to do this and the Word with the water, which is used in accord with the institution and practices and administers the same, then this is called a baptism and is a baptism.

This is the principal part, which we must see and be concerned with here, namely, Who is the Founder who has ordained and commanded such baptism? For it makes a great difference between this baptism and all others which are invented by men and then considered to be a baptism which counts for something before God. For example, the magicians, witches, and weather prophets also employ a sign or creature, such as a root or herb, and speak over it the Lord's Prayer or some other holy word and name of God. This, they say, is not an evil thing but rather both: a creation of God and precious words and holy names; therefore it should possess power and accomplish what it is used for; just as the pope also juggles and conjures with his chrism, holy water, and salt.

But here one must look to the third part and ask: My friend, where and who is the Founder who commanded this? Do you too have a word and command of God which says you should do this, that you should consecrate salt or water and speak such words over them? When there is no such command, then it is nothing and it stands for nothing, no matter what sign or word is used. Even baptism would not be a sacrament without this word of command, even though water and the Word spoken over it were present, as the papacy plays the fool with such fake, lying baptisms as blessing and baptizing inanimate bells in which both water and Word are used as in proper baptism. What is lacking in this? Nothing else but this part, that there is no divine institution and command which has commanded and ordered such a thing, but rather men have introduced such practice on their own discretion; just as the whole papacy is purely human doctrine and nothing but their own junk. Therefore such baptizing is not a sacrament, but just a pure perversion, indeed, a mockery and blasphemy of baptism.

You see, then, that this is the most necessary thing which we must learn and know about baptism—that here we have the Founder from heaven, who gives us both the command to baptize and also the form and the manner of baptism. In the first place God himself must command it. Then afterwards he must himself name the creature or element, and then also prescribe the words which are to be used with it, in order that all may be done according to his command, not according to human choice or devotion, which everywhere in the Scriptures the Holy Spirit condemns and calls idolatry and magic. He speaks of this in the prophet Jer. 7 [:31], *Quod non praecepi, neque ascendit in cor meum,* that is, "Which I did not command, nor did it come into my mind." Therefore he does not want us to adopt anything except that which he himself institutes and orders, which, of course, is also the best and most profitable for us, since then we do not need to waver and hover in doubt, but can say with certainty: I know that the baptism which I have received is not man's, but God's work and baptism, even though it is administered by a man, for it is His own institution and ordinance.

Now, when we have this understanding of what baptism is, we can guard and defend ourselves against the sectarians, who consider baptism to be simply water and a human thing, and also against all the conjuring and abomination of the pope, who misuses both the creatures and God's Word without having a command of God. For when God institutes and ordains something, this will not be merely a human sign, which one can recognize and distinguish from others, but a salutary, holy, godly thing, which is powerful and conducive to salvation. Where there is water along with God's Word and God's command, there our hearts can be certain that this is a real, divine baptism, even though we are not confronted by any great, external spectacle, for this, even though it were the most glorious imaginable, would still not make it a baptism.

For a person is brought here completely stripped and naked, and nothing happens except that by God's command he is immersed in water or water is poured over him and these words spoken: "I baptize you, etc." And when this happens you should have no doubt that this is a right, perfect baptism, nor ask whether he who administers the baptism is devout and believing or not. Let him be godless and unbelieving, for what he is in his person does not affect the baptism, nor will it harm you; as long as he adheres to the institution of Christ and does not add wine, beer, lye, or any other thing, but uses water with the Word of God added to it, it is a holy baptism. For then everything is here that belongs to the essence of baptism, namely, natural water, with the Word, by God's institution and command.

Therefore it must inevitably effect and accomplish that for which it was instituted, namely, as St. Paul teaches in Titus 3 [:5], "regeneration and renewal in the Holy Spirit." For as we are born of Adam and Eve for this life, so the same old man, born before in sin and unto death, must be born again and anew to righteousness and eternal life by the power of the Holy Spirit. And yet outwardly, nothing more is there and nothing more is perceived than water and the Word, which is all that is seen with the eyes and heard with the ears. Nevertheless it has such power that the man who was so conceived and born in sin is now born anew in the sight of God and he who before was condemned to death is verily a child of God. Who can ever grasp this glory and power of holy baptism with human senses or understanding?

Therefore in baptism do not look to the minister's hand, which takes simple water, and his mouth, which speaks a few words over it, which is a trivial act that only fills the eyes and ears and otherwise accomplishes nothing, as blind reason permits itself to think. But rather look to the Word and act of God, by whose command baptism was instituted, indeed, who is himself the baptizer. That's why it has such power. As the Holy Spirit declares through St. Paul, it is a "washing of regeneration and renewal in the Holy Spirit" [Titus 3:5], which changes, cleanses, and removes the inherited disease of our impure and condemned birth from Adam, in which we are all born in sin and therefore are so full of filth and leprosy that our hearts and the highest faculties of reason resist God's command and will, and of which we cannot cleanse ourselves. And then it makes us innocent, so that, without sin and without death, we shall rise on the last day, more beautiful and pure than the sun, righteous in body and soul, and live to all eternity.

Therefore one must not hold baptism in low esteem, as do the devil's sectarians, who make of it simply a sign, but rather highly honor and exalt it as our highest and most precious treasure. And this despite the fact that we see nothing of it but the water and hear no more than the words spoken by the baptizer, of whom we cannot know whether he himself believes or not, which, as has been said, neither takes anything from baptism nor harms you. For I should not and will not stake it all upon what the minister is or believes. Rather, if I am to be certain of my baptism, I must look to the Founder and listen to what his Word and command say. True, the minister must be there, he must lend his hand and mouth; but I must not allow my attention to be fixed upon the visible baptizer, but rather upon the unseen Baptizer, who instituted and ordained the baptism; to him I must look, no matter who the minister may be.

Then I also hear that these words which are spoken do not read: I baptize you in my name or in the name of St. Peter, St. Paul, or the name of any other man; but rather "in the name of the Father, Son, and Holy Spirit." In addition to this I see that the child is immersed in water or sprinkled with it. Accordingly, I know that this is a true baptism, for the Scriptures clearly testify that when these three parts are present, it is a true baptism, which creates a new man, and if he remains a new man, he is holy in body and soul.

Therefore I say that we should both speak and think highly of holy baptism, in order that it may be completely distinguished from all other washing and bathing; for here it is God himself, Father, Son, and Holy Spirit, who is baptizing and bathing. Therefore this act must be so powerful that it makes a man altogether new. This is why St. John the evangelist is fond of speaking of this dear baptism as water mingled with the blood of Christ, as in John 19 [:34], when Christ was crucified and dead and one of the soldiers pierced his side with a spear, he says, "at once there came out blood and water." And then he goes on to confirm this with this strong statement: "He who saw it has borne witness—his testimony is true, and he knows that he tells the truth—that you also may believe" [v. 35].

Likewise in the last chapter of his epistle he says of Christ, "This is he who came by water and blood, Jesus Christ, not with the water only but with the water and the blood" [I John 5:6]. Thus he is always wanting to mingle the blood in the baptism in order that we may see in it the innocent, rosy-red blood of Christ. For human eyes, it is true, there appears to be nothing there but pure white water, but St. John wants us to open the inward and spiritual eyes of faith in order that we may see, not only water, but also the blood of our Lord Jesus Christ.

Why? Because this holy baptism was purchased for us through this same blood, which he shed for us and with which he paid for sin. This blood and its merit and power he put into baptism, in order that in baptism we might receive it. For whenever a person receives baptism in faith this is the same as if he were visibly washed and cleansed of sin with the blood of Christ. For we do not attain the forgiveness of sins through our work, but rather through the death and the shedding of the blood of the Son of God. But he takes this forgiveness of sin and tucks it into baptism.

This is what St. John was looking to when he mingled water and blood together, for, after all, it has in it that which was gained through the blood. And thus St. John deems the person who is baptized as having been washed in the blood of Christ. His blood is not that of a sinful man or the blood of a dead goat or ox; it is innocent, just, and holy, it is a blood of life. Therefore it also contains such strong salt and soap that, wherever it touches sin and uncleanness, it bites and washes it all away, eats and destroys both sin and death in an instant.

Thus St. John pictures our dear baptism for us in this way, so that we shall not regard and look only at the clear water, for, he says, Christ comes "not with water only (as the Anabaptists blaspheme, saying it is nothing but water) "but with the water and the blood" [I John 5:6]. Through such words he desires to admonish us to see with spiritual eyes and see in baptism the beautiful, rosy-red blood of Christ, which flowed and poured from his holy side. And therefore he calls those who have been baptized none other than those who have been bathed and cleansed in this same rosy-red blood of Christ.

So St. Peter, too, says in I Pet. 1 [:2], that those who have been baptized have been sprinkled with the innocent blood of Christ. How were they sprinkled? Who has ever seen anybody sprinkled in this way? True, in the Old Testament there was much sprinkling, since in Num. 19 [:2-10] there was a commandment concerning the water for impurity made of the ashes of a burned red heifer by which those who were unclean were to have their sin removed. But the sprinkling of which St. Peter is speaking (and which is signified by this sprinkling) is none other than preaching. Holy water or water for impurity is the Holy Scriptures.[1] The tongue of the preacher or Christian is the aspergillum.[2] He dips it into the rosy-red blood of Christ and sprinkles the people with it, that is, he preaches to them the gospel, which declares that Christ has purchased the forgiveness of sins with his precious blood, that he has poured out his blood on the Cross for the whole world, and that he who believes this has been sprinkled with this blood.

Therefore this preaching and the baptizing that follows it is the equivalent of being sprinkled with the blood of Christ himself, except that here it is done spiritually (for physical sprinkling will not do it), in that we believe and declare: I have been washed of sin and death by the blood of my Lord Christ. How? By the preaching of the gospel. There I hear that Christ died and shed his blood in order that all who believe in him might have forgiveness of sins and be justified and saved.

It is the same as in absolution; we believe that through absolution the sins of those who have fallen are forgiven, not because of the laying on of hands, for my laying on of hands does nothing of itself, but rather because Christ has commanded and said, "Whatever you loose on earth shall be loosed in heaven" [Matt. 18:18], and again, "If you forgive the sins of any, they are forgiven" [John 20:23]. It is upon these words that I accept absolution as that which God himself has instituted and commanded, and I know that in

---

[1] Cf. Sermon at the Dedication of the Church at Torgau, Oct. 5, 1544, pp. 331-354.
[2] Brush used to sprinkle holy water.

this too I am sprinkled with the innocent blood of Christ, with which he has stained the absolution, baptism, and the sacrament.

Thus St. John wanted to show us in this passage, in which he says that Christ "came by water and blood" [I John 5:6], that baptism is such a glorious and powerful thing that it washes away sin, drowns and destroys death, and heals and cleanses all disease. It is true that we do not see this with our eyes, but Christians are the kind of people who should not insist upon seeing, but rather hold fast to the Word and believe.

Nevertheless, at the same time the dear God is so concerned for us that we do not go astray and grope for him in vain, that he has given us outward, visible signs upon which we are to fix our eyes and ears. Otherwise we might object that we did not know how or where to find him, or go wandering and fluttering hither and yon after our own thoughts, as was done in time past in the papacy, some running to St. James,[3] others to Rome, and so on.

Therefore he well provides us with such signs, so that we do not need to search hither and yon. He says: Look to the Word, baptism, the sacrament, the keys [absolution]. True enough, he says, all this is external, but it is necessary and helpful to you, in order that you may have a definite image by which you can take hold of me, for you will never reach me in naked majesty; therefore I must present myself to you in these external images, in order that you may grasp me.

And we should stick to these images and signs which he himself has given us. Otherwise the same thing will happen to you as with the whole rabble of monks, who forgot their baptism, went into the cloister, put on a cowl, and thus contrived for themselves a sign in which they proposed to find and meet God, and then claimed that this is the right way to serve God and attain to heaven. Then they went on to feed the laity with hopes of getting their surplus merit and attributed as much power to their trumped up consecrated salt and water as to holy baptism itself. All this is to fail God, yea, to tempt God, and to dish up idolatry for true service of God; for what is lacking here is the Word which institutes and commands these things.

Therefore let us magnify and value our precious holy baptism.

---

[3] St. James of Compostella.

First, because it is a true and sure image and sign, erected by God himself, in which we surely find and meet with his grace. Secondly, in order that we may learn to avoid all other images and signs which have been invented and erected by men, no matter how fine and holy they may seem, and know with certainty that we shall never find nor meet God in them, but that they only lead us farther away from him.

But you may say: I do not see such great and glorious things in baptism as you have been talking about. I said a while ago that Christians are people who should believe and not see. Even though God were to reveal visibly how the Holy Spirit and the whole Trinity works in baptism, as was said above, and how all the angels are present, you still would not be able to stand it, you could not endure such majesty for an instant.

Therefore he must so cover and veil himself that you may be able to endure it and say: True, I see nothing in baptism except water, into which the baptizer dips the child or which he pours upon it, and I hear nothing but the words which he speaks over it, "I baptize you in the name, etc." This my eyes and ears tell me. But the Word and faith tell me that God himself is present, doing the work. Therefore it is such a potent fountain of youth that it causes a man to be born again, washes away and drowns every sin within him.

Therefore you should take it as a very special grace that he should deal so kindly with you, so kindly that none could ever be more kindly. For he simply presents a man; he does not put a sword, a gun, or any kind of weapon in his hand, but simply commands him to take a little water with his bare, empty hand and say these words, "I baptize you in the name, etc." Thus he lays nothing hard or unbearable upon us, nor does he burden us with any expenditure, as with the Jews, who were obliged to be circumcised, to slaughter and make sacrifices; but, as we said, simply commands us to take a little water, which is familiar to everyone and so necessary that we cannot get along without it for an hour, and then say the words, "I baptize you, etc." In the Lord's Supper also he bids us eat and drink and to do this in remembrance of him, etc.

Now he who has this understanding of holy baptism which we have indicated, who knows what it is, what it does, what its benefits are, and who the Founder and real baptizer is, will also experience the power of it in his heart and be bettered by it. He will thank and praise God for his great grace, that he has liberated him from the false kingdom of the Antichrist in which this teaching concerning baptism is kept silent and, indeed, is unknown; and he will know how to judge with certainty all kinds of doctrines as to whether they are right or wrong. He will extort nothing from his neighbor or be hard on him in any way, but rather treat him with all kindness, counsel and help him whenever he can, and gladly suffer and bear the holy cross. Such fruits will surely follow. If not, then this is a sure sign that he has no understanding either of faith or of baptism, no matter how much he may talk about it.[4]

We shall leave it at that now and earnestly entreat Christ our Lord to preserve us in pure understanding of the Word and the holy sacrament and defend us from all error, and to this end may he grant us his grace. Amen.

---

[4] There is an untranslatable play on words here; the word *waschen* means both "to wash" and "to chatter."

SERMON AT THE DEDICATION OF CASTLE CHURCH, TORGAU

1544

SERMON AT THE DEDICATION OF CASTLE CHURCH, TORGAU 1544

Sermon at the Dedication of the Castle Church in Torgau,

Luke 14:1-11, October 5, 1544

This sermon has classical significance because of its thoroughly evangelical definition of worship, a salutary antidote for muddled liturgical thinking. The text is the Gospel for the Seventeenth Sunday after Trinity (Luther rarely chose special texts for special occasions) and the occasion was the dedication of the first new church to be built in Saxony since the Reformation. This sermon was preached in the morning and Luther preached again in the afternoon on Eph. 4:1-10. The Weimar edition prints two versions: Rörer's notes and Caspar Cruciger's version based on Rörer's notes. The present translation is based on Cruciger's version and compared with Rörer's notes.

Text in German; WA 49, 588-615.

My dear friends, we are now to bless and consecrate this new house to our Lord Jesus Christ. This devolves not only upon me; you, too, should take hold of the aspergillum[1] and the censer, in order that the purpose of this new house may be such that nothing else may ever happen in it except that our dear Lord himself may speak to us through his holy Word and we respond to him through prayer and praise.[2] Therefore, in order that it may be rightly and Christianly consecrated and blessed, not like the papists' churches

---

[1] Cf. 326 n. 2. Luther here uses the brush and censer as symbols of the Word of God and prayer, which alone impart true consecration.
[2] Luther's famous definition of worship.

333

with their bishop's chrism and censing, but according to God's command and will, we shall begin by hearing and expounding God's Word, and then, in order that this may be done fruitfully, following his command and gracious promise, call upon him together and say the Lord's Prayer.

The Gospel: Luke 14 [:1-11]
On the Dropsical Man Healed on the Sabbath

"One sabbath when he went to dine at the house of a ruler who belonged to the Pharisees, they were watching him. And behold, there was a man before him who had dropsy. And Jesus spoke to the lawyers and Pharisees, saying, 'Is it lawful to heal on the sabbath, or not?' But they were silent. Then he took him and healed him, and let him go. And he said to them, 'Which of you, having an ass or an ox that has fallen into a well, will not immediately pull him out on a sabbath day?' And they could not reply to this.

"Now he told a parable to those who were invited, when he marked how they chose the places of honor, saying to them, 'When you are invited by any one to a marriage feast, do not sit down in a place of honor, lest a more eminent man than you be invited by him; and he who invited you both will come and say to you, 'Give place to this man,' and then you will begin with shame to take the lowest place. But when you are invited, go and sit in the lowest place, so that when your host comes he may say to you, 'Friend, go up higher'; then you will be honored in the presence of all who sit at table with you. For every one who exalts himself will be humbled, and he who humbles himself will be exalted."

This Gospel presents us with a disputation concerning the sabbath which Christ was obliged to enter into with the Jews; for they were especially troubled by their sabbath. So here the Lord also troubled them with it and right gladly too, and also quite rightly. On the sabbath when the people assembled, as we do on Sunday, the Lord usually preached and after the sermon, performed a miracle to help the poor people, and particularly to substantiate his teaching. Now the Jews could tolerate the preaching, when he did not revile them; but that he should deal with the sick and perform

334

miracles on the sabbath displeased them and they called it breaking the sabbath.

Now this part concerning the sabbath belongs in the preaching of the catechism, when one deals with the [third] commandment: You shall keep the sabbath, or day of rest, holy [Exod. 20:8]. This, being the third commandment in the first table, was for the Jews a particularly serious one, and they were obliged to observe it on the particular, appointed day, namely, the seventh. Therefore, for them the sabbath was no joke, and so they were much annoyed that Christ should heal the sick on the sabbath, of all days, and accused him of not keeping the sabbath [Matt. 12:10]. Thus wisdom was obliged to allow herself to be justified by her children [Luke 7:35], just as they revile us Christians to this day, saying that we preach the Ten Commandments and the sabbath and yet do not keep them in their way. But what they gain from their reviling and blaspheming of Christ and his church we can see in this Gospel also; they had to swallow their own words and were publicly shamed by having their own example compared with oxen and asses.

But by God's grace we know how the sabbath is to be kept, for we have learned it from this our Lord, the Son of God. It is true that at that time the particular day of the sabbath was fixed for the Jewish people, and also a specified place, a special tribe or [group of] persons, and a particular priesthood or service of worship was appointed. For all this must take place only in their country and in the temple at Jerusalem, conducted by the Levites, who belonged to the priestly tribe, from which tribe alone the ministers of the church were drawn.

But we, who are in the kingdom of our Lord Christ, are not thus bound to a tribe or place, so that we must adhere to one place alone and have only one race or one particular, separate kind of persons. Rather we are all priests, as is written in I Pet. 2 [:9]; so that all of us should proclaim God's Word and works at every time and in every place, and persons from all ranks, races, and stations may be specially called to the ministry, if they have the grace and the understanding of the Scriptures to teach others. So we, too, are lords of the sabbath with Christ and through Christ, as he himself says in Matt. 12 [:8], "The sabbath was made for man, not man for the sabbath; so the Son of man is lord even of the sabbath" [Mark

2:27-28]. Accordingly, all those who believe in him are likewise lords of the sabbath.

There, in the Jewish nation, it had to be so, that they observed a particular, separate, definite day, and adhered to a particular tribe, persons, and place, until the coming of Christ, in order that they might be distinguished from the heathen in this external way which was appointed and commanded by God himself, and also that they might possess an external evidence that they were God's people among whom God's Son was to be born. But now that this Christ, our Lord, has come and a new kingdom has been inaugurated throughout the whole world, we Christians are no longer bound to such external, particular conduct, but rather have the freedom, if the sabbath or Sunday does not please us, to take Monday or any other day of the week and make a Sunday of it; though this must be done in an orderly way. And it should be a day or a time which is convenient for all, and not left to the choice of each individual to make something special for himself in matters which concern the whole congregation or even the whole church, or to change appointed times or days unless it is required by an unusual common need. Likewise, the one who is called to the office and commissioned to preach should not preach to himself alone, but to the whole congregation. Therefore it should also be arranged in such a way that they may all assemble at a definite and convenient time, when the ordinary man can be away from his trade or work, and at a definite place where they may know and hear their preacher. However, in case the circumstance should arise that it were impossible to preach or to assemble today, which is the appointed day, then one might well do so tomorrow or some other day.

However, since Sunday is now universally accepted as our sabbath or day of rest, let it remain so, provided, however, that we remain lord over it, and not it over us. For if every one were to start something new as he pleased, changing days, hours, and places, this would not be right either. Rather every one should agree in these things, make themselves ready, and come together to hear God's Word and to respond to him by calling upon him together, praying for every kind of need, and thanking him for benefits received. If this cannot be done under roof or in the church, then let it be done out of doors or wherever there is room. St. Paul preached at the riverside in Philippi (Acts 16 [:13]), and in a hall at Troas (Acts 20 [:8-12]). Just so that it be an orderly, public, reverent assembly, since one cannot and should not appoint a special place and location for each individual, and one should not seek out secret corners to hide away, as the Anabaptists do.[3]

We Christians receive this freedom through the teaching of today's Gospel and we should insist that we are the lords of the sabbath and of other days and places and not attribute special holiness or service of God to a particular day, as the Jews or our papists do.

Therefore this house shall be built and appointed according to this freedom for those who dwell here in this castle and court or any others who desire to come in. Not that we are making a special church of it, as if it were better than other houses where the Word of God is preached. If the occasion should arise that people did not want to or could not assemble, one could just as well preach outside by the fountain[4] or somewhere else. For neither did the prophets have such great regard for the temple in Jerusalem (particularly because they could not stand the high priests there), nor did they always preach there, but in various places, wherever it suited them, as may be seen in their writings. Nevertheless they often wished to be with the multitude and in the place where people assembled publicly, as Ps. 42 [:4], "I went with the throng, and led them in procession to the house of God, with glad shouts and songs of thanksgiving, a multitude keeping festival." Now this multitude must have some kind of a room and its days or hours, which will be convenient for the listeners. Therefore God very wisely arranged and appointed things, and instituted the holy sacrament to be administered in the congregation at a place where we can come together, pray, and give thanks to God. Just as is done in worldly affairs when something which concerns the community must be dealt with, so much the more should this be done where we are to hear the Word of God.

And here the advantage is that when Christians thus come together their prayers are twice as strong as otherwise. One can and one really should pray in every place and every hour; but prayer

---

[3] Rörer's transcript says: "the conventicles of the Anabaptists are prohibited."
[4] A fountain in the court yard next to the church.

is nowhere so mighty and strong[5] as when the whole multitude prays together. Thus the dear patriarchs gathered with their families, and anybody else who happened to be with them, under a tree, or put up a tent, and erected an altar, and this was their temple and house of God, where they talked about Christ, the coming seed who was promised to them, sacrificed together, called upon God, and gave thanks to him. And thus they were always glad to be with the multitude whenever they could, even though they also meditated upon God's Word and promise and prayed by themselves in private.

How often we read in Holy Scriptures that even the prayer of a single man has been very effectual, as in Gen. 18 [:23-33], where Abraham prays to God for the people of Sodom and the adjacent cities and prevails upon him and wins him over to such a degree that he was willing to spare them even if only ten righteous persons were to be found in them; and Christ makes another and even stronger promise in Matt. 18 [:20, 19], that where only two or three are gathered in his name, he would be in the midst of them, and what they agreed upon to pray for together would be done for them by his heavenly Father. How much more, then, should not this assurance comfort a whole congregation of Christians when they pray together in unity for something in Christ's name? And even if no other fruit came of it, it would still be altogether sufficient that, if two or three or a whole multitude of you were together, Christ himself would be present among you. And there, most certainly, God the Father and the Holy Spirit, too, would not be absent, and the holy angels would not be far away, but the devil and his hellish troops would not willingly be anywhere near.

Let this be said with regard to the beginning of this Gospel concerning the sabbath and how and why and to what extent we Christians should make use of it, namely, that we are to come together at a time and place which we are agreed upon, deal with and listen to God's Word, bring to God our ordinary and unusual needs and those of others and thus launch up to heaven a strong, effectual prayer, and also together laud and praise God's goodness with thanksgiving. And of this we know that it is the right service and worship of God, a service which is well-pleasing to him and in which he himself is present. We know that we need not build

---

[5] Rörer's transcript reads "so warm and efficacious."

any special church or temple at great cost or burden and that we are not necessarily bound to any place or time, but have been granted liberty to do this whenever, wherever, and as often as we are able and are agreed together. We know that, just as we are always obliged in our whole Christian life to use our liberty in these external things in love and for the service of our neighbor, so in this matter also we should be in harmony and conformity with others.

Secondly, we see how Christ rebukes the Jews for their blindness and puts to shame those who would censure and cavil at him, and demonstrates to them by their own example how the sabbath may be used in freedom according to our own and our neighbor's need. For here is where they began to argue with him about his healing the dropsical man, accusing him of breaking the sabbath, imagining that now they had really hit home. Just as before, in the thirteenth chapter of Luke [13:11-17], when Christ healed in the synagogue on the sabbath a poor woman who for eighteen years had walked bent over, the ruler of the synagogue, or, as we would say, the parson, rose up and spoke to the congregation, "There are six days on which work ought to be done; come on those days and be healed, and not on the sabbath day," when one should rest and not do any work. With that speech he felt he had administered a severe rebuke to Christ, whom, however, he did not dare to address to his face.

But he gave him a proper answer, which made his and his adherents' faces red and put them to silence: "You hypocrites! Does not each of you on the sabbath untie his ox or his ass from the manger, and lead it away to water it? And ought not this woman, a daughter of Abraham whom Satan bound for eighteen years, be loosed from this bond on the sabbath day?" [Luke 13:15-16]. And here again he says the same thing: "Which of you, having an ass or an ox that has fallen into a well, will not immediately pull him out on the sabbath day?" What he really wanted to say to them in our plain German was: You are just plain oxen and asses yourselves and even more stupid than those you untie, and it may well be that the ass can read better than you can, and the ox might lead you to school, for he can well teach you to untie him when he is thirsty and to water him on the sabbath, or to pull him out of the well if he has fallen into it, so that he will not perish. Can't you understand or learn how much more necessary it is to help a person when he needs help? No, you are such utter blockheads that you even forbid anybody to help a person when he is in distress, even though you yourselves would not allow your cattle to go unhelped in even less distress. For your ox or cow would not die of thirst so quickly, even though you did not water them on the sabbath, but yet you think that you must not let them suffer thirst for the sabbath's sake. You therefore have far more regard for the need of a dumb animal than that of a man, who is your neighbor, created after God's image, and whom you have been commanded by God to love, since he says, "You shall love your neighbor as yourself" [Luke 10:27].

Beloved, put it on the scales and weigh it according to God's Word. You consider that it would be a great lack of mercy not to lead your cattle to water when they are thirsty; and yet you are the kind of devil who leaves in a lurch a man, to whom, according to God's commandment, you owe love and kindness and even your own life, and still you insist you are right in the bargain and want to punish me for helping a sick person. Yet you would want some-body to help you on the sabbath if you were in need, and you would not like it or consider it good if your neighbor let you stick and then started debating about the sabbath, as you are doing now against your neighbor, and then wanted to be considered a great saint, imagining that you have kept the sabbath well. You don't under-stand what the sabbath is or how it is to be kept; even your cow and your ass is wiser here than you, you scribes, who teach you what you should do to them in need, when they ought to be teaching you what you should do toward your neighbor.

But that's the way these hypocrites are, who neither know nor want to hear anything of the gospel and allow themselves to think that they are the masters and teachers of all the world, whereas they are the blindest and the most ignorant. It looks to me as if these fellows who had this argument with Christ were the same persons as the priest and the Levite (or their followers), of whom Christ spoke in Luke 10 [:30-37], who passed by the wounded man who lay half-dead on the road and let him lie there and, as far as they were concerned, perish in his need.

That certainly must have happened on a sabbath day, when they were going to worship and wanted a good excuse for letting the wounded man lie. They doubtless said: Ah, God preserve me from touching this man today; I must not make myself unclean now and I must not miss the service, and so on. Just as the remainder of the dregs, their children of harlotry,[6] are doing to this day; they dare not bake an apple on their sabbath, much less lend a hand to a poor man in his need (especially a Christian); they would much rather help to strike all Christians dead. But when it comes to hatred and jealousy and also their usury and skinning and scraping the Christians, they have no conscience at all, regard neither the sabbath nor God's commandment, but wherever it is a question of their own advantage they will not allow a chicken or a goose to be killed, on account of the sabbath, which they nevertheless pretend to keep so strictly. In short, they are still the same pious, holy children (though as far as blood is concerned they themselves do not know where they come from) whom the prophet Isaiah rebukes concerning their sabbath in Isa. 58 [:4], telling them that on the sabbath they do only what they want to do, observing forbidden worship, and despising or oppressing their neighbors; except that these are much worse; who are forever eager to shed the blood of Christ and his Christians and yet with great seriousness pretend to serve God by observing the sabbath, even though they themselves see that it's all up with their worship, priesthood, temple, and sabbath, and nothing is left of it.

Therefore it serves these hypocrites right to have to blush before Christ and be publicly put to shame. This is what should happen to those who want to lecture and censure Christ, the Son of God; they themselves are befouled and shown up to be more crazy and foolish than an ox or an ass, because they hold these dumb animals in more and higher regard than a man. Therefore they are quite properly paid back with interest by Christ, so that instead of gaining honor and respect for their mastery, which they tried to get by exposing him, they publicly exposed themselves to shame before everyone.

Therefore, learn here from Christ what is the right understanding of the sabbath, and how one should maintain the distinction between the outward use of the sabbath, with regard to time, hour, or place, and the necessary works of love, which God requires at all

---

[6] In the sense of Hos. 2:4-5; the reference is to the Jews.

times and hours and all places wherever there is need; so that we may know, as he says elsewhere [Mark 2:27], that the sabbath was made for man, not man for the sabbath; and that therefore man is the lord of the sabbath and should use it according to his and his neighbor's need, in such a way that he may keep this and other commandments of God without let or hindrance. For the real meaning of the third commandment is that we should use the sabbath to hear God's Word and learn that we are to keep all the other commandments, both toward God and our neighbor, and also serve and help others in love.

The hypocrites know nothing of this distinction, nor can they know anything of it, because they see in this commandment only the external work of observing the day and consider that this is the only thing necessary, and yet when it is profitable or necessary to them they do not keep it themselves. They will not allow their ox or ass to go unwatered, but they have no regard at all for their neighbor's need. Here they want to keep the commandment so strictly that they will not move a hand when they see he needs their help. Here the ox or the ass must have preference before the neighbor, and whatever they do, the sabbath must not be said to be broken; but if they were to serve or help their neighbor in his need or if they see others doing this, this would be to desecrate and break the sabbath. As they say about Christ elsewhere in the gospel, "This man is not from God, for he does not keep the sabbath" [John 9:16].

But by the grace of God we know how this commandment concerning the sabbath is to be understood, for it reads thus: You shall keep the sabbath or day of rest holy. Here pay attention to the words. What does it mean to "keep holy" or "sanctify" a day, an hour, or a week? Obviously it does not mean, as the Jews and our false saints dream, to sit in idleness and do nothing. It means rather, in the first place, to do something on that day which is a holy work, which is owing only to God, namely, that above all other things one preaches God's Word purely and holily, not as these scribes and Pharisees who falsify and pervert God's commandment because they have more regard for an ox or animal than a man. And likewise, that the others hear and learn God's Word and help to see to it that it is purely preached and kept. This is what it means rightly to observe the day of rest and to "consecrate" or "sanctify" the place or the church: as we, praise God, are consecrating this house! Yes, this preaching of the Word is the aspergillum, which all of us together should grasp and with it bless and sanctify ourselves and others.

Secondly, it means that we receive the Word of God, which we have heard in our hearts and with which we have thus been sprinkled, in order that it may bring forth power and fruit in us, and that we may publicly confess it and intend to hold on to it through life and through death.

Thirdly, it means that when we have heard God's Word we also lift up to God our common, united incense, that is, that we call upon him and pray to him together (which we know is certainly pleasing and acceptable to him, particularly in common assembly), and also praise and thank God together with joy for all his benefits, temporal and eternal, and all the wonderful works he does in his church. Thus everything that is done in such an assembly of the whole congregation or church is nothing but holy, godly business and work and is a holy sabbath, in order both that God may be rightly and holily served and all men be helped.

For when I preach, when we come together as a congregation, this is not my word or my doing; but is done for the sake of all of you and for the sake of the whole church. It is only that it is necessary that there be one who speaks and is the spokesman by the commission and consent of the others, who, by reason of the fact that they listen to the preaching, all accept and confess the Word and thus also teach others. Thus, when a child is baptized, this is done not only by the pastor, but also the sponsors, who are witnesses, indeed, the whole church. For baptism, just like the Word and Christ himself, is the common possession of all Christians. So also they all pray and sing and give thanks together; here there is nothing that one possesses or does for himself alone; but what each one has also belongs to the other.

You see, then, that this is the way the sabbath is rightly hallowed and God rightly served to our salvation, and in this way our neighbor is also served through preaching and prayer, which is the highest service and benefit, through which he is helped eternally.

Then afterwards you come down to the second table,[7] which deals particularly with our neighbor, and tells you to help him in physical need and wherever you see that he needs your help. For God has commanded this too, and his commandment should be kept not only outside the sabbath but in every time and hour, and yet in such a way that the ministry of the church, God's Word, and prayer are not neglected. For in the commandment, "You shall keep the day of rest holy," and in the other commandments, the works of love are neither forbidden nor curbed, but only those works which hinder the ministry of preaching God's Word and prayer.

Thus this commandment concerning the sabbath includes the whole law, so that the other commandments are not made null and void through it. For example, when I see my neighbor in need and in danger of life and limb, that I do not pass him by, like the priest and the Levite, and let him lie there and perish [Luke 10:31-37], so that in my very pretension of keeping the sabbath pure I become a murderer of my brother, but rather serve and help him, like the Samaritan, who bound up the wounded man, set him on his beast, and brought him to an inn.

So we also see what our Lord Christ himself did and taught us to do by his example. For as the story of the gospel shows it was his custom to go regularly on the sabbath to the synagogues, which among them were like our parish churches, and there preached a sermon to the congregation which was gathered to pray and sing psalms. There, after the sermon was over, or later at table, if he was invited by someone, he healed the sick who were present or were brought to him. These were his good works and alms, which he scattered about him along with the lovely gifts of saving teaching and alms of health, besides granting the forgiveness of sins and God's grace to all who sought it from him; as he still does to this day in his church through the same ministry of the Word which he himself carried on.

On the other hand, there is nothing to be seen in these hypocrites, who were censuring and rebuking Christ as one who did not keep the sabbath, except the very opposite of this and the other commandments, both in their teaching and their life. For in the first place they did not teach rightly, they distorted God's command-

---

[7] The second table of the commandments.

ment and did not teach men either to pray or to give thanks to God. In fact, they taught men to neglect the right works of love toward one's neighbor, helping him both spiritually to come into the kingdom of God, and physically in his need. And yet they themselves perform the kind of works on the sabbath (and insist that they are justified in doing so) which minister to their own need and serve their own bellies, such as not letting their oxen and asses suffer when they are thirsty or have fallen into a pit. Or again, as Christ says elsewhere [Matt. 12:5], they slaughter oxen, calves, and sheep and prepare them for sacrifice on the sabbath day and they teach the people this only in order to get them to bring many such sacrifices to them [Num. 28:9-10]. Isn't that, too, working with one's hands? Ask any butcher about it.

And they do this, not for God's sake, as they claim, but rather for the sake of their belly and their enjoyment; as they themselves proved by the fact that at the great festivals they brought sheep, oxen, and doves to be sold in the temple in order that people might bring them as many sacrifices as possible. Otherwise they, too, could well have said to the people what the ruler of the synagogue said: There are six days in the week, bring and prepare your sacrifices on those days, and not on the sabbath day [Luke 13:14].

We did the same thing in the past under the papacy. I may very well use myself as an example; for I lived for more than fifteen years in pure idolatry and blasphemy, in unbelief in God and false trust in the dead saints whom I invoked and in my masses and monastic life. And so I would have helped (as they are now doing in their impenitence), to condemn, persecute, and kill devout, innocent Christians, who will not laud such idolatry, and I would have thought I was doing God a great service, all the while continuing to observe my daily offices and celebrations in the church with great reverence and devotion.

But now God has mercifully liberated me from this and given me to see that this is pure perversion and godlessness and that the whole papacy is nothing else and nothing better than simply a pack of these crude teachers and pupils who belong in a school for oxen and asses. Indeed, they are not even worthy to be compared with them; for they are not even as good as the Jews, who kept their sabbath because, after all, it was commanded by God. But these have nothing on their side except their own fabricated human trash and self-chosen works and life, which they elevate far above God's commandment.

Then, besides the fact that they desecrate and blaspheme God every day with their idolatry and godless doctrine, they also have no regard for any work of love toward their neighbor. Indeed, they would rather let a man die and perish in his need rather than lend him a hand. And in this they are so scrupulous that they dare not move a hairbreadth contrary to their human regulations, rules, and ordinances. Just as the Jews were not allowed to pour a little wine or mustard on the Sabbath, and though they would be doing wrong if they were to put off or omit the works of their self-invented service of God for the sake of their neighbor; but meanwhile they had no qualms of conscience, not only about leaving their neighbor unhelped, but also misleading him with false doctrine and diddling him out of money and goods besides, in order to fill their bellies, to have enough of everything for themselves, and not to stint themselves for anything. They claim that they must guard these things as church property and not allow them to be impaired in any way, no matter what happens in the meantime to God or one's neighbor.

Such false, foolish saints, yes, more foolish than oxen and asses, are also Mohammed's crowd, the Turks, and whatever else those who do not hear and accept Christ are called. Therefore we should really praise and thank God that we hear and have his Word purely preached, that we know how we are to act both toward God and our neighbor, to practice true service of God, and lead our whole life aright in all things. And we should also earnestly call upon God and beseech him to preserve us that we may remain in his Word, in right faith, and the true hallowing of the sabbath.

Let this be sufficient for the first part of this Gospel concerning the sabbath, which teaches us how it is to be kept holy; that we are not bound to a particular time, place, house, or persons, but rather that we are to accept it and use it according to our opportunity and need to hear God's Word together and pray and give thanks with one another. All of which is done best in the assembly, when people come together solely for this purpose and hearts and thoughts are less distracted than when each one is dealing with himself or with others. In this way and for this purpose may this house too be now consecrated, not for its sake, but for our sakes, that we ourselves may be and remain consecrated through God's Word, so that we, too, may help to keep and to spread that which God has so graciously given to us.

Then comes the second part.

The second part of this Gospel is a lecture which Christ delivered against those who chose to sit at the head of the table, etc. Thus this may not appear to be any very remarkable teaching, nevertheless it was necessary in order to rebuke the hypocrisy and false ideas of the Jews who thought the only thing that mattered was their holiness and services to God so that they might be proud and have prestige and honor above that of others. And just as they perverted the commandment concerning the sabbath, which they observed solely in order to be considered holy, and thus served, not God according to his commandment, but themselves, so they also did the same thing in their outward station and conduct before the world. This they used, not to serve God or their neighbor, but only to elevate themselves. They read the Scriptures and Moses with blind eyes, as if it were not commanded that they were to befriend the poor and the lowly and serve and help them, but only in order that they might sit at the head of the table on the sabbath and be lords on earth. Just as they imagine even now that their law implies that they should be lords over the Gentiles and we should be their servants. Just as the Turks, too, believe and hold that they must be the lords of the world, strutting around like lords and noblemen with their Mohammedans and Mamelukes clothed in gold and silk; but we must go barefoot like their lowest cowherds and bow down to them. They think that they are offering a great service to God when they do this [John 16:2], and when they are successful they consider this a sign that God is their friend and on their side, just as our Antichrist, the pope, also sought after this and taught it.

So this hypocritical preaching and acting was likewise all directed toward their being considered great and noble by everyone, toward being free to be unmerciful and proud with their neighbors; and, what is more, they insisted that this was right. Thus they fabricated another Moses and another law, just as they made of the sabbath something different from what God had commanded them. Therefore the Lord had much trouble with them on this point also, as he cries woe upon them in Matt. 23 [:13-15] and tells his disciples to beware of the Pharisees and scribes, who love the best seats in the synagogues and the salutations in the market places [vv. 6-7].

Now, how can these two things be reconciled: to sit in the place of honor is not right and yet it is right? For, after all, it is not prohibited, and Christ himself says in the text, "When you are invited, go and sit in the lowest place, so that when your host comes he may say to you, 'Friend, go up higher.'" How can he say one should not sit in the place of honor and yet at the same time say that he who sits in the lowest place shall be placed at the head of the table?

This is the answer. Here the emphasis is upon the word, "chose," as the text says, "When he marked how they chose the places of honor" [Luke 14:7]; just as in the preceding section, in which they are rebuked concerning the sabbath, it says that "they were watching him" [Luke 14:1]. There must be those who sit higher and those who sit lower; for, as I said above, one cannot set aside a special place, time, temple, or chapel in the congregation for each individual. Likewise, we cannot all be princes, counts, preachers, noblemen, citizens, men, women, and servants. Rather, there must be many stations, and each one has enough to do in his own station. So all of us should not and cannot sit above or below at the same time. There must be the destination, ordained by God, that he who is in the higher station should also sit higher than the others; a count should not seat himself higher than the princes and the servant should not sit higher than the master. Thus there must also be a distinction among other stations, citizens, peasants, etc.

But what is important is that you rightly understand what Christ means by these words and realize that, if you are of a higher rank or are in some way above others, this is something that has been given to you by God, but not in order that you may put on airs on account of this gift and ride roughshod over everybody else, as if you were better than others in the sight of God because of it. On the contrary, he has commanded that you be humble and serve your neighbor with it. For example, I am a preacher because God has given me the grace to be one, but he has also commanded me not to pride myself on this gift but rather to go down and serve every man that he may be saved, as Paul says in Rom. 15 [:2-3], "Let each of us please (not himself, but) his neighbor for his good, to edify him. For Christ did not please himself, etc." Thus he made others princes, lords, noblemen, regents, scholars and to this end gave them sovereignty, power, honor, great understanding, etc. And he wills that they should be held in honor and sit at the head of the table, but in such a way that they do not exalt themselves above everybody because of this. But most of them sin by their pride and arrogance, especially in these days when there is altogether too much insolence and presumption among the upper classes and also gross peasant's pride among others.

Therefore, if you have received this gift from God of being more powerful, higher, more learned, nobler than others, then remember that he has commanded you to take this gift and serve your neighbor with it. If you do not, then you should know that even a poor shepherd boy, who, compared with you, has no gifts or standing whatsoever in the world, is far greater and far closer to heaven in the sight of God and the angels. You, however, with your fine, high dignity and your trappings, will be cast into hell. For God did not create only princes, counts, noblemen, and scholars nor invite only them into his kingdom, and to him one man is as good as another as long as he is a Christian; as our Creed says: I believe in God, Creator of heaven and earth. So do not think that you alone must sit at the head of the table or that you must not give way to anybody. For the God who made you a lord, a regent, a doctor, or a teacher, is just as much the God of the poor beggar at your door, and his eyes look just as straight at him as at the greatest lords or princes on earth. In short, whether you are at the top or the middle or at the bottom, all are made equal by faith, which says: "We all believe in one God, Creator of heaven and earth, etc."[8] Therefore, nobody has any reason for being proud toward others. Rather the one who is highest should take this lesson of Christ to heart and not exalt himself above others and thus be sent down in shame; but rather consider: The God who has made me a prince has also made my subject, and I have nothing more nor better than does the humblest peasant in the field. Indeed, if you propose to be proud and arrogant in your lordly rank, despising others; then perhaps God will take some peasant's servant who walks in humility and esteem

---

[8] Luther's versification of the Creed, vid. PE 6, 180, 304.

and elevate him above all emperors and kings, as he did with Joseph, David, Daniel, and others.

Well, you say, if that's the case, then I must not be a king, prince, lord, doctor, or be something above others, or sit at the head? No, that's not the way it is. Be and remain what you are, and do what is commanded you and your station demands, but see to it that you are not proud and that you do not exalt yourself before this Lord who has invited you and others. For He will not suffer anybody to exalt himself; but he whom He exalts and sets in the high place is exalted in good conscience and honor. And even though one may be placed in a higher station and estate, before him all alike are his beloved guests, so long as they keep his Word and command, so that here every maidservant has the same dignity as the noblest empress or queen; for she can say: I believe in the same God, I have been baptized in his name, I call upon my Lord Christ. If I am not a noblewoman or rich freewoman, what does that matter to me? I still have just as much before God as they. And as I am believing and humble, let me be satisfied with my modest station, for I know that God respects me and I can well let the great empress sit where she is.

Therefore, among Christians, nobody need complain that he is too poor or in too humble a station. Beloved, do you not have as much as a king or sovereign prince—a golden crown, power, goods, honor? After all, you have the same God, Creator of heaven and earth, the same Christ, the same baptism, and his whole heavenly kingdom; as St. Paul says of the Christians, they have nothing and yet possess everything [II Cor. 6:10], for, as he says in I Cor. 3 [:22-23], "all things are yours; and you are Christ's; and Christ is God's." Therefore, under this Lord you are rich and blessed enough, so that even an emperor cannot have more than you. But remain in your station and be content, whether you sit above or below, and guard against this scrambling up higher, so that you will not think: Because I am a prince, because I am noble, learned, powerful, I alone must be respected and elevated; but rather say: Defend me, heavenly Father, from pride, for I know that the humblest plowman can be better in thy sight than I.

So you see that God creates one and the same standing within the great inequalities of many different stations and persons as he himself ordains how they must live in this life, and yet in such a way that each one perform his office and do the work of that office as his station requires in the humility which renders all stations and persons equal in the sight of God, since he has created them all alike and to him one is as good as the other. Therefore, no one should vaunt himself before God and put himself above his neighbor because he is in a higher station, but realize that, if he does not remain humble in his high station, he is sinning abominably and will be far more severely condemned than the others.

On the other hand, even though all persons, both in high station and low, are equal and have all things in common before God, as the Epistle for today says (Eph. 4 [:4-5]), "One body and one Spirit . . . one Lord, one faith, one baptism, etc.," it does not say and it will not do that a servant behind the plow or a maidservant in the house should walk up to masters and mistresses and say: I am just as noble and good as you are in the sight of God; therefore I cannot be subject to you or obedient to you, and so on. Unfortunately, it is all too common and widespread these days that even the lower stations want to out-swagger the upper classes; just as the Junkers do to their princes and lords, and even the servants and maidservants to their masters and mistresses, quite wantonly, especially when they see that one needs them. This does not befit any Christian, for it, too, is contrary to this rule and teaching of Christ. For while it is forbidden to anybody in a higher station to show pride and arrogance to those in the lower station, God would have this forbidden even more among persons of a lower and subject class.

This humility belongs to being a Christian as one of the primary and most necessary virtues, and it is also the greatest bond of Christian love and unity; as St. Paul says, again in the Epistle for today [Eph. 4:2], he does not puff himself up in his office or station and exalt himself above others, even though he is more than others, but rather knows that, like others, he should in his office serve his Lord, who has given to each his office and work and will draw him into his kingdom as a beloved guest and seat him at his table, if he serves him faithfully in that office. For he has need of many and various offices and stations and therefore he bestows many different kinds of gifts, so contriving things that one always needs the other and none can do without the other. What would princes, nobles, and regents be if there were not others, such as pastors, preachers, teachers, farmers, craftsmen, etc.? They would not and could not learn or do everything alone and by themselves.

Therefore none should look to himself alone, but rather each should look up to heaven and say: God has created all stations and before him none is the lowest, except those who are arrogant and proud, and none is better, except those who cast themselves down to the lowest place. You may well be of high rank and in high office, but if you were required to give an accounting of the gifts which you have received, you would be worse off than a poor cowherd. I myself have known several great doctors who were considered to be great lights in the world and had high standing among lords and princes, but when the hour came for them to die they said: Oh, Lord God, if I had only been a swineherd, and so on. Yes, if you had said this from your heart before, when you were living amidst great honor and dignity, and thus humbled yourself, God would have said to you too: Friend, you are sitting in the lowest place; come up higher.

For he appoints many different offices, and Christ, the Son of God who sits at the right hand of the Father, bestows many gifts, in order that he may test us and see whether we fear him and are willing to serve him therein and thus humble ourselves. For, as we said, he demands this humility of us and it is also his due. If we do not do so in this life, we shall nevertheless be grievously cast down in the end when we die. He wants all to have stations and persons alike, to care for them as his guests and seat them and honor them, so that none may complain; except that each must be satisfied with his own place and not exalt himself above others, even though he may be higher and greater than others in the eyes of the world.

Christ, the Son of God, was also high and noble, and yet he made himself equal to us poor men, indeed, he humbled himself beneath everybody. A woman must be a woman and cannot be a man. She, too, is God's creature and her divine station is that she should bear and care for and rear children. So I am a man, created for another office and work. But should I be proud because of this and say: I am not a woman, therefore I am better in the sight of God? Should I not rather praise God for creating both the woman and me also through the woman and putting me in this my station? What an un-Christian thing it is that one should despise another because he is in another station or is doing something other than he is doing? It is like what happens among the Junkers nowadays; often one assaults another for trifling reasons, one calls the other a clerk and they can kill each other on this account; but they are more likely to do this to others, poor pastors, preachers, or humble people. Very well, but be careful and arm yourself against this saying: "Everyone who exalts himself will be humbled." For God will not and cannot tolerate such pride and arrogance. What do you have that you should be so proud? What do you have of yourself? And is not another just as much God's creature as you are, no matter who he is? He will not have him despised; for he who despises his creature also mocks his Creator, says Solomon [Prov. 14:31; 17:5], and he who scoffs at a station scoffs at the Lord himself.

Therefore, even where you would not otherwise give respect or regard, you should have regard for God. But if you despise him, then know that he can despise you and make you despised and will cast you down, no matter how high you are sitting. For hereby you have incurred the wrath, not of a man, but of the Majesty in heaven. If a secular prince entrusted an office in court to someone, and someone else were to mock, deride, or murder him, you would soon find out whether the prince would tolerate such a thing. What would you, nobleman, do if somebody else were wilfully to mock and insult someone in your household? As strongly as you feel about your dog, your horse, your trooper, so strongly does God feel about his creatures.

Therefore, even though another station may be more humble than yours, you must nevertheless know that it, too, has been created and ordained by God. Contrariwise, you must know that you, too, have been put in your station in order that you may humble yourself and serve others, as, for example, a nobleman serves his prince at court or in the field, or a servant or maidservants serve their master and mistress; and you should do this for God's sake. This is really to humble oneself, as Christ calls it. Then God on his part will exalt you and lift you up before all the world with all honor.

Let this be sufficient to be said concerning this Gospel for the consecration of this house. And now that you, dear friends, have

helped to sprinkle with the true holy water of God's Word, take hold
of the censer with me, that is, seize hold upon prayer, and let us call
upon God and pray. First, for his holy church, that he may preserve
his holy Word among us and extend it everywhere. And then that
he may keep this house pure, as it now is, God be praised, consecrated and sanctified through God's Word, that it may not be
desecrated or defiled by the devil and his lies and false doctrine.
And then also for all governments and public peace in German
lands, that God may graciously preserve and strengthen the same,
and guard us against the devil and his servants, the pope, bishops,
papists, and wicked Turks; for here we have need of a strong prayer.
For it is a grievous torment to see and endure such discord and
arrant cunning of the devil and his rabble. And finally, also for our
beloved government, the sovereign prince and the whole nobility
and all ranks, high and low, rulers and subjects, that they may all
honor God's Word, give thanks to God for it, administer their offices
well, be faithful and obedient, and show Christian love to their
neighbors. For this is what God would have from us all, and this is
the true incense of Christians—to pray earnestly for all of these
necessities. Amen.

SERMON AT MARRIAGE OF SIGISMUND VON LINDENAU

1545

SERMON AT MARRIAGE OF
SIGISMUND VON LINDENAU
1545

Sermon Preached at the Marriage of Sigismund von
Lindenau in Merseburg, Heb. 13:4, August 4, 1545

In 1544 Luther had already declared his intention of leaving Witten-berg but was dissuaded by Bugenhagen and others. His disgust with the moral conditions in Wittenberg and his own physical debility prompted him to carry out his resolve and he left the city toward the end of July, 1545. On July 28, he wrote to his wife, "I should like to arrange not to have to go back to Wittenberg." "Away with this Sodom!" Upon the urging of Prince Georg of Anhalt, coadjutor and canon of the cathedral in Merseburg, he went there to preach at the marriage of Sigismund von Lindenau, dean of the cathedral. Sigismund had lived in secret marriage for seven years "under com-pulsion" not to declare it publicly. Now by order of the coadjutor marriage of the clergy was permitted and concubinage strictly for-bidden and the pair were married by the coadjutor in the cathedral. The sermon is printed with another preached in Merseburg and was given to the printer by Magister Matthias Wanckel, pastor in Halle, who may well have been the transcriber.

Text in German; WA 49, 797-805.

"Let marriage be held in honor among all, and let the marriage bed be undefiled; for God will judge the immoral and adulterous" (Heb. 13:4).

This is a sermon concerning the holy estate of matrimony which is highly necessary, especially among Christians, that all men may know what the holy estate of matrimony really is and where it comes from, so that we shall not go on living so casually from day to day, like the heathen and dumb brutes who neither ask nor think about these things, but simply go on interbreeding and cohabiting promiscuously. No, among Christians, it must not be so; but rather as St. Paul says in I Thess. 4 [:3-5], "This is the will of God, your sanctification: that you abstain from immorality; that each one of you know how to take a wife for himself in holiness and honor, not in the passion of lust like heathen who do not know God."

Therefore Christians should live in sanctification, not like swine and animals, nor like the heathen, who neither regard nor honor this estate.

There is much to preach concerning this holy estate and divine ordinance of marriage, for it is the oldest of all estates in the whole world; indeed, all others are derived from that estate in which Adam and Eve, our first parents, were created and ordained and in which they and all their God-fearing children and descendants lived.

For there it is, written in the first book of Moses: "God created man in his own image, in the image of God he created him; male and female he created them. And God blessed them, and God said to them, 'Be fruitful and multiply, and fill the earth and subdue it'" [Gen. 1:27-28].

There it is; these are not my words nor those of any other man, but God's Word. This is the way he created and ordained it, and he who will not believe it, let him leave it. Moreover, the daily birth and arrival of all men proves that God wants his creation and ordinance, the holy estate of matrimony, to be maintained, in that little men and women are born and begin to grow up every day.

So every single one of us must declare and confess that we have not made or created ourselves; nor can we do it, neither could our parents do it. Who, then? The almighty, eternal God, the creator of all things, who first created and ordained little men and women for the marriage estate, he created us too for this estate. For I must freely confess and declare that I was created a male child, another a female child; I must confess that I am not a stone or a stick, but rather born and created a human being, man or woman. No man in the whole world, from the first to the latest, can say anything else. The people, especially the papists, are still raging and fuming beyond all bounds against this glorious creation of God, as if it

358

should not exist. And if it were in the pope's hand and power to create men, it would surely not exist; for he would not create or allow a single woman to exist in the whole world. What would happen then? Human beings would pass away. For it is certain that nobody is born without a mother; but what is born comes from the mother. And just as Adam did not make himself, but was created by God, so all men must be created by God in the womb and there sustained and later be born with God's help into the world.

Therefore all men should marry and be married, and since through the fall of our first parents we have been so spoiled that we are not all fit for marriage, yet those who are not fit for the married state should so live that they walk chastely and honorably and give offense to no one, though at the beginning it was not so and all were fit to become married. But now it happens that some do not want to enter the state of matrimony even though they are fit and qualified to marriage. Some, on the other hand, would like to be married and are unable to do so. Neither do I condemn and disapprove of these. The third group, however, who desire and want to be married and are also fit and competent to do so, even though they enter the marriage state contrary to human laws, do what is right, and nobody should be scandalized by what they do. For the married state should not be forbidden to anyone who is competent to be married, but should be free and open to everyone. And this estate should not be condemned and rejected as something foul and unclean, as the pope and his followers do. For to be married is an ordinance and institution of God, since when God created man and woman, he himself placed them in this estate in which they not only could but should live godly, honorable, pure, and chaste lives, bearing children and peopling the world, indeed, the kingdom of God.

Who, then, would be so bold as to tear down the glorious, holy ordinance of God or to say anything against it? Who, then, is so bold as to condemn this ordinance and despise it as useless, unholy, and unnecessary?

The pope and his cardinals, monks, nuns, and priests have tried to improve things and ordain a holy estate in which they might live in holiness and chastity. But how holy, pure, and chaste the lives of popes, cardinals, bishops, monks, priests, and nuns have been is so apparent that the sun, moon, and stars have cried out against it.

Pigsties are nasty, dirty places, but they are clean and pure compared with the cloisters; for they have been leading such a chaste and pure life in the cloisters that one cannot very well even speak of it. Why, then, did this happen? Because they tore down and despised God's holy ordinance of the estate of matrimony and they were not worthy to enter into marriage. But here those who have entered into holy matrimony in accord with God's ordinance should love and esteem this saying of St. Paul:

"Let marriage be held in honor among all, and let the marriage bed be undefiled, etc."

They should also pride themselves upon and comfort themselves with the fact that they are married; for here a man can say: I thank God that I have been created a man by God; or a woman: I thank God that I have been created a woman; and that we have also been placed by God in the holy estate of marriage in order to bring forth children according to his blessing and will. This honor, which those who are married have, is far greater. Therefore, nobody should hate or condemn this estate and ordinance of God, as the pope and his followers do, but rather highly exalt it and love and esteem it.

Here let the pope, cardinals, monks, nuns, and priests pull a sour face; what do we care about that? If they will not look at us with friendly and pure eyes, then let them look at the whorehouses and the impure, filthy, and befouled cloisters. We are content to know that we are esteemed by God and his only Son, our Lord Jesus Christ, who sits at the right hand of God and rules all things, the one who ordained the marriage estate and placed us in it and watches over this estate until the last day. Because I know this and most certainly believe it, I am happy and confident, and I live in the holy ordinance of marriage with a good conscience and a happy mind. For here God says to the man: You are my man; and to the woman: You are my woman. And because I know that God speaks so to me, I also know that all the angels speak so to me, and love me and respect me. I also know that the sun, moon, and all the stars look upon me and minister to me with their light and influence, even though this terribly vexes the devil with his scales, the popes, cardinals, and monks, who also are the devil's. I don't care a snap for them; even though they were a thousand against one, I don't care. If they don't want to regard me or listen to me, then in the devil's name let them take a look in Morolf's looking glass.[1]

Here it is written: "God will judge the immoral and adulterous."

It is not written that God will judge and condemn the married, but rather the whoremongers and adulterers. For if God were to condemn and judge the married people, he would have to condemn himself. But God does not do this, but rather is well pleased with married people, as those who live and walk in his ordinance and creation. So, if God does not judge me, why should I care if the pope judges and condemns me; after all he himself was born of a woman and sucked a woman's—his mother's—breast.

At this point they bring forth a passage from the prophet Isaiah, who says in chapter fifty-two: "Go out from the midst of her, purify yourselves, you who bear the vessels of the Lord" [Isa. 52:11]. This passage they use to defend their celibacy (meaning that priests should not be married) and to condemn the married estate as unclean. It is in fact a fine, excellent passage, but it does not fit here at all. For in the Old Testament the priests were required to have wives and be married; it is to these who were married that the prophet says, "Purify yourselves." Why then does the pope, the devil in Rome, use this passage against those who are married, when it was actually spoken by God to the married? The pope nevertheless uses it against those who are married. So our adversaries, the miserable papists, interpret purity to mean unmarried and without a wife, and thus want their priests to be pure, that is, not to have wives, despite the fact that God wants the priests to be married and thus to live purely in the marriage estate. Therefore, those who are married should be cheerful and confident and grateful to God that they are in an estate which has been ordained and blessed by God, of sure hope and assurance that God will keep his ordinance and blessing, regardless of whether it annoys the devil, the pope in Rome, and therefore prompts them to condemn this estate.

But here you say: Yes, but we have vowed and sworn to God that we shall be chaste and live without women; I am obliged to keep this vow; therefore I cannot be married. My answer to that is:

---

[1] The allusion is to the sixteenth-century folk tale character, akin to the later Til Eulenspiegel; the meaning: to look up his posterior.

Right, do what you have vowed to do; be chaste and pure. Why don't you keep it, why don't you do it? Who is stopping you from being chaste and pure? Yes, you say, but I can't keep it. What a proper fool you are; why do you vow what you neither know nor can keep? There is only one thing I can vow which I can also keep, and that is that I will not bite off my own nose. Who commanded you to vow and swear something which is contrary to God and his ordinance, namely, to swear that you are neither a man or a woman, when it is certain that you are either a man or a woman, created by God. Why, then, do you swear that you are not a man or a woman?

If you are able to remain chaste and be pure by your own strength, why then do you vow to be chaste? Keep it, if you can; but it is a mere nothing that you should want to boast about your vow and then plead that they have led you astray. Do you want to know to whom you have vowed to keep chastity? I'll tell you: the miserable devil in hell and his mother.

I say this for the comfort of all those who are in the married state, that they may be emboldened and encouraged. If all of you who are married are not rich, as not all of you can be rich, then be satisfied with what you have, and let it be your strong consolation that you have been married in accord with divine ordinance, and be assured that God will keep watch over this his ordinance and blessing. Nor do we desire to prevent or force anybody in this matter. Here we have a sure and strong word of comfort:

"Let marriage be held in honor among all, and let the marriage bed be undefiled."

Hold fast to that, those of you who are married.

St. Augustine writes in one place concerning married people, that even if one of them is somewhat weak, etc., he should not be afraid of the sudden and infallible Day of the Lord; even if the Day of the Lord were to come in the hour when man and wife were having marital intercourse, they should not be afraid of it.[2] Why is this so? Because even if the Lord comes in that hour he will find them in the ordinance and station in which they have been placed and installed by God.

---

[2] A note in WA states that this citation cannot be verified in Augustine's writings.

Now, since this is so, nobody, no mandate of emperor, pope, or bishop, shall stand in my way and prevent me. I am content that I have a gracious God, who is pleased with this ordinance, and who also regards me and blesses and protects me. Who made them so bold and who commanded them to tear down this glorious ordinance of God?

Therefore it will not do for you to try and defend yourself by pointing to your vow of chastity, which you are not able to keep. If you have vowed it, you have vowed it to the devil, and you are not obliged to keep it, for it is against God. Besides, this vowing is not something ancient and of long standing. In the time of St. Augustine and St. Ambrose nothing whatsoever was known of this vow and vowing; rather everybody was free to remain single or to marry as he pleased. This binding and this vowing to keep chastity and remain unmarried is something new, invented and devised by the devil and the miserable monks, the defamers of God's ordinance and the holy estate of matrimony.

The marriage estate is God's ordinance and we shall stick to this no matter whether they hate and persecute us and will neither regard nor listen to us; this bothers us not at all. We have God; he regards us, along with all the angels and heavenly hosts, he also defends us against all the darts of the devil and our adversaries.

Then, if our dear God and Father in heaven grants you children, nurture and care for them, raise them up in the discipline, fear, and admonition of the Lord. Then you will be doing right and performing better and nobler good works than all the monks and nuns; then you will be living in God's vocation and ordinance and they contrary to God's vocation and ordinance. Because I am certain that I have a gracious God, who regards me, nourishes me, and protects me, I do not care that the louse in Rome, the pope, and his lice, the cardinals and bishops, monks and nuns, do not regard or respect me. I pay no attention to it; I am content that God, my dear Father, sees me and has regard for me.

Therefore we also lead brides and grooms to the church, in order that they may publicly confess that they are entering into the holy estate of matrimony in accord with God's ordinance, that they do not intend to live in concubinage, and they are blessed, and they have no doubt that they are blessed by God. But they must take care that they remain blessed and lead their married life as married persons should, God-fearingly, purely, and unblemished, then they will remain blessed.

Now we know what the marriage estate is, namely, the creation and ordinance of God, and what is essential to it, namely, a man and a wife. Therefore it should also be considered pure by all men. And if the pope were a Christian, he, too, would hold the marriage estate to be holy and pure. But since he is not a Christian, but the Antichrist and the devil himself, he despises holy matrimony and considers it unclean. But God, who ordained and appointed and blessed the marriage estate, honors marriage. Therefore, we, who are Christians and children of God through faith in Christ, should also honor, uphold, cherish, and esteem the marriage estate. And it should also be kept pure by all; which means that no whore nor adulterer should be found among you, but rather each of you should have his own wife. Moreover, it was for the sake of the marriage estate that God gave us the fourth commandment and made it the first commandment following the first table, thereby declaring that he wants marriage to be upheld and honored, for he says, "Honor your father and your mother, etc." [Exod. 20:12]. Why should I honor father and mother; after all they lead a carnal life? No, the life father and mother lead is an honorable and godly life. Just as it would be a dishonor for you, if you were born of a whore out of wedlock, so it would be a dishonor if parents lived together unmarried. Therefore to be married is honorable and pleasing to God. But if for a time you have lived outside of this state in concubinage and led a life of fornication, ah, then stop it and repent, enter into marriage and henceforth live a married and godly life. Then you will be doing the right and Christian thing.

Those who bring forth children outside of marriage are parents too, it is true; but there is no honor in it. Therefore it is said, "Let the marriage bed be undefiled." In other words, let it not be a whore's bed or an adulterous bed. But here you object: How can the marriage bed be undefiled; after all, there is much impurity in the marriage bed too? This is true, there is not much that is pure in it. But if you want to see impurity, then look at the state of maidens and bachelors; everything is not pure there either, for as they eat and drink they cannot be clean; they must be hawking, sniffling, and snuffling, and whatever other uncleanness there may be. Look here, since you find it in the unmarried state too and are not troubled by such impurity there, why do you look only at the impurity that occurs also in the married state? Indeed, if we are going to talk about the purity and chastity which the angels possess, you will not find it anywhere, either in marriage or outside of marriage in the unmarried state; that kind of purity is gone. Nor are children pure; there you have nose dirt, filth, scabs, and much else that is unclean. But St. Paul is not speaking of that kind of impurity here; for in this respect all men are blemished and impure. He is speaking of the purity which should obtain in the marriage estate, that married people should not be fornicators or adulterers and adulteresses. Whatever else occurs in the married state God covers up, for, after all, it is done in order to bring forth children and God approves of this, for it is his ordinance. This kind of impurity, says God, I do not see. Here parents, fathers and mothers, or married people, are excused; God will not consider it impurity on account of inherited sin, nor will he consider it to be a sin. God will rather build his kingdom of heaven over this work and cover up everything that is unclean in it for the sake of his ordinance and creation.

This is the kind of purity St. Paul means when he says: "Let the marriage bed be undefiled." He is not talking about cleanness in eating and drinking, but rather about marital faithfulness and duty, in which one trusts the other, keeps away from all other persons, and is content with his own spouse; this is what he calls purity. We should therefore thank and praise God, and we should also glory over against the miserable devil and the pope that we have been born of a pure and undefiled marriage bed; for the marriage bed is pure in the sight of God. Even though this vexes the devil, who would like to have it considered impure and wants to make it impure, this does not trouble us at all. This assurance and boast is given us by this text: "Let the marriage bed be undefiled among all." But this is followed by these words:

"God will judge the immoral and adulterous."

Here is pronounced the judgment that no whoremonger or adulterer will escape God's judgment. Here our adversaries, the enemies of marriage, must stop, and it will be no help for them to boast and appeal to their vows; for they are the real, true adulterers, who prevent marriage and forbid people to be married. But when our Lord Jesus Christ comes on the last day to judge the living and the dead, God will not judge the married, for they are in his ordinance. Oh, what an unspeakable comfort that is for all married people in their estate! How confidently they can await the glorious coming of our Lord Jesus Christ! For an apple tree or some other tree which bears its kinds of fruit will not be judged on the last day because it bears apples or is defiled by caterpillars and worms. No, for it was created by God for the purpose of bearing apples and fruit. So married people, who are wedded and bear children and live pure wedded lives, will not be judged because of this.

But the immoral and adulterous, who live outside of this state in defilement and impurity, such as the pope and cardinals, bishops, canons, monks, nuns, etc., who forbid marriage and themselves engage in all kinds of abominable lust and vileness and so woefully befoul the holy estate of matrimony, God will judge on that day. Then the true judgment will be made. Indeed, God does not leave everything until that glorious day of Christ, but also punishes here in this life. I am not very old and yet I have lived almost three times longer than those in one or four convents I know of, where the bishop, canons, and vicars have passed away, and, as St. Peter says in II Pet. 2 [:1, 3], they "bring upon themselves swift destruction" and "their destruction has not been asleep." Our dear Lord God and Father in heaven does not grant and bestow upon them a long life, or at least very seldom, and few old people are to be found in convents, simply because they rage and rant against God's holy ordinance and violently tear it down and abominably befoul it.

You ought to thank the almighty, eternal God, the Father of our Lord Jesus Christ, that you can boast of the ordinance of God and the holy estate of matrimony. Keep it and raise up your children in the name of God. You don't need to worry about whether you are condemned by God for it, nor will he judge you for the work's sake; this I know for certain. Indeed, the fact that you are married, as long as you are a Christian, will be a great glory and honor to you on the last day. And now, and as long as you live, be confident in every hour that you are living in an estate which was instituted by God and is pleasing to him. Let pope and bishops who are opposed to it fulminate and growl and the more they boast of their vow and condemn the married state the more let us be proud of the ordinance of God in which we live, for this God and his only Son, our Lord Jesus Christ, and the Holy Spirit, is and will remain an everlasting God, whereas the pope and his rabble will wither like the grass of the field or quickly vanish away like a bubble.

But it is also required that every Christian should remain in the estate and calling in which he has been placed by God and faithfully discharge its duties; then God adds felicity and blessing. May God grant us this and be praised to all eternity. Amen.

THE LAST SERMON
IN WITTENBERG

1546

THE LAST SERMON
IN WITTENBERG
1546

The Last Sermon in Wittenberg, Rom. 12:3,

January 17, 1546

The title of the printed version of this sermon reads: "The Last Sermon of Doctor Martin Luther of Hallowed Memory which He Preached on the Second Sunday after the Epiphany, January 17, 1546." It is the last sermon of which we possess a transcript (Rörer's). The printed verion of 1549 was prepared by Stephan Tucher, pastor in Magdeburg, who heard the sermon himself but followed Rörer's transcript with remarkable faithfulness. After this sermon Luther preached five others before his death, on January 26 in Halle and on January 30, February 2, 7, and 15 in Eisleben. The present translation is based on both Rörer's macaronic and Tucher's German text.

Text in WA 51, 123-134, compared with CL 7, 411-417.

"For by the grace given to me I bid [every one among you not to think of himself more highly than he ought to think, but to think with sober judgment, each according to the measure of faith which God has assigned him"] Rom. 12 [:3[1]].

---

[1] The register of pericopes in Luther's *Neues Testament Deutsch* (1546) begins the Epistle for this day with verse 3, though Luther's earlier *Fastenpostille* (1525) began it with verse 6. In any case, Luther limited himself in this sermon to this one verse.

St. Paul, as was his custom, taught first the great chief articles of Christian doctrine—the law, sin, and faith, how we are to be justified before God and live eternally. As you have often heard and still hear every day, namely, that there are two points to be taught and preached: first we must see to it that faith in Christ is rightly preached, and second, that the fruits and good works are rightly taught and practiced.

Faith requires that we know what sin is, what the law is, what death is, and what it does, and also how we return to life and abide in it. This is the way Paul teaches in all his epistles; first concerning faith in Christ. First he plants the good tree, just as anybody who wants to have a good garden must have good trees. This is what Paul does; first he sets out the wild trees [cf. Rom. 11:24] and teaches how we should become good trees, that is, how we are to believe and be saved.

This he has been describing up to this point in the twelfth chapter. From here to the end of the epistle he teaches the fruits of faith, in order that we may not be false Christians, who have only the name of Christian, but rather real, true believers. This is the preaching concerning good works, which God commands, especially in the first and second table [i.e., of the Ten Commandments], that we, who have been redeemed through the blood and death of the Son of God, should live godly lives, as those who do not belong to this transitory life but rather to eternal life, provided that we rightly believe; in order that after believing we may not again follow the world, as Paul says in the preceding verse: "Be transformed by the renewal of your mind," etc. [Rom. 12:2]. Review therefore the good works, which are to be done, to the end of the Epistle. First he deals with the good fruits which the Christians bring forth among themselves as if there were no government except the government of the church through baptism, etc. Then in the thirteenth chapter he deals with worldly authority and the attitude of Christians toward it [Rom. 13:3]. In the fourteenth chapter he admonishes the strong to receive the weak in faith [Rom. 14:1].

Here he is teaching concerning the works of Christians. Now, he is saying, now that we have been made rich through Christ the Lord, transferred from the dominion of the devil and the world to his kingdom [cf. Col. 1:13], that is, into the church of Christ; now that we have the Word and the sacraments, now that we have been baptized, now that we are sons and heirs of God and fellow heirs with Christ the Son of God [cf. Rom. 8:17], who has given us eternal life, now it is necessary that we look to and really devote ourselves to the glorious calling and gifts.

After baptism there still remains much of the old Adam. For, as we have often said, it is true that sin is forgiven in baptism, but we are not yet altogether clean, as is shown in the parable of the Samaritan, who carried the man wounded by robbers to an inn [Luke 10:30-37]. He did not take care of him in such a way that he healed him at once, but rather bound up his wounds and poured on oil. The man who fell among robbers suffered two injuries. First, everything that he had was taken from him, he was robbed; and second, he was wounded, so that he was half-dead and would have died, if the Samaritan had not come to him. Adam fell among the robbers and implanted sin in us all. If Christ, the Samaritan, had not come, we should all have had to die. He it is who binds our wounds, carries us into the church and is now healing us. So we are now under the Physician's care. The sin, it is true, is wholly forgiven, but it has not been wholly purged. If the Holy Spirit is not ruling men, they become corrupt again; but the Holy Spirit must cleanse the wounds daily. Therefore this life is a hospital; the sin has really been forgiven, but it has not yet been healed.

So there must be preaching and everyone must also take care that his own reason may not lead him astray. For, behold what the fanatics do. They have accepted the Word and faith, but then, added to baptism, there comes wisdom, which has not yet been purged, and wants to be wise in spiritual things. They want to master both the Scriptures and faith by their own wisdom, and they perpetrate heresy. If we were wholly clean, we should not need everywhere the ministry of the Word. If we were altogether pure, we should have no need to be admonished, but would be like the angels in heaven with no need for a schoolmaster, and do everything willingly of ourselves. But since we are still confined to this miserable carcass—which in time the worms will devour, though it deserves something worse, to burn in hell eternally—it is necessary constantly to resist and put off the old man and his works and put on the new man, which is being renewed in knowledge after the image of him that created him [cf. Col. 3:10]. Usury, gluttony, adultery, manslaughter, murder, etc., these can be seen and the world understands that these are sins. But the devil's bride, reason, the lovely whore comes in and wants to be wise, and what she says, she thinks, is the Holy Spirit. Who can be of any help then? Neither jurist, physician, nor king, nor emperor; for she is the foremost whore the devil has. The other gross sins can be seen, but nobody can control reason. It walks about, cooks up fanaticism [Schwärmerei] with baptism and the Lord's Supper, and claims that everything that pops into its head and the devil puts into its heart is the Holy Spirit. Therefore Paul says: As I am an apostle and God has given me the Spirit, so I appeal to you [cf. Rom. 12:1; I Cor. 4:16].

But you may say: Am I not a Christian nevertheless? Very well, but take heed, take heed to yourself, the sin has not yet been fully purged and healed. If I say to a young man or girl, "You should not have your father's or your mother's sickness," this is impossible. But if you follow your lusts you will become a fornicator. Here the gospel admonishes you: Don't do it, don't follow your evil desires. The sin is forgiven, but see to it that you remain in grace. The remaining evil that still clings to the flesh is forgiven, but not yet fully purged, as in the case of him who fell among robbers. I am talking about lewdness, which is a gross sin and everybody feels it. Thus if a man does not heed the admonition of God to resist the devil when he is tempted, his sin has not been forgiven.

And what I say about the sin of lust, which everybody understands, applies also to reason; for the reason mocks and affronts God in spiritual things and has in it more hideous harlotry than any harlot. Here we have an idolater running after an idol, as the prophets say, under every green tree [cf. Jer. 2:20; I Kings 14:23], as a whorechaser runs after a harlot. That's why the Scriptures call idolatry whoredom, while reason calls it wisdom and holiness. How the prophets inveighed against this lovely whoredom, idolatry! It is a wild thing which is not easily caught and its foolishness is inborn, but it considers itself the height of wisdom and justice, and still it cannot understand the things of God. We must guard against it, as the prophets say: You must not serve God on the mountains or in the valleys or under the trees, but in Jerusalem, which is the place that God appointed for his worship and where his Word is. But here again, reason says: True enough, I have been called, circumcised, and adjured to go to Jerusalem, but here is a beautiful meadow, a fine green mountain; if we worship God here this will please God and all the angels in heaven. After all, is God the kind of God who binds himself only to Jerusalem? Such wisdom of reason the prophets call whoredom.

Therefore, when we preach faith, that we should worship nothing but God alone, the Father of our Lord Jesus Christ, as we say in the Creed: "I believe in God the Father almighty and in Jesus Christ," then we are remaining in the temple at Jerusalem. Again, "This is my beloved Son; listen to him" [Matt. 17:5]. "You will find him in a manger" [cf. Luke 2:12]. He alone does it. But reason says the opposite: What, us? Are we to worship only Christ? Indeed, shouldn't we also honor the holy mother of Christ? She is the woman who bruised the head of the serpent.[2] Hear us, Mary, for thy Son so honors thee that he can refuse thee nothing. Here Bernard went too far in his "Homilies on the Gospel 'Missus est Angelus.' "[3] God has commanded that we should honor the parents; therefore I will call upon Mary. She will intercede for me with the Son, and the Son with the Father, who will listen to the Son. So you have the picture of God as angry and Christ as judge; Mary shows to Christ her breast and Christ shows his wounds to the wrathful Father. That's the kind of thing this comely bride, the wisdom of reason cooks up: Mary is the mother of Christ, surely Christ will listen to her; Christ is a stern judge, therefore I will call upon St. George and St. Christopher.

No, we have been by God's command baptized in the name of the Father, the Son, and the Holy Spirit, just as the Jews were circumcised. Therefore, just as the Jews set up all over the land

---

[2] Gen. 3:15. The Vulgate translates: "*She* shall crush thy head, and thou shalt lie in wait for *her* foot," and the Roman church refers this to Mary.

[3] Bernard of Clairvaux (1091-1153). The reference is to *Homilia II super "Missus est"* [Luke 1:26], *Opera* (Mabillon), I, 2, Cols. 1672-1673. Cf. WA 47, 99-100 for another sermonic reference to Bernard's ascription of divine honor to Mary.

their own self-chosen shrines, as if Jerusalem were too narrow, so we also have done. As a young man must resist lust and an old man avarice, so reason is by nature a harmful whore. But she shall not harm me, if only I resist her. Ah, but she is so comely and glittering. That's why there must be preachers who will point people to the catechism: I believe in Jesus Christ, not in St. George or St. Christopher, for only of Christ is it said, "Behold, the Lamb of God, who takes away the sin of the world" [John 1:29]; not of Mary or the angels. The Father did not speak of Gabriel or any others when he cried from heaven, "Listen to him" [Matt. 17:5].

Therefore I should stick to the catechism; then I can defend myself against reason when the Anabaptists say, "Baptism is water; how can water do such great things? Pigs and cows drink it. The Spirit must do it." Don't you hear, you mangy, leprous whore, you holy reason, what the Scripture says, "Listen to him," who says, "Go and baptize all nations" [Matt. 28:19], and "He who believes and is baptized [will be saved"]? [Mark 16:16]. It is not merely water, but baptism given in the name of the holy Trinity.

Therefore, see to it that you hold reason in check and do not follow her beautiful cogitations. Throw dirt in her face and make her ugly. Don't you remember the mystery of the holy Trinity and the blood of Jesus Christ with which you have been washed of your sins? Again, concerning the sacrament, the fanatical antisacramentalists say, "What's the use of bread and wine? How can God the Almighty give his body in bread?" I wish they had to eat their own dirt.[4] They are so smart that nobody can fool them. If you had one in a mortar and crushed him with seven pestles his foolishness still would not depart from him.[5] Reason is and should be drowned in baptism, and this foolish wisdom will not harm you, if you hear the beloved Son of God saying, "Take, eat; this is my body, which is given for you;[6] this bread which is administered to you, I say, is my body." If I hear and accept this, then I trample reason and its wisdom under foot and say, "You cursed whore, shut up! Are you trying to seduce me into committing fornication with the

[4] *Ich wolt, das du müstest mit dem hindermaul etc.*; cf. CL 7, p. 414n.
[5] Cf. Prov. 27:22 and Ernst Thiele, *Luthers Sprichwörtersammlung, op. cit.*, p. 222.
[6] The form which appears in the Small Catechism.

devil?" That's the way reason is purged and made free through the Word of the Son of God.

So let us deal with the fanatics as the prophets dealt with the spiritual harlots, the idolaters, the wiseacres, who want to do things better than God does. We should say to them, "I have a Bridegroom, I will listen to him. Your wisdom is utter foolishness. I destroy your wisdom and trample it under foot." This struggle will go on till the last day. This is what Paul wants; we are to quench not only the low desires but also the high desires, reason and its high wisdom. When whoredom invades you, strike it dead, but do this far more when spiritual whoredom tempts you. Nothing pleases a man so much as self-love,[7] when he has a passion for his own wisdom. The cupidity of a greedy man is as nothing compared with a man's hearty pleasure in his own ideas. He then brings these fine ideas into the Scriptures, and this is devilishness pure and simple. This sin is forgiven, but when it reigns in one's nature, not yet fully purged, then assuredly the true doctrine is soon lost, however willingly one preaches and willingly one listens. Then Christ is gone. Then they fall down before the devil on the mountain and worship him (Matt. 4 [:8-10]).

Therefore I exhort you, says Paul, by the grace God has given me, not to think of yourselves more highly than you ought to think [cf. Rom. 12:3]. What he is saying is: You still have your own proud ideas, as well as other gross sins; therefore take heed to yourselves. Hitherto you have heard the real, true Word, now beware of your own thoughts and your own wisdom. The devil will kindle the light of reason and rob you of your faith. This is what happened to the Anabaptists and the antisacramentarians, and now we have nothing left but instigators of heresy. I have had more than thirty fanatics come to me and try to teach me; but I refuted all their arguments with this passage: "This is my beloved Son, with whom I am well pleased; listen to him" [Matt. 17:5]. And up to now I have by God's grace been sustained by this passage; otherwise I should have had to accept thirty different faiths.

The heretics are always looking for quarrels and dodges to make us retreat, and relax, and give in. But I say to them, we shall

---

[7] The word *philautia*, coined here by Luther, exists only in the Greek adjectival form *philautos;* cf. II Tim. 3:2.

not do it, God helping us. When they hear this they say: You are proud dunces. Well, I will suffer all kinds of reviling from them, but not one fingerbreadth will I depart from the mouth of Him who says, "Listen to Him." I foresee that, if God does not give us faithful ministers, the devil will tear our church apart through the sectarians and he will never cease until he has accomplished it. In a word, that is simply what he has in mind. If he cannot do it through the pope and the emperor, he will accomplish it through those who are still in accord with us in doctrine.

Therefore we need to pray from our hearts that God may give us pure teachers. Now we are so secure and we do not see how horribly the prince of this world is taking possession of us through the pope, the emperor, and our learned doctors, who say, What harm is there if we yield here? No, we should not yield a hair's breadth. If they will stick with us, very well; if not, let them go. I did not receive the doctrine from them, but by divine grace from God. I have been taught wisdom by experience. Therefore earnestly pray God that he may leave the Word with you, for some surprising things are going to happen. "Ah!" say the jurists and the wiseacres at court, "you're proud, the result will be an uprising," and so on. Our Lord God help us confidently to resist these perilous temptations!

You may think that you have been blessed above others with splendid gifts and sincerely thank God for them, but don't go too far, but only as far as accords with faith and is like faith. If an idea occurs to you, I would not throw it out altogether, but let it have some value. But go easy; St. Paul says, "in proportion" [Rom. 12:6]; don't be misled by it. How can I know, then, how far? Paul answers, "in proportion to our faith,"[8] that is, as far as it is in accord with faith. So you must keep your own ideas in check. Just as the evil lusts of the flesh are to be bridled, so conceit is original sin. Thus one may have a desire for a young woman which is "according to the measure of faith." How? The answer is that you should love the young woman (or young man) only in such a way as to desire her (or him) as a married partner, for the sixth commandment prohibits illicit love. Lust is in our corrupt nature; but when you "proportion" it thus: "I want to love the young woman, not to

---

[8] The original reads: *secundum analogiam fidei.*

commit fornication with her"; then the desire has its proportion, namely, that it is not contrary to the sixth commandment, and the sixth commandment becomes the measure by which the desire is controlled.

So it is with this hellish, whorish lust of thinking that everything was fine under the papacy; you are taking pleasure in your own conceit. Hang a clog on the neck of that lust, set a limit to it, so that it will not become presumptuous, but rather remain subject to faith, which is the overlord of all the gifts we have, not only of our conceit. Everything should be subject to faith, or rather, the fine gift of conceit should not be wiser than faith. See to it that it is in accord with it.

When you hear a fanatical antisacramentalist say, "There is only bread and wine in the sacrament of the altar," or "Do you think that at your word Christ is going to descend from heaven into your mouth and your belly?" You just say to him, "Ah, I like what you say; what a learned bride the devil has! But what do you say to this: 'This is my beloved Son, listen to him?' And he says, 'This is my body' [Matt. 17:5; 26:26]. Go, trot to the privy with your conceit, your reason! Shut up, you cursed whore, do you think you are master over faith, which declares that the true body and the true blood is in the Lord's Supper, and that Baptism is not merely water, but the water of the Father, the Son, and the Holy Spirit?" Reason must be subject and obedient to this faith.

Likewise, those who say that we are proud and ought to give in; are they talking about material things? No, they are really talking about matters of faith. But it is written here that we are to accept conceit and reason only in so far as it is not contrary to faith; you must not make faith a servant nor cast Christ out of heaven [i.e., rob Christ of his divinity].

Therefore Paul has exhorted us to withstand the high evil lusts, not only the low and mean ones. I must hang the word of faith like a clog on the neck of the high lusts. Reason, wisdom, would you lead up a green mountain, there to worship contrary to the commandment of God? No, I will not do it, I will worship him in Jerusalem. I don't care whether you can worship God in other places too: God has forbidden us to worship him under a green tree. I know very well that God is able to help us through the mother of the Son; but he does not will to help us except only through the Son, Jesus Christ the Lord, in whom we should put all our trust and hope. God could have said: If you say a *Paternoster* [the Lord's Prayer] to this saint, you will be saved. But God doesn't want you to do this; in fact, he has sternly forbidden it. This is the evil which St. Paul means in this passage—that we should be on our guard, not only against the gross lusts, but also against the high lusts, which break the unity of faith and bring about whoredom, which is idolatry.

THE LAST SERMON, EISLEBEN

1546

THE LAST SERMON, EISLEBEN
1546

The Last Sermon, Preached in Eisleben,

Matt. 11:25-30, February 15, 1546

On the Saturday following the preceding sermon Luther set out for Mansfeld to mediate a dispute between Count Albert and Count Gebhard. Most likely his last sermon was preached on Monday, February 15, not on February 14, to a large crowd which gathered from all over the countryside to hear him. On the day afterward while confined to his bed, he signed the treaty between the brothers, on the eighteenth he died, and on the twenty-second his body was buried in Wittenberg. The last four sermons, preached in Eisleben, were published in Wittenberg, 1546. Who the transcriber was cannot be determined.

Text in German; WA 51, 187-194.

This is a fine Gospel and it has a lot in it. Let us talk about part of it now, covering as much as we can and as God gives us grace.

The Lord here praises and extols his heavenly Father for having hidden these things from the wise and understanding. That is, he did not make his gospel known to the wise and understanding, but to infants and children who cannot speak and preach and are not knowing and wise. Thus he indicates that he is opposed to the wise and understanding and dearly loves those who are not wise and understanding but are rather like young children.

But to the world it is very foolish and offensive that God should be opposed to the wise and condemn them, when, after all, we have the idea that God could not reign if he did not have wise and under-

383

standing people to help him. But the meaning of the saying is this: the wise and understanding in the world so contrive things that God cannot be favorable and good to them. For they are always exerting themselves; they do things in the Christian church the way they want to themselves. Everything that God does they must improve, so that there is no poorer, more insignificant and despised disciple on earth than God; he must be everybody's pupil, everybody wants to be his teacher and preceptor. This may be seen in all heretics from the beginning of the world, in Arius and Pelagius, and now in our time the Anabaptists and antisacramentarians, and all fanatics and rebels; they are not satisfied with what God has done and instituted, they cannot let things be as they were ordained to be. They think they have to do something too, in order that they may be a bit better than other people and be able to boast: This is what I have done; what God has done is too poor and insignificant, even childish and foolish; I must add something to it. This is the nature of the shameful wisdom of the world, especially in the Christian church, where one bishop and one pastor hacks and snaps at another and one obstructs and shoves the other, as we have seen at all times in the government of the church to its great detriment. These are the real wiseacres, of whom Christ is speaking here, who put the cart before the horse and will not stay on the road which God himself has shown us, but always have to have and do something special in order that the people may say: Ah, our pastor or preacher is nothing; there's the real man, he'll get things done!

But is this behavior not a disgusting thing, and should not God grow impatient with it? Should he be so greatly pleased with these fellows who are all too smart and wise for him and are always wanting to send him back to school? As it says later in the same chapter, "Wisdom must be justified by her own children" [Luke 7:35]. Things are in a fine state, indeed, when the egg wants to be wiser than the hen. A fine governance it must be when the children want to rule their father and mother, and the fools and simpletons the wise people. You see, this is the reason why the wise and understanding are condemned everywhere in the Scriptures.

The pope has also done the same thing. For example, when Christ established and instituted the ministry [*Predigtamt*] and the sacrament of his body and blood in order that Christians should use it to strengthen and fortify their faith, the pope cried: No, that's not the way it should be; it must be wisely handled! For his decree says that it is not good that the sacrament should be administered for the strengthening of the faith of Christians, but that when the priest reads the mass for the living or the dead it must be a sacrifice; for example, when a merchant is about to go on a journey, he should first have a mass read for him, and then it will turn out fortunately for him.

Likewise, the fact that God instituted baptism is a trifling thing to the pope and with him it soon became lost and impotent. In its place he created his shavelings, who wear cowls and tonsures; they are the ones who were going to save 'the world with their orders and monkery, so that anybody who entered such an order possessed a new and better baptism, by which not only he but also other people were to be helped if they wished to be saved. Such is the pope's wisdom and understanding. So it is with our Lord God in the world; whatever he institutes and ordains must always be not only perverted but also reviled and discredited by the devil and his followers. And then the world even thinks that God should be pleased and look with approval upon the fact that every fool wants to master and rule him.

In worldly affairs and government the same thing happens, as Aristotle too has written. A few people are often endowed with great wisdom and understanding, unlike ordinary people. Often God gives us a fine, noble, intelligent man, who could serve principalities and people with wisdom and counsel. But such persons flee from the business of government and it is hard to bring them to govern. On the other hand, however, there are others who want to be and to do it, but they have no ability. In worldly government these are called jackanapes and wiseacres. These fellows are inveighed against and we are quite rightly hostile to them; everybody mourns the fact that we can never be safe from these fools, for they are good for nothing and they do nothing but put flies in the ointment. That's why the people say of them: The devil has slobbered us with fools.[1] And Aristotle,[2] who observed in governments that

---

[1] *Hat uns der Teufel mit Narren beschiessen.*
[2] Luther may have had in mind Aristotle's reference to *epistēmē* and *doxa* in *Nichomachean Ethics*, VI, 10; cf. *WA* 51, *Nachträge und Berichtigungen.*

few people are properly qualified to govern, makes a distinction between the truly wise and understanding and others whom he calls *doxa, id est opinione sua sapientes,* the wise who only think they are wise and understanding; just as we say in German: Conceit keeps the dance going. They imagine that because they are in the government and are higher-ups they must surely be wise. And one such fool in counsel hinders the others from getting on with anything at all; for he wants to be wise by force in the devil's name, and still he is a fool.

Now, if in worldly affairs one is quite rightly opposed to these people who want to be wise and are not, how much more irksome are those people, whom both God and men rightly dislike, who want to be wise in the holy Christian church and are not. For these people hinder the ministry, so that the people cannot come to God. Such in our time were Münzer,[3] and the antisacramentarians, who prevent and obstruct the course of the gospel and mislead the people, imagining that they alone are wise and understanding because they are in the office and government of the church.

So the pope, too, wants to be a very wise man, indeed, the wisest of the wise, simply because he has a high position and claims to be the head of the church; whereupon the devil so puffs him up that he imagines that whatever he says and does is pure divine wisdom and everybody must accept and obey it, and nobody should ask whether it is God's Word or not. In his big fool's book,[4] he presumes quite shamelessly to say that it is not likely that such an eminence, meaning himself, could err. So, too, the emperor, kings, and cardinals; because they sit in such high places, they too think they cannot err or be wrong.

This is just the kind of wisdom that Caiaphas had when he was in council with the Jews [John 11:49-50]: You utter fools, you have no heads, you know nothing and understand nothing at all; is it not better that one man should die rather than the whole nation should perish? This was wise and shrewd counsel: better kill one man than ruin the whole country. But how did this counsel turn out? This was precisely the thing by which he brought it about that the whole country had to perish and go down. This is what all such wise-

---

[3] Thomas Münzer, leader in the Peasant's War (d. 1525).
[4] I.e., the papal decretals, part of the *Corpus Iuris Canonici.*

acres do in the Christian church and in the secular government.

This, then, is what the Lord Christ is saying here. He is opposed to the wiseacres, he will not tolerate them in his Christian church, whether they be pope, emperors, kings, princes, or learned men, because they want to make themselves masters of his divine Word and with their own wisdom rule in the high, great matters of faith and our salvation. We ourselves have experienced many such instances in a short time. These wiseacres have undertaken to institute agreements and reformations by which unity is to be achieved in the Christian church. And the reasons they bring forward are priceless: the emperor, the kings, the princes, and lords should do so and so; then the country and the people would be helped and much good would be accomplished in Christendom. But it is all too evident what is accomplished by such schemes and such wisdom.

But most of all and for the longest time it has been the pope and the cardinals who have promoted this kind of wisdom and understanding and wanted to be God's master and rule Christendom themselves. But this God will not tolerate. He has no intention of being a pupil; they are to be the pupils. He is the eternal wisdom and he knows very well what he wishes to do or not to do. They think that, because they sit at the top of the government, they are the wisest, that they see more deeply into the Scriptures than other people. Therefore God brings them to terrible destruction; for he will not and cannot, nor should he, tolerate it. And so he brings it to pass that the gospel remains hidden from the high and the wise, and he rules his church quite differently from what they think and understand, even though they imagine they know and understand everything and that, because they are in the government, God cannot get along without their counsel and rule.

It sounds almost as if, when Christ spoke these words: "I thank thee, Father, Lord of heaven," etc. [Matt. 11:25], they were spoken with ill will. And yet there was no ill will or hatred in his heart; for, since he gave himself, body and life, for us, how could there be any ill will there? But his annoyance and displeasure comes from the fact that these miserable, foolish people presume to become masters of the divine Majesty. This he cannot and should not tolerate, and all devout hearts thank him for it, for otherwise there would be no end to this affected wisdom and mastery. The devil so rides these people that all they want from the Holy Scriptures and God's Word is a big name and their own praise and honor, and they want to be more than other people. But here we ought to say: Dear heavenly Father, speak thou, I am willing to be a fool and a child and be silent; for if I were to rule with my own understanding, wisdom, and reason, the cart would long since have been stuck in the mire and the ship would long since have been wrecked. Therefore, dear God, do thou rule and guide it thyself; I will gladly put out my eyes, and my reason besides, and let thee alone rule through thy Word.

But this cannot be achieved with the world. The sectarians rise up and at bottom seek nothing else except to gain great honor among the people, so that people will say of them: There's the right man; he'll do it! And with this praise they also want to strut and tickle their own vanity: This you have done, this is your work, you are the first-rate man, the real master. But that isn't even worth throwing to the dogs. For right preachers should diligently and faithfully teach only the Word of God and seek only his honor and praise. Likewise, the hearers also should say: I do not believe in my pastor, but he tells me of another Lord, whose name is Christ; him he shows to me; I will listen to him, in so far as he leads me to the true Teacher and Master, God's Son.

Then things would be right in the church and it would be well governed, and there would be harmony all around. Otherwise there will be the same displeasure as there is in secular government. A city council will not tolerate a fool who frequently gets the whole town into confusion, but casts him out, and the whole country is glad about it. The same thing should happen here in the Christian church; none other should be preached or taught except the Son of God alone. Of him alone is it said, "This is my beloved Son; listen to him" [Matt. 17:5]—and of no other, be he emperor, pope, or cardinal.

Therefore this is what we say: I grant that emperor, pope, cardinals, princes, and nobles are wise and understanding, but I shall believe in Christ; he is my Lord, he is the one God bids me to listen to, from him he bids me to learn what real, divine wisdom and understanding is.

But right here the pope and those who follow him cry out: No, no, this you should not do; you should be obedient to the governing authorities and do what we tell you to do. Yes, I reply, this I should do, but first you become one with the Lord, who here says: "All things have been delivered to me by my Father" [Matt. 11:25]. Therefore, dear pope, emperor, king, prince, and lord, do not go on this way; I will gladly listen to you so far as secular government is concerned, but when you presume to be master in Christendom and claim power to determine what I should believe and do, this I will not accept, for then you are claiming to be wise and understanding at the point where you are a fool and nothing has been revealed to you. For here is the Lord, who is the only one we ought to hear in these matters, as he himself says: "No one knows the Father except the Son and any one to whom the Son chooses to reveal him" [Matt. 11:27], that is, to the childlike and simple, who consider themselves neither wise nor understanding, but rather hear and accept his Word. So, if it is his Word you hold up to me and command, I shall gladly accept it, even though it be spoken by a little child, or even the ass that spoke to Balaam [Num. 22:21-30]. Here I will make no distinction between the persons who speak, whether they be wise men or fools; for it has been decided and commanded: "All things have been delivered to me" [Matt. 11:27], I alone am the Man who should teach and rule, despite all the wise and understanding, who should allow their eyes to be blinded, and their reason too.

For our wisdom and understanding in divine things is the eye which the devil opened for us in paradise, when Adam and Eve, too, wanted to be wise in the devil's name. God himself taught them and gave them his Word, which they were to adhere to, if they wanted to be really wise. Then came the devil and made improvements; he closed the eyes with which they had previously seen God and not seen the devil. This is the plague which still continues to cling to us—that we want to be wise and understanding in the devil's name.

But to combat this we must learn what this means: "All things have been delivered to me." In other words: I must rule, teach, counsel, give orders, and command in my church. And when he said that, Christ openly confessed that he is true God; for no angel nor any other creature can say that all things have been delivered to him. It is true that the devil once tried to seat himself on the throne and be like God; but he was soon flung out of heaven for it. Therefore Christ says, "All things have been delivered to me," that is, to me, to me you must be obedient. If you have my Word, then stick to it, and pay no attention to anybody who teaches and commands you differently. I will rule, protect, and save you well. Let the pope, emperor, the mighty, and the learned be wise; but don't you follow them, even though they were a thousand times wiser than they are. Don't you do what even an angel in heaven dare not do, take over the sovereignty and the power of being wise yourself or exercising power and rule in God's government. And yet these poor, miserable people, the pope, emperor, kings, and all sectarians, do not hesitate to arrogate this to themselves. But God has set his Son at his right hand and said in Ps. 2 [:7], "You are my son"; I have made the whole world and all nations your possession; hear him, you kings and lords, if you would be wise; do homage to him as your Lord; and know that what he says to you I am saying to you.

This we Christians should learn and acknowledge, even though the world does not want to do it, and we should be grateful to God that he has so richly blessed us and granted that we ourselves are able to hear him, just as Christ himself here gives joyful thanks to his heavenly Father. In times past we would have run to the ends of the world if we had known of a place where we could have heard God speak. But now that we hear this every day in sermons, indeed, now that all books are full of it, we do not see this happening. You hear at home in your house, father and mother and children sing and speak of it, the preacher speaks of it in the parish church—you ought to lift up your hands and rejoice that we have been given the honor of hearing God speaking to us through his Word.

Oh, people say, what is that? After all, there is preaching every day, often many times every day, so that we soon grow weary of it. What do we get out of it? All right, go ahead, dear brother, if you don't want God to speak to you every day at home in your house and in your parish church, then be wise and look for something else: in Trier is our Lord God's coat, in Aachen are Joseph's pants and our blessed Lady's chemise; go there and squander your money, buy indulgence and the pope's secondhand junk; these are valuable things! You have to go far for these things and spend a lot of money; leave house and home standing idle!

But aren't we stupid and crazy, yes, blinded and possessed by the devil? There sits the decoy duck in Rome with his bag of tricks, luring to himself the whole world with its money and goods, and all the while anybody can go to baptism, the sacrament, and the pulpit! How highly honored and richly blessed we are to know that God speaks with us and feeds us with his Word, gives us his baptism, the keys [absolution], etc.! But these barbarous, godless people say: What, baptism, sacrament, God's Word?—Joseph's pants, that's what does it! It is the devil in the world who makes the high personages, the emperor and the kings, oblivious to such things and causes them to allow themselves to be so grossly duped and fooled and bespattered with filth by these first-class rascals and liars, the pope and his tonsured shavelings. But we should listen to God's Word, which tells us that he is our schoolmaster, and have nothing to do with Joseph's pants or the pope's juggling tricks.

This is the first point in this Gospel—that Christ and God the Father himself are opposed to the wise and understanding. For they vex him greatly; they mangle the sacrament and the church, and set themselves up in God's place and want themselves to be masters. To such all the angels in heaven and all Christians are opposed and we should say to them: If you want to teach Christ to me, I shall gladly listen to you, otherwise not, even if you were an angel from heaven, as St. Paul says in Gal. 1 [:8]. "Even if we, or an angel from heaven, should preach to you a gospel contrary to that which we preached to you, let him be accursed."

When, therefore, the great lords, the emperor, pope, cardinals, and bishops are hostile and wrathful toward us because of all this, excommunicate us, and would gladly burn and murder us all, we must suffer it and say: We did not start this on account of the pope, the bishops, and the princes, nor shall we stop it on account of them. Christ says, "Come to me, all who labor and are heavy-laden" [Matt. 11:28], and it is as though he were saying: Just stick to me, hold on to my Word and let everything else go. If you are burned and beheaded for it, then have patience, I will make it so sweet for you that you easily would be able to bear it. It has also been written of

391

St. Agnes[5] that when she was led to prison to be killed, it was to her as if she were going to a dance. Where did she get this? Ah, only from this Christ, from believing this saying, "Come to me, all who labor and are heavy-laden, and I will give you rest." That is to say: If things go badly, I will give you the courage even to laugh about it; and if even though you walk on fiery coals, the torment shall nevertheless not be so severe and the devil shall nevertheless not be so bad, and you will rather feel that you are walking on roses.[6] I will give you the heart to laugh even though Turk, pope, emperor, and everybody else be filled with horrible wrath and rage. Only come to me; and if you are facing oppression, death, or torture, because the pope, the Turk, and emperor are attacking you, do not be afraid; it will not be heavy for you, but light and easy to bear, for I give you the Spirit, so that the burden, which for the world would be unbearable, becomes for you a light burden. For when you suffer for my sake, it is my yoke and my burden, which I lay upon you in grace, that you may know that this your suffering is well pleasing to God and to me and that I myself am helping you to carry it and giving you power and strength to do so. So also say Ps. 31 [:24] and Ps. 27 [:14]: "Let your heart take courage, all you who wait for the Lord," i.e., all you who suffer for his sake. Let misfortune, sin, death, and whatever the devil and the world loads upon you assail and assault you, if only you remain confident and undismayed, waiting upon the Lord in faith, you have already won, you have already escaped death and far surpassed the devil and the world.

Lo, this means that the wise of this world are rejected, that we may learn not to think ourselves wise and to put away from our eyes all great personages, indeed, to shut our eyes altogether, and cling only to Christ's Word and come to him, as he so lovingly invites us to do, and say: Thou alone art my beloved Lord and Master, I am thy disciple.

This and much more might be said concerning this Gospel, but I am too weak and we shall let it go at that.

---

[5] St. Agnes who died *ca.* 304 is commemorated in the Roman church on January 21 and 28.

[6] The allusion is to St. Vincentius, early Christian martyr who was laid on fiery coals, etc.

INDEXES

INDEX OF NAMES AND SUBJECTS

INDEX TO SCRIPTURE PASSAGES